Dave Veerman and Dana Nies

SPORTS TRIVIA DEVOTIONAL

Inspiration for Kids from Sports and Scripture

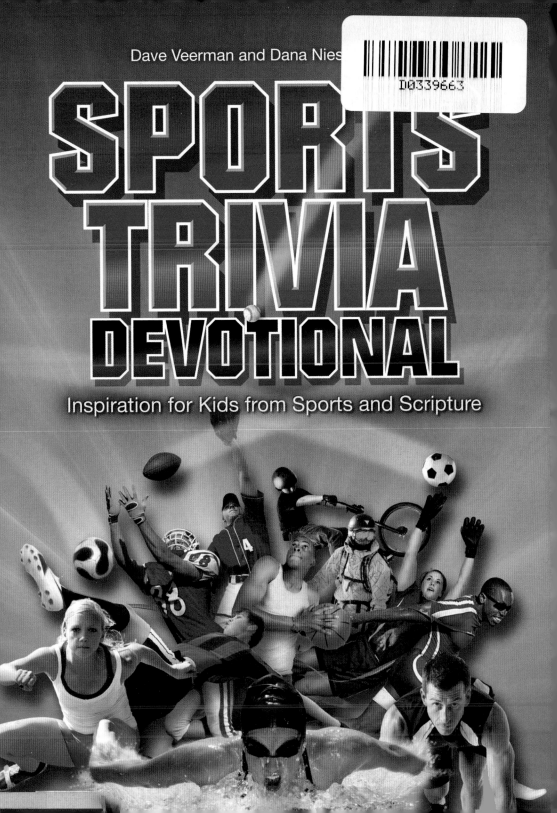

We want to hear from you. Please send your comments about this book to us in care of zreview@zondervan.com. Thank you.

ZONDERKIDZ

Sports Trivia Devotional
Copyright © 2010 by The Livingstone Corporation

This title is also available as a Zondervan ebook
Visit www.zondervan.com/ebooks.

Requests for information should be addressed to:

Zonderkidz, *Grand Rapids, Michigan 49530*

ISBN 978-0-310-721857

Produced with the assistance of The Livingstone Corporation (www.livingstonecorp.com). Project staff includes
Dave Veerman, Dana Niesluchowski, Neil Wilson, Linda Washington, and Ashley Taylor.

Zonderkidz is a trademark of Zondervan.

Creative direction: Larry P. Taylor, Livingstonecorp.com
Cover design: John Wolinka, Design Corps
Interior design: Larry P. Taylor, Livingstonecorp.com
Interior production: Lindsay Galvin, Tom Shumaker, and Kirk Luttrell, Livingstonecorp.com

Printed in China

10 11 12 13 14 15 /TLC/ 23 22 21 20 19 18 17 16 15 14 13 12 11 10 9 8 7 6 5 4 3 2 1

Dedication

To Edmund David Niesluchowski
and Natalie Beth, Amy Ellen, and
Lindsey May Conrad.

*As you grow in stature, may you also grow in wisdom
and in your relationships with God and others.
(See Luke 2:52.)
Run, jump, ride, throw, hit, catch, cheer, serve, pass,
stroke, shoot, kick, score, win, and lose . . .
for Jesus.*

Welcome to a full year of sports facts, unusual happenings, insights, and fun. Beginning on January 1, just about every day will highlight a sports-related event that happened on that day at some point in history. You'll also find a devotional, beginning with more information about the featured athlete, sport, or event and ending with a spiritual challenge and a key verse. Then follows a listing of a few more significant events and birthdays related to the day. Finally, at the bottom of the page sits a Fun Fact related to the featured athlete or event.

If we've done our job right, as you read the daily devotionals you'll learn some cool stuff about lots of sports and athletes. But you'll also see how the Bible relates to life—your life—and, hopefully, deepen your relationship with God.

We've combined every sixth and seventh day; and instead of a devotional, we've written a sports quiz. This will give you a break in the routine and broaden your sports IQ. You may even want to amaze your family and friends with your knowledge and see how well they can do in answering the questions.

At the very back of the book, you'll find an index of all the key verses along with the dates they were used and the related topics and sports. This will be helpful when you're studying a passage on your own or in Sunday school, or when you're supposed to give a devotional, say, for a team or before a sporting event.

We hope you'll enjoy this book—every page. More important, however, we hope you will strengthen your commitment to Christ and God's Word.

Dave and Dana

The **Game's On**

On this day in 1923, the Tournament of Roses Association sponsored the first football game played in the Rose Bowl.

What's your usual routine for New Year's Day? When you eventually get out of bed (sleeping in after staying up past midnight), you probably watch the Rose Parade and then the Rose Bowl and other football games, sandwiched around the big meal. A nice tradition. For the athletes in the games, this day marks the *end* of a successful season—even the losing teams finish with winning records. For most, January 1 marks a fresh start. Turning the calendar to a new month and year, we put the previous 365 days behind and begin again—we may even make "resolutions."

Beginning and ending—every year we look back and reflect, and we look ahead and

plan. Some people remember the previous year with regret, like the also-ran teams that didn't come close to being bowl eligible—they can focus on what they did *wrong*, what they didn't do that they should have, what went awry. That's easy to do, especially with first semester grades about to hit (if only we had studied more or turned in those papers on time). But we may also think of a relationship gone sour, an unfinished project, or the pain of not making the squad or cast or being cut from the team.

So we resolve to do better—to lose weight, to improve those grades, to have a regular time of prayer and Bible reading, to save money, to be a better friend, or to get

along with a brother or sister. Resolutions can be good, motivating us to make important changes—especially if the ultimate goal is to do what God wants, to become his person . . . and to do it in his strength.

That's pretty much what the apostle Paul is saying in the passage below: he's looking ahead, focusing on God's goals and ultimate prize. That's where our resolutions should begin and end.

Happy New Year!

ALSO ON THIS DAY . . .

1935—The first Sugar Bowl and first Orange Bowl football games were played.

1970—Charles "Chub" Feeney became president of baseball's National League.

1990—The Sports News Network began operation on cable TV.

BIRTHDAYS:

1863—Pierre de Coubertin of France, the baron who revived the Olympic games

1911—Hank Greenberg, New York, NY, Hall-of-Fame first baseman, Detroit Tigers

1967—Derrick Thomas, Miami, FL, NFL linebacker for the Kansas City Chiefs

Forgetting what is behind and straining toward what is ahead, I press on toward the goal to win the prize for which God has called me heavenward in Christ Jesus. **Philippians 3:13–14**

FUN FACT The Rose Bowl game, "The Granddaddy of Them All," has been sold out every year since 1947. With a seating capacity at approximately 93,000, a record crowd of 106,869 attended the game on January 1, 1973.

2 Fanatics!

ON THIS DAY IN 1971, A BARRIER COLLAPSED AT IBROX PARK FOOTBALL STADIUM AT THE END OF A SOCCER MATCH IN GLASGOW, SCOTLAND, KILLING SIXTY-SIX.

What's your favorite sport? How about your favorite professional team? If you're a true fan, you check the scores and stats regularly, read the stories about the games, and view or attend as many games as possible (tough with the high prices). When watching certain sporting events, what do you think of the fans who paint themselves in the team's colors or wear wild outfits? And how about those guys who stand bare-skinned in sub-zero temps, with letters painted on their chests, screaming at the top of their lungs? Definitely fanatics . . . and, you think, maybe a little bit out of their minds.

Actually, that's nothing compared to many European soccer fans. Some spend the whole time singing. Others bring obnoxious noise-makers they use nonstop. Many, angered by a referee's call or an athlete's play, litter the field with anything they can throw. In England, "hooligan" fans cause mayhem inside and outside the stadium.

The Ibrox tragedy in Scotland occurred mainly because of too many fans jammed into poorly constructed stands. But in other games, referees and athletes have been assaulted and spectators have been trampled by the out-of-control crowds.

Cheering for a favorite team can be exciting and fun, but we shouldn't get carried away. Many other areas of our lives should be way more important to us than winning or losing a game: family and friends, school and career, health and finances . . . . You can probably think of examples in each of those categories where fanataticism for a sport, team, or game has caused big problems.

And our most important interest of all should be our faith! Our relationship with God should be at the forefront and should impact every area of our lives, including athletics. So do you read the sports pages more than your Bible? Do you skip church to make the kickoff? Do you know more sports stats than Scriptures? Do you talk more about the team than Christ? If so, your priorities may be out of whack.

Be a *faith* fanatic—keep God "number one" in your life.

ALSO ON THIS DAY . . .

1945—The University of Kentucky began their 130-home-basketball-game win streak. It ended in 1955.

1965—The New York Jets signed quarterback Joe Namath, Alabama all-American.

1977—Bowie Kuhn suspended Atlanta Braves owner Ted Turner for one year due to tampering charges in the Gary Matthews free-agency signing.

But seek first his kingdom and his righteousness, and all these things will be given to you as well. **Matthew 6:33**

BIRTHDAYS:

1927—Gino Marchetti, Smithers, WV, NFL great, defensive end for the Dallas Texans and Baltimore Colts

1947—Calvin Hill, Baltimore, MD, NFL running back for the Dallas Cowboys

1971—Lisa Harrison, Louisville, KY, WNBA basketball player for the Phoenix Mercury

FUN FACT In 1978, Geral Fauss, a former high school teacher, invented the #1 foam hand, which has become one of the most popular pieces of US sports merchandising.

What a **Rush!**

On this day in 1983, Tony Dorsett, running back for the Dallas Cowboys, set the NFL record with a ninety-nine-yard rush against the Minnesota Vikings.

In football, the worst place to begin an offensive drive is on your own one-yard line. And that's where the Cowboys were, their backs against their end zone. The outlook was bleak. Perhaps they would move a few yards on three downs to get out of the shadow of their goalposts, far enough to make a safe punt. Or, a more optimistic scenario would have them move slowly down the field, one first down after another. Instead, against all odds, Tony Dorsett took the handoff, burst off left tackle, cut to his right, wove through defensive backs, and ran untouched ninety-nine yards for the touchdown.

You may never become a Hall-of-Fame running back, but the chances are good that you'll find yourself on life's one-yard line, facing fierce opposition and very little hope for a positive future. (Maybe you're there right now.) Perhaps in school, your assignments and tests seem insurmountable. Maybe your friends have boxed you in and are pressuring you to do what you know you shouldn't. Or perhaps your family is unraveling, falling apart.

In times like those, you can assume that all is lost or that the least you can hope for is a little relief, a little progress. Just remember Tony's great run. More important, remember God's promise "to do immeasurably more than all we ask or imagine."

Did you catch that? The verse says, "immeasurably more" that you can "ask or imagine." God has great plans for you and will accomplish those plans "according to his power that is at work within [you]."

This doesn't mean you will run to pay dirt every time. But it does mean you can hope as you depend on him. Take his handoff and run.

....

ALSO ON THIS DAY ...

1920—The New York Yankees purchased Babe Ruth from the Boston Red Sox for $125,000 (the deal was signed in December but announced in January).

1973—George Steinbrenner III bought the New York Yankees from CBS for $12 million.

1981—Mary Terstegge Meagher swam a female record 100 meter butterfly (58.91).

1991—Los Angeles Kings' Wayne Gretzky, "the great one," scored his 700th goal, against the New York Islanders.

BIRTHDAYS:

1939—Bobby Hull, Point Anne, Ontario, Hall-of-Fame NHL forward (Chicago Blackhawks)

1972—Deborah Carter, WNBA forward (Utah Starzz)

1981—Eli Manning, New Orleans, LA, NFL quarterback (New York Giants)

Now to him who is able to do immeasurably more than all we ask or imagine, according to his power that is at work within us, to him be glory in the church and in Christ Jesus throughout all generations, for ever and ever! Amen. **Ephesians 3:20–21**

FUN FACT »
What made Tony Dorsett's record-breaking run even more amazing is that Dallas had only ten players on the field at the time. They were missing the fullback.

JANUARY 4 — In a **League** of Their **Own**

NATIONAL NEGRO BASEBALL LEAGUE

ON THIS DAY IN 1920, THE FIRST BLACK BASEBALL LEAGUE (NATIONAL NEGRO BASEBALL LEAGUE) WAS ORGANIZED.

Today, most sports feature colorful competitors from a wide variety of countries and cultures. But for many years, and in many sports, that wasn't the case. Professional baseball, for example, was for whites only. So black players formed their own league, giving them the opportunity to develop as athletes and to play the game they loved. Eventually many of those excellent players were inducted into the Hall of Fame—Satchel Paige, Josh Gibson, Cool Papa Bell, Judy Johnson, Oscar Charleston, Buck Leonard, Willard Brown, and several more—all well deserving.

Looking back, we may wonder how that could happen, how athletes could be excluded from a sport or team simply because of their race or skin color. But we do the same when we form cliques, avoid "undesirables," and don't associate with people who are different. And this can happen in all sorts of groups—even in church. What do kids at school say, for example, about the new student who speaks with a thick accent? If your neighborhood is made up mostly of people of one race, how do your neighbors react when someone of a different race moves in? How do you feel around someone with a physical or mental handicap?

In John's vision of heaven, he sees that God's kingdom is made up of people from "every nation, tribe, people and language" (Revelation 7:9), all praising God together. All those who love Jesus will be there, from all over the world. Clearly God doesn't discriminate on the basis of race or nationality, and neither should we.

....

ALSO ON THIS DAY . . .

1887—Thomas Stevens was the first man to bicycle around the world.

1977—Mary Shane was hired by the Chicago White Sox as the first woman TV play-by-play announcer.

1986—NCAA basketball's David Robinson blocked a record fourteen shots in a game for the U.S. Naval Academy.

BIRTHDAYS:

1930—Don Shula, Grand River, OH, the NFL's winningest coach (Miami Dolphins)

1951—Barbara Ann Cochran, Claremont, NH, slalom skier (Olympic gold medal winner, 1972)

1989—Graham Rahal, Columbus, OH, American race car driver and son of Bobby Rahal

There is neither Jew nor Greek, slave nor free, male nor female, for you are all one in Christ Jesus. Galatians 3:28

Fun Fact Satchel Paige, the first player to be inducted from the Negro leagues (1971), had these rules for staying young: Avoid fried meats which angry up the blood; if your stomach disputes you, lie down and pacify it with cool thoughts; keep the juices flowing by jangling around gently as you move; go very light on the vices, such as carrying on in society—the social ramble ain't restful; avoid running at all times; don't look back—something might be gaining on you.

Big Business, **Big Bucks**

On this day in 1989, Major League Baseball signed with ESPN for $140 million, to televise 175 games in 1990.

Sports are big business—one hundred forty million dollars is a lot of money. But salaries have grown since 1989, and these days some individual athletes make that much in a year or two (in 2010, baseball's TV contracts totaled more than 3 billion dollars a year).

Many professional athletes still play for the love of the game. Too often, however, money and greed take over. That's why we continue to hear reports of athletes doing just about anything to get ahead (using performance-enhancing drugs and cheating in other ways), agents driving up the price of their clients, and owners treating players like commodities. The athletes and their managers may "win" for a while, but every year numerous highly paid professionals lose big time—bankruptcies, failed marriages, drug abuse, crime, and worse.

So much God-given talent, so much potential, wasted!

Athletes aren't the only ones susceptible to greed. We don't have to look far to find greedy coaches, politicians, business people, doctors, lawyers, teachers, blue-collar workers, administrators, students, parents, kids . . . . No one is immune. Greed is the lust for *more*—usually money or what money can buy—and leads to people revolving their lives around getting and spending.

In discussing this problem, Jesus clearly told his disciples that having two leaders doesn't work: "No one can serve two masters. Either he will hate the one and love the other, or he will be devoted to the one and despise the other. You cannot serve both God and Money" (Matthew 6:24). God will never let you down; money *always* will.

This is a good lesson to learn when you're young. Let God call the shots—keep focused on him and his values—and don't worry about being rich and famous.

ALSO ON THIS DAY . . .

1951—Babe Didrikson-Zaharias won the LPGA Ponte Vedra Beach Women's Golf Open.

1957—The Brooklyn Dodgers' Jackie Robinson retired rather than be traded to baseball's New York Giants.

2003—The San Francisco 49ers came back from a twenty-four-point deficit to beat the New York Giants in the NFC wildcard game, 39-38.

BIRTHDAYS:

1945—Chuck McKinley, St Louis, MO, U.S. tennis player

1947—Mercury Morris, Pittsburgh, PA, NFL running back (Miami Dolphins)

1968—Andrew Golota, Polish boxer

1975—Warrick Dunn, Baton Rouge, LA, NFL running back (Tampa Bay Buccaneers and Atlanta Falcons)

People who want to get rich fall into temptation and a trap and into many foolish and harmful desires that plunge men into ruin and destruction. For the love of money is a root of all kinds of evil. Some people, eager for money, have wandered from the faith and pierced themselves with many griefs. **1 Timothy 6:9–10**

Fun Fact
The most legendary quarterback Johnny Unitas was ever paid in a year was $250,000 (one year, double his previous salary). At the height of his career, Walter Payton was reported to be making $475,000 per season, the highest salary in the NFL at the time. In 2009, the New York Jets signed their first-round draft choice, QB Mark Sanchez, to a five-year contract worth $50.5 million with $28 million in guarantees.

MATCH the NFL city to its mascot.

1. Chicago
2. Baltimore
3. Washington
4. Seattle
5. Green Bay
6. Minnesota
7. Detroit
8. New York
9. Tampa Bay
10. Pittsburgh
11. Cincinnati
12. New England
13. Miami
14. Carolina
15. New Orleans
16. Tennessee
17. New York
18. Kansas City
19. Indianapolis
20. Denver
21. San Francisco
22. Oakland
23. San Diego
24. Houston
25. Dallas
26. Arizona
27. Buffalo
28. Cleveland
29. Jacksonville
30. Philadelphia
31. St. Louis
32. Atlanta

a. Seahawks
b. Broncos
c. Saints
d. Chargers
e. Bengals
f. Panthers
g. Bears
h. Colts
i. Jaguars
j. Rams
k. Ravens
l. Chiefs
m. Jets
n. Raiders
o. Cardinals
p. Redskins
q. Browns
r. Steelers
s. Bills
t. Packers
u. Texans
v. Buccaneers
w. Giants
x. Dolphins
y. Lions
z. Falcons
aa. Eagles
bb. Cowboys
cc. Patriots
dd. 49ers
ee. Titans
ff. Vikings

Answers: 1-b; 2-k; 3-p; 4-a; 5-t; 6-ff; 7-y; 8-m or w;
9-v; 10-r; 11-e; 12-cc; 13-x; 14-f; 15-c; 16-ee; 17-m or w;
18-l; 19-h; 20-b; 21-dd; 22-n; 23-d; 24-u; 25-bb; 26-o;
27-s; 28-q; 29-i; 30-aa; 31-j; 32-z

12

A **Rose** is a Rose

On this date in 2004, Pete Rose admitted that he gambled on baseball.

Pete Rose was one of professional baseball's all-time great players (mostly for the Cincinnati Reds). Always playing with great enthusiasm and effort, Pete earned the nickname "Charlie Hustle" and was one of the most popular and admired players of his era.

He won three World Series rings, three batting titles, one Most Valuable Player Award, two Gold Gloves, the Rookie of the Year Award, and made seventeen all-star appearances at five different positions (2B, LF, RF, 3B, and 1B). When he retired in 1986, he held the record for the most hits (4,256).

Unfortunately, Rose was also addicted to gambling, and in 1989 he was banned from Major League Baseball for allegedly betting on the game. For fourteen years, he denied ever betting on baseball. But, then, in his tell-all book *My Prison Without Bars*, he admitted having done just that.

While in his prime, Pete Rose was the hero of thousands of kids, representing all that was good about sports, especially baseball. Coaches would point to him as a great example of how the game should be played—with total dedication and all-out effort. While Pete Rose was a great player, he was also a flawed human being and a *terrible* example off the field.

Here's the deal: we should be careful about who we idolize, put on a pedestal, pattern our lives after. Human beings will *always* let us down. Eventually they will mess up—some a little and some a lot. In fact, we could take up all the space on this page just listing famous "heroes" who recently have been caught or convicted.

No one is perfect; every person ever born is a sinner: parents, pastors, best friends, leaders in government and business, sports stars, even Mother Theresa and Billy Graham . . . everyone, that is, except One—Jesus. That's why we should keep our eyes on him, see him as our hero, copy the way he lived.

If you want to improve at a sport, mirror the attitudes and actions of great players. But if you want to improve at life—to really live—look to Christ.

ALSO ON THIS DAY . . .

1955—Furman set an NCAA basketball single-game scoring record with 154 points.

1962—Golfer Jack Nicklaus, 21, made his first professional appearance—he came in 50th.

1972—The NCAA announced that freshmen could play on teams starting in the fall.

1980—New York Islander Glenn Resch recorded his twentieth shut-out, against the Vancouver Canucks, 3-0.

BIRTHDAYS:

1953—Bruce Sutter, MLB Pitcher (Cubs, Cardinals, Braves)

1967—Willie Anderson, NBA guard (New York Knicks, Olympic bronze in 1988)

1971—Jason Giambi, MLB infielder (Oakland Athletics and New York Yankees)

Let us fix our eyes on Jesus, the author and perfecter of our faith, who for the joy set before him endured the cross, scorning its shame, and sat down at the right hand of the throne of God. Consider him who endured such opposition from sinful men, so that you will not grow weary and lose heart. **Hebrews 12:2–3**

Fun Fact Billy Joel's 1978 song "Zanzibar" mentions Pete Rose. The original version says, "Rose, he knows he's such a credit to the game/ but the Yankees grab the headlines every time." Joel updated the lyrics to reflect the changes in Rose's career since the song was written, rewriting the first part to, "Rose, he knows he'll never reach the Hall of Fame."

9 In That **Number**

ON THIS DAY IN 1967, THE NATIONAL FOOTBALL LEAGUE'S NEW ORLEANS' FRANCHISE TOOK THE NAME "SAINTS."

New Orleans is known for its history (Spanish, French, Louisiana Purchase, Battle of New Orleans), traditions (festivals, Mardi Gras), politics (the Long family, Edwin Edwards, and others), weather (Hurricane Katrina), food (Creole and Cajun cooking), and music (think Louis Armstrong, Al Hurt,

Pete Fountain, Dr. John, the Neville brothers, the Marsalis family, Harry Connick Jr., and Preservation Hall).

Speaking of music, one of the most well-known Gospel/Dixieland songs associated with this city is "When the Saints Go

Marching In." Just about everyone has heard and sung this popular tune. So the team's owners, with the blessing of the NFL, chose "Saints" as their name—and the song is played with great enthusiasm before, during, and after home games.

The word *saint* comes from the Bible and means someone who is a follower of Christ. That's why Paul wrote to the believers in Rome, whom he hadn't met, "To all in Rome who are loved by God and called to be saints: Grace and peace to you from God our Father and from the Lord Jesus Christ" (Romans 1:7). And some churches honor great men and women of faith by giving each the title of "saint."

So we can see why people would sing about men and women entering heaven—"Oh, when the saints go marching in"—and then almost shout, "Lord,

how I want to be in that number when the saints go marching in." What began as a folk worship hymn has become an athletic anthem.

The New Orleans professional football players may or may not be true "saints." But you are, if you have put your trust in Christ as your Savior. In that case, you *will* go marching in one day. Thank God for his gift of salvation and for making you one of his "saints" (even if you don't live in New Orleans).

ALSO ON THIS DAY . . .

1811—The first women's golf tournament held.

1977—In Super Bowl XI, the Oakland Raiders beat the Minnesota Vikings, 32-14.

1991—Dean Smith of UNC/Chapel Hill became the sixth college basketball coach to win 700 games.

BIRTHDAYS:

1971—Bill Schroeder, NFL Wide Receiver (Green Bay Packers, Super Bowl XXXI)

1972—Jay Powell, MLB pitcher (Florida Marlins)

1978—Chad Johnson (changed to Ochocinco), NFL football player (Cincinnati Bengals)

And I pray that you, being rooted and established in love, may have power, together with all the saints, to grasp how wide and long and high and deep is the love of Christ, and to know this love that surpasses knowledge—that you may be filled to the measure of all the fullness of God. **Ephesians 3:17–19**

Fun Fact
In 1980, the Saints lost their first fourteen games, so many Saints fans began wearing paper bags over their heads at the team's home games with the word "Ain'ts" written on them. But in 2010 the team finally became champions, winning the Super Bowl!

Chosen and **Elected**

On this day in 1945, the baseball writers again failed to elect any new members to the Hall of Fame.

Every major sport has a Hall of Fame, and the ultimate honor is to someday be elected as a member. Baseball's Hall of Fame is probably the oldest and most well known.

Named in 1936, the first five inductees to Cooperstown were Ty Cobb, Babe Ruth, Honus Wagner, Christy Mathewson, and Walter Johnson. Since then, about 290 more have been enshrined, including 203 former Major League players, 35 Negro Leaguers, 19 managers, 9 umpires, and 26 pioneers, executives, and organizers. League play began in 1876, so that's a small percentage of the thousands who have played at least one game in the National and American leagues. And during a few years, as in 1945, no new members were elected at all. This is a select group—no doubt about it.

Everyone wants to be valued. We want to be complimented, thanked, and recognized for our work, our achievements. Even little league teams highlight their "most valuable players" and give other

significant awards. And we hurt when we fall short of the mark or are overlooked and ignored.

Did you know that God has a Hall of Fame? Not officially, but that's what Bible teachers call Hebrews 11, where a bunch of Old Testament heroes are mentioned. The men and women described are listed in that chapter because of their great

faith. Despite fierce opposition, they stood firm for God.

But you know what's really cool? Eventually all believers will be able to hang with those spiritual giants. That's because we've been *chosen*. The Bible uses the word "election" (2 Peter 1:10) to describe the process. God loved you so much that he chose you to be his, and faith sealed the deal.

If you have trusted in Christ as your Savior, you have been elected to God's eternal Hall of Fame. On top of that, he has adopted you as his son or daughter, his highly valued child. So don't get down on yourself—God thinks you're special.

....

ALSO ON THIS DAY . . .

1982—The Bengals beat the Chargers in -9°F weather in the "Freezer Bowl" to win the AFC Championship.

1990—The NCAA approved random drug testing for college football players.

1996—Jimmie Johnson was announced as the new head coach of the Miami Dolphins.

BIRTHDAYS:

1938—Frank Mahovlich, NHL Hall of Famer

1949—George Foreman, world heavyweight boxing champion (1973-74, '95)

1975—Jake Delhomme, NFL quarterback (Carolina Panthers)

For it is by grace you have been saved, through faith—and this not from yourselves, it is the gift of God—not by works, so that no one can boast. For we are God's workmanship, created in Christ Jesus to do good works, which God prepared in advance for us to do. **Ephesians 2:8–10**

FUN FACT » The Giants have the most members of baseball's Hall of Fame, with twenty-three. The Royals have only one. More pitchers are in the Hall than any other position (seventy). Only thirteen third basemen have made it in.

11 A **Great** Catch

On this day in 1977, the Chicago Cubs traded outfielder Rick Monday to the Los Angeles Dodgers for first baseman Bill Buckner.

Bill Buckner was a great baseball player, enjoying a long career with the Dodgers, Cubs, Red Sox, Angels, and Royals. During his twenty-year career, he accumulated over 2,700 hits. Yet he is remembered most for his error in the sixth game of the 1986 World Series that led to Boston losing the game, and eventually the series, to the Mets.

Rick Monday was an excellent player, too, but he also is not most remembered for any outstanding baseball plays.

Instead, he became famous for his quick thinking and act of patriotism on April 25, 1976. During a game at Dodger Stadium, two protesters ran into the outfield and tried to set fire to an American flag they had brought with them. Monday, then playing with the Cubs, saw what they were doing and ran over and grabbed the flag from the ground. Later he said, "If you're going to burn the flag, don't do it around me. I've been to too many veterans' hospitals and seen too many broken bodies of guys who tried to protect it."

We can't control what people think, and we don't know what we'll be remembered for. But many crucial decisions and actions are under our control and help build our reputations. Someone who doesn't follow through on a job may be thought of as "lazy." A person who bends the truth may be seen as a "liar." Someone who often

doesn't show up on time (or at all) may be considered "unreliable." The person who is caught stealing, even something small, can be branded as a "thief." The problem with a bad reputation is that it's difficult to live down, to erase in people's minds.

Wouldn't you rather be known as a "hard worker," "truthful," "trustworthy," "honest," and, most important of all, a "true Christian"? We may say that we believe a certain way, but our actions speak much louder . . . and build our reputations.

What reputation are you building these days?

ALSO ON THIS DAY . . .

1960—Lamar Clark set a professional boxing record of forty-four consecutive knockouts.

1995—National Hockey League Players Association and owners agreed to end the NHL strike.

1997—Martina Hingis defeated Jennifer Capriati at Sydney Tennis International Tournament.

A good name is more desirable than great riches; to be esteemed is better than silver or gold. **Proverbs 22:1**

BIRTHDAYS:

1972—Rey Ordonez, MLB infielder

1987—Scotty Cranmer, American professional BMX rider

FUN FACT You can see this event on YouTube: "The Greatest Play in Baseball—Rick Monday Saves U.S. Flag." When asked how he feels after nineteen years in baseball being remembered mainly for this one incident, Rick replies, "If that's all you're known for, it's not a bad thing at all."

No Match on Paper

ON THIS DAY IN 1969, THE NEW YORK JETS BEAT THE BALTIMORE COLTS IN SUPER BOWL III, 16-7, IN MIAMI WITH JOE NAMATH, NY JETS QUARTERBACK, NAMED THE MVP.

After the AFL (American Football League) and the NFL (National Football League) merged, they held a final championship game called the Super Bowl. In the first two Super Bowls, the powerful Green Bay Packers easily defeated their young AFL opposition. The AFL was not generally respected as having the same caliber of talent as the NFL, and the Colts were loaded with outstanding players—even touted by the sports media as "the greatest team in pro football history." So the experts predicted another lopsided NFL victory in this game. Instead, in one of sport's great upsets, Joe Namath and his Jets beat the mighty Colts.

On paper it was no contest—the Colts were by far the better team. But that's why the games are played. Statistics, past accomplishments, and press clippings don't win games—the athletes do.

According to the scouting reports, the Israelites were no match for the giant Canaanites (Numbers 13:25–29). On paper, Gideon's tiny army was no match for the hordes of Midianites (Judges 7). None of the experts thought David had a chance against mighty Goliath (1 Samuel 17:1–51). And who would have predicted that a small band of followers of a man named Jesus could turn the world upside down (Acts 17:6)? In each of those situations, the underdog won—God brought the victory. The common factor in all these events was God's participation.

During your lifetime, you will face many powerful foes, insurmountable obstacles, and daunting tasks. At those times, you could easily give up without a fight—you don't have a chance "on paper." But with God anything is possible. Determine to do what he wants you to do, to give it your all, and leave the results to him. Anything is possible—even great upsets!

ALSO ON THIS DAY . . .

1958—The NCAA added the two-point conversion to football scoring.

1966—Red Auerbach won his 1,000th game as coach of the NBA Boston Celtics.

1997—Annika Sorenstam won the LPGA Chrysler-Plymouth Tournament of Champions.

BIRTHDAYS:

1944—Joe Frazier, heavyweight boxing champion

1977—Sara Walsh, South Bend IN, fencer—foil (Olympics, 1996)

1982—Dontrelle Willis, MLB pitcher (Marlins and Tigers)

> Jesus looked at them and said, "With man this is impossible, but not with God; all things are possible with God." **Mark 10:27**

FUN FACT This was the first time that famous celebrities appeared for the Super Bowl festivities. Entertainer Bob Hope led a pregame ceremony honoring the astronauts of Project Apollo and the recently completed Apollo 8 mission, the first manned flight around the Moon.

In the beginning God . . .

APOLLO 8 · SIX CENTS · UNITED STATES

Basketball Nicknames

1. Shaquille O'Neal
2. Clyde Drexler
3. Julius Erving
4. Allen Iverson
5. Anthony Webb
6. Pete Maravich
7. Phil Jackson
8. Chris Webber
9. Charles Barkley
10. Dennis Rodman
11. Dwayne Wade
12. David Robinson
13. John Wooden
14. Isiah Thomas
15. Karl Malone
16. Kobe Bryant
17. Kevin Garnett
18. Bob Knight
19. Bill Bradley
20. Jason Kidd
21. LeBron James
22. Mike Krzyzewski
23. Larry Bird
24. Michael Jordan
25. Ray Allen
26. Wilt Chamberlain
27. Steve Nash
28. Toni Kukoc
29. Tracy McGrady
30. Shawn Kemp

a. The Stilt
b. The Legend
c. Coach K
d. The Black Mamba
e. Air
f. The Big Ticket
g. Zeke
h. J-Kidd
i. The Zen Master
j. Jesus Shuttlesworth
k. Mailman
l. The Round Mound of Rebound
m. The Croatian Sensation
n. C-Webb
o. Spud
p. Tmac
q. King James
r. Dr. J
s. The Worm
t. The Wizard of Westwood
u. Rain Man
v. Captain Canada
w. The Glide
x. Flash
y. Dollar Bill
z. Diesel
aa. Al
bb. Pistol
cc. The General
dd. The Admiral

In the **Blink** of an **Eye**

ON THIS DAY IN 1990, TRENT TUCKER OF THE NEW YORK KNICKS HIT A LAST-SECOND SHOT TO DEFEAT THE CHICAGO BULLS 109-106.

What Trent Tucker did may not seem like a big deal; after all, lots of games are decided on the last shot. But Tucker's shot caused the NBA to change their rules. Here's why. When play stopped with the ball out of bounds, the game clock showed 0.1 second (that's 1/10 of a second). New York inbounded the ball to Tucker, who caught it twenty-six feet from the basket, turned, and launched a three pointer before the timekeeper could start the clock. The Bulls protested that his shot would take more than 0.1 second, and time should have expired. Later, NBA officials agreed (but didn't change the outcome) and made a new rule. Dubbed the "Trent Tucker Rule," they said that no shot taken with less than 0.3 on the clock could count, and that only a tip-in or dunk could be accepted with that much time remaining.

A person can only do so much in 0.1 second. Count from 1 to 10 as fast as you can, and you'll see how fast a tenth is—like a blink of an eye, and evidently quicker than the time-keeper's finger.

The Bible talks about something amazing that will happen that quickly. Get this: "But let me reveal to you a wonderful secret. We will not all die, but we will all be transformed! It will happen in a moment, in the blink of an eye, when the last trumpet is blown. For when the trumpet sounds, those who have died will be raised to live forever. And we who are living will also be transformed. For our dying bodies must be transformed into bodies that will never die; our mortal bodies must be transformed into immortal bodies" (1 Corinthians 15:51–53, NLT). The Apostle Paul is talking about when Christ returns to earth. Suddenly, faster than we can imagine, everything will change—the world, our bodies, our situation, our future, everything. And with God as Timekeeper, we know that this will happen at just the right time. Trumpet sounds! Game over!

This is a great promise that should give us hope. No matter how bad the outlook, we know that Jesus will return and get things right. Every time you hear the final horn at a game, remember this truth.

....

ALSO ON THIS DAY . . .

1934—Babe Ruth signed a contract for $35,000 ($17,000 cut).

1967—In Super Bowl I the Green Bay Packers beat the Kansas City Chiefs, 35-10, in Los Angeles.

1990—Forty-two-year-old George Foreman knocked out Gerry Cooney in the second round of their heavyweight boxing match.

BIRTHDAYS:

1841—Lord Frederick Stanley, presenter of hockey's Stanley Cup

1979—Drew Brees, NFL football player (New Orleans Saints quarterback) and MVP of Super Bowl XLIV

1980—Matt Holiday, MLB player

. . . while we wait for the blessed hope—the glorious appearing of our great God and Savior, Jesus Christ. **Titus 2:13**

FUN FACT »
Sixteen years passed before someone actually tipped in a shot with only 0.1 second remaining—David Lee did it against Charlotte. That game also took place at Madison Square Garden, with Bobcats owner—and former Bull—Michael Jordan watching from the sideline. Once again, New York hit the winner, and once again, Michael Jordan was on the losing end.

JANUARY 16 Running to **Honor God**

On this day in 1902, famed Scottish Olympian Eric Liddell was born in Tientsin, China.

At the Summer Olympic Games in Paris in 1924, there was one thing you were guaranteed not to find on any given Sunday: Eric Liddell running. Liddell, a Christian, believed that competing on Sunday dishonored God. But his best event, the 100-meter race, was scheduled for Sunday.

Imagine the pressure of being the fastest runner in Scotland, one who trained at Edinburgh University and was called "the Flying Scotsman." Imagine the hopes of people all over Scotland and the entire British Empire, people who are hungry for their first gold medal ever—if only you would run.

So what did Eric Liddell do? He gave up his dream of running in the 100-meter race and endured the scorn of those with disappointed hopes and who probably pegged him as a "loser." But contrary to their beliefs, Liddell's Olympic run was not over. He could still compete in the 400-meter race later that week—a race for which he hadn't yet trained.

Liddell was given a verse that became a motto for his life: 1 Samuel 2:30. This was a message that God spoke to the priest Eli (1 Samuel 2) about Eli's family. Those who honored God would be honored by God. And on the day that Liddell ran the 400 meters, Liddell learned the truth of that verse. He crossed the finish line in the gold-medal position and established a new world record. One year after the Olympics, he became a missionary to China but still competed in races.

Like Liddell, there may be some decisions you have to make that might make you seem like a loser in the eyes of your friends. But if your goal is to honor God, you're already a winner in God's eyes.

············

ALSO ON THIS DAY . . .

1905—Ottawa Silver beat Dawson City (Yukon) for the Stanley Cup, with one player, Frank McGee, scoring 14 goals.

1970—The NFL went from 4 divisions to 2 conferences of 3 divisions each (6 total divisions) after the NFL/AFL merger.

1981—Ivan Lendl intentionally lost a match at the Volvo Masters Tournament in order to avoid having to play Bjorn Borg.

2005—NHL commissioner Gary Bettman cancelled the season, the first time a North American professional sports league had to cancel a season due to a labor dispute.

BIRTHDAYS:

1935—A. J. Foyt, a four-time winner of the Indianapolis 500

1972—Jerome Bettis, running back for the Pittsburgh Steelers

1980—Albert Pujols, MLB All-Star first baseman (St. Louis Cardinals)

The LORD declares: "Far be it from me! Those who honor me I will honor, but those who despise me will be disdained." **1 Samuel 2:30**

Fun Fact In 1981, *Chariots of Fire*, a movie based on Eric Liddell's life, won the Academy Award for Best Picture.

Movin' On

On this day in 1995, the Los Angeles Rams announced that they would be moving to St Louis.

Diehard fans were distraught, jilted, enraged—how could their beloved team leave them? They had been the *Los Angeles* Rams since 1946—nearly fifty years, but they would be relocating several states and more than 2,000 miles to the east.

This had happened before to other professional franchises (for example, baseball's Brooklyn Dodgers to Los Angeles, New York Giants to San Francisco, Milwaukee Braves to Atlanta, basketball's Minneapolis Lakers to Los Angeles, and New Orleans Jazz to Salt Lake City) and has happened since (for example, football's Baltimore Colts to Indianapolis, Cleveland Browns to Baltimore, hockey's Winnipeg Jets to Phoenix, and Hartford Whalers to Raleigh [North Carolina]). In every move, local fans of the moving team feel cheated.

In each case, the decision is explained in business terms—the team was losing money in one place and the new location offered more (fan base, tax incentives, new stadium). But the "reasons" don't fill the void in the heart of the loyal fan.

We value loyalty and expect it in our loved ones, friends, co-workers, team members, and even sports franchises. And when our loyalty seems to be disrespected, trashed, we feel hurt and angered.

But have *we* ever been disloyal? How about not setting the record straight when we hear gossip about a friend? What about switching sides when it helps us get ahead? What about ignoring someone or not inviting him or her because that person isn't popular? And how about keeping quiet in class or a conversation when the topic of God or faith comes up? Remember the Apostle Peter? He was totally disloyal to Jesus when he denied even knowing him (see Matthew 26:60–75).

Proverbs reminds us, "Many will say they are loyal friends, but who can find one who is truly reliable?" (Proverbs 20:6, NLT). Choose to be that kind of person—loyal to the truth, to friends and family, and, most important of all, to your Savior. Don't "relocate" for a "better offer."

....

ALSO ON THIS DAY . . .

1916—Jim Barnes won the first PGA Championship at Siwanoy Country Club, Bronxville, NY.

1963—Wilt Chamberlain of the NBA San Francisco Warriors scored 67 points versus Los Angeles.

1989—The Phoenix Suns canceled their game at the Miami Heat due to racial unrest in Miami.

BIRTHDAYS:

1931—Don Zimmer, American baseball player, manager, and coach

1942—Muhammad Ali (Cassius Clay), heavyweight champion boxer (1964-67 and 1974-78)

1982—Dwyane Wade, NBA star (Miami Heat)

Create in me a pure heart, O God, and renew a steadfast spirit within me. **Psalm 51:10**

FUN FACT Basketball great Wilt Chamberlain never fouled out of a game.

18 In Our **Place**

ON THIS DAY IN 1973, THE BOSTON RED SOX SIGNED ORLANDO CEPEDA AS THE AMERICAN LEAGUE'S FIRST DH (DESIGNATED HITTER).

Most Major League baseball pitchers aren't very good hitters. That's because they spend most of the practice time working on their pitching, not their hitting; they aren't paid to have a good batting

D.H.

average or hit home runs; and they only get into about every fifth game. When pitchers bat, they often strike out, unless they're told to lay down a sacrifice bunt.

Because of this, and to make the game more interesting, in 1973 the American League created the position of "designated hitter." This player, the DH, doesn't play in the field but just hits for the pitcher, allowing the pitcher to keep pitching but

not bat. (In the National League pitchers still have to hit for themselves.)

At times we'd love to have someone like a DH to take our place. Say you're unprepared for a big test—wouldn't a DT (designated test-taker) be nice? Or suppose you have a job at home that you're supposed to do; instead of having to stop watching TV, your DC (designated chore-doer) jumps in and does the work—sweet! You can probably imagine other times and places for a DH.

Of course someone taking our place would really help in a situation where we are *totally helpless on our own*—even worse than a pitcher in the batting box. And that's exactly the case with our sin. The Bible points out that our sins—disobeying God by doing or thinking what we shouldn't and *not* doing what we should—separate us from him. In fact, we cannot be forgiven and have eternal life, including heaven, on our own. We're toast.

The good news is that Jesus is our DS (designated sin-taker). The Bible says that even though Jesus was perfect and perfectly sinless, he "became sin for us" (2 Corinthians 5:21). And he died on the cross in our place, paying the penalty for our sins (Romans 5:6–8). So now, because of Jesus and by faith in him, we can know God, be forgiven of all our sins, and have eternal life.

Orlando Cepeda may have been the first DH, but Jesus is the first and *only* DS. If you have put your faith in him, thank him for all that he has done for you.

....

ALSO ON THIS DAY . . .

1886—Modern field hockey was born with the formation of the Hockey Association in England.

1958—The NHL had its first black player—William O'Ree, Boston Bruins.

1983—The International Olympic Committee restored Jim Thorpe's Olympic medals seventy years after they were taken from him for being paid $25 in semipro baseball.

1996—Baseball owners unanimously approved interleague play, beginning in 1997.

And [Jesus] died for all, that those who live should no longer live for themselves but for him who died for them and was raised again. **2 Corinthians 5:15**

FUN FACT
All major league umpires must wear black underwear while on the job.

BIRTHDAYS:

1938—Curt Flood, Major League baseball player (St. Louis Cardinals); his lawsuit opened the way for free agency.

1980—Julius Peppers, NFL football player (Carolina Panthers and Chicago Bears)

1985—Riccardo Montolivo, Italian soccer player

Keep **Peddlin'**

On this day in 1903, a new bicycle race, the Tour de France, was announced.

Every July, nearly 200 cyclists from around the world race approximately 2,200 miles throughout France and bordering countries. Lasting three weeks, it is probably the most demanding athletic event because of the distance and the type of terrain. Competing in this race has been compared to running a marathon several days a week for nearly three weeks. And the total elevation is comparable to climbing three Mt. Everests.

For anyone to just make it through the whole race takes tremendous dedication, time, and hard work. Becoming a world-class cyclist begins with serious training, the right equipment and nutrition, helpful coaching, and personal commitment. It means riding thousands of miles in all types of conditions and fighting through aches and pains. With the desire to reach that goal,

daily workouts would become almost an obsession. Eventually, after several years, competing in the Tour de France might be possible.

The Bible often compares the Christian life to a long-distance endurance race—like a Tour de France, not a sprint. Listen to what Paul says about the race and about conditioning: "Do you not know that in a race all the runners run, but only one gets the prize? Run in such a way as to get the prize. Everyone who competes in the games goes into strict training. They do it to get a crown that will not last; but we do it to get a crown that will last forever. Therefore I do not run like a man running aimlessly; I do not fight like a man beating the air. No, I beat my body and make it my slave so that after I have preached to others, I myself will not be disqualified for the prize" (1 Corinthians 9:24–27).

Our prize is to become all that God wants us to become, to hear him say, "Well done!"

(Matthew 5:23). Just like the endurance runner or biker, that begins with focusing on the goal, following the instructions of our "spiritual trainer" (Jesus), and then exercising our "spiritual muscles" (praying, reading the Bible, showing love for others). But we won't be doing this on our own—God is in us, giving us the strength to do what he wants. "Being confident of this, that he who began a good work in you will carry it on to completion until the day of Christ Jesus" (Philippians 1:6).

ALSO ON THIS DAY . . .

1952—The PGA voted to allow black participants.

1956—Hoboken dedicated a plaque at Elysian Field honoring the achievements of Alexander Cartwright in organizing early baseball.

1974—Notre Dame beat UCLA, ending their NCAA-record eighty-eight-game basketball winning streak.

BIRTHDAYS:

1932—Joe Schmidt, NFL Hall of Famer (Detroit Lions)

1979—Svetlana Khorkina, Russian gymnast

1992—Shawn Johnson, American gymnastics champion

Continue to work out your salvation with fear and trembling, for it is God who works in you to will and to act according to his good purpose. **Philippians 2:12–13**

Fun Fact

In 1999, demonstrating firemen stopped the Tour de France and pelted riders with stink bombs.

Winter Olympics

1. In what year were the Winter Olympics held for the first time in order to not coincide with the Summer Olympics?
   a. 1975
   b. 1986
   c. 1992
   d. 2000

2. Where were the 1972 Olympics held for the first time?
   a. England
   b. Australia
   c. South Africa
   d. Asia

3. Which direction do long-track speed skaters move around the rink?
   a. Clockwise
   b. Counterclockwise

4. The Winter Olympics have never been held in the southern hemisphere.
   a. True
   b. False

5. Which country will host the 2014 Winter Olympic games?
   a. Russia
   b. India
   c. Scotland
   d. New Zealand

6. Where were the first Winter Olympics held?
   a. USA
   b. France
   c. Italy
   d. Sweden

7. Who won the first gold medal ever at the Winter Olympics?
   a. Scott Hamilton
   b. Kristi Yamaguchi
   c. Shaun White
   d. Charles Jewtaw

8. Before the existence of the Winter Olympics, which of these events was held during the summer games?
   a. Figure skating
   b. Ice hockey
   c. Both of the above
   d. None of the above

9. How many sports did the first Winter Olympics have?
   a. 14
   b. 9
   c. 25
   d. 2

10. Which of these events was not included in the first Winter Olympics?
    a. Luge
    b. Figure skating
    c. Ice hockey
    d. Bobsled

ANSWERS: 1.c, 2.d, 3.b, 4.a, 5.a, 6.b, 7.d, 8.c, 9.b, 10.a

Crash!

On this day in 1988, Mike Tyson knocked out (TKO) Larry Holmes in the fourth round to claim the heavyweight boxing title.

Muscular, skilled, and "mean," Mike Tyson was a boxing machine. Nicknamed "Kid Dynamite" and "Iron Mike," he won his first nineteen professional bouts by knockout, twelve in the first round. Tyson reigned as the undisputed heavyweight champion and was (and still is) the youngest man ever to win the WBC, WBA, and IBF world heavyweight titles. Iron Mike had it all—money, fame, power—and he was flying high. Being one of the world's strongest men and arguably its best fighter, he probably felt invincible. But he spun out of control and crashed.

Among other problems and conflicts, in 1992, Mike was convicted of sexual assault, and he served three years in prison. A couple of years later, he was disqualified in his fight with Evander Holyfield for biting off part of his ear. In 2003, Tyson declared bankruptcy, despite earning over 300 million dollars during his career.

Mike Tyson isn't alone in this tragic career path. Many people with great talent and potential have fallen short. Like a bottle rocket, they zoom up and light the sky but then crash to earth. The possible reasons for the crash are many. Iron Mike was surrounded by lots of people—hangers-on, groupies—who spoke his praises. Listening to them, sheltered from the real world, and with so much money and power, perhaps Mike assumed he could do whatever he wanted, with no consequences—he could get away with it. He was wrong.

God warned about that kind of attitude when he said, "be sure that your sin will find you out" (Numbers 32:23). Regardless of a person's status, wealth, or position, eventually the truth will come out. Jesus said, "For whatever is hidden is meant to be disclosed, and whatever is concealed is meant to be brought out into the open" (Mark 4:22). Many powerful people have discovered that to be true, to their sorrow.

You may not have as many temptations as Mike Tyson, but you still can fall just the same. So be careful to follow Christ, relying on God's strength for each day.

ALSO ON THIS DAY . . .

1857—The National Association of Baseball Players was founded.

1973—George Foreman TKOed Joe Frazier in the second round for the heavyweight boxing title.

1984—Annette Kennedy of SUNY sets the women's basketball scoring record for one game with seventy points.

1998—The World League of American football became the NFL East Division.

BIRTHDAYS:

1927—Joe Perry, Stephens, AK, NFL Hall-of-Fame fullback (San Francisco 49ers and Baltimore Colts)

1952—Karen Moe-Thornton, Del Monte, Philippines, American butterfly swimmer who won the gold medal in the 1972 Olympics

1988—Greg Oden, Buffalo, NY, NBA center (Portland Trailblazers)

Do not be deceived: God cannot be mocked. [A person] reaps what [he or she] sows. **Galatians 6:7**

FUN FACT "Another thing that freaks me out is time. Time is like a book. You have a beginning, a middle, and an end. It's just a cycle." Mike Tyson

 23 Straight **Arrow**

On this day in 1879, the National Archery Association was formed in Crawfordsville, Indiana.

To participate in archery, you'll need three things: a bow, arrows, and a target. To have **success** in archery, you'll need these three things: a **good** bow, with the right tension for you, **good** arrows, and a **realistic** target at a **realistic** distance (too close, say a few feet, or too far, say a mile, would be silly). Let's imagine that you've read up on archery, you've taken a course on it, and you've visited the sporting-goods store and bought the perfect bow for you. Behind your house, you've set up a target at the other end of the yard. Now you set your arrow, pull back the bow string, and let it fly . . . but you don't come close to the target. What's the problem? Probably the arrow.

Arrows need to have an "arrowhead" at one end, a "fletching" with "vanes"

at the other end, and a strong and straight "shaft," and, they must be properly weighted. All those factors are important in an arrow. But let's look at the word *straight*. Imagine shooting an arrow with a crooked shaft—you'd be lucky to come near your target.

You may have heard the expression "straight arrow" when referring to someone. It usually means the person has his or her act together, especially regarding morals and values. This person knows what's important in life and always tries to do what is right. We can depend on straight-arrow people—they keep their word and won't let us down. And we know they're heading straight for the bull's-eye.

Followers of Christ should have a straight-arrow reputation. People should know what we stand for, that we will try hard to always do what glorifies God and is right, and that we will stand for God's truth. As John wrote to his friend Gaius centuries ago, "Dear friend, you are faithful in what you

are doing for the brothers, even though they are strangers to you. They have told the church about your love" (3 John 5–6).

What do you think a friend might write about you and your character? Are you a straight arrow?

ALSO ON THIS DAY . . .

1943—The Detroit Red Wings scored an NHL-record eight goals in one period.

1955—Babe Didrikson-Zaharias won the LPGA Tampa Golf Open.

1983—Bjorn Borg announced his retirement from professional tennis.

It teaches us to say "No" to ungodliness and worldly passions, and to live self-controlled, upright and godly lives in this present age, while we wait for the blessed hope. **Titus 2:12–13**

FUN FACT » The first arrows were made of pine and had a main shaft and a six-to-eight-inches-long foreshaft with an arrowhead made of flint.

BIRTHDAYS:

1963—Hakeem Olajuwon, Lagos, Nigeria, NBA center (Houston Rockets)

1971—Julie Foudy, San Diego, CA, Olympic and World Cup soccer midfielder

1980—Theresa Kulikowski, Tacoma, WA, gymnast (Olympics, 1996)

Refs and **Rules**

ON THIS DAY IN 1947, THE
NATIONAL FOOTBALL LEAGUE ADDED
A FIFTH OFFICIAL, THE BACK JUDGE
(TODAY THEY USE SEVEN).

Are you blind?" "What do you mean foul? She hardly touched her!" "Kill the umpire!" "Come on, ref—give us a break!"

Shouts like those are common at athletic events. With every foul, infraction, or close call, half the crowd is convinced that the referee, umpire, or judge made the wrong decision. Have you ever felt that way? Even fans on the last row of the bleachers can think they saw the play better and know the truth. And lots of the comments seem to imply that the game would go better without any refs. But think how that would go, with every player deciding if someone fouled, went out of bounds, made an illegal move or hit, or took too long.

The whole time would be spent arguing—it would be chaos.

Having rules and rule enforcers makes athletic contests work. What if a football field had no sideline markers, a basketball court had no out-of-bounds, a race had no official start or finish line, a swimming pool had no lane markers, a wrestling match had no time limit or illegal holds . . . ? And what if the events had no one to make sure that no contestant had an unfair advantage over another?

Life has rules, too. They were given to us by God not to keep us from being free but to help us to get the most out of life, to succeed. Sometimes we'd rather not play by his rules,

to ignore them or to cheat. If everyone lived that way, imagine the mess, the chaos. God's rules were given long ago, in the Ten Commandments (you can look them up in Exodus 20). And Jesus summarized the rules in what has been called the Great Commandment (Matthew 22:37–40).

God designed the "game," wrote the rules, and is the referee! To win at life, play the game his way, by his rules.

ALSO ON THIS DAY . . .

1901—The first games were played in baseball's American League.

1962—Jackie Robinson became the first African American elected to the Baseball Hall of Fame.

1964—CBS purchased the NFL 1964 and 1965 television rights for $28.2 million.

BIRTHDAYS:

1916—Jack Brickhouse, Peoria, IL, Hall-of-Fame American sports broadcaster

1968—Mary Lou Retton, Fairmont, WV, American gymnast, winner of one gold, two silver, and two bronze medals in the 1984 Olympics

1983—Scott Speed, Manteca, CA, American race car driver

Jesus replied: "'Love the Lord your God with all your heart and with all your soul and with all your mind.' This is the first and greatest commandment. And the second is like it: 'Love your neighbor as yourself.' All the Law and the Prophets hang on these two commandments." **Matthew 22:37–40**

Fun Fact
According to Major League Baseball rules, players can get to first base in twenty-three ways. The most unusual is if a runner is on first base when the game is suspended and that runner gets traded before the make-up game, a new player is allowed to take that runner's place when the game is resumed, without being a "pinch runner."

Let the Games Begin

On this day in 1924, the first Winter Olympic Games opened in Chamonix, France.

What's your favorite part of the Olympics? Some like the opening ceremonies, with amazing performances, a light show, music, fireworks, and the parade of athletes from all the participating countries. Many prefer the closing ceremonies, with another spectacular show. For most, however, a special sport captures their attention. In the Winter Olympics, it may be the downhill or slalom ski races, the skeleton, snowboard aerials, short-track speed skating, figure skating, or hockey. (Some even like curling!) Some of those sports hadn't even been invented back in 1924.

What seems most impressive about the Olympics, however, is the international flavor. Athletes from all over the world—from some countries that we've hardly ever heard of—come to one city to compete. And, at least for a couple of weeks, this mixture of races, nationalities, cultures, and languages seems to work—people actually living together in peace, getting along. If only we all lived that way the rest of the time! Instead, new conflicts pop up almost daily between bordering communities and nations, ethnic groups, religions, political affiliations, and the like. And we see the same pattern much closer to home, even at school, with kids fighting because of their differences.

The Bible tells us why this happens: "What causes fights and quarrels among you? Don't they come from your desires that battle within you?" (James 4:1). In other words, our sin nature—the inward push to be selfish and do only what pleases us—is the culprit. Fortunately, through his Holy Spirit, God gives us the ability to make the right choices, to become "peacemakers" instead of conflict starters.

And Jesus said that peacemakers are "blessed" (Matthew 5:9).

Do your part for world peace. Be a peacemaker in your home, your school, your church, and your neighborhood.

ALSO ON THIS DAY . . .

1978—The San Diego Padres traded pitcher Dave Tomlin and $125,000 to the Rangers for Gaylord Perry, who went on to win the 1978 Cy Young Award.

1989—Michael Jordan scored his 10,000th NBA point in just his 5th season.

1998—Spice Girl Victoria Adams (Posh) and soccer star David Beckham got engaged.

BIRTHDAYS:

1918—Ernie Harwell, Washington, GA, Hall-of-Fame American baseball sportscaster

1937—Don Maynard, Crosbyton, TX, NFL receiver (New York Jets)

1962—Chris Chelios, Chicago, IL, NHL defenseman (Chicago Blackhawks, Detroit Red Wings)

> Blessed are the peacemakers, for they will be called sons [and daughters] of God. **Matthew 5:9**

FUN FACT The first gold medal awarded in the Chamonix Olympic Winter Games was won by Charles Jewtraw of the United States in the 500-meter speed skate. Also, Charles Granville Bruce won a prize for alpinisme (mountain climbing), a sport that would be difficult to have at the Olympics. Bruce led the expedition that had tried to climb Mount Everest in 1922.

Defense!

On this day in 1986, the Chicago Bears beat the New England Patriots, 46-10, in New Orleans in Super Bowl XX.

Chicago entered this game as huge favorites, and they lived up to it, winning easily. The Bears' lineup featured several colorful and talented players on both sides of the ball, including arguably the greatest running back ever, Walter Payton. But the secret of their success was their defense. Led by eventual Hall of Famers Mike Singletary and Dan Hampton and Super Bowl MVP Richard Dent, the team had shut out their previous two playoff opponents. During the regular season, the Bears' defense allowed the fewest points (198), total yards (4,135), and rushing yards (1,319) of any team. And they led the league in interceptions with thirty-four. This Bears team has been recognized as one of the all-time best defensive units.

Coaches say, "Defense wins championships." That seems to be true in sports. It definitely is true in life. Drivers-ed students are taught about "defensive driving"—being aware of other drivers and not assuming that everyone will turn, change lanes, stop, or go at the right times. Many people learn self-defense skills, knowing that the world is not always safe. And certainly we should be careful about what we eat and drink, where we invest money, and who we hang around with.

The Bible also talks about defense. Peter writes, "Be self-controlled and alert. Your enemy the devil prowls around like a roaring lion looking for someone to devour. Resist him, standing firm in the faith" (1 Peter 5:8–9). His point is that we should know our opponent and be ready for his attacks. And Paul talks about wearing defensive armor: "In addition to all this, take up the shield of faith, with which you can extinguish all the flaming arrows of the evil one" (Ephesians 6:16).

Clearly, spiritual defense is important. Just as in football, this means knowing your opponent and being trained and alert so you can resist his attacks. Teamwork makes the defense stronger. So find a friend to join the team. You can pray together and encourage each other as you move toward victory.

ALSO ON THIS DAY . . .

1913—Jim Thorpe relinquished his 1912 Olympic medals for being a professional.

1960—High-school basketball sensation Danny Heater scored 135 points in a game.

1960—Pete Rozelle was elected NFL commissioner on the twenty-third ballot.

BIRTHDAYS:

1819—Abner Doubleday, Ballston Spa, NY, a Union general-major and the inventor of baseball

1961—Wayne Gretzky, Brantford, Ontario, Canadian hockey player and one of the NHL's all-time greats (Oilers, King, Rangers)

1977—Vince Carter, Daytona Beach, FL, NBA guard/forward (Raptors, Nets, Magic)

Therefore put on the full armor of God, so that when the day of evil comes, you may be able to stand your ground, and after you have done everything, to stand. **Ephesians 6:13**

Fun Fact So confident of victory, in the middle of the season the Chicago Bears recorded the "Super Bowl Shuffle," which instantly became a mainstream phenomenon. The song sold more than a half-million singles and reached number forty-one on the music charts.

On what team was Trent Tucker playing when he beat the Chicago Bulls on a last-second shot? (Jan. 15)

What is the NAA? (Jan. 23)

In 1945, what did the baseball writers fail to do? (Jan. 10)

When was the first football game played in the Rose Bowl? (Jan. 1)

Who is known as Mr. Cub? (Jan. 31)

In what country were the first Winter Olympic Games played? (Jan. 25)

In what baseball league (not AL or NL) did Satchel Paige and Josh Gibson play? (Jan. 4)

What did Pete Rose admit in 2004? (Jan. 8)

What boxer is known as "Iron Mike"? (Jan. 22)

How many points did the winning team score in the most lopsided high school basketball game in history? (Jan. 29)

In what country was the stadium barrier that collapsed in 1971 and killed sixty-six people? (Jan. 2)

What's the name of the famous bicycle race around France? (Jan. 19)

In 1983, against what team did Tony Dorsett make his ninety-nine yard run? (Jan. 3)

What's a DH, and who was the first one in Major League Baseball? (Jan. 18)

What great Super Bowl football team recorded the "Super Bowl Shuffle"? (Jan. 26)

What do most people remember about Rick Monday? (Jan. 11)

What college men's basketball team won eighty-eight games in a row? (Jan. 30)

In 1989, who signed with ESPN to televise 175 games the next year? (Jan. 5)

In what country was the famous runner Eric Liddell born? (Jan. 16)

What city is the home of the Saints? (Jan. 9)

How many officials are used in a typical NFL game these days? (Jan. 24)

Who was the quarterback when the New York Jets upset the Baltimore Colts in Super Bowl III? (Jan. 12)

In 1995, to what city did the Los Angeles Rams move? (Jan. 17)

Not Even **Close**

On this day in 1964, the high school basketball game with the most lopsided score was played (in Louisiana): 211-29.

How would you like to have been on the losing team in that game? Talk about humiliating! And think about the stats! The high scorer for the winning team probably scored more than seventy points, way more than lots of high school teams score for the whole game. When we see a score like that, we wonder how it could be possible. A high school game only has thirty-two minutes of playing time. Thus the winning team scored an average of 6.6 points per minute. Was one team that good and the other team that bad (maybe they just had a really off shooting night)? But a more important question is how could the one coach allow his or her team to run up the score like that? Talk about poor sportsmanship!

Playing sports, especially through high school, is supposed to be about learning life lessons, exercising, developing skills, and having fun. Sure teams want to win and should try hard to do so; otherwise, why keep score? But they shouldn't win at all costs, disrespect the opponent, or injure the competition. In many cases, unfortunately, that's what it has come to. Coaches and parents scream. Fights break out. Athletes cheat—in conditioning and in the events themselves. We need to play fair and learn to be good losers and good winners. Postgame congratulations should be sincere.

The truth—winning *isn't* everything. Many things are more important—faith, family, and friends, to name just three. God wants us to use our gifts well, to do our best, and if that leads to wins, great. But being his kind of person means so much more.

You'll see plenty of great examples of good sportsmanship, too. Thank God for those athletes, and ask him to help you compete his way.

ALSO ON THIS DAY . . .

1900—The American League was organized in Buffalo, Chicago, Cleveland, Detroit, Indianapolis, Kansas City, Milwaukee, and Minneapolis.

1936—The first players were elected to the Baseball Hall of Fame: Ty Cobb, Babe Ruth, Honus Wagner, Christy Matthewson, and Walter Johnson.

1995—Andre Agassi defeated Pete Sampras to win the Australian Open.

BIRTHDAYS:

1960—Steve Sax, West Sacramento, CA, MLB second baseman (Dodgers, Yankees, White Sox, Athletics)

1965—Peter Lundgren, Gudmundra, Sweden, Swedish tennis star

1969—Karen Fonteyne, Canadian synchronized swimmer (Olympics silver, '96)

Each of you should look not only to your own interests, but also to the interests of others. **Philippians 2:4**

FUN FACT Babe Ruth wore number three because he batted third.

30 **Winning** Streek

ON THIS DAY IN 1971, UCLA BEGAN ITS EIGHTY-EIGHT-BASKETBALL-GAME WINNING STREAK.

When coach John Wooden sent his players out to play the University of California, Santa Barbara, he didn't say, "All right, men, let's win and start a record-setting winning streak." In fact, no one dreamed that this would be the first in a string of eighty-eight victories. The players just went out and played their best and emerged with a 74-61 win. They did the same in the next game and the next and the next . . . and they had a winning streak.

Winning and losing streaks are built over one season and beyond, one contest at a time.

That's true in other areas, too. A person becomes a straight-A student one class and one assignment at a time. A successful salesperson makes one call,

one sale at a time. A bestselling author has to write one book, one chapter, and, actually, one line at a time. Even a marathon runner has to take one stride at a time.

The Bible is clear that God's purpose for us is to become like Jesus (Romans 8:29). That's a huge goal, much greater than any winning streak, national championship, or personal achievement. And we may think that it's way beyond us and get discouraged or not even try. But as with everything else, becoming like Christ is a process that takes place one day, one decision at a time.

Jesus said, "Seek first [God's] kingdom and his righteousness, and all these things will be given to you as well. Therefore do not worry about tomorrow, for

tomorrow will worry about itself. Each day has enough trouble of its own" (Matthew 6:33–34). This means taking each day as it comes, living for Christ in it, and letting God take care of the rest. And we're not alone in this: God is helping us do what he wants.

Win today—then tomorrow and the next day. Start your own winning streak!

ALSO ON THIS DAY . . .

1948—The fifth Winter Olympics opened in Moritz, Switzerland.

1993—In the sixty-seventh Australian Women's Tennis Open, Monica Seles beat Steffi Graf (4-6, 6-3, 6-2).

2000—In Super Bowl XXXIV, the St. Louis Rams beat the Tennessee Titans 23-16 at the Georgia Dome in Atlanta, with MVP Kurt Warner at quarterback.

BIRTHDAYS:

1957—William Payne Stewart, Springfield, MO, PGA golfer

1966—Danielle Goyette, St-Nazaire, Quebec, Canadian ice hockey forward

1973—Jalen Rose, Detroit, MI, NBA guard (Nuggets, Pacers, Bulls, Raptors, Knicks, Suns)

Therefore, since we are surrounded by such a great cloud of witnesses, let us throw off everything that hinders and the sin that so easily entangles, and let us run with perseverance the race marked out for us. **Hebrews 12:1**

Fun Fact Because a lot of players were called up to duty during WWII, the Pittsburgh Steelers and Philadelphia Eagles combined to become the Steagles.

Let's **Play Two!**

On this day in 1931, Ernie Banks, "Mr. Cub" and Chicago Cubs Hall-of-Fame shortstop and first baseman, was born.

Ernie Banks played in the major leagues eighteen years, all with the Chicago Cubs. The Cubs last won the World Series in 1908 and haven't even appeared in the Fall Classic since 1945. Since then they often have been the worst team in the National League. Yet in good or bad seasons, Ernie Banks always came to the ballpark with an optimistic, upbeat attitude and a pure love for the game. He would say, "It's a beautiful day for a ball game. Let's play two!"

The opposite kind of person is one for whom the present and future always look gloomy. He or she seems to complain constantly—about weather, teachers, coaches, parents, food, computers,

traffic, friends, some slight or insult . . . . This person looks like he or she is sucking on a lemon or dill pickle—sour. So, who would you rather hang with— people who bring you down or those who lift you up and make you feel good? The answer is obvious.

Of course, Christians, of all people, should be positive and hopeful. Regardless of the news reports of terrible world events, we know that God is in control. No matter how depleted our finances, we know that God cares about us and will care for us. When we experience loss, we know that we can never lose our God connection. And whatever people say about us—good or bad—we know that God's opinion of us is all that matters.

Almighty God is good, and he loves you. Jesus died for you—you're forgiven. The Holy Spirit lives inside you, changing you and empowering you. God has a great future for you, eventually ending in heaven. Remember all that . . . and smile.

Hey, it's a beautiful day for a ball game!

ALSO ON THIS DAY . . .

1920—Quebec's Joe Malone set a NHL record of seven goals in a game.

1975—UCLA won the men's college basketball championship.

1992—Sportscaster Howard Cosell retired.

BIRTHDAYS:

1919—Jackie Robinson, Cairo, GA, the first black major league baseball player (Dodgers)

1947—Nolan Ryan, Refugio, TX, Hall-of-Fame pitcher with the Mets, Angels, and Astros (seven no-hitters, 5,714 strikeouts)

1976—Buddy Rice, Phoenix, AZ, American race car driver and winner of the 2004 Indy 500

But in your hearts set apart Christ as Lord. Always be prepared to give an answer to everyone who asks you to give the reason for the hope that you have. But do this with gentleness and respect. **1 Peter 3:15**

Fun Fact A "face-off" in hockey was originally called a "puck-off."

The Big **Win**

ON THIS DAY IN 1977, HILLSDALE HIGH SCHOOL DEFEATED PERSON HIGH SCHOOL 2-0 IN BASKETBALL.

Only 1-0 would be a lower possible score for a basketball game, with someone making just one free throw out of two. For this game, the coach for Person High School decided to slow the game way down and only took shots as time was running out. Obviously his team missed all those shots, and Hillsdale emerged with the victory.

If you played on the Hillsdale team, how would you feel about the victory? What if you won 75-73 in overtime—would that make a difference, even though the margin of victory in both games would be the same? Or suppose you played on the Person team and Hillsdale was a huge favorite. Do you think you would feel good for only losing by two points?

The phrase "winning ugly" refers to a victory that was achieved despite poor play. In a basketball game, for example, a team could have stumbled and bumbled their way to victory over an inept opponent. The team would have won "ugly." The score

2-0 seems to qualify as an ugly win. Some say that *how* you get the win, how you play, doesn't matter—a win is a win. So how would you feel about winning ugly?

Many years ago, sports reporter Grantland Rice wrote:

For when the One Great Scorer comes
To write against your name
He marks—not that you won or lost—
But how you played the Game.

That famous poem highlights the Bible truth that God is concerned with *how* we live. He wants us to use our gifts well and to always do our best in everything we do. For a Christ-follower, then, *how* the game is played does matter, even more than the victory. So when you win a match, game, race, or other athletic contest, ask these questions about your performance: Did I give it my best effort? Did I follow the coach's instructions? Was I a good teammate? Did I use my abilities well? Did I respect the officials?

Answering yes means that you played the way God would want you to play.

Sure, you'll feel bad about a loss and good about a win. But you'll feel better about yourself if you played right.

ALSO ON THIS DAY . . .

1968—Vince Lombardi resigned as coach of the Green Bay Packers.

1992—Barry Bonds signed baseball's highest single-year contract ($4.7 million) with the San Francisco Giants.

1998—In the NFL Pro Bowl game, the AFC beat the NFC 29-24.

BIRTHDAYS:

1948—Debbie Austin, Oneida, NY, LPGA golfer

1966—Michelle Akers, Santa Clara, California, soccer forward (Olympics, '96)

1983—Kevin Martin, Zanesville, OH, NBA guard (Houston Rockets)

And whatever you do, whether in word or deed, do it all in the name of the Lord Jesus, giving thanks to God the Father through him. **Colossians 3:17**

FUN FACT »
The first basketball game was played in 1892 with nine players, and the final score was 1-0.

What a **Change!**

On this day in 1970, Pete Maravich became the first college basketball player to score 3,000 points.

"P istol" Pete holds nearly every major NCAA basketball scoring record, including most career points (3,667), highest career scoring average (44.2 points per game), most field goals made (1,387) and attempted (3,166), and most career 50-point games (28).

During his three years of varsity basketball at LSU, he led the nation in scoring each year and was College Player of the Year in 1970. In his senior season Pete scored 50 or more points in 10 of LSU's 31 games, setting an NCAA record for most points (1,381) and highest scoring average in a single season. He did all this without the three-point basket, which wasn't introduced into the college game until 1986.

Pete was also known for his playing style—

dribbling moves, circus shots, and hotdog passes—and his trademark floppy hair and socks. In the pros, he played for the Atlanta Hawks, New Orleans Jazz, and Boston Celtics. Inducted into the Basketball Hall of Fame in 1987, Pete was, and still is, the youngest player to be inducted.

With all the fame and money came the temptations, and eventually Pete's life was torn by personal tragedy and alcoholism, leading to despair and thoughts of suicide. But at his lowest, he found Christ. In his desperation, Pete prayed through his tears, "Jesus, I know you're real because I've tried everything else. I've got nowhere to go. If you don't save me, I won't last two more days."

"From that moment on," he said, "my life was never to be the same again. When I took God into my heart, it was the first true happiness I ever had." Later he added, "I want to be remembered as a Christian, a person that serves him to the

utmost. Not as a basketball player" (from *Pete Maravich*, by Federman and Terrill; Tyndale House, 2008). Pete spent time studying the Bible and telling others about Christ, not knowing he only had a few more years to live.

Tragically, on January 5, 1988, while playing a game of pickup basketball, he collapsed and died of a heart attack at the age of only forty.

Life is short, even for a great athlete like Pete Maravich. But he found the One who mattered, and Pete's story still helps bring people to the Savior.

ALSO ON THIS DAY . . .

1876—Baseball's National League formed with teams in Boston, Chicago, Cincinnati, Hartford, Louisville, New York, Philadelphia, and St. Louis.

1949—Golf champion Ben Hogan was seriously injured in an auto accident.

1959—Vince Lombardi signed a five-year contract to coach the Green Bay Packers.

1974—The Cleveland Cavaliers played the Golden State Warriors in front of the smallest crowd (1,641).

BIRTHDAYS:

1895—George S. Halas (Papa Bear), Chicago, IL, end and legendary coach of the Chicago Bears and cofounder of the NFL

1908—Clarence "Buster" Crabbe, Oakland, CA, swimmer and winner of the Olympic gold medal in 1932, later became an actor

1979—Lindsay Langston, Modesto, CA, archer (Olympics, 1996)

Why, you do not even know what will happen tomorrow. What is your life? You are a mist that appears for a little while and then vanishes. Instead, you ought to say, "If it is the Lord's will, we will live and do this or that." **James 4:14–15**

Fun Fact Compared to right-handed individuals, left-handed people are better at sports that require good spatial judgment and fast reaction.

Sports **Terms**

MATCH the term with the sport.

1. **Drafting**
2. Jab
3. **Medley**
4. Setter
5. **Checking**
6. Throw-in
7. **Bull pen**
8. Dead rubber
9. **Double dribble**
10. Clipping
11. **Tee (not golf)**
12. Icing
13. **Hit and run**
14. Pick and roll
15. **Drop shot**
16. Handicap
17. **Dig**
18. Fore
19. **Drag**
20. Dive shot

a. **Soccer**
b. Volleyball
c. **Baseball**
d. Basketball
e. **Golf**
f. Tennis
g. **Football**
h. Boxing
i. **Swimming**
j. Ice Hockey
k. **Tennis**
l. Golf
m. **Lacrosse**
n. Swimming
o. **Football**
p. Basketball
q. **Baseball**
r. Bicycling
s. **Ice hockey**
t. Volleyball

ANSWERS: 1. r, 2. h, 3. i, 4. b, 5. j, 6. a, 7. c, 8. f, 9. d, 10. g, 11. o, 12. s, 13. q, 14. p, 15. k, 16. e, 17. t, 18. l, 19. n, 20. m.

36

Get **Real!**

Wrestling is a great sport, featured in the summer Olympics, pitting well-conditioned and skilled athletes in one-on-one combat. But professional wrestling, complete with cartoon personalities in outlandish outfits, is something else altogether. Primarily entertainment, it's a show with choreographed and rehearsed acts. In short, as far as sports go, pro wrestling is phony. Those choosing this line of work are usually decent athletes themselves, many having previously competed in football or other sports. But the televised contests are staged, rigged.

Suppose you were to meet a new kid at school who had just moved into the neighborhood. She knows very little about sports but happens to

watch a professional wrestling match on TV. Then, at school, she begins to tell you all about it—very excited about the wrestling moves and the championship won in the match. How would you respond? In a nice way, you probably would explain the difference between what she saw and *genuine* wrestling. One is phony; one is real.

Now suppose you were to meet another new student who knows very little about Jesus. Over the weekend, he hears some people talk about Christian stuff, but it all seems to be a show. Their lives don't match their words. How would you explain the difference between phony believers and real ones?

Unfortunately, some people make a show of faith, but their "faith" is phony, not real. They

might pretend to be Christians to make money, get votes, or to fit into a certain group. Jesus confronted some people like that: the Pharisees. He told his followers to not be like them and that a person's true beliefs count, not his or her religious show (Matthew 23:1–33). Jesus said we should get our hearts right, focusing on him and his kingdom—what's on the inside counts! Then our actions should match what we say we believe.

So are you the real deal? What do people learn about Jesus and true Christianity by watching you?

....

ALSO ON THIS DAY . . .

1948—Dick Button became the first US figure skating Olympic champion.

1948—Gretchen Fraser became the first US woman Olympic slalom champion.

1972—Bob Douglas became the first African American elected to the Basketball Hall of Fame.

1989—Kareem Abdul-Jabar became the first NBA player to score 38,000 points in his career.

BIRTHDAYS:

1891—Elizabeth Ryan, Anaheim, CA, doubles tennis champ, a six-time winner at Wimbledon

1934—Hank Aaron, Mobile, AL, baseball's greatest home-run hitter—755 for his career—and the 1957 NL MVP

1942—Roger Staubach, Cincinnati, OH, Hall-of-Fame NFL quarterback (Dallas Cowboys)

1947—Darrell Waltrip, Owensboro, KY, American race car driver and NASCAR TV analyst

So then, just as you received Christ Jesus as Lord, continue to live in him, rooted and built up in him, strengthened in the faith as you were taught, and overflowing with thankfulness. **Colossians 2:6–7**

FUN FACT André the Giant was also an actor and is most known for his role as Fezzik in 1987's *The Princess Bride*.

Doing His **Part**

On this day in 1927, Smokey Burgess, professional baseball catcher, was born.

You probably never have heard of Forest Harrill "Smokey" Burgess. Here's a quick career summary. During eighteen years in the majors (he retired in 1967), Smokey played for the Cubs, Phillies, Reds, Pirates, and White Sox. He was a five-time all-star and had his best season in 1954, batting .368 in 108 games for the Phillies. But what set Smokey apart from other players was his ability to pinch-hit, and for many years he held the record for career pinch hits with 145.

Pinch-hitting is one of the most difficult, yet valuable, roles in baseball. The player needs to come off the bench, often in a crucial situation and facing a relief pitcher, and be warmed up and ready to swing the bat. That job seems small, and pinch hitters don't get the big headlines and huge salaries, but their work often makes the difference in the game.

Being faithful in the little things matters. That's what Jesus taught in his parable of the talents: "His master replied, 'Well done, good and faithful servant! You have been faithful with a few things; I will put you in charge of many things. Come and share your master's happiness!'" (Matthew 25:21). Jesus wasn't talking about pinch-hitting exactly, but he could have been.

Most people want to be the stars and be in the spotlight, to have the solo or the lead in the play, to be the clean-up hitter and captain. But someone has to play those other, supportive roles. What skills and abilities has God given you? How can you use them, even behind the scenes or in a bit role, to help further his mission on earth? Think of God as your heavenly Coach. You're sitting on the bench when he calls your name to get in the game. Are you ready?

....

ALSO ON THIS DAY . . .

1932—The Olympics had its first dog sled race, Lake Placid, NY (demonstration sport).

1958—Ted Williams signed with the Boston Red Sox for $135,000, making him the highest-paid baseball player.

1983—Nancy Lopez won the LPGA Elizabeth Arden Golf Classic.

2005—In Super Bowl XXXIX, the New England Patriots beat the Philadelphia Eagles 24-21.

BIRTHDAYS:

1895—George Herman (Babe) Ruth, Baltimore, MD, Hall-of-Fame baseball player (Boston Red Sox and New York Yankees)

1953—Susie Hutchison, Flintridge, CA, equestrian show jumper (Olympics, '96)

1976—Kim Zmeskal, Houston, TX, US gymnast (Olympics, '92)

[Jesus said,] "Whoever can be trusted with very little can also be trusted with much, and whoever is dishonest with very little will also be dishonest with much." Luke 16:10

FUN FACT » The first time a golf ball was hit on the moon was in 1971 (by Alan Shepherd).

The "Greatest"

On this day in 1965, Cassius Clay announced that he had become a Muslim and changed his name to Muhammad Ali.

Cassius Clay burst onto the sporting scene when at the 1960 Summer Olympics in Rome he won the gold medal in the light heavyweight division. After turning professional, he went on to become the first boxer to win the heavyweight championship three times. Clay was vocal, both about himself and when taunting his opponents, earning the nickname phrase "The Louisville Lip." Of all his words, the most remembered is "I am the greatest!" This he would proclaim, especially after his victories.

Many disliked this brash fighter simply because of that boast. Others said that claiming to be "the greatest" was all right if someone could back up those words

with actions—and this Cassius seemed to do.

But the "greatest," the "greatest of all time"? Claims like that remind us of individuals and teams in many sports who claim to be "number one" after a victory. But even if they win the *world's championship*, how long does that last? A year at the most . . . until the next "greatest" is crowned.

The truth is that only one person in history actually was and is the *greatest*. And eventually everyone will know that he is King of kings and Lord of lords. And Jesus left us with instructions for being truly great. When the disciples asked what it would take to be the greatest in the kingdom of heaven, Jesus replied, "whoever humbles himself like this child is the greatest in the kingdom of heaven" (Matthew 18:4). The way to greatness with God is humility—serving without looking for the credit, building up others instead of our egos, glorifying God and not ourselves.

Do you want to be "great"? Do it God's way.

ALSO ON THIS DAY . . .

1942—Cornelius Warmerdam (Netherlands) became the first person to pole vault over fifteen feet indoors (15' 3/8").

1986—Debi Thomas won the US Female Figure Skating championship.

1987—Dennis Conner and "Stars & Stripes" brought America's Cup back to the US.

1990—Basketball player Lisa Leslie of Morningside High School in Inglewood, CA, scored 101 points in the first half; South Torrance High School decided not to play the second half and lost 102-24.

BIRTHDAYS:

1964—Cynthia "Sippy" Woodhead, Riverside, CA, swimmer (Olympic silver medalist, '84)

1974—Steve Nash, Charleston, WV, Canadian NBA all-star guard (Dallas Mavericks and Phoenix Suns)

1977—Hillary Wolf, Chicago, IL, extra lightweight judoka (1996 Olympics)

The greatest among you will be your servant. For whoever exalts himself will be humbled, and whoever humbles himself will be exalted. **Matthew 23:11–12**

FUN FACT In one of boxing's biggest upsets, Muhammad Ali regained his title on October 30, 1974, by defeating champion George Foreman in Zaire. In "the Rumble in the Jungle," Ali won by tiring out the champion, leaning on the ropes, covering up, and absorbing ineffective body shots. His strategy was later called "Rope-A-Dope."

The **Little Guy**

ON THIS DAY IN 1986, 5'7" SPUD WEBB OF THE ATLANTA HAWKS WON THE NBA SLAM DUNK COMPETITION.

Each year basketball players seem to get taller and taller. Now almost every college team has at least one seven-footer on the squad. Certainly height gives a player a great advantage in this game, since the goal is to get the basketball through a hoop that stands at ten feet above the floor. And think of the advantage for a tall player who also has a huge vertical leap. So you can see why everyone was surprised that such a relatively short man could win the NBA All-Star Slam Dunk Competition. For Spud

Webb to dunk the ball at all, he had to jump more than four and a half feet off the floor. In the contests, Spud's dunks included the elevator two-handed double-pump dunk, the one-handed off-the-backboard one-handed jam, a 360-degree helicopter one-handed dunk, a 180-degree reverse double-pump slam, and finally, the 180-degree reverse two-handed "strawberry jam" from a lob bounce off the floor. Wow!

Spud didn't let the supposed "handicap" of his size limit what he could do.

Some people think they can't do much because of their gender or family background or race or neighborhood or whatever. But God can use us to do great things for him, regardless of our body shape or other personal characteristics. Remember little David, the shepherd boy? He didn't stand a chance against mighty Goliath (talk about big guys—about 9' tall!). Yet he trusted God and took his shot . . . and the giant fell (see 1 Samuel 17). We may not win a slam-dunk contest,

but we can do God's great work.

The key is depending on God and trusting him to work in us and through us.

So what does God want you to do? Don't let any supposed drawback draw you back. Move forward in faith.

ALSO ON THIS DAY . . .

1936—In the first NFL draft, the Eagles selected Heisman Trophy winner Jay Berwanger.

1985—Bruce Morris of Marshall University made a 92' 5" basketball shot.

1998—Finland beat Sweden 6-0 in the first female ice hockey game in Olympic history.

2010—In Super Bowl XLIV, the New Orleans Saints beat the favored Indianapolis Colts 31-17.

> "Not by might nor by power, but by my Spirit," says the Lord Almighty. **Zechariah 4:6**

BIRTHDAYS:

1925—Raimondo d'Inzeo, Italy, equestrian, and winner of seven Olympic medals (2 gold, 2 silver, and 3 bronze, 1948-76)

1963—Raleigh McKenzie, Knoxville, TN, NFL center/guard (Philadelphia Eagles, San Diego Chargers, Green Bay Packers)

1978—Christa Williams, Houston, TX, softball pitcher, winner of the 1996 Olympic gold medal

Fun Fact
The tallest player in college these days is Mountain State's 7'8" Paul Sturgess. The tallest NBA player is Yao Ming of the Houston Rockets at 7'6", and the tallest basketball player in the world is Sun Mingming of China at 7'9".

Doing It **Right**

On this date in 1980, Rick Barry of the Houston Rockets became the first player in NBA history to score eight three-point field goals in a game.

Rick Barry, named one of the fifty greatest players in NBA history, could score from almost anywhere on the court, including the freethrow line. In fact, during the course of his thirteen-year professional basketball career, he made about ninety percent of his free throws. Rick had a very unusual free throw shooting style—two hand, underhand. He would hold the ball with a hand on each side of the ball, bend at the waist with the ball down low between his legs, and then shoot underhanded. Called a "granny shot," it sure looked different, even silly.

Rick didn't care how the shot looked or what anyone said, even if they made fun of him. He just cared about the results, and he was very effective shooting that way.

Sometimes we know that we should do something a certain way. But because of what we think people might say—that we look funny or no one else does it that way or we're old-fashioned—we may be tempted to do something else. Has that ever happened to you?

Consider these possibilities: Let's say you were to choose to go to church on Sunday instead of play soccer—what would your teammates say? Or if you were to spend a week of vacation helping poor people, what would your friends think? Or if you were to sit at lunch with an unpopular and shy kid, what would your lunch buddies say? Or if you were to use some money you saved to help earthquake victims in another country instead of buying the Xbox or Wii system you had been saving for, what would your family think?

Doing what you know is right in the face of opposition or ridicule can be tough. But that's way better than giving in and doing something else just because another person or group thinks you should. And remember, God's opinion of your actions is the only one that really counts.

ALSO ON THIS DAY . . .

1900—Dwight Davis established a new tennis trophy, the Davis Cup.

1920—The Major League Baseball Joint Rules Committee banned foreign substances and alterations to baseballs.

1992—Earvin "Magic" Johnson came back after his announcement that he was infected with the AIDS virus to play in the NBA All-Star Game.

1997—Scotty Bowman became the first NHL coach to win 1,000 games.

BIRTHDAYS:

1965—Benito Santiago, Ponce, Puerto Rico, Major League catcher (Padres, Marlins, Reds, Phillies, Blue Jays, Cubs, Giants, Royals, Pirates)

1971—Bev Oden, Millington, TN, volleyball middle blocker (Olympics, '96)

1984—Julia Mancuso, Reno, NV, American Olympic skier who won the gold medal in the giant slalom in 2006 and the silver medal in the downhill and combined in 2010

Peter and the other apostles replied: "We must obey God rather than men!"
Acts 5:29

FUN FACT When basketball was first created, the basket was set at ten feet exactly because that was the highest the ceiling would allow at the YMCA gym.

Sports Clusters

1. driver, green, ball, strokes, glove—
2. **driver, green, pit, start, finish—**
3. pit, shoe, post, toss, ringer—
4. **ball, strike, glove, hit, spikes—**
5. ball, strike, lane, split, turkey—
6. **ball, net, volley, set, spikes—**
7. ball, net, volley, set, love—
8. **start, lane, suit, strokes, water—**
9. ball, pass, block, goal, water—
10. **ball, pass, block, guard, punt—**
11. ball, pass, block, guard, rebound—
12. **ball, pass, dribble, tackle, goal—**
13. goal, pass, helmet, line, check—

What sport **matches** each **cluster** of words?

Fully **Equipped**

On this day in 1876, Al Spalding opened his sporting goods store.

Al Spalding was an outstanding baseball player and one of the organizers of the National League. But you probably recognize the name for what he did off the field, not on it. You may have used a Spalding basketball, volleyball, softball, golf ball, or football. Spalding has become one of the foremost names in sports equipment, and it began shortly after Al and his brother opened their store.

In 1877, Spalding began to use a glove to protect his catching hand. Baseball players had used gloves before, but never a star like Spalding. He and his brother sold baseball gloves, and his wearing one was good for sales. Spalding's business grew rapidly, and by 1901 they had fourteen stores and had begun manufacturing baseball equipment.

Wise athletes use the right equipment—and every sport has its own needs. Think of what these sports require in equipment: bicycling, swimming, golf, football, lacrosse, badminton, bowling, and archery. And the equipment should be of good quality and in good shape.

Christian living is not a sport, but we also need the right equipment. Check out the apostle Paul's instructions to Timothy, a young Christian leader: "All Scripture is God-breathed and is useful for teaching, rebuking, correcting and training in righteousness, so that the man of God may be thoroughly equipped for every good work" (2 Timothy 3:16–17).

So let's consider your equipment. Where is your Bible, the most important one? What kind of shape is it in? How are you using it to "thoroughly equip" you "for every good work"? You don't have to go to the sporting goods store—the Bible has everything you need.

....

ALSO ON THIS DAY . . .

1949—Team Canada beat Denmark 47-0 in ice hockey.

1991—North and South Korea formed a joint team for table tennis competition.

1995—Sun Cayun set the female indoor pole-vault world record (4.13m [13.55 ft.]).

1995—Bonnie Blair set the female 500m speed skating world record (38.69 seconds).

BIRTHDAYS:

1934—Bill Russell, Monroe, LA, NBA Hall-of-Fame player with the Boston Celtics and gold medal winner at the 1956 Olympics

1948—Cindy Hill, LPGA golfer

1984—Brad Keselowski, Rochester Hills, MI, NASCAR driver

Do your best to present yourself to God as one approved, a workman who does not need to be ashamed and who correctly handles the word of truth.
2 Timothy 2:15

FUN FACT Albert Spalding's nephew, also named Albert Spalding, was a renowned violinist.

Hair Today, **Gone** Tomorrow

On this day in 1976, Dorothy Hamill won the Olympic figure skating gold medal in Innsbruck, Austria.

Dorothy Hamill was an amazing skater, winning many international competitions. In fact, she developed a new skating move known as the "Hamill camel"—a camel spin that turns into a sit spin. When Dorothy won Olympic gold, she immediately became America's new sweetheart, with a Dorothy Hamill doll made and sold in 1977. And her bobbed hairstyle, a "wedge" that she sported during the Olympics, started a fad. Girls and women of all ages wanted to look like nineteen-year-old Dorothy.

Fads seem to pop up often. These are styles and choices of entertainment, refreshment, speech, clothing, or, in this case, hair that many people copy. A rock star wears a flashy outfit, and suddenly teenagers everywhere want one just like it. A movie star sports a unique tattoo, and fans line up to get similar body work. A sports hero promotes a certain drink, and they fly off store shelves. Fads usually are short-lived—they come and go quickly ("pet rock" anyone?).

There's nothing inherently wrong with being stylish, with listening to the latest song or having the latest hairstyle, unless those styles are extreme or harmful. But lots of times God wants us to act much differently than everyone else—to be very "unfaddish." And copying someone we admire is okay, too, as long as they're leading us in the right direction.

The apostle Paul, in fact, told some young believers to copy him (not his hairstyle, but his actions). Listen to his words: "Follow my example, as I follow the example of Christ" (1 Corinthians 11:1). Paul was modeling the way he lived after Jesus, and he was trying to be a good example to those who looked up to him.

Who sets the standards, the example, for how you live? Follow Jesus, no matter what anyone else does.

ALSO ON THIS DAY . . .

1937—The NFL Boston Redskins moved to Washington, DC.

1954—Frank Selvy scored 100 points in a Division I college basketball game (Furman University vs. Newberry College).

1988—Ronald Weigel (East Germany) set an unofficial speed walking world record.

2010—Georgian luger Nodar Kumaritashvili died in a crash during a training run for the Vancouver Olympics hours before the opening ceremonies.

BIRTHDAYS:

1918—Patty Berg, Minneapolis, MN, LPGA golfing legend

1944—Sal Bando, Cleveland, OH, all-star third baseman for the Oakland Athletics

1977—Randy Moss, Rand, WV, NFL wide receiver (Minnesota Vikings, Oakland Raiders, and New England Patriots)

Remember your leaders, who spoke the word of God to you. Consider the outcome of their way of life and imitate their faith. Jesus Christ is the same yesterday and today and forever. Hebrews 13:7–8

FUN FACT In 1993, a national sports study had Dorothy Hamill tied for first place with fellow Olympian Mary Lou Retton as the most popular athlete in America, ranking far ahead of other major sports stars such as Michael Jordan, Magic Johnson, Troy Aikman, Dan Marino, Wayne Gretzky, Joe Montana, Nolan Ryan, and 800 other athletes.

Going **Nowhere Fast**

ON THIS DAY IN 1988, BOBBY ALLISON, AT FIFTY, BECAME THE OLDEST DRIVER TO WIN THE DAYTONA 500.

Happy Valentine's Day! That has nothing to do with sports, but, after all, this is February 14. Now back to our program already in progress . . .

Are you a NASCAR fan? Each race draws hundreds of thousands, and the most popular is the Daytona 500. Even though this race **begins** the NASCAR season every year, it is seen as the

"Super Bowl" of racing and has the largest television audience and purse, with the winner receiving over 1.5 million dollars.

Some people don't think that race car drivers should be considered "athletes,"

because driving a car isn't physically challenging. But racing a stock car with an average interior temperature of 120 degrees for 500 laps at speeds close to 200 mph takes superior depth perception, hand-eye coordination, and physical fitness, not to mention courage. So drivers follow an intense conditioning and weight-lifting program. A good race car driver is a good athlete.

Sometimes drivers will make jokes about their sport, explaining that most of the time they just turn left and drive in circles (for hours!). That's true, but the competition is intense.

Actually, life can seem that way. At times we can feel as though we're just going in circles, with no end in sight, just hoping to avoid crashes along the way. We follow the same routine, day after day, week after week, month after month, and year after year—going nowhere. You may not feel that way yet, but ask some adults—that's

what many will admit.

Solomon reflected that attitude when he wrote in Ecclesiastes, "'Meaningless! Meaningless!' says the Teacher. 'Everything is meaningless!'" (12:8). Yes, without Christ, life certainly can seem meaningless. But with him, we're not just running in circles, we're going somewhere—life has meaning. Jesus said, "I have come that they may have life, and have it to the full" (John 10:10). Follow him, and you'll make the "right turns" and win the race, and find meaning along the way.

....

ALSO ON THIS DAY . . .

1936—Maribel Vinson won the US Female Figure Skating championship.

1951—Sugar Ray Robinson defeated Jake LaMotta to take the boxing middleweight title.

1957—The Georgia Senate unanimously approved Senator Leon Butts' bill barring blacks from playing baseball with whites.

1992—Merlene Ottey (Jamaica/Slovenia) ran a world-record 60m indoor (6.96 sec); she competed in seven Olympics from 1980 to 2004.

Do you not know that in a race all the runners run, but only one gets the prize? Run in such a way as to get the prize. **1 Corinthians 9:24**

FUN FACT »

Richard Petty has won the Daytona 500 more times than any other driver (seven).

15 Loser?

On this day in 1973, Friendsville Academy in Tennessee ended their 138-game basketball losing streak.

The losing streak was broken when the Friendsville Foxes defeated St. Camillus Academy of Corbin, Kentucky, 62-43. The streak had lasted six years. Think of it—six years of losing. If you had played on that team beginning in 8th grade, you would have graduated high school without ever winning a game, not a single one. Do you think the players felt like losers?

Losing streaks aren't limited to sports. We can feel like losers in class or in social situations. Some people never shake the feeling of being a "loser," like a big "L" has been placed on their forehead for all to see. And it doesn't have to be a streak at all; sometimes just one loss can trigger those feelings. We fail a test; we hurt a friend; we give a poor performance; we break a valued possession; we can't find our way. Sometimes we feel like losers just because someone else labeled us that way. And in a world that often divides into "winners" and "losers," we know our category.

But do you know the gospel—the good news proclaimed and offered by Jesus? It begins with bad news: you *are* a loser; in fact, everyone who has ever lived is one—a sinner who cannot win God's favor. We're all lost in our sins, doomed (bummer, right?). But here comes the good news: We can be *winners*, spectacular, grand champion–type winners, because of what Christ has done for us on the cross. And he takes all our sins away—the penalty for those sins too—when we put our faith in him. We're forgiven, embraced, and on our way to heaven. God's kingdom, his team, his family, has no losers, only winners. And that's you!

Celebrate your victory!

ALSO ON THIS DAY . . .

1916—The New York Yankees bought Frank "Home Run" Baker from the Athletics for $37,500.

1932—US bobsled team member Eddie Eagan became the only athlete to win gold in both Summer and Winter Olympics (1920 boxing).

1982—Dan Issel of the NBA (Denver Nuggets) began his streak of making sixty-three free throws in a row.

2006—Jason McElwain, seventeen-year-old student with autism, scored twenty points in four minutes for Greece Athlena High School (Rochester, NY).

BIRTHDAYS:

1960—Darrell Green, Houston, TX, NFL cornerback (Washington Redskins)

1972—Jaromir Jagr, Czechoslavkia, NHL right wing (Pittsburgh Penguins, Washington Capitals, and New York Rangers and Olympic gold medal winner, 1998)

1974—Seattle Slew, American racehorse, the only undefeated Triple Crown winner and probably thoroughbred racing's greatest champion

This is the victory that has overcome the world, even our faith. Who is it that overcomes the world? Only he who believes that Jesus is the Son of God. **1 John 5:4–5**

FUN FACT
The California Institute of Technology (CalTech) has the longest losing streak in NCAA basketball—207 losses in Division III play and 245 losses in conference play over twenty-one years.

All **Downhill**

ON THIS DAY IN 1984, BILL JOHNSON BECAME THE FIRST AMERICAN TO WIN OLYMPIC DOWNHILL SKIING GOLD.

Johnson predicted he'd win the gold. Then he went out and did just that, stunning the ski world. Johnson would recklessly careen down the hill at top speed. That worked in Sarajevo and at the two World Cup victories that followed. At the top of his sport, Johnson reigned as an Olympic champion, and he finished third in the world that year. But his life soon went downhill, almost as fast as his skiing. After that season, his best results were two seventh place finishes. Then, because of injuries to his knee and back, Johnson was left off the US team for the 1988 Winter Olympics in Calgary. In 1990, he was finished as a serious competitor.

Bill's heartaches multiplied in 1992 when he and his wife lost their first child in a drowning accident, and then a few years later when his wife divorced him and moved out of state with their two other sons. Then, in 2001, while attempting a skiing comeback, Bill had a terrible crash at the end of a run that left him in a coma for three weeks. He survived but with brain damage. Today, the once-proud skier walks with a cane, the right half of his body virtually useless. He can remember standing at the top of the mountain in Sarajevo, but he might not remember what he did earlier in the day.

How quickly life can turn! The future isn't guaranteed, and someone can fall quickly from the heights of fame and fortune. Usually we live as though we know what will happen in the months and years ahead and act as though we have everything in control. But only God sees the future; only he controls events and lives.

James wrote: "Now listen, you who say, 'Today or tomorrow we will go to this or that city, spend a year there, carry on business and make money.' Why, you do not even know what will happen tomorrow. What is your life? You are a mist that appears for a little while and then vanishes. Instead, you ought to say, 'If it is the Lord's will, we will live and do this or that'" (4:13–15).

All we can do is trust our loving God. He is in control; he loves us; he will be with us no matter what.

....

ALSO ON THIS DAY . . .

1962—Jimmy Bostwick defeated his brother Pete to win the US Open Tennis championship.

1972—Wilt Chamberlain hit the 30,000-career-point mark during a game with the Phoenix Suns.

1992—The Los Angeles Lakers retired Magic Johnson's number thirty-two uniform.

2005—Commissioner Gary Bettman cancelled the 2004-05 NHL season, the first time a North American professional sports league had to cancel a season due to a labor dispute.

BIRTHDAYS:

1959—John P. McEnroe, Weisben, West Germany, American professional tennis player (winner of the US Open 1979-81, 1984, and Wimbledon 1981, 1983)

1973—Cathy Freeman, Australian 100m, 200m, and 400m runner (Olympic silver medalist in 1992 and 1996)

1977—Ahman Green, Omaha, NE, NFL running back (Green Bay Packers, Houston Texans)

How can a young man keep his way pure? By living according to your word. Psalm 119:9

Fun Fact The USA has won a total of 253 medals at the winter Olympics (1924–2010): 87 gold, 95 silver, and 71 bronze.

Sports Trophys and Awards

1. For which sport would you receive the Stanley Cup?
   a. Hockey
   b. Baseball
   c. Football
   d. Soccer

2. For which sport would you receive the Heisman Trophy?
   a. Hockey
   b. Football
   c. Golf
   d. Volleyball

3. For which sport would you receive the Ryder Cup?
   a. Swimming
   b. Hockey
   c. Baseball
   d. Golf

4. For which sport would you receive the World Cup?
   a. Soccer
   b. Tennis
   c. Football
   d. Baseball

5. For which sport would you receive the Cy Young Award?
   a. Football
   b. Hockey
   c. Tennis
   d. Baseball

6. For which sport would you receive the Vince Lombardi Trophy?
   a. Volleyball
   b. Gymnastics
   c. Football
   d. Wrestling

7. For which sport would you receive the Lady Byng Trophy?
   a. Tennis
   b. Football
   c. Soccer
   d. Hockey

8. For which sport would you receive the Norman Brookes Challenge Cup?
   a. Swimming
   b. Golf
   c. Tennis
   d. Hockey

9. For which sport would you receive the green jacket?
   a. Tennis
   b. Swimming
   c. Golf
   d. Hockey

10. For which sport would you receive the Rosewater Dish?
   a. Tennis
   b. Football
   c. Soccer
   d. Baseball

ANSWERS: 1.a, 2.b, 3.d, 4.a, 5.d, 6.c, 7.d, 8.d, 9.c, 10.a

Strike **Out!**

On this day in 1982, Sharie Langford of California set a women's bowling series record of 853.

A perfect bowling game is 300—strikes in every frame and three in the tenth. A perfect score for a series of three games would be 900. Sharie came pretty close! She was on a roll . . . and she set the record.

Usually talk about "striking out" means that something bad happened. A person tried but failed. That's because we associate "strikes" with baseball—three strikes and "you're out!" No one wants to strike out that way and then have to walk slowly back to the bench.

But in bowling, a strike is good. It means knocking down all the pins on your first ball in a frame. And then you can add to your total pins for that frame the number of pins you knock down with the *next two balls*. So in the tenth frame, if you get a strike with your first ball, you get to roll two more times. And if you knock down all ten with each ball, you've **struck out**. Now that's a great feeling!

Sometimes we fail, or strike out, and feel terrible. We may even think that life is terrible, that no one likes us, and that things will never be good again. But God can take that bad "strikeout" and turn it into good, sort of like turning baseball into bowling. Remember Joseph (the guy with the colorful coat)? His brothers threw him in a pit and left him for dead, but God had other plans, and eventually, Joseph became assistant Pharoah in Egypt and was able to save his family from starvation. Here's what he told his brothers: "'Don't be afraid. Am I in the place of God? You intended to harm me, but God intended it for good to accomplish what is now being done, the saving of many lives. So then, don't be afraid. I will provide for you and your children.' And he reassured them and spoke kindly to them" (Genesis 50:19–21). God turned bad into good.

So when something bad happens—you have a strike against you—trust God and look for how he can make it a strike *for* you, for your good.

ALSO ON THIS DAY . . .

1942—The NY Yankees announced that 5,000 uniformed soldiers would be admitted free at each of their upcoming home games.

1984—Phil and Steve Mahre became the first brother combo to win gold and silver in the same event in the Olympics (slalom skiing).

1988—The US Olympic hockey team destroyed their rooms at the Olympic village in Japan.

BIRTHDAYS:

1916—Eddie Arcaro, Cincinnati, OH, Hall-of-Fame jockey (two triple crowns)

1957—Dave "Smoke" Stewart, Oakland, CA, Major League Baseball pitcher (Oakland Athletic)

1966—Matthew Ryan, Port Jefferson, NY, team handball circle (1996 Olympics)

1971—Becky Droen-Lancer, San Jose, CA, synchronized swimmer, gold medal winner in the 1996 Olympics

And we know that in all things God works for the good of those who love him, who have been called according to his purpose. **Romans 8:28**

Fun Fact Another form of bowling is played outdoors where players throw a ball, sometimes electrically weighted, trying to put it closest to a designated point or slot in the bowling area.

The Rest of **the Week**

ON THIS DAY IN 1927, GOLFERS IN SOUTH CAROLINA WERE ARRESTED FOR VIOLATING THE SABBATH.

The Sabbath was Sunday, a day for rest and worship, when stores were closed and people did very little business or work. And in South Carolina, in 1927, evidently they took that tradition seriously.

Certainly, arresting someone for playing golf on Sunday is extreme, but we've gone way in the opposite direction. These days Sundays are jammed with athletic events: youth soccer, baseball, and other sports, college games, and professional competitions. In fact, Sunday seems to be the *main* day for sporting activities. And all the stores are open and many other businesses humming. At least the schools are closed!

In the Ten Commandments we read, "Remember the Sabbath day by keeping it holy. Six days you shall labor and do all your work, but the seventh day is a Sabbath to the Lord your God. On it you shall not do any work.... For in six days the Lord made the heavens and the earth, the sea, and all that is in them, but he rested on the seventh day. Therefore the Lord blessed the Sabbath day and made it holy" (Exodus 20:8–11). Obviously God wants us to take one day a week to rest, to reflect on him, and to worship.

In Jesus' day, some religious people were taking this to extremes and implying that God would zap people who didn't obey their Sabbath rules. But God isn't like that, and Jesus told those Pharisees that they were wrong. Just because *they* were wrong, however, doesn't mean we should treat Sunday like any other day. We should honor God by setting aside one day for him, just as he said.

What's your typical Sunday like? How do you observe Sabbath in your life—breaking the busy routine for rest? Resting doesn't mean lying around (although that would be restful); it might involve play—swimming, golfing, hanging with friends, messing around. But this day should also involve focusing on God, spending time with him.

Take a break.

....

ALSO ON THIS DAY . . .

1929—The Red Sox announced that they would be playing Sunday games at Braves Field.

1953—The US Court of Appeals ruled that Organized Baseball was a sport and not a business, affirming the twenty-five-year-old Supreme Court ruling.

1998—Tara Lipinski won the Olympic figure skating gold medal.

Then [Jesus] said to them, "The Sabbath was made for man, not man for the Sabbath." Mark 2:27

FUN FACT In golf, it is a rule that you keep score on your own scorecard or you are disqualified.

BIRTHDAYS:

1928—Elroy Face, Stephentown, NY, Major League Baseball pitcher (Pittsburgh Pirates)

1934—Bobby Unser, Colorado Springs, CO, auto racer (1968, '75, '81 Indianapolis 500 winner)

1963—Charles Barkley, Leeds, AL, NBA forward (Phoenix Suns and Houston Rockets, 1996 Olympic gold medal winner)

1967—Tom Waddle, Cincinnati, OH, NFL wide receiver (Chicago Bears and Cincinnati Bengals)

Finally!

On this day in 1953, Niagara beat Siena 88-81 in the longest collegiate basketball game up till then, lasting six overtimes.

Will this game ever end?!" That must be what the players, coaches, and fans thought that night. Think of it—six overtime periods, until finally, somehow, Niagara won. By then, a number of players must have fouled out; for sure, everyone was exhausted. And think of the emotional ups and downs, as a team would tie the score to send it to overtime, or a team would miss the winning basket, sending the game to the extra session.

In many ways, overtime periods are like new games, second chances to win. It's as though both teams are starting the game again, only with a shorter time to play. For many teams, overtimes are gifts, especially if they had been losing most of the game in regulation.

Have you ever wished for an "overtime" in life? Maybe you didn't finish your homework and needed just one more day to get it done. Perhaps your vacation was ending and you would love to stay another few days. Perhaps you failed a test and would like a do-over. Or maybe you messed up and wished you could start again in that messy situation.

And you'd love to have a fresh start with God, especially when coming face to face with your sin, right?

That last situation definitely is possible—and it's the most important one. Jesus promises that when we give our lives to him, we are made totally clean, forgiven, born again. It's like an eternal overtime of the best kind. And God's "do-over" isn't one and done—we can start fresh with him every day, every moment. That's an extra period that we're glad never ends!

ALSO ON THIS DAY . . .

1979—In Iowa two girls' high school basketball teams played four scoreless quarters, and the game was won 4-2 in the fourth overtime period.

1992—Kristi Yamaguchi of the US won the Olympic gold medal in women's figure skating.

1993—Sergei Bubka pole-vaulted an indoor world record, 6.15 m (20.18 ft).

BIRTHDAYS:

1958—Alan Trammell, Garden Grove, CA, MLB all-star infielder (Detroit Tigers)

1966—Edie Boyer, St. Paul, MN, discus thrower

1976—Robin Confer, Clearwater, FL, soccer forward (Olympics, '96)

Because of the Lord's great love we are not consumed, for his compassions never fail. They are new every morning; great is your faithfulness. Lamentations 3:22–23

FUN FACT The 1992 Winter Olympic Games were the last ones played the same year as the summer games.

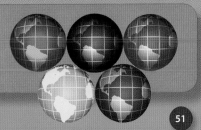

22 **Miracle** on Ice

ON THIS DAY IN 1980, THE USA BEAT THE USSR IN OLYMPIC HOCKEY 4-3 ON THE WAY TO A GOLD MEDAL.

This victory by the Americans against the highly favored Soviets was a huge upset. The United States team was a collection of amateur and collegiate players, while the Soviet team was basically

professional and considered the best hockey team in the world. As the last seconds were clicking off, announcer Al Michaels exclaimed, "Do you believe in miracles?" And the game became known as the "miracle on ice." In 2008,

the International Ice Hockey Federation chose this game as the number-one international hockey story of the twentieth century.

Well, do *you* believe in miracles? Many people don't. When they see an amazing healing or other occurrence, they write it off to coincidence. But then they may refer to a long basketball shot, a "Hail Mary" pass, a fielding gem, or, as in the 1980 Olympics, a big upset as "miraculous."

Sports heroics aren't miracles—victories come because athletes work hard and play together, for the whole contest. But miracles *do* occur. God says that we can ask for his divine intervention, and, if it is in his will, he will do it. That's why we pray for healing, for guidance, and for provision—for

all our needs to be met. And sometimes God answers those prayers in ways that can only be described as "miraculous."

But you know the greatest miracle? God changing a person from the inside out. It's an amazing transformation—from death to life. Every person who trusts Christ as Savior gets this miracle, this new life. But some stories of life change are dramatic, spectacular.

Do you believe in miracles? *You* are a miracle!

ALSO ON THIS DAY . . .

1888—John Reid of Scotland demonstrated golf to Americans in Yonkers, New York.

1962—Wilt Chamberlain set the NBA record with thirty-four free throw attempts in one game.

1969—Barbara Jo Rubin became the first female jockey to win at a major US track.

BIRTHDAYS:

1934—George "Sparky" Anderson, Bridgewater, SD, Hall-of-Fame baseball manager of the World Champion Cincinnati Reds and Detroit Tigers

1950—Julius Erving, Roosevelt, NY, Hall-of-Fame ABA/NBA forward (Virginia Squires, New York Nets, Philadelphia 76ers)

1956—Amy Alcott, Kansas City, MO, LPGA golfer

1972—Michael Chang, Hoboken, NJ, professional tennis star (1989 French Open winner)

> Therefore, if anyone is in Christ, he is a new creation; the old has gone, the new has come! **2 Corinthians 5:17**

FUN FACT » The movie *Miracle*, depicting the famous USA/Russia game, was released in 2004. Al Michaels re-recorded all of his commentary; but in the final ten seconds of the movie, Al Michaels' original broadcast was used so as to keep the full emotion of the moment.

Naming Rights

On this day in 1994, Richard Jacobs, owner of the Cleveland Indians, announced that he would pay $10 million to name the Indians' baseball field "Jacobs Field."

In the last couple of decades, naming rights have become a big deal in sports. This is the practice of putting the name of a business on a sports stadium or arena for a price. Considering this to be a good advertising

investment, companies pay millions of dollars for this right. So we have the United Center, Citi Field, Monster Park, U.S. Cellular Field, Barclays Center, Bank of America Stadium, Heinz Field, and

so forth. The business owners believe that all the publicity will pay off.

Did you know that someone has bought "naming rights" to *you*? Here's what God told his people through the prophet Isaiah: "The nations will see your righteousness. World leaders will be blinded by your glory. And you will be given a new name by the Lord's own mouth. . . . Never again will you be called 'The Forsaken City' or 'The Desolate Land.' Your new name will be 'The City of God's Delight' and 'The Bride of God,' for the Lord delights in you and will claim you as his bride" (Isaiah 62:2-4, NLT). God was saying that Israel should find their true identity in him. No matter what any nation or person said about them, they were special because they were his.

Maybe you've thought of yourself as "Desolate" or

"Forsaken": a loser, a failure, a nobody, not liked, not good looking, nothing special. God wants to change your name. This doesn't mean that you'll lose the one you got right after birth (you'll still be Natalie, Edmund, Amy, Colin, Justine, Daren, Lindsey, Juan, Dana, Makaila, Rose, Kara, Michael, or whatever). But instead of all those negative labels you've heard or given yourself, God calls you "Forgiven," "Special," "Honored One," "Chosen," "Blessed," "Child," "Mine."

He paid for you on the Cross. His banner is flying over you and you bear his name. And everyone who knows you will know him better.

Isn't that great!

ALSO ON THIS DAY . . .

1934—Casey Stengel became manager of the Brooklyn Dodgers.

1986—Mary Beth Zimmerman won the LPGA Standard Register/Samaritan Golf Classic.

1980—Eric Heiden won all five speed skating gold medals at the Lake Placid Olympics.

1988—Chicago gave the Cubs the right to install lights and play up to eighteen night games.

BIRTHDAYS:

1937—Tom Osborne, Hastings, NE, college football coach (Nebraska, national championships in 1994, '95, '97), US Congressman, and athletic director

1949—Anna-Maria Muller, German DR, Luge (Olympic gold medal winner, 1972)

1981—Charles "Peanut" Tillman, Chicago, IL, NFL cornerback (Chicago Bears)

He has taken me to the banquet hall, and his banner over me is love. **Song of Songs 2:4**

FUN FACT Prior to the mid-twentieth century, many baseball fields included a dirt path from the home plate to the pitcher's mound. In recent years, some ballparks have revived the feature for nostalgic reasons.

1. In 1981, how many penalties were given for a brawl at the NHL Minnesota versus Boston game? (Feb. 26)
2. **Who was the first college basketball player to score 3,000 points? (Feb. 2)**
3. How tall was Atlanta Hawks basketball player Spud Webb? (Feb. 8)
4. **What baseball position did John "Pepper" Martin play? (Feb. 29)**
5. In what state were golfers arrested for violating the Sabbath? (Feb. 20)
6. **How old was Bobby Allison when he won the Daytona 500? (Feb. 14)**
7. Who is called the "Houdini of the Hardwood"? (Feb. 27)
8. **In 1977, what was the final score of the Hillsdale High School versus Person High School basketball game? (Feb. 1)**
9. To what did Cassius Clay change his name? (Feb. 7)
10. **How long was Friendsville Academy's basketball losing streak? (Feb. 15)**
11. How many overtimes was the Niagara versus Siena game? (Feb. 21)
12. **Whom did Hulk Hogan defeat in the first primetime television professional wrestling match in thirty years? (Feb. 5)**
13. In what Olympic event did Dorothy Hamill compete? (Feb. 13)
14. **What baseball position did Smokey Burgess play? (Feb. 6)**
15. How long is a marathon? (Feb. 28)
16. **What USA Olympic event is referred to as the "Miracle on Ice"? (Feb. 22)**
17. For what NBA team did Rick Barry play? (Feb. 9)
18. **What is the score for a perfect bowling game? (Feb. 19)**
19. What year did Al Spalding open his sporting goods store? (Feb. 12)
20. **How much did Richard Jacobs pay the Cleveland Indians to have their baseball field called "Jacobs Field"? (Feb. 23)**
21. In what sport did Bill Johnson win an Olympic gold medal? (Feb. 16)

In the **Penalty Box**

On this day in 1981, 84 penalties, totaling 406 minutes, were assessed for a brawl between NHL teams Minnesota and Boston.

In sports, the emotions get involved. The purpose of pregame speeches by coaches or captains is to get the team or individual competitor motivated and fired up emotionally, ready to give his or her all in the contest. Sometimes those emotions can turn ugly. Tempers can flare and fights break out in almost any sport, but especially in contact sports, like football and hockey. Fighting happens so often in hockey that someone said, "I went to a fight the other day, and a hockey game broke out!" The one between Minnesota and Boston was a brawl.

Players fight for many reasons: retaliating for a cheap shot, protecting a teammate, responding to taunting or trash talk, or even trying to injure someone. And some may fight just because they're having a bad day.

Unless part of the sport itself (such as boxing), fighting should have no place in any competition. Holding those emotions in check is often very difficult, but we must. Imagine the chaos if every competitor decided to fight whenever he or she felt angry. Now that would be chaos.

Christians should be role models, good examples, in this regard. Remember when Jesus gave what is known as the Sermon on the Mount? In it he said we should not return violence for violence and should instead "turn the other cheek" (Matthew 5:39). He also said that we should be "peacemakers" (Matthew 5:9). And get this: We are supposed to *love our enemies* (Matthew 5:43–44). This relates to all of life, not just sports.

How we react to those who treat us wrong—at home, in school, on the playground, in the neighborhood, in sports—says lots about our character and who we follow.

What do people learn about you by watching you in those tense moments?

ALSO ON THIS DAY . . .

1935—The New York Yankees released Babe Ruth, and he signed with the Boston Braves.

1941—Two boxers were unable to continue their slugfest, and the referee declared a double knockout.

1973—Triple Crown winner Secretariat was bought for a record $5.7 million.

1978—Nancy Lopez won the LPGA Bent Tree Golf Classic.

BIRTHDAYS:

1918—Edwin Charles "Preacher" Roe, Major League baseball pitcher (Brooklyn Dodgers)

1957—Connie Carpenter-Phinney, Madison, WI, a 79k cyclist (winner of Olympic gold medal in 1984)

1973—Marshall Faulk, New Orleans, LA, NFL running back (Indianapolis Colts and St. Louis Rams)

1973—Jenny Thompson, Danvers, MA, 400m freestyle (won Olympic gold medals in 1992 and 1996)

Do not repay anyone evil for evil. Be careful to do what is right in the eyes of everybody. If it is possible, as far as it depends on you, live at peace with everyone. Romans 12:17–18

FUN FACT Tiger Williams holds the record for the most hockey penalty minutes in a career with 3,966 over fourteen years.

27 Assisted **Living**

The point guard takes the ball from the in-bounds pass, dribbles down the court, and crosses midcourt. A forward sets a screen, and, keeping his dribble, the guard drives toward the basket. As the defense collapses on him, he whips a pass to the other forward, now wide open, who lays it in. The forward gets credit for the basket, the two points, but it was made possible by the play of the guard—his "assist."

Bob Cousy, "Houdini of the Hardwood," led the league in assists eight consecutive times in his first eleven seasons in the NBA, and he introduced a new blend of ball-handling and passing skills. One of the all-time greats, he's in the Basketball Hall of Fame.

Often sports reports center on the top scorers, but those who make the assists are vital to the game. These days, basketball teams (hockey and soccer, too) won't be successful without them. These athletes work hard at serving, at making others look good and get the glory.

That sounds a lot like what Jesus expects of his followers. He wants us to serve others, to help them. Along the way, we might get praised for our work, but often we may be unnoticed, almost invisible. We should follow Jesus' example, as he told his disciples: "Whoever wants to become great among you must be your servant, and whoever wants to be first must be your slave—just as the Son of Man did not come to be served, but to serve, and to give his life as a ransom for many" (Matthew 20:26–28).

Serving may mean helping prepare a meal, picking up clothes and toys, taking out garbage, making phone calls, babysitting, and working behind the scenes doing lots of other necessary but not very glamorous tasks.

See if you can set a record for assists!

ALSO ON THIS DAY . . .

1874—Baseball was first played in England, at Lord's Cricket Grounds.

1982—Earl Anthony became the first professional bowler to win more than $1 million.

1987—Mike Conley triple jumped to a world indoor record (17.76m).

1988—Katarina Witt (GDR) won her second consecutive Olympic figure skating gold medal (Calgary).

BIRTHDAYS:

1933—Raymond Berry, Corpus Christi, TX, NFL Hall-of-Fame receiver (Baltimore Colts)

1962—Veronica Ribot-Canales, Buenos Aires, Argentina, US diver (Olympics, '96)

1976—Tony Gonzalez, Torrance, CA, NFL tight end (Kansas City Chiefs and Atlanta Falcons)

[Jesus said] "Now that I, your Lord and Teacher, have washed your feet, you also should wash one another's feet. I have set you an example that you should do as I have done for you. I tell you the truth, no servant is greater than his master, nor is a messenger greater than the one who sent him. Now that you know these things, you will be blessed if you do them." **John 13:14–17**

FUN FACT Bob Cousy married his college sweetheart, Missie Ritterbusch, in December 1950, and they have been married over sixty years.

Running **Smart**

On this day in 1970, Caroline Walker set the world female record for a marathon (3:02:53).

A marathon is a long race—26.2 miles! Obviously to run this race successfully, runners need to be in great physical condition. For a person who runs regularly, this

means a three-month workout routine. Beyond the physical challenge, the greatest battle during the race is mental, a mind game—competitors need to run "smart." This begins by understanding

that the race is *long*, that doing what they should at the *beginning* will make a big difference at the end. Here are a few examples:

❶ At the start, everyone is excited. But runners should know their appropriate pace and stick to it. For most this means slowing down.

❷ All along the route, water stations are available. Runners shouldn't wait until they feel dehydrated (too late); they should hydrate early, when they don't feel like it, because they'll need it later.

❸ Runners should run their race and not worry about who passes them or who they pass.

Later, when they "hit the wall" and feel like quitting, runners should trust their conditioning and push through to the finish.

In each of these situations, the runner must remember the truth and act on it and not rely on his or her feelings.

Life is a marathon (you've heard that before). Some don't

realize that and burn out early. Others don't do what they should when they're young to prepare for later life (education, for example). Some are so worried about everyone else that they lose focus. Instead, they should run smart.

Most important is to listen to the One who made us and designed the course. Running smart begins and ends with following the instructions of our Coach, our Trainer, our Creator. Run smart!

BIRTHDAYS:

1940—Mario Andretti, American racecar driver (1969 Indianapolis 500 winner)

1954—Brian Billick, Fairborn, OH, NFL football coach (Baltimore Ravens, winner of Super Bowl XXXV)

1973—Eric Lindros, London, Ontario, great NHL center (Philadelphia Flyers)

1979—Virginia Ledgerwood, Chester, VA, rhythmic gymnast (Olympics, '96)

Don't let the excitement of youth cause you to forget your Creator. Honor him in your youth before you grow old and say, "Life is not pleasant anymore." Ecclesiastes 12:1, NLT

Fun Fact Even though the marathon was one of the original modern Olympic events in 1896, it wasn't until 1921 that the distance became standardized.

On this day in 1904, John "Pepper" Martin, Major League third baseman and outfielder (St. Louis Cardinals) and the National League stolen base leader in 1933, 1934, and 1936, was born.

People born on this day face an unusual dilemma—knowing when to celebrate their birthday! Because the 29th comes around just once every four years, some older people claim that they're only ten on their fortieth birthday (they're kidding

of course). Anyway, it's an unusual day, and Pepper Martin was an unusual ball player.

Martin, a third baseman and outfielder for the St. Louis Cardinals' "Gashouse Gang" during the 1930s, was also called "Wild

Horse of the Osage." According to one description, Pepper was a *scrappy* player whose game featured *aggressive* base running and speed. Someone else noted that he played every aspect of the game with *passion*, sliding headfirst when stealing bases and running for every batted ball as though he were playing in the seventh game of the World Series. No wonder he was called "Pepper" and "Wild Horse."

Maybe Pepper got that way because he was born on February 29 . . . or because he had to fight his way for everything growing up . . . or because he had a competitive spirit—whatever the reason, he threw himself into the game, every game.

Coaches love that kind of athlete, one who will work hard, play aggressively and with enthusiasm, and never give up—with "passion."

That's a good way to live in whatever we do. Some people

seem to lazily float through the days, allowing life to happen to them. But time moves quickly, and our years are few, so we should make every day count. Moses prayed, "Teach us to realize the brevity of life, so that we may grow in wisdom" (Psalm 90:12, NLT)—living with no regrets.

Christians especially should live that way, with passion. After all, we have a mission from God that we need to fulfill—telling the world about his great love, about Jesus. In everything we should live with purpose and determination, to do what God wants . . . even if we weren't born on February 29.

ALSO ON THIS DAY . . .

1952—The Ladies Figure Skating Championship in Paris was won by Jacqueline du Bief of France.

1964—Two North Carolina high school basketball teams played to a 56-54 score in thirteen overtimes.

1980—Gordie Howe became the first NHL player to score 800 career goals.

1996—Kenya defeated West Indies (all out 93) in Cricket World Cup.

BIRTHDAYS:

1936—Henri "Rocket" Richard, Montreal, Canada, NHL center (Montreal Canadians)

1952—Raisa Smetanina, USSR, cross country skier and Olympic gold medal winner in 1976, 1980, and 1992

1976—Bryan Gillooly, Auburn, NY, American Olympic diver, 1996

Whatever your hand finds to do, do it with all your might. Ecclesiastes 9:10

FUN FACT

Carlos Beltrán has the highest career success rate, with over 300 stolen base attempts, at 88.3%.

World **Class**

ON THIS DAY IN 1992, JENNY THOMPSON SWAM THE 100M FREESTYLE IN WORLD-RECORD TIME (1:01.40).

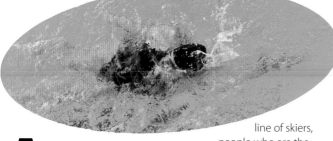

A world record—that's pretty cool, even if it only lasts a short time. Athletes who compete at that level are called "world class"—an elite group in any sport.

People want to be known as "great" or "the best" at something. Every year the *Guinness Book of World Records* lists record holders in a wide variety of categories such as fastest violin player, person eating the most meatballs in one minute, largest playing card structure, most people static cycling, longest line of skiers, people who are the tallest or shortest or whatever, and on and on. They sell lots of books, and people will do all sorts of crazy stunts to get listed in the book.

One strong reason behind this craze is the desire to be noticed and known, to be valued. It's as though they're shouting, "Look at me! I'm somebody—I mean something. I have value."

Having world-class goals is fine, if that means working hard to be the best at whatever we do. But we shouldn't confuse our achievements with our worth. Just because we don't hold a world record doesn't mean we're worthless. God loves *all* people, champs and chumps, overachievers and underachievers, in-crowd and out-crowd, veterans and rookies, winners and also-rans—and everyone in between. We have value, not because of what we do but because God made us, and he doesn't make junk.

That includes the person reading this sentence. God made you, loves you, sent Jesus to die for you, and is with you. You are his.

Now that's cool, world-class cool.

....

ALSO ON THIS DAY . . .

1941—Elmer Layden became the first NFL commissioner.

1949—Joe Louis retired as heavyweight boxing champion.

1969—New York Yankee Mickey Mantle retired from baseball.

1973—Robyn Smith became the first female jockey to win a major race.

1993—George Steinbrenner was reinstated as the owner of the New York Yankees.

BIRTHDAYS:

1920—Harry Caray, St. Louis, MO, American baseball announcer (St. Louis Cardinals, Chicago Cubs)

1963—Ron Francis, Sault Ste. Marie, NHL center for the Pittsburgh Penguins and Team Canada

1971—Tyler Hamilton, Marblehead, MA, cyclist in the 1996 Olympics

But we have this treasure in jars of clay to show that this all-surpassing power is from God and not from us. **2 Corinthians 4:7**

FUN FACT » The first four
Olympic swimming competitions were not held in pools, but in open waters.

Where do they Play?

MATCH the NHL team with the city.

1. Red Wings
2. **Blackhawks**
3. Predators
4. **Blues**
5. Flames
6. **Avalanche**
7. Canucks
8. **Devils**
9. Islanders
10. **Oilers**
11. Blue Jackets
12. **Bruins**
13. Rangers
14. **Flyers**
15. Sabres
16. **Penguins**
17. Canadians
18. **Wild**
19. Senators
20. **Thrashers**
21. Ducks
22. **Hurricanes**
23. Stars
24. **Panthers**
25. Kings
26. **Lightning**
27. Coyotes
28. **Capitals**
29. Sharks
30. **Maple Leafs**

a. New Jersey
b. **Carolina**
c. Vancouver
d. **New York**
e. Phoenix
f. **Boston**
g. Ottawa
h. **Montreal**
i. Nashville
j. **Florida**
k. Los Angeles
l. **Dallas**
m. Columbus
n. **Edmonton**
o. St. Louis
p. **Detroit**
q. Tampa Bay
r. **Buffalo**
s. New York
t. **San Jose**
u. Minnesota
v. **Philadelphia**
w. Chicago
x. **Toronto**
y. Anaheim
z. **Pittsburgh**
aa. Washington
bb. **Atlanta**
cc. Calgary
dd. **Colorado**

ANSWERS: 1.p, 2.w, 3.i, 4.o, 5.cc, 6.dd, 7.c, 8.a, 9.d, 10.n, 11.m, 12.f, 13.s, 14.v, 15.r, 16.z, 17.h, 18.u, 19.g, 20.bb, 21.y, 22.b, 23.l, 24.j, 25.k, 26.q, 27.e, 28.aa, 29.t, 30.x

In the **Gap**

ON THIS DAY IN 1941, NHL CHICAGO GOALIE SAMUEL LoPRESTI STOPPED A RECORD EIGHTY OF EIGHTY-THREE BOSTON SHOTS.

A standard ice hockey puck is black, hard rubber, and round. It is 1 inch thick, 3 inches in diameter, and weighs about 6 ounces. During a game, hockey pucks can reach speeds of more than 100 miles per hour when struck. Obviously they can be quite dangerous to players and spectators. So can you imagine what it must have been like to have eighty-three shots blasted at you in one game? And for a while, hockey goalies didn't wear masks.

Playing goalie in hockey means dealing with lots of pressure. In every game, this athlete stands as the last line of defense and often means the difference between winning and losing. A hot goalie can almost carry his team to the Stanley Cup. A goalie needs to have quick reactions, great vision, and excellent hand-eye coordination. A *great* goalie knows the game, his or her team, and the opponent and has great courage.

At times God wants us to be his "goalies," standing as almost the last line of defense and making the difference between victory and defeat. He may need you to say no to something you know is wrong when everyone else seems to be saying yes. He may need you to speak up for the truth when everyone else seems to believe a lie. He may ask you to do what is right even though it may cost you some friends.

Being this kind of person, "God's goalie," won't be easy. You won't face 100 mph pucks, but sharp words and hateful stares can be even more painful. But God is looking for his people who will take the shots and stand in the gap. Will you be the one?

....

ALSO ON THIS DAY . . .

1928—Andy Payne won the first Bunion Run race from Los Angeles to New York City.

1930—Emma Fahning bowled the first sanctioned 300 game by a woman.

1970—Jacksonville University was the first college basketball team to average 100+ points per game.

1995—Michael Johnson ran a world-record 400m indoor (44.63 sec).

BIRTHDAYS:

1891—Dazzy Vance, Orient, IA, Hall-of-Fame pitcher who led the NL in strikeouts for seven years

1964—Linda French, Oak Park, IL, badminton player in the 1996 Olympics

1966—Kevin Johnson, Sacramento, CA, NBA guard for the Phoenix Suns

1974—Sherry Wigginton, Austin, TX, diver in the 1996 Olympics

[God said,] "I looked for someone who might rebuild the wall of righteousness that guards the land. I searched for someone to stand in the gap in the wall so I wouldn't have to destroy the land, but I found no one." **Ezekiel 22:30, NLT**

FUN FACT » Although NHL goaltenders can wear any number between one and ninety-eight, the most popular number is thirty.

Winning **Right**

On this day in 1982, pitcher Gaylord Perry (with 297 wins) signed with the Seattle Mariners.

Gaylord Perry, a right-handed pitcher, was a five-time all-star and the first pitcher to win the Cy Young Award (given to the best pitcher) in both leagues, winning it in the American League in 1972 with the Cleveland Indians and in the National League in 1978 with the San Diego Padres. Perry won 314 games over a twenty-two-year career starting in 1962, playing for seven different Major League teams.

Managers, coaches, and especially batters suspected that Perry threw a spitball, a pitch outlawed in 1920. Many tried to catch him through the years, but no one had any proof until his twenty-first season, at age forty-three. Even after admitting he had used foreign substances on the baseball for years, Perry was still inducted into the Hall of Fame in 1991.

Doctoring the baseball is cheating, and it is wrong. But Gaylord Perry's attitude—one shared by many athletes—was that cheating in sports is all right if the person doesn't get caught. Cheating in sports has taken many forms, including wearing illegal equipment, having others do class work (in college), hurting competitors, and taking steroids and other performance-enhancing drugs.

Athletes are tempted to cheat because they feel the pressure to win at almost any cost. But cheating is wrong, flat-out wrong—and cheating athletes should be punished.

Cheating is wrong because it is both lying and stealing. When we cheat, we are pretending that we performed to a certain level naturally, on our own, that we were playing by the rules, but, in fact, we weren't—that's lying. And when we cheat, we are robbing someone else of the opportunity to succeed—that's stealing. Cheating isn't limited to sports; people cheat in school, in relationships, and in business. Cheating is always wrong.

The Ten Commandments, God's rules for living, prohibit both lying and stealing. But more than simply not doing wrong, Christians should do what is right. We should be known for speaking and living the truth and loving others.

What God thinks of us is way more important than any other victory.

ALSO ON THIS DAY . . .

1864—The first college track meet was held, between Oxford and Cambridge.

1966—Bob Seagren pole-vaulted 5.19m (17.028 ft.) for an indoor world record.

1981—Jayne Torvill and C. Dean (Great Britain) won the Ice Dance Championship at Hartford, CT.

1996—Earl Weaver and Jim Bunning were elected to the Baseball Hall of Fame.

BIRTHDAYS:

1945—Randy Matson, Kilgore, TX, US shot-putter who won Olympic gold in 1968

1946—Rocky Bleier, Appleton, WI, NFL running back (Pittsburgh Steelers)

1967—Nicole Boegman, Australian long jumper (Olympics, 1988, '92, '96)

1976—Paul Konerko, Providence, RI, Major League baseball player (Chicago White Sox)

"You shall not steal. You shall not give false testimony against your neighbor." **Exodus 20:15–16**

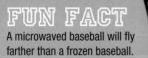

FUN FACT
A microwaved baseball will fly farther than a frozen baseball.

Keeping **Score**

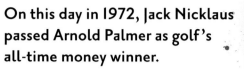

On this day in 1972, Jack Nicklaus passed Arnold Palmer as golf's all-time money winner.

How do we keep score? You may answer that it depends on the athletic event. Scoring and keeping score are quite different between football and fencing, basketball and bowling, racquetball and running, or soccer and skiing. In each sport, however, the winner is determined by numbers, either the highest or lowest points (including goals, strokes, baskets, hits, etc.), place, or time.

Well then, how do we keep score in life? That is, how do we know who is winning and losing? Often the answer is "money." That's why someone thought the amount of money Jack Nicklaus won playing golf compared to Arnold Palmer was important enough to remember.

Many years ago, a popular bumper sticker read, "He who dies with the most toys wins." The message was clear: We keep score by how much money a person makes, how many "toys"—computer, electronic gadget, home entertainment system, car, pool, and so forth—they have. And those who amass cash and stuff are considered "winners," successful.

Jesus had a very interesting response to this way of thinking when he said, "And what do you benefit if you gain the whole world but lose your own soul? Is anything worth more than your soul?" (Matthew 16:26, NLT). Some people seem willing to trade their "souls"—integrity, values, character . . . even eternal life—for things. That may seem satisfying for a short time, but eventually life and money run out. And the person who has invested himself or herself this way ends up with nothing . . . or worse.

Don't fall for the foolish idea that your value is somehow based on money and possessions. And don't trade your relationship with God and your future for "toys."

ALSO ON THIS DAY . . .

1895—England beat Australia to win one of the best cricket series ever, 3-2.

1923—The St. Louis Cardinals announced that their players would wear numbers on their uniforms.

1982—In the NBA's highest-scoring game, San Antonio beat Milwaukee 171-166 (three overtimes).

1988—Julie Krone became the winningest female jockey, with 1205 victories.

BIRTHDAYS:

1926—Ann Curtis, San Francisco, CA, 400m/800m US swimmer, gold medal winner in the 1948 Olympics

1931—Willie Mays, Westfield, AL, Hall-of-Fame baseball centerfielder of the Giants

1970—Eric Robert Carter, Long Beach, CA, former American professional "Old/Mid School" Bicycle Motocross (BMX) rider

1972—Shaquille O'Neal, Newark, NJ, NBA center for the Orlando Magic, Los Angeles Lakers, Phoenix Suns, and Cleveland Cavaliers (won 1996 Olympic gold)

[Jesus said,] "No one can serve two masters. Either he will hate the one and love the other, or he will be devoted to the one and despise the other. You cannot serve both God and Money." **Matthew 6:24**

Fun Fact
The drink consisting of half iced tea and half lemonade is called the "Arnold Palmer" in honor of the golf legend and his favorite drink.

Physically **Challenged**

On this day in 1988, Jim Abbott, a one-handed pitcher, won the fifty-eighth James E. Sullivan award, given to the nation's best amateur athlete in the United States.

Jim Abbott was born without a right hand. Yet he played high school and college (1985–88) baseball, leading Michigan to two Big Ten Championships. Then he pitched in the Major Leagues from 1989 to 1999 for the California Angels, New York Yankees, Chicago White Sox, and Milwaukee Brewers.

You may be wondering how that could work, how he could pitch at all, much less be successful—baseball takes *two* hands, right? Here's how Jim did it. He wore a right-hander's fielder's glove over the stump at the end of his right arm. After releasing the ball, while completing his follow-through, he would quickly slip his left hand into the glove in time to field any balls sent his way. Then he would remove the glove by putting it between his right forearm and body, usually in time to throw out the runner. It worked! And he actually pitched a 4-0 no-hitter for the New York Yankees against the Cleveland Indians (Sept. 4, 1993).

Jim was successful, however, because he was determined to play the game he loved despite his handicap. He says, "I've learned that it's not the disability that defines you, it's how you deal with the challenges the disability presents you with."

What real or perceived handicap has been keeping you from doing your best—in your studies, in sports, in other interests and activities? Stressful home environment? Physically limited? Learning disability? Emotionally wounded? You may not ever pitch in the majors, but God can use you to great things for him. Are you up to the challenge?

ALSO ON THIS DAY . . .

1857—Baseball decided that nine innings constitutes an official game, not nine runs.

1954—Russia won the championship in their first international ice hockey competition.

1982—The NCAA Tournament Selection was televised live for the first time.

1992—Nicole Stevenson swam a world-record 200m backstroke time (2:06.78).

I can do everything through him who gives me strength. **Philippians 4:13**

FUN FACT Jim Abbott used to throw balls against the side of his family's house, pretending to be his favorite pitchers. When the balls bounced off the house, he had to put on his glove incredibly fast if he didn't want to chase the balls down the street. He says, "I would recommend a rubber-coated ball for this method!"

BIRTHDAYS:

1960—Joe Carter, Oklahoma City, OK, Major League outfielder (Toronto Blue Jays)

1969—Anne Marie Lauck, Rochester, NY, marathoner (tenth in 1996 Olympics)

1970—James Calvin Spivey, Schiller Park, IL, miler and three-time Olympian (1984, '92, '96)

High **Hopes**

ON THIS DAY IN 1967, THE NEW ORLEANS SAINTS BEGAN SELLING SEASON TICKETS AND SOLD 20,000 THE FIRST DAY.

When awarded an NFL franchise, the people of New Orleans were excited—at last, a professional football team of their own! And hopes were high, proven by the great number of tickets sold. Yet in the early 1980s, after a string of losing seasons, locals were calling their team the "Aint's" and wearing bags over their heads, embarrassed because of the terrible play. The great expectations crashed into reality.

That often happens. Every March, for example, during baseball's spring-training season, most of the Major League baseball teams talk as though they are legitimate candidates for the World Series. A few months into the season, however, the contenders are separated from the pretenders. And fans wait again "for next year."

How do you handle defeats

and disappointments when your ideals and goals don't work out? Some people make excuses for their performance (injuries, bad luck, stress elsewhere, "sun got in my eyes"...), others blame their teammates or coaches, and

some just get discouraged and may even quit. How you deal with losses *now* will determine how you handle them in the future.

The apostle Paul had his share of troubles. He was hassled and hounded, beaten, jailed, and chased out of town. He was even shipwrecked—all while doing God's work. Talk about a losing streak! Yet he wrote to the Corinthian believers, "We are

hard pressed on every side, but not crushed; perplexed, but not in despair; persecuted, but not abandoned; struck down, but not destroyed" (2 Corinthians 4:8–9). Paul knew what God wanted him to do, and he kept doing it, leaving the results to God.

Aren't you glad he did? If Paul had packed it in, had given up and gone home, the gospel may never have spread to Turkey, Greece, Italy, and the rest of the world—to us and to you.

What has God called you to do in your home? In your school? In your community? In your church? Regardless of the opposition or setbacks, keep doing it and leave the victory to him.

....

ALSO ON THIS DAY . . .

1941—Hugh Mulcahy of the Philadelphia Phillies became the first baseball player to be drafted during World War II.

1971—Joe Frazier beat Muhammad Ali in fifteen rounds to retain his heavyweight boxing title.

1986—Martina Navratilova became the first tennis player to earn $10 million.

BIRTHDAYS:

1953—Jim Rice, Hall-of-Fame Boston Red Sox outfielder (eight time all-star and AL MVP in 1978)

1965—Kenny Smith, Rochester, NY, NBA guard (Houston Rockets) and broadcaster

1966—Laura McCabe, cross country skier, 1994 Olympics

1976—Hines Ward, Seoul, South Korea, American NFL wide receiver (Pittsburg Steelers)

So we tell others about Christ, warning everyone and teaching everyone with all the wisdom God has given us. We want to present them to God, perfect in their relationship to Christ. That's why I work and struggle so hard, depending on Christ's mighty power that works within me. **Colossians 1:28–29, NLT**

FUN FACT Large portions of New Orleans are below sea level, and civil engineers believe that it is continually sinking due to being built on thousands of feet of soft sand, silt, and clay.

Basketball

1. What team won the very first NBA game?
   a. New York Knicks
   b. Philadelphia Warriors
   c. Toronto Huskies
   d. Chicago Stags

2. What player won All-Star Game MVP, NBA MVP, and NBA Finals MVP in 2000?
   a. Michael Jordan
   b. Kobe Bryant
   c. Shaquille O'Neal
   d. Tim Duncan

3. Who scored the first three-point basket in NBA history?
   a. Wes Unseld
   b. Gene Stump
   c. Chris Ford
   d. Larry Bird

4. Who was the first Chinese player to play in a NBA game?
   a. Hai Rui
   b. Yao Ming
   c. Wang Zhizhi
   d. Mao Zedong

5. What team did Wilt Chamberlain finish his NBA career with?
   a. Philadelphia 76ers
   b. Dallas Mavericks
   c. Chicago Bulls
   d. Los Angeles Lakers

6. What NBA player scored 100 points on March 2, 1962?
   a. Bill Russell
   b. Wilt Chamberlain
   c. Kareem Abdul-Jabbar
   d. Elgin Baylor

7. What basketball player played the most seasons in the NBA?
   a. Robert Parrish
   b. Kareem Abdul-Jabbar
   c. Gene Stump
   d. Michael Jordan

8. What trophy is now awarded to the winner of the NBA Finals?
   a. The Larry Bird Championship Trophy
   b. The John Paxton Championship Trophy
   c. The Michael Jordan Championship Trophy
   d. The Larry O'Brien Championship Trophy

9. How many times did Michael Jordan win the NBA's MVP award?
   a. 3
   b. 7
   c. 5
   d. 10

10. What NBA coach holds the record for the most NBA championships?
   a. Red Auerbach
   b. Phil Jackson
   c. Patrick Ewing
   d. Pat Riley

You Make **the Call**

On this day in 1986, the National Football League adopted instant replay.

These days, the NFL uses seven officials to run and officiate their games. Even with that many, they can't see everything, especially with such quick and powerful athletes running and jumping fullspeed. But sometimes a call or missed call can make a huge difference in a game. Was it a fumble or not? Was that a catch, or did the ball hit the ground? Did the receiver get both feet in bounds? Where should the ball be placed? To help make sure the calls are correct, the league uses instant replay. A couple of times a game, each coach can challenge a call and have it reviewed by having officials check out the video of

the play in question. And at the end of games, all the important plays are reviewed. The person in the video booth will run a play over many times, in slow motion, looking at different camera angles—to get it right.

The person in the video booth has a lot of knowledge . . . and power. This person has many views of every play and player. Any official who wants the truth can call the booth.

Do you know that God sees everything you do, every move you make (he knows every thought, too)? And he sees and knows about everyone else, too. That's why he makes the correct call *every* time. And that's why we should always trust his judgment—not questioning his "calls"—and why we should trust his plan and guidance.

When playing "hide-and-seek," little children often hide in plain sight or just cover their eyes, thinking because they can't see us, we can't see them. We think that's cute but, obviously, very childish. Yet we do the same when we think we can hide from God, keep secrets from him, or get away with something.

We can't. But that's good because God loves us and wants the best for us. He's not watching like a referee, umpire, or judge, but like our loving Father.

Will you trust him? You make the call.

ALSO ON THIS DAY . . .

1892—The first public basketball game was played in Springfield, Massachusetts.

1948—Reginald Weit became the first black athlete to play in the US Tennis Open.

1979—Randy Hold received sixty-seven minutes in penalties in a sixty-minute NHL hockey game.

1991—Monica Seles ended Steffi Graf's streak of 186 weeks at number 1 in tennis.

BIRTHDAYS:

1885—Malcolm Campbell, English racer and first person to drive an automobile more than 300 mph

1923—Louise Brough Clapp, Oklahoma City, OK, tennis player (four-time Wimbledon champion)

1977—Becky Hammon, Rapid City, SD, WNBA player (New York Liberty, San Antonio Silver Stars)

1979—Elton Brand, Cortland Manor, NY, former College Player of the Year (Duke) and current NBA forward (Chicago Bulls, Los Angeles Clippers, Philadelphia 76ers)

O Lord, you have searched me and you know me. You know when I sit and when I rise; you perceive my thoughts from afar. You discern my going out and my lying down; you are familiar with all my ways. Psalm 139:1–3

FUN FACT Although NFL instant replay began in 1986, the current system began in 1999 and allows coaches to "challenge" field calls of play.

Go-To **Teammate**

On this day in 1985, Larry Bird scored a Boston–Celtic record sixty points against the Atlanta Hawks.

Larry Bird was one of the all-time great basketball players, in college and in the pros. During his thirteen seasons with the Boston Celtics (1979–1992), he showed how the game should be played, with his hustle and excellence in all areas: scoring, passing, ballhandling, and defending. He was a great team player too and is probably remembered most as a clutch performer. When the game was on the line, the Celtics wanted the ball in his hands.

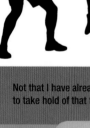

Larry was a gifted athlete to be sure, but he played with and against many who were more athletic; that is, they were bigger, stronger, faster, and better leapers. Yet Larry would outperform them, night after night, especially with his shooting. Larry was such a deadly shooter that he sometimes would practice shooting three-pointers with his eyes closed.

God-given traits and abilities can take a person just so far. Every person in every area of life (not just sports) needs to add practice and discipline to what comes naturally. Consider the high school phenom who never made it in college; instead of studying and practicing, he partied and flunked out. Or the high draft pick college all-American who grabbed his signing bonus and big contract and wasted it and himself on wild living. Think of how many of your friends seem to be satisfied with doing as little as possible to get by.

To make an impact, especially an impact for God, we need to dedicate ourselves to developing and using the mental, social, and physical abilities that he has given us. Those are gifts to be used, not abused or squandered. A fast runner can use that ability to win sprints . . . or escape the police. A genius can use that gift to invent life-saving medical equipment . . . or to plan "perfect" crimes. A natural salesperson can use that gift to tell people about God's good news . . . or rip people off. Larry Bird enhanced his natural abilities and became a champion. How can you become a champion for Christ?

. . . .

ALSO ON THIS DAY . . .

1966—Bobby Hull (Chicago Blackhawks), the Golden Jet, scored his fifty-first goal, setting a record for most goals in a season.

1972—NHL great Gordie Howe (Detroit Red Wings) retired after twenty-six seasons.

1987—David Robinson scored fifty points in a basketball game for the Naval Academy against Michigan.

BIRTHDAYS:

1963—Candy Costie, Seattle, WA, synchronized swimmer and winner of a 1984 Olympic gold medal

1963—John Andretti, Bethlehem, PA, race car driver, winner (CART, NHRA Top Fuel Dragsters NASCAR stock racing and endurance racing)

1978— Cristina Teuscher, New Rochelle, NY, 4X200m freestyle swimmer and winner of a 1996 Olympic gold medal

Not that I have already obtained all this, or have already been made perfect, but I press on to take hold of that for which Christ Jesus took hold of me. **Philippians 3:12**

FUN FACT » Larry Bird's hometown is French Lick, Indiana, which is why he had the nickname "the Hick from French Lick" later in his basketball career.

What's in **a Name?**

On this day in 1960, the Chicago White Sox unveiled new road uniforms with players' names above the number.

A team could have many reasons for putting the last names of the players on the uniforms. Certainly that would be helpful for those fans without printed programs. And radio and TV announcers probably appreciate it from time to time. Notice that the White Sox did this on their "road" uniforms, probably because the home fans knew the players by sight and position and didn't need the printed names.

In the years since, some teams have decided not to feature the players' names on the uniforms. The usual explanation given is that because baseball is a *team* sport, with everyone performing an important role, individual players shouldn't be highlighted. Good point.

Legendary basketball coach John Wooden said, "It's amazing how much can be accomplished if no one cares who gets the credit." That was his philosophy, and his UCLA teams won *ten national championships* in twelve years (1964–1975). Teamwork counts—all the players sacrificing individual glory and pulling together.

John Wooden was a strong Christian, and that philosophy certainly lines up with what the Bible teaches. When Paul wrote about the church (believers), he compared it to a body. He said that this body is made up of many members, each with special gifts and contributions to make. Then he said, "so that there should be no division in the body, but that its parts should have equal concern for each other. If one part suffers, every part suffers with it; if one part is honored, every part rejoices with it" (1 Corinthians 12:25–26).

Did you catch that phrase about every part rejoicing when someone else is honored? That's tough because most people, not just athletes, want recognition, glory, props. And only unusual people can be genuinely happy with someone else's success. But think what can be accomplished for Christ and his kingdom when we aren't concerned about who gets the credit.

So don't worry if your work goes unnoticed or your name is missing or misspelled on your "uniform." God knows, and he is glorified by your humility and team approach.

....

ALSO ON THIS DAY . . .

1915—The Brooklyn Dodgers manager Wilbert Robinson tried to catch a baseball dropped from an airplane, but the pilot substituted a grapefruit. Robinson was surprised but not hurt.

1954—The Milwaukee Braves' Bobby Thomson broke his ankle and was replaced by Hank Aaron.

1982—Elaine Zayak (US), landed six triple jumps to win the world skating championship.

1985—Michael Secrest (US) began a twenty-four-hour cycling ride of 516 miles, 427 yards.

BIRTHDAYS:

1886—John "Home Run" Baker, Trappe, MD, Hall-of-Fame third baseman (hit two HR in 1911 World Series)

1967—Colleen Rosensteel, S. Greensburg, PA, heavyweight judoka, 1996 Olympics

1972—Trent Dilfer, Santa Cruz, CA, NFL quarterback (Tampa [Pro Bowl], Baltimore [Super Bowl], Seattle, Cleveland, San Francisco)

Instead, speaking the truth in love, we will in all things grow up into him who is the Head, that is, Christ. From him the whole body, joined and held together by every supporting ligament, grows and builds itself up in love, as each part does its work. **Ephesians 4:15–16**

FUN FACT The Chicago White Stockings (now White Sox) captured the American League's first major league pennant in 1901.

14 Family **Ties**

ON THIS DAY IN 1997, GORDIE HOWE BECAME THE SECOND NHL PLAYER TO SCORE 500 GOALS.

One of the all-time great hockey players, Gordie Howe spent most of his professional career with the Detroit Red Wings. Often called "Mr. Hockey," Howe is the only player to have competed in the NHL in five different decades (1940s through 1980s). Able to use the straight sticks of his era to shoot left- or right-handed, Howe won six Hart Trophies as the league's most valuable player and six Art Ross Trophies as the leading scorer. He also was a four-time Stanley Cup champion with the Red Wings. In 1997, at the age of sixty-nine, Howe played one game, the season opener, with the Detroit Vipers (IHL). Thus his career spanned six decades. Now that's staying power!

During his long career, Howe was also able to fulfill a dream and play professional hockey with his two sons, Marty and Mark—on the Houston Aeros (1973-77) and the Hartford Whalers (1977-80). Imagine that—lacing up the skates and playing at such a high level with what used to be your babies, your little boys. What a thrill that must have been!

Everyone has a family—some with more love and closeness than others. But every person came from a mother and father. Even with a family broken in some way, we have connections to parents, siblings, and other relatives.

The Bible has much to say about family relationships—children relating to parents and parents to children. How we relate to each other is important to God. Unfortunately, we often take those relationships for granted or we drift apart through the years.

How do you relate to your brother or sister? You should be his or her biggest fan, encouraging and cheering. Also, you should be there to listen, console, protect, stand with, and pickup. And if you get to be on the same team— what a great bonus!

You won't always get along—family conflicts are natural and inevitable. But with love as the foundation, you should be willing to ask for and extend forgiveness. Families are forever.

Thank God for your family.

ALSO ON THIS DAY . . .

1899—The Montreal Shamrocks beat the Winnipeg Victorias 6-2 to win the Stanley Cup.

1993—Oksana Baiul (UKR) won the World Ladies Figure Skating Championship in Prague.

1996—Australia beat West Indies by five runs in an amazing cricket match in the World Cup semi-final, 207-202.

2007—The Phoenix Suns and Dallas Mavericks played a two-overtime thriller with the Suns, winning 129-127.

BIRTHDAYS:

1920—Dorothy Tyler-Odam, Great Britain, high jumper and Olympic silver medalist in 1936 and 1948

1944—Clyde Lee, Nashville, TN, arguably Vanderbilt University's greatest basketball player, played ten NBA seasons with the Warriors, Hawks, and 76ers

1962—Kirby Puckett, Chicago, IL, Hall-of-Fame centerfielder (Minnesota Twins)

1976—Sarah Elizabeth Ulmer, Auckland, New Zealand, 3k individual pursuit cyclist in the 1996 Olympics

If anyone does not provide for his relatives, and especially for his immediate family, he has denied the faith and is worse than an unbeliever. **1 Timothy 5:8**

FUN FACT Flying elbows and flying pucks come with hockey, so, especially with no helmets in its early years, facial cuts and stitches were common. Howe estimated that he had received three hundred stitches in his face.

Flying **High**

ON THIS DAY IN 1897, THE FIRST INDOOR FLY-CASTING TOURNAMENT OPENED AT MADISON SQUARE GARDEN.

As you've already figured out, sports come in a wide variety, everything from the more well-known ones, like soccer and swimming, to the much more obscure, like curling and cricket. Chances are good that more athletes in your school are involved in football than fencing.

Lots of the familiar, popular sports involve running, jumping, and pushing. So the bigger kids have a big advantage. No one likes to be chosen last for a team, but that happens to those who don't measure up physically. The problem is that we can get down on ourselves because we're not as physically gifted as someone else—we're not very tall, strong, and fast . . . yet.

That's when we need to remember that God made us the way we are for a purpose.

And he will help us grow at his speed and timing, exactly the right pace for us. As the former little shepherd boy David wrote, "I praise you because I am

fearfully and wonderfully made; your works are wonderful, I know that full well" (Psalm 139:14).

In the meantime, we can still be involved in sports. Take fly fishing for example. This ancient and unique method is used for catching many different kinds of fish, including trout, salmon, pike, bass, pan fish, and more.

Fishing this way takes skill—and being tall, strong, or fast doesn't matter. As a bonus, fly fishermen (and women) get to enjoy God's peaceful and beautiful creation as they do their sport.

That's only one example, of course. Many other fascinating sports are available to try. So don't worry if you'll never dunk a basketball, throw a 100 mph fastball, or bench press hundreds of pounds. You can still be an athlete. Look for sports that use your unique physique and abilities. Remember, you are "fearfully and wonderfully made."

ALSO ON THIS DAY . . .

1869—The Cincinnati Red Stockings became the first professional baseball team.

1912—Pitcher Cy Young retired from baseball with 511 wins.

1958—Royals' basketball star Maurice Stokes collapsed with encephalitis during a playoff game, went into a coma, and became permanently disabled.

1997—Pittsburgh Penguins' Joe Mullen became the first American to score 500 goals in the NHL.

BIRTHDAYS:

1926—Norm Van Brocklin, Parade, SD, Hall-of-Fame quarterback and coach (Los Angeles Rams)

1946—Bobby Bonds, Riverside, CA, Major League baseball player (Giants, Yankees) and father of Barry

1956—Clay Matthews, Palo Alto, CA, NFL linebacker (Cleveland Browns and Atlanta Falcons) and father of Clay and Casey

1965—Marianne Morris, Middletown, OH, LPGA golfer

But in fact God has arranged the parts in the body, every one of them, just as he wanted them to be. If they were all one part, where would the body be? As it is, there are many parts, but one body. **1 Corinthians 12:18–20**

Fun Fact Recently, interest in fly fishing has picked up as middle-aged adults have discovered the sport. Movies such as Robert Redford's film *A River Runs Through It*, starring Brad Pitt, cable fishing shows, and the emergence of a competitive fly-casting circuit have also added to the sport's visibility.

Who played what **Sport?**

1. Joe DiMaggio
2. **Nadia Comaneci**
3. Bobby Hull
4. **Justine Henin**
5. Mia Hamm
6. **Phil Mickelson**
7. Michael Phelps
8. **Nancy Kerrigan**
9. Evan Lysacek
10. **Annika Sörenstam**
11. Drew Brees
12. **Shaun White**
13. Ron Santo
14. **Roger Federer**
15. Anton Ohno

a. Figure skating
b. Golf
c. Speed skating
d. Gymnastics
e. Baseball
f. Tennis
g. Ice hockey
h. Golf
i. Baseball
j. Figure skating
k. Soccer
l. Tennis
m. Swimming
n. Football
o. Snowboarding

MATCH the **player** with the **sport.**

ANSWERS: 1.e, 2.d, 3.g, 4.f, 5.k, 6.b, 7.m, 8.a, 9.j, 10.h, 11.n, 12.o, 13.i, 14.l, 15.c

Nicknamed

ON THIS DAY IN 1945, MAURICE "ROCKET" RICHARD BECAME THE FIRST NATIONAL HOCKEY LEAGUE PLAYER TO SCORE FIFTY GOALS IN A SEASON.

With a name of Joseph Henri Maurice Richard Sr., maybe that's why he was called "Rocket." Actually, Maurice earned that nickname because of his burst of speed and his hard slapshot that allowed him to score so many goals. Rocket Richard played for the Montreal Canadians from 1942 to 1960. During that time he won the Stanley Cup eight times and the Hart Trophy (league MVP) in 1947. He was a fixture in the all-star games, playing in every one from 1947 to 1959, eight times on the first team and seven times on the second.

Lots of athletes have nicknames, for example, "Crazy Legs," "Magic," "Air," "Hands of Stone," "Sweetness," and "Human Eraser." Each one highlights a feature of the individual's play. Elroy Hirsch carried the football on "crazy legs." Earvin Johnson could do "magic" with the ball. Michael Jordan seemed to be floating on "air" when he dunked. Roberto Duran's punches landed like "stone." Walter Payton ran with "sweet" moves. And Marvin Webster would block shots, wiping them out like an "eraser."

In the Bible, we find a few nicknames, as well—and they tell us about the people who carried them. James and John were named "Sons of Thunder," probably because of their temper (Mark 3:17), and Jesus called Peter "stone" or "rock," encouraging him to stand strong. And then we find this man: "For instance, there was Joseph, the one the apostles nicknamed Barnabas (which means 'Son of Encouragement'). He was from the tribe of Levi and came from the island of Cyprus" Acts 4:36 (NLT). How wonderful to be known as someone who encourages others.

If you could choose a nickname that would speak about your character, what would you choose? "Loyal one"? "Truthful"? "Friend"? "Courageous"? "Strong"? "Smart"? "Cool"? Those are certainly better than "Hothead," "Lazy," or "Weirdo." Hopefully others see positive qualities dominating your lifestyle.

But how about "Lover of Jesus"? Now that would be great!

ALSO ON THIS DAY . . .

1942—Two black players, Jackie Robinson and Nate Moreland, requested a tryout with the Chicago White Sox; they were allowed to work out.

1953—The University of Indiana beat the University of Kansas 69-68 to win the fifteenth NCAA basketball national championship.

1985—Baseball Commissioner Peter Ueberroth reinstated Willie Mays and Mickey Mantle.

1995—Michael Jordan announced that he was ending his seventeen-month retirement and returning to the NBA.

BIRTHDAYS:

1964—Bonnie Blair, Champaign, IL, speed skater and winner of five gold medals—1988, 1992, 1994 Olympics—and one Bronze Medal—1988 Olympics

1969—Sheila Taormina, Livonia, MI, 4X200m freestyle swimmer and winner of 1996 Olympics gold

1976—Scott Podsednik, West, TX, Major League baseball player (Brewers, White Sox, Royals)

[Jesus said,] "I no longer call you servants, because a servant does not know his master's business. Instead, I have called you friends, for everything that I learned from my Father I have made known to you." **John 15:15**

FUN FACT Maurice Richard retired before the huge salaries. His largest yearly salary was $25,000 (equivalent to $200,000 in 2008).

19 **Together**

On this day in 1975, Pennsylvania became the first state to allow girls to compete with boys in high school sports.

People probably could debate for days about what specific sports girls and boys can and should compete in together. Football? Wrestling? Rhythmic gymnastics? But the real issue is that for many years girls were not allowed to compete *at all*, except in intramurals. Then, when they were allowed, they received very little financial support (at least much less than the boys).

That's not right. Although God created males and females different in many ways, he created *both* in his image and equal in his sight, both with roles and responsibilities in this world. Check out Genesis 1:27: "So God created man in his own image, in the image of God he created him; male and female he created them." And he declared this "good." But for a long time, girls felt unequal, inferior, on the outside looking in. Fortunately, these days girls have lots of opportunities in just about every field of study, athletics, and employment.

When these changes came, some men and boys went along with them reluctantly, sort of putting up with the fact that they had to work (or compete) with women. But God expects us to do better than that. He wants us to treat each other with respect, as brothers and sisters in his family.

Hopefully you are learning *now* how to treat the opposite sex, not just because society thinks it may be a good idea but because God says that's how we should act. Some day you'll meet the person you'll marry, and that person will know that you, and God, think he or she is special, valued, and worthy.

ALSO ON THIS DAY . . .

1956—The Minnesota Lakers beat the St. Louis Hawks 133-75 for the NBA's biggest margin of victory.

1987—Bonnie Blair skated to a women's world speed skating record in the 500m (39.43 sec).

1990—The first world ice hockey tournament for women was held, in Ottawa, Canada.

1991—The NFL owners stripped Phoenix of the 1993 Super Bowl game because Arizona did not recognize Martin Luther King Jr. Day.

BIRTHDAYS:

1927—Richie Ashburn, Tilden, NE, Major League infielder for the Philadelphia Phillies and sportscaster

1939—Joe Kapp, Santa Fe, NM, NFL quarterback (Minnesota Vikings, Boston Patriots, Houston Oilers)

1971—Whitney Hedgepeth, Colonial Heights, VA, 100m/200m backstroke swimmer and two-time silver medal winner in the 1996 Olympics

1979—Hee-Seop Choi, Major League baseball player from Korea (Chicago Cubs, Florida Marlins, Los Angeles Dodgers)

> For you are all children of God through faith in Christ Jesus. And all who have been united with Christ in baptism have put on Christ, like putting on new clothes. There is no longer Jew or Gentile, slave or free, male and female. For you are all one in Christ Jesus.
> Galatians 3:26–28, NLT

FUN FACT The popularity of women's tennis and figure skating rivals or exceeds that of their male counterparts.

One of **a Kind**

ON THIS DAY IN 1990, THE LOS ANGELES LAKERS RETIRED KAREEM ABDUL-JABBAR'S NUMBER THIRTY-THREE.

When a team retires a former player's number, it means the team's management (and their fans) think that player is a unique talent, one of a kind, who has performed at the highest level. This is a great honor, for it means that no one else will ever wear that number, be confused or compared with that player.

Kareem Abdul-Jabbar was one of the all-time great basketball centers in high school, college (UCLA), and the pros (Milwaukee Bucks and Los Angeles Lakers). His high school team won seventy-one consecutive games. During his years in college, Kareem played on three national championship teams. Then, in the pros, from 1969 to 1989, he won a record six MVP awards and six championships, scored more points than any player in NBA history. What a career! No wonder they retired number thirty-three.

How would you like to have *your* number retired eventually? Imagine that you're standing on the platform, and the crowd is going wild as your number is raised to the rafters. What a thrill that would be!

Here's a greater truth and a much greater thrill—*God* has retired your number. You see, he created you as a unique, special person with a role in this world that only you can fulfill. No one else has been, is, or will be exactly like you—no one can fill your jersey. And God has given you everything you need to succeed. God is very proud of you, and he's your biggest fan. Think of him as the audience and the announcer and the one raising the banner with your number on it.

Now live like the "all-pro" that you are!

....

ALSO ON THIS DAY . . .

1897—Yale University beat the University of Pennsylvania 32-10 in the first known intercollegiate basketball game.

1934—Female Babe Didrickson pitched a hitless inning for the Philadelphia A's in an exhibition game against the Brooklyn Dodgers.

1962—Sjoukje Dijkstra won the world figure skating championship.

1989—Major League Baseball announced that legendary player and Cincinnati Reds manager Pete Rose was under investigation for gambling.

BIRTHDAYS:

1945—Pat Riley, Schenectady, NY, NBA coach (Los Angeles Lakers, New York Knicks, Miami Heat)

1948—Bobby Orr, Parry Sound, Ontario, Hall-of-Fame NHL defenseman (Boston Bruins)

1971—Janis Kelly, Winnipeg, Manitoba, volleyball player, 1996 Olympics

Not many of you were wise by human standards; not many were influential; not many were of noble birth. But God chose the foolish things of the world to shame the wise; God chose the weak things of the world to shame the strong. He chose the lowly things of this world and the despised things . . . so that no one may boast before him. **1 Corinthians 1:26–29**

FUN FACT »

In Kareem Abdul-Jabbar's farewell game, all the players wore his trademark goggles and tried a sky hook at least once.

The Agony **of Defeat**

On this day in 1970, Yugoslavian ski jumper Vinko Bogataj crashed dramatically at the International Ski Flying Championship.

You've probably never heard of Vinko Bogataj, but certainly you've seen his famous crash. For decades following that fateful event, ABC ran a video clip of Vinko at the introduction to their *Wide World of Sports*, with Jim McKay's trademark audio introduction: "Spanning the globe to bring you the constant variety of sport—the thrill of victory . . . and the agony of defeat."

During that last line, "the agony of defeat," viewers saw Vinko nearing the end of the ski jumping chute, slipping on the ice, losing control, and, then, head-over-heels with arms and legs flailing, crashing to the end of the ramp and falling to the slope below. (Fortunately, as bad as the crash looked, he escaped with a minor concussion.) Vinko's crash perfectly pictured defeat . . . and the agony.

Hopefully you'll never experience a crash like that, but you *will* experience defeat (if you haven't already)—the score that beats your team at the buzzer, the list with those who made the roster and you're not on it, the last-place finish, the failing grade, the breakup. And each defeat can be agonizing. Through your tears, you may question God and how he could allow you to experience such pain. Just remember: God does not promise a life filled with only victories and good times. But he does promise to be with us in everything we experience.

Just before leaving them and going to the cross, Jesus told his disciples, "I have told you these things, so that in me you may have peace. In this world you will have trouble. But take heart! I have overcome the world" (John 16:33). Jesus knew that his followers would experience many agonizing defeats—that's the nature of life in this world. But he promised to be with them. They could have peace in their problems.

Remember Jesus' promise and lean on him in your defeats. Then get up, dust yourself off, and keep hustling. And get this—God can take those defeats and transform them into victories after all. Just watch!

ALSO ON THIS DAY . . .

1946—Kenny Washington signed with Rams—the first black NFL player since 1933.

1953—In the game between Boston and Syracuse, an NBA record 106 fouls were called, with twelve players fouling out of the game.

1980—President Jimmy Carter announced that the United States would boycott the Moscow Olympics because of the USSR's involvement in Afghanistan.

2009—Eric Rupe won the USA Cycling BMX National Championship.

BIRTHDAYS:

1939—Martha Hudson, Eastman, GA, 4X100m relay runner and winner of Olympic gold in 1960

1956—Ingrid Kristiansen, Norwegian marathoner, placed fourth in the 1984 Olympics and won the Boston Marathon in 1986 and 1989

1985—Adrian Peterson, Palestine, TX, University of Oklahoma all-American and all-pro NFL running back (Minnesota Vikings)

Who shall separate us from the love of Christ? Shall trouble or hardship or persecution or famine or nakedness or danger or sword? ... No, in all these things we are more than conquerors through him who loved us. **Romans 8:35, 37**

FUN FACT When ABC flew Bogataj to New York City to celebrate the twenty-fifth anniversary of the *Wide World of Sports*, the former skier and factory worker was stunned to learn that he had a wide following in the United States. Then he said, "Every human being must be glad he's famous at one time."

Fame

On this day in 1928, Ed Macauley, NBA player for the Boston Celtics, was born.

Have you ever heard of Ed Macauley? Probably not. How about these athletes who also were born on this day: Lyndsay Stephen, golfer (1956), Juan Aguilera, Spanish tennis star (1962), Mario Cipollini, Italian cyclist (1967), and Philippe Clement, Belgian soccer player (1974)? All were big stars at one time but now are all but forgotten, except for their family and close friends, of course.

You may be thinking, "Well obviously I wouldn't remember them. Some played before I was even born and some in different countries!" Good point. But what about this: Who won the Super Bowl two years ago? Who won the last World Cup in soccer? How about the NCAA Basketball Championship last year? The Boston Marathon? The US Open? The Stanley Cup? And don't even

bother trying to remember who came in second.

The fact is, fame doesn't last. And today's hero is tomorrow's has-been. One of the saddest sights is watching former high school stars walk around the stadium wearing their old letter jackets, almost like they are shouting, "Look at me! Remember me? Cheer again for me. I'm important!"

Is anything wrong with playing to win, wanting to be the best, the champion? No. And when we win and are, truly, number one in the conference, state, or even the world, celebrations are in order—it feels great! We just have to keep it all in perspective and remember that *everything* in this world,

including all those trophies and medals, will pass away and be forgotten. Only what is done for Christ will have any lasting value. And God will remember what we've done for him—for eternity!

······································

ALSO ON THIS DAY . . .

1894—In the first playoff game ever for the Stanley Cup, Montreal AAA beat the Ottawa Generals 3-1.

1934—The first Masters Golf Tournament began in Augusta, GA.

1989—Clint Malarchuk of the Buffalo Sabres suffered a near-fatal injury when another player accidentally slit his throat with a skate.

1997—Tara Lipinski (USA) won the Women's Figure Skating Championship in Lausanne, Switzerland.

BIRTHDAYS:

1938—Vivian Pulliam, horse trainer

1952—Bob Costas, Queens, NY, sportscaster

1969—Russell Maryland, Chicago, IL, NFL defensive tackle (Dallas Cowboys, Oakland Raiders)

[Jesus said,] "Do not store up for yourselves treasures on earth, where moth and rust destroy, and where thieves break in and steal. But store up for yourselves treasures in heaven, where moth and rust do not destroy, and where thieves do not break in and steal. For where your treasure is, there your heart will be also." **Matthew 6:19–21**

Fun Fact Philippe Clement plays defensive midfielder for Germinal Beerschot. His former clubs include Genk and Coventry City in England and Club Brugge. Philippe played for the Belgium team for the Euro 2000 and the 1998 World Cup. (Impress your friends with this knowledge.)

Hockey Arenas

MATCH the **city** to the **arena.**

1. Chicago
2. **Anaheim**
3. Detroit
4. **New York**
5. New Jersey
6. **Philadelphia**
7. Pittsburgh
8. **Boston**
9. Montreal
10. **Buffalo**
11. Carolina
12. **Ottawa**
13. Atlanta
14. **Florida**
15. Toronto
16. **Tampa Bay**
17. Columbus
18. **Nashville**
19. Washington
20. **St. Louis**
21. Calgary
22. **Dallas**
23. Colorado
24. **Edmonton**
25. Minnesota
26. **Vancouver**
27. Los Angeles
28. **Phoenix**
29. San Jose
30. **New York**

a. Madison Square Garden
b. **BankAtlantic Center**
c. Bell Centre
d. **General Motors Place**
e. Nationwide Arena
f. **Bridgestone Arena**
g. Xcel Energy Center
h. **Pengrowth Saddledome**
i. HP Pavilion at San Jose
j. **Rexall Place**
k. Joe Lewis Arena
l. **Pepsi Center**
m. Jobing.com Arena
n. **Honda Center**
o. TD Garden
p. **Staples Center**
q. St. Pete Times Forum
r. **Nassau Veterans Memorial Coliseum**
s. Scotiabank Place
t. **Mellon Arena**
u. Philips Arena
v. **Wachovia Center**
w. United Center
x. **Scottrade Center**
y. Prudential Center
z. **RBC Center**
aa. American Airlines Center
bb. **Air Canada Centre**
cc. Verizon Center
dd. **HSBC Arena**

ANSWERS: 1.w, 2.n, 3.k, 4.a, 5.y, 6.v, 7.t, 8.o, 9.c, 10.dd, 11.z, 12.s, 13.u, 14.b, 15.bb, 16.q, 17.e, 18.f, 19.cc, 20.x, 21.h, 22.aa, 23.l, 24.j, 25.g, 26.d, 27.p, 28.m, 29.i, 30.r.

Name **Change**

On this day in 1971, the Boston Patriots became the New England Patriots.

College and professional teams seem to change names quite a bit. Sometimes it's because the team moves to a new city. So the New Orleans Jazz became the Utah Jazz, and the Chicago (football) Cardinals became the St. Louis Cardinals, then later became the Phoenix Cardinals. Some names are changed because of sensitivity to certain groups or to change the team's image. So the Stanford University Indians became the Cardinal; the Wheaton College Crusaders became the Thunder; the Marquette University Warriors became the Golden Eagles. But some, like the Boston Patriots, changed their name so that they would represent a larger geographical region.

Names signal who we are, and we grow up identifying with that name and listening for it. In a noisy crowd you'll hear your name when someone almost whispers it. Thus, a team that changes its name is sending a message.

The Bible reports God changing a few names. He changed Abram to Abraham, which means "father of many nations" (Genesis 17:5). For some strange-sounding names, check out the book of Hosea, where God told the prophet to give his kids names that would send a message to the people (for example, Lo-Ruhamah—"not loved" [1:6]). Also, Jesus changed Simon to Cephas or Peter (John 1:42).

What's even more important than a person's name is his or her character. That's what God was saying when he changed those names—what's inside a person is what truly counts. And that's where God makes his biggest changes. When Jesus told a religious leader he had to be "born again" (John 3:3), he was explaining that Nicodemus needed to be transformed, made new, on the inside. Doing religious rituals and ceremonies and having a fancy title wouldn't cut it. Being "born again" only happens when a person puts his or her faith in Jesus as Savior. And when that happens, the person becomes a member of God's family . . . so I guess the name is changed after all—to Christian, meaning "Christ-one."

Are you in his family? Do you bear his name?

....

ALSO ON THIS DAY . . .

1896—The modern Olympics began in Athens, Greece.

1937—It was revealed that Quaker Oats was paying Babe Ruth $25,000 per year for his involvement in their advertisements.

1958—Sugar Ray Robinson became the first boxer to win the championship five times.

1972—UCLA won its sixth consecutive basketball national championship, 81-76 over Florida State.

BIRTHDAYS:

1966—Tom Glavine, Concord, MA, Major League pitcher (Atlanta Braves and New York Mets), Cy Young Award winner in 1991

1971—Sheryl Swoopes, Brownfield, TX, WNBA forward (Houston Comets and Seattle Storm), winner of three Olympic gold medals (1996, 2000, 2004)

1982—Danica Patrick, Roscoe, IL, auto racing driver

This means that anyone who belongs to Christ has become a new person. The old life is gone; a new life has begun! **2 Corinthians 5:17, NLT**

Fun Fact
Between 2001 and 2005, the New England Patriots became the second team to win three Super Bowls in four years.

26 Never Give Up

On this day in 2005, in the NCAA Elite Eight, the University of Illinois had one of the most memorable comebacks in tournament history, beating the University of Arizona.

With only four minutes remaining in the game, the Arizona Wildcats were leading by a whopping fifteen points over Illinois. But the Fighting Illini outscored Arizona 20-5 the rest of the way, tying the game at eighty on a Deron Williams three-point shot with thirty-eight seconds to go. In overtime, Illinois kept the momentum and held on for a gut-wrenching 90-89 victory, advancing to their first Final Four appearance in sixteen years. Arizona went home, devastated.

Interviewed after the game, all-American guard Deron Williams explained, "We just kept fighting. We never gave up. It looked like the game was over. ... We've got to keep going, keep playing. I'm trying to tell my teammates out on the floor, 'This game's not over.'"

Deron's words are similar to what Sir Winston Churchill told the English during World War II— "Never, never, never give up!" And what Dr. V. Raymond Edman used to tell students at Wheaton College—"It's always too soon to quit."

But the greatest example of never giving in or giving up has to be the apostle Paul, who said, "We are pressed on every side by troubles, but we are not crushed. We are perplexed, but not driven to despair. We are hunted down, but never abandoned by God. We get knocked down, but we are not destroyed" (2 Corinthians 4:8-9, NLT).

Persecuted, isolated, hunted—if anyone seemed to be losing the game badly it was Paul. But he knew that in the ultimate game, fulfilling God's purpose for him, he was not a loser and would ultimately win. And he knew that God was with him every step of the way.

Regardless of what you're going through right now— conflicts, disappointments, sickness or injury, loss—don't quit, throw in the towel, walk away. Keep doing what you know God has called you to do, and keep your eyes on his prize. Never give up.

....

ALSO ON THIS DAY . . .

1937—Joe DiMaggio took Ty Cobb's advice and replaced his forty-ounce bat with a thirty-six-ounce bat.

1979—Larry Bird and Magic Johnson faced off in their first meeting as opponents in the NCAA Men's basketball tournament.

1988—Janet Evans swam the 1500m freestyle in a female world record (15:52.10).

1992—The NHL New York Rangers clinched their first regular season championship in fifty years.

BIRTHDAYS:

1937—Barbara Pearl Jones, Chicago, IL, 4X100m relay runner, winner of Olympic gold medals in 1952 and 1960

1960—Marcus Allen, San Diego, CA, NFL running back (Los Angeles Raiders and Kansas City Chiefs) and winner of the Heisman Trophy in 1981

1962—John Stockton, Spokane, WA, all-star NBA point guard (Utah Jazz) and winner of the Olympic gold medal in 1996

> Brothers, I do not consider myself yet to have taken hold of it. But one thing I do: Forgetting what is behind and straining toward what is ahead.
> **Philippians 3:13**

FUN FACT Illinois went on to beat Louisville in the Final Four, moving their season record to 37-1. In the championship game, the Illini were able to keep it close, but in the end they fell, 75-70, to North Carolina.

No **Excuses**

ON THIS DAY IN 1991, THE NATIONAL COLLEGIATE ATHLETIC ASSOCIATION BANNED THE UNIVERSITY OF MINNESOTA FOOTBALL TEAM FROM POSTSEASON PLAY IN 1992.

Just about every year, we read headlines like the one about the 1991 University of Minnesota football team—colleges and coaches getting caught breaking the rules and then paying the price. Some of the violations involve recruiting by coaches and alumni. At times, the whole athletic department seems to be involved, especially when we hear that certain athletes don't write their own papers, take their own tests, or even go to class. And in some cases the athletes alone are responsible.

Winning at all costs is the basic reason for this widespread cheating. Successful athletic programs lead to big payouts for their universities—attendance at events, media contracts, bowl games, and more. If coaches win,

they get rewarded with huge contracts; if not, they're fired. Imagine the pressure they must feel.

Usually this kind of behavior falls into the category of "the end justifies the means." In plain English, this is saying that the goal is all-important, so how we reach that goal doesn't matter. By this reasoning, a person can lie, cheat, and steal as long as that helps him or her reach the goal, the achievement. Thinking like this can be very tempting, and we can easily explain away our unethical, immoral, sinful actions. Other common excuses (lies) include "everybody's doing it," "no one will get hurt," and "no one will ever know."

God has a different point of view. Certainly he wants us to have good goals (for example, help hurting people, get into a great college, make money so we can give more away, see people

come to Christ), but how we achieve those goals is even more important. Remember the Great Commandment, the one about loving God totally and loving others as much as we love ourselves? This means that doing what God wants in every situation should be our guide for how we live, how we relate to others, and how we play the game. We must live morally and be above reproach, even if that means losing on the field or in the classroom.

Don't let the pressure to win push you to do wrong. Determine to live God's way.

....

ALSO ON THIS DAY . . .

1871—In the first international rugby game, Scotland beat England 1-0.

1902—After using a variety of names for the Chicago National League baseball team (White Stockings, Colts, Orphans, and Remnants), the team became the Chicago Cubs.

1939—In the first NCAA Men's Basketball Championship, the University of Oregon beat Ohio State University 46-33.

1988—Katarina Witt won the Women's Figure Skating World Championship in Budapest.

BIRTHDAYS:

1950—Vic Harris, Los Angeles, CA, Major League baseball player, second baseman for the Rangers, Cubs, Cardinals, Giants, and Brewers

1963—Randall Cunningham, Santa Barbara, CA, NFL quarterback for the Philadelphia Eagles and Minnesota Vikings

1968—Irina Belova, Russian pentathelete who set the world record in 1992

Do not conform any longer to the pattern of this world, but be transformed by the renewing of your mind. Then you will be able to test and approve what God's will is—his good, pleasing and perfect will. **Romans 12:2**

FUN FACT In 1984, Katarina Witt was voted "GDR female athlete of the year" by the readers of an East German newspaper.

28 Clutch **Player**

On this day in 1990, Michael Jordan scored sixty-nine points, the fourth time he had scored sixty points in a game.

When the game is on the line, certain players want the opportunity to win. They want to be standing at home plate with two outs in the ninth inning, receiving the puck in overtime, swimming or running the anchor leg, standing over the ball on the last green, receiving the handoff at the goal-line. For this person in basketball, it means taking the last, game-winning shot.

Michael Jordan epitomized that attitude. At the end of a close game, everyone knew that the ball would be passed to him and that he would shoot it at the last second; yet he did and often scored the game-winner. The go-to player is not a glory hog, demanding to take every shot. He or she is someone the team can count on—confident, cool, and determined.

This kind of athlete *thrives* on pressure, steps up, and delivers.

The opposite is what we know as a "choker." This kind of player doesn't come through under pressure, often even missing a relatively easy opportunity to put the game away.

So are you a "go-to" player? You may not get many opportunities to win games at the buzzer, but you'll have plenty of chances to come through under pressure—in the classroom, in conversation, or just hanging out. Picture yourself in English class and one of the students says something insulting about Jesus. Will you come through and defend the truth, or will you give in to the pressure and stay silent? Or suppose you're at church and the youth leader is asking for a volunteer to lead a Bible study. Will you accept the challenge, or will you duck, avoiding eye contact, and let someone else do it? Or what if you hear your mom talk about an older woman down the street who really could use some help? Will you go to her and offer to clean her house and do other jobs, or will you think of excuses for not going?

Do it for Jesus. Come through for his team. Be a clutch player.

....

ALSO ON THIS DAY . . .

1963—The American Football League's New York Titans became the New York Jets.

1982—In the first NCAA Women's Basketball Championship, Louisiana Tech beat Cheney State 76-62.

1984—At night, under the cover of darkness, Robert Irsay, the owner of the Baltimore Colts, moved his team to Indianapolis, Indiana.

1992—In perhaps the greatest college basketball game ever, with 2.1 seconds left in over-time and trailing 103-102, Duke's Christian Laettner shot a field goal to defeat Kentucky in the tournament semifinals.

Whatever you do, work at it with all your heart, as working for the Lord, not for men, since you know that you will receive an inheritance from the Lord as a reward. It is the Lord Christ you are serving. Colossians 3:23–24

FUN FACT » Michael Jordan's biography on the National Basketball Association's website says that he is "the greatest basketball player of all time."

BIRTHDAYS:

1940—Kevin Loughery, Brooklyn, NY, NBA star (Baltimore Bullets and Philadelphia 76ers) and coach

1958—Bart Wayne Conner, Morton Grove, IL, gymnast and winner of two gold medals in the 1984 Olympics

1972—Jonathan Edwards, Boston, MA, doubles luger in the 1994 Olympics

Included

ON THIS DAY IN 1989, THE FIRST SOVIET HOCKEY PLAYERS WERE PERMITTED TO PLAY IN THE NATIONAL HOCKEY LEAGUE.

The Soviet Union and western nations, including the United States and Canada, didn't like each other very much. For many years they were in what was called the Cold War—they weren't shooting at each other but were against each other in many ways. So athletes from that group of formerly independent countries (Russia, Czechoslovakia, Ukraine, Belarus, Yugoslavia, Romania, and others) weren't allowed to be part of many international professional sporting associations, such as the NBA, NFL, and NHL. This was a big deal for the NHL because many of the world's best hockey players lived behind the "Iron Curtain." In the late 1980s, when the USSR began to open up and then break up, some hockey players were allowed in and then played in the NHL.

People are excluded from organizations for many reasons, some very complex, including politics. Sometimes, however, certain people are left out simply because they are different. That still happens in social groups at school where kids would rather be with their friends, naturally, but then don't widen the circle for anyone else. And we certainly don't want anything to do with people who *don't like us*.

Aren't you glad that God doesn't treat us that way? Our sins are insults to God. All of our lives we have disobeyed and disrespected him. We've treated him worse than in a "cold war." In fact, the Bible says that we were God's "enemies." But listen to this amazing passage from God: "You see, at just the right time, when we were still powerless, Christ died for the ungodly. Very rarely will anyone die for a righteous man, though for a good man someone might possibly dare to die. But God demonstrates his own love for us in this: While we were still sinners, Christ died for us" (Romans 5:6–8).

We deserved to be totally excluded from God and his good plans. Instead, he sent his Son to pay the penalty for our sins so that we could be *included*, be his friends and part of his family. All we have to do is ask.

That's called grace.

ALSO ON THIS DAY . . .

1953—Patty Berg won the LPGA New Orleans Women's Golf Open.

1992—The Ladies Figure Skating Championship in Oakland, CA, was won by Kristi Yamaguchi (USA).

1997—In the first game played at Turner Field in Atlanta, the Braves beat the Yankees 2-0 (exhibition).

BIRTHDAYS:

1867—Cy Young, Gilmore, OH, Hall-of-Fame Major League pitcher after whom the annual award for being the best pitcher in a league was named

1945—Walt "Clyde" Frazier, Atlanta, GA, NBA guard (New York Knicks)

1976—Jennifer Capriati, Long Island, NY, tennis professional and winner of the Olympic gold medal in 1992

For since our friendship with God was restored by the death of his Son while we were still his enemies, we will certainly be saved through the life of his Son. So now we can rejoice in our wonderful new relationship with God because our Lord Jesus Christ has made us friends of God. **Romans 5:10-11, NLT**

FUN FACT

The NHL was organized in 1917 in Montreal, Canada, and consisted of four teams: Montreal, Ottawa, Quebec, and Toronto.

1. What one-handed pitcher won the fifty-eighth James E. Sullivan award? (March 7)

2. **What hockey team did Gordie Howe play with most of his career? (March 14)**

3. In what swimming race did Jenny Thompson break the world record? (March 1)

4. **Who is known as the greatest basketball player of all time? (March 28)**

5. What sport did Ed Macauley play? (March 22)

6. **What tournament opened in Madison Square Garden in 1897 (hint: flies were involved)? (March 15)**

7. What was Kareem Abdul-Jabbar's jersey number? (March 20)

8. **For what NHL team did goalie Samuel LoPresti play? (March 4)**

9. How many tickets did the New Orleans Saints sell on their first day selling season tickets? (March 8)

10. **Who won the American League's first major-league pennant in 1901? (March 13)**

11. When were the Soviets first allowed to play in the National Hockey League? (March 29)

12. **What was Maurice Richmond's nickname? (March 18)**

13. From where are the New England Patriots originally? (March 25)

14. **Gaylord Perry was the first pitcher to win what award in both leagues? (March 5)**

15. Against whom did Larry Bird score a record sixty points? (March 12)

16. **For what is ski jumper Vinko Bogataj most known? (March 21)**

17. What NCAA football team was banned from postseason play in 1992? (March 27)

18. **In 1972, whom did Jack Nicklaus pass as golf's all-time money winner? (March 6)**

19. What year did the NFL begin using instant replay? (March 11)

20. **What was the first state to allow girls to compete with boys in high school sports? (March 19)**

21. In the 2005 NCAA Elite Eight basketball game, who did the University of Illinois come back to defeat? (March 26)

Winner or **Whiner?**

On this day in 1992, the National Hockey League players began the first strike in the league's seventy-five-year history.

Through the years, occasionally individual players would threaten to not play unless their demands were met (usually more money). Then labor unions got involved with the formation of players associations: MLB (1953), NBA (1954, recognized by owners in 1964), NFL (1956), and NHL (1957). Since then, every major sport has experienced some sort of work stoppage, either a strike by the players or a lockout by the owners.

As in other occupations, job actions arise from differences between the workers (in this case the athletes) and management (team owners). Players may want more money, but the differences may involve working (playing) conditions, benefits, and other issues. Players will say the owners are unfair; owners will say the players are unreasonable. In the end, usually neither side gets everything it wants. And both sides often look like whiners, especially with most players and owners in those leagues making millions of dollars.

Athletes used to play for the love of the game. Many still do. But some act like spoiled brats, demanding a new contract, more scoring opportunities, a trade, or a new manager (or coach). Forget their fans or teammates or the contracts they already signed, it's all about them and their egos. They pout and complain, all the while cashing their enormous checks. But nobody likes a self-centered whiner—especially the fans who are watching the ticket prices climb (and the team lose).

A person's focus and attitude say much about his or her character. And one word that you'll find often when God talks about the attitude he wants us to have is "humility." God isn't saying we shouldn't stick up for what is right and fair or that contracts are bad. But he wants his people to focus on him and others, not themselves, and to speak gently, honor individuals, and treat people (including coaches, owners, fans, and competitors) with respect. Christians in all endeavors should be peacemakers and known for their love.

Do you ever feel like those whining players and threaten to quit or take your ball and go home if you don't get your way? Be a winner, not a whiner!

ALSO ON THIS DAY . . .

1912—The Greek athlete Konstantinos Tsiklitiras broke the world record in the standing long jump, jumping 3.47 meters.

1984—Eight men recorded the longest distance (thirteen miles) rowed in twenty-four hours.

1985—Villanova (number eight) defeated top-ranked Georgetown in the NCAA men's basketball national championship, 66-64.

BIRTHDAYS:

1965—John "Jumbo" Elliot, Lake Ronkonkoma, NY, NFL tackle (New York Giants and New York Jets)

1975—Kristine Quance, Los Angeles, CA, 100m breaststroke and 200m medley, 1996 Olympics gold medal winner in the 400m relay

1988—Brook and Robin Lopez, North Hollywood, CA, NBA basketball players (twins); Brook plays for the New Jersey Nets, and Robin plays for the Phoenix Suns

"For everyone who exalts himself will be humbled, and he who humbles himself will be exalted." Luke 14:11

FUN FACT The strike lasted ten days. The players got a large increase in playoff bonuses, increased control over the licensing of their likenesses, and changes to the free agency. The strike greatly changed the relationship between the league and its players.

2 Overcomer

On this day in 1931, seventeen-year-old Jackie Mitchell struck out Babe Ruth and Lou Gehrig.

Jackie Mitchell was a remarkable athlete. She entered the world at just over three pounds, but as soon as she could walk, she went with her dad to the baseball field and there learned the game. Her neighbor, Dazzy Vance (future Hall-of-Fame pitcher for the Brooklyn Dodgers), taught Jackie how to throw the drop pitch, which would drop suddenly, just before reaching the plate. Jackie was only five when she learned this pitch.

Jackie loved baseball and at sixteen played for the Chattanooga Lookouts, a class AA minor-league team. The owner offered her a contract to play for the entire 1931 season.

That special day in April, in an exhibition game against the New York Yankees, Jackie faced Babe Ruth and Lou Gehrig in succession. Her first pitch to Ruth sailed high for a ball. Her next two were strikes. Then she dropped one across the plate for a called third strike. The crowd of 4,000 went wild. But Jackie wasn't finished. The next batter was the Yankees' clean-up hitter, the great Lou Gehrig. She struck him out, too—on three pitches.

In her life, Jackie had to overcome a lot: her premature birth, her age, and her gender in a man's sport. But she succeeded, despite her odds. She was a sports "overcomer."

Early Christians had to overcome lots of adversity. They weren't allowed to have jobs; they were persecuted; many were tortured and, then, killed—just because they believed in Jesus. But listen to what Paul wrote to these believers: "What, then, shall we say in response to this? If God is for us, who can be against us? . . . No, in all these things we are more than conquerors through him who loved us" (Romans 8:31, 37). They could persevere; they could hang tough because Jesus was with them in their struggles and sufferings. They could be spiritual "overcomers," "more than conquerors."

What odds are against you? What do you have to overcome to reach your goals, to live for Christ?

God was with them, and he's with you. God and you—a great team!

ALSO ON THIS DAY . . .

1908—The Mills Committee declared that baseball was invented by Abner Doubleday.

1955—Pancho Gonzales retained his tennis title by winning a tournament playing under table tennis rules.

1986—The NCAA adopted the three-point basketball rule (19 feet 9 inch distance).

2005—James Stewart Jr. became the first African American to win a major motor sports event.

The Lord is with me; I will not be afraid. What can man do to me?
Psalm 118:6

FUN FACT Shortly after Mitchell struck out Ruth and Gehrig, baseball commissioner Landis voided her contract, declaring women unfit to play baseball as the game was "too strenuous." Jackie continued to play professionally, barnstorming with the House of David, a men's team famous for their very long hair and long beards. While traveling with this team, sometimes she would wear a fake beard for publicity.

BIRTHDAYS:

1945—Don Sutton, Clio, AL, Hall-of-Fame baseball pitcher (Los Angeles Dodgers)

1966—Bill Romanowski, Vernon, CT, NFL linebacker (Philadelphia Eagles and Denver Broncos—Super Bowl XXXII)

1970—Tammi Reiss, Mid-Hudson, NY, WNBA guard (Utah Starzz)

1982—Jeremy Bloom, Loveland, CO, World Champion and Olympic skier and football player (Philadelphia Eagles and Pittsburg Steelers)

Underdogs

On this day in 2010, Butler University beat Michigan State University in the NCAA Basketball Tournament, 52-50, to continue its unlikely journey to the championship game.

March Madness" has become almost a national celebration, with massive television ratings and sports enthusiasts filling in their brackets, trying to predict the eventual national champion. The 2010 tournament featured the most upset wins in a long time, with teams such as Murray State, Ohio University, Northern Iowa, Baylor, Cornell, and Butler gaining national attention through their big victories. And one of them made it to the championship in Indianapolis.

Not only was Butler a longshot in this tournament, but their campus is just a short ride from the stadium where the Final Four games were held. And here's another coincidence: "Hoosiers," released in 1986, tells the story about another underdog, Milan, a small-town Indiana high school

basketball team that won state in 1954. The championship game took place, and was later reenacted and filmed, in Hinkle Fieldhouse on the Butler campus.

In the film, the small-town players were struck with awe by the fieldhouse when they checked it out and seemed intimidated by the prospect of playing there. So the coach got a measuring tape and a stepladder and measured the distance from the basketball rims to the floor—ten feet, just like everywhere else. His message: The game is the same everywhere. Don't be afraid; just play your game. You've shot and made baskets in your driveway, in our gym, and all over the state. Remember that and you'll be fine.

It's a great lesson. Often we can be psyched out by events or intimidated by circumstances. That's when we should remember similar situations in the past where we made it

through, where we succeeded, and, most important, where we trusted in God. He was with us then; he'll be with us now.

Joshua had that in mind when he told the people to build a monument of stones (Joshua 4:1–9). He said, "In the future, when your children ask you, 'What do these stones mean?' tell them . . . . These stones are to be a memorial to the people of Israel forever" (vv. 6–7).

When did God give you strength? When did he answer your prayer? When did you feel him close? Remember that and you'll be fine.

....

ALSO ON THIS DAY . . .

1936—The shortest boxing bout with gloves was held; it lasted only ten seconds.

1962—Jockey Eddie Arcaro retired after thirty-one years and 24,092 races.

1988—Mario Lemieux won the NHL scoring title, stopping Wayne Gretzky's seven-year streak.

1991—Bo Jackson (NFL running back) signed a one-year contract to play for the Chicago White Sox.

BIRTHDAYS:

1963—Jack Del Rio, Castro Valley, CA, NFL football player (Chiefs, Cowboys, Vikings, and Dolphins) and coach (Jacksonville Jaguars)

1971—Picabo Street, Triumph, ID, American champion skier and winner of an Olympic gold medal in 1994 (downhill)

1993—Dakoda Dowd, Palm Harbor, FL, American professional golfer

For the Lord your God dried up the Jordan before you until you had crossed over. The Lord your God did to the Jordan just what he had done to the Red Sea when he dried it up before us until we had crossed over. He did this so that all the peoples of the earth might know that the hand of the Lord is powerful and so that you might always fear the Lord your God. **Joshua 4:23–24**

FUN FACT By reaching the Final Four in 2010, Butler became the first team since 1972 (UCLA) to advance to the Final Four in which the host city was also the city where the campus was located.

4 Inside **Operation**

On this day in 1989, New York Yankee Tommy John tied the record of playing twenty-six seasons, and his 287th win put him nineteenth overall as the Yankees beat the Twins on opening day, 4-2.

Although Tommy John was an excellent left-handed pitcher with a long and successful career with the Indians, Dodgers, White Sox, Yankees, Angels, and Athletics, he is known more for the surgery he had on his pitching arm. In 1974, John was doing great, with a 13-3 record with the Dodgers when, suddenly, he permanently damaged his ulnar collateral ligament (very serious injury). He could no longer pitch. That's when Dr. Frank Jobe operated and replaced that damaged ligament in the elbow with a tendon from some place else on his body. The operation was successful and has been repeated on many other pitchers. In fact, those who have undergone "Tommy John surgery" (position players, too) often return to the game even stronger than before.

This may come as a surprise, but the Bible talks about surgery—not on elbows but on hearts. And God is the surgeon. Listen to this interesting passage: "I will give you a new heart and put a new spirit in you; I will remove from you your heart of stone and give you a heart of flesh. And I will put my Spirit in you and move you to follow my decrees and be careful to keep my laws" (Ezekiel 36:26–27).

Through the prophet Ezekiel, God was making this promise to Israel; they just had to surrender to him, to submit and obey him. Then, after God's spiritual "heart surgery," they would be free from their sins and free to do his will because his Spirit would be in them. Through Christ, we can have the same surgery—God wants to transform us in the inside, to remake us.

Some people try to change on their own. But that would be like Tommy John putting a bandage on his arm and thinking it would help. Instead, he needed a new, reconstructed elbow.

How's your heart—stone or flesh? Ask God to remake you into his kind of person.

ALSO ON THIS DAY . . .

1937—Byron Nelson won the fourth golf Masters Championship, shooting a 283.

1983—Jimmy Valvano and North Carolina State stunned heavily favored University of Houston to win the NCAA basketball championship.

1989—Kareem Abdul-Jabbar played his last professional basketball game, in Seattle.

1994—Arkansas defeated top-ranked Duke University in the NCAA basketball championship game—Arkansas' only national title.

BIRTHDAYS:

1888—Tris Speaker, Hubbard, TX, Hall-of-Fame centerfielder, hit more doubles than Pete Rose

1944—Lawrence A. Hough, US rower (pairs w/o cox) who won the 1968 Olympic silver medal

1975—Kisha Ford, Baltimore, MD

I will give them an undivided heart and put a new spirit in them; I will remove from them their heart of stone and give them a heart of flesh. Then they will follow my decrees and be careful to keep my laws. They will be my people, and I will be their God. **Ezekiel 11:19–20**

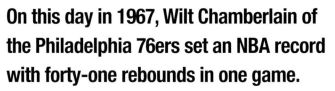

Dirty **Work**

On this day in 1967, Wilt Chamberlain of the Philadelphia 76ers set an NBA record with forty-one rebounds in one game.

The game of basketball has many facets, including shooting field goals and free throws, setting screens, playing man-to-man and zone defense, executing plays, passing, dribbling, cutting, blocking, and diving for loose balls. One of the most important, but often overlooked, is rebounding. About half of the shots taken don't go in, and that percentage increases the farther away the shooter is from the basket. Missed shots result in caroms, meaning that the ball bounces off the rim or backboard and away from the basket. When the shooting team grabs one of those, it's an offensive rebound and gives that team another chance to score. Defensive rebounds give the ball to the other team. So having more rebounds means having more shots (and, usually, more points).

Rebounding isn't the glory part of basketball. It involves smart positioning (blocking out), good timing (knowing when to go to the basket and when to jump for the ball), and lots of pushing and shoving. Rebounding is part of the "dirty work" of basketball, the necessary job that players have to do if they want their team to win.

That's true in all sports—blocking in football, moving a runner over in baseball, tackling in soccer, blocking shots in hockey. It also happens in most other areas of life. Some people just want to take the shots and get the glory, but true team players will do anything the team needs, including the dirty work, to gain a victory.

In a successful family, everyone pitches in, doing important jobs like cleaning a room, taking out garbage, raking leaves, pulling weeds, and other "dirty work." In a successful

church, some members work behind the scenes cleaning, setting up chairs, stuffing bulletins, changing flowers, and other "dirty work." And in living for Christ at school and in the neighborhood, Christians need to do their best, visit the sick, feed the hungry, listen to the hurting, and other "dirty work."

You won't get much glory—you may not even be noticed. But you'll be doing what God wants.

ALSO ON THIS DAY . . .

1915—Jess Willard knocked out Jack Johnson in twenty-six rounds for the heavyweight boxing title.

1973—The NFL adopted a jersey numbering system (for example, quarterbacks would wear one to nineteen).

1989—Orel Hershiser (Los Angeles Dodgers) ended his fifty-nine consecutive scoreless pitched inning streak.

1993—During the NCAA basketball championship game, Chris Webber of Michigan called for a timeout in the final seconds; however, the team was out of timeouts, and Michigan lost to North Carolina.

Now that I, your Lord and Teacher, have washed your feet, you also should wash one another's feet. **John 13:14**

FUN FACT After his basketball career, Wilt Chamberlain played volleyball in the International Volleyball Association and was the president of the organization.

Rules of the Game—Baseball

1. How many players are on the field at a time (not including batter or base runners)?
   a. 7
   b. 11
   c. 9
   d. 3

2. How many sides make up home plate?
   a. 4
   b. 5
   c. 8
   d. None, it's a circle

3. The pitcher's glove may not be white or gray.
   a. True
   b. False

4. When the game is set to start, the umpire says:
   a. It's go time!
   b. Bring it!
   c. Game on!
   d. Play!

5. If a foul tip hits the umpire and is caught by a fielder on the rebound, the runner:
   a. Is called out
   b. Takes first base
   c. Does nothing and the ball is considered dead

6. No player, coach, or manager may interact with a spectator before or during a game.
   a. True
   b. False

7. Who decides if a game is played during bad weather or poor field conditions?
   a. Umpire-in-chief
   b. Home team owner
   c. Visiting team manager
   d. Home team manager

8. In baseball, the battery refers to:
   a. The pitcher and catcher
   b. The two team managers
   c. The umpires
   d. The scoreboard

9. A player may be appointed the manager.
   a. True
   b. False

10. When a team tries to score a runner on third during a bunt, it is called:
    a. A run-off
    b. Cat and mouse
    c. A squeeze play
    d. A triple steal

ANSWERS: 1. c, 2. b, 3. a, 4. d, 5. c, 6. a, 7. c, 8. a, 9. a, 10. c

What's **Important?**

ON THIS DAY IN 1968, MAJOR LEAGUE BASEBALL POSTPONED THE OPENING-DAY GAMES BECAUSE OF MARTIN LUTHER KING JR.'S ASSASSINATION.

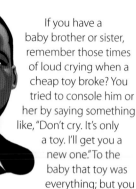

America is sports crazy. Every early April, three professional sports are in full swing: the NHL and NBA are nearing the playoffs, and MLB is celebrating opening days. And March Madness has just officially ended with the crowning of new national champions in both men's and women's college basketball. We have sports on TV, radio, Internet, and phones. And everyone talks about the "big game" last night or coming up!

So cancelling or postponing a prominent athletic contest because of another event is very rare. But it happens—and rightfully so. When Martin Luther King Jr. was murdered, the nation was stunned and grief-stricken. Suddenly the idea of playing a baseball game seemed trivial, even silly.

Events like that shock us back to reality, and we focus, even for just a short time, on what is much more important. Sometimes this happens with teams or individual players when a loved one is fighting to live. The affected athlete will reflect about priorities and real meaning in life. Or when disaster strikes a community or country and the coach or team owner will comment on putting things into perspective.

Winning isn't most important, and sports shouldn't be everything. We condition ourselves to get in shape so we can perform well. We play hard and fair, trying to win. But the games are not life-and-death struggles. Even when we lose a heartbreaker, a new day dawns, and life goes on.

If you have a baby brother or sister, remember those times of loud crying when a cheap toy broke? You tried to console him or her by saying something like, "Don't cry. It's only a toy. I'll get you a new one." To the baby that toy was everything; but you knew better.

God is giving us the same message when we get all caught up emotionally in sports and other trivial pursuits. Listen carefully, and you'll hear him saying, "Don't cry. It's only a game. So much more important are people and love and my Word and church . . . . I have something much better for you—trust me!"

ALSO ON THIS DAY . . .

1974—Henry Aaron replaced Babe Ruth as home run king with 715.

1982—Tracy Caulkins, nineteen, won her thirty-sixth US swimming title.

1991—Oakland A's stadium became the first outdoor arena to ban smoking.

2001—Tiger Woods won the Master's Golf Tournament, his second of four (so far).

BIRTHDAYS:

1912—Sonja Henie, Norwegian figure skater, winner of Olympic gold medals in 1928, 1932, and 1936

1940—John Havlicek, Martins Ferry, OH, NBA Hall-of-Fame forward for the Boston Celtics

1954—Gary Carter, Fullerton, CA, Hall-of-Fame catcher for the Montreal Expos and New York Mets

1970—Derek D. Brown, Washington, DC, team handball right wing in the 1996 Olympics

But seek first his kingdom and his righteousness, and all these things will be given to you as well. **Matthew 6:33**

Fun Fact
Martin Luther King Jr. skipped both the ninth and twelfth grades and started at Morehouse College at age fifteen without formally graduating from high school.

Beginning **Again**

On this day in 1985, White Sox pitcher Tom Seaver started a record fifteenth opening day baseball game.

Nothing is quite like opening day, especially on a sunny spring afternoon. Fans pack the park, team owners and past heroes stand to wild applause, vendors hawk hot dogs, peanuts, and other wares, a celebrity sings the National Anthem, a politician throws out the ceremonial first pitch, and the crowd cheers as the home team takes the field. It's a beautiful day for a ballgame, and most feel that this will be the year!

A new season. A fresh start. Last year forgotten, only good awaits. Just like the green shoots pushing through brown earth, buds on the branches, and the robin's chirp, the sights and sounds of opening day renew hope. We experience

similar feelings in other settings: the first day of school, the new (and latest) video game or bike, the new wardrobe . . . . Each brings excitement and the feeling that life is good.

At other times, we wish we could have a do-over and start again with the past wiped clean, forgotten. The time we blew up at a friend. The test we forgot about and failed. The terrible tryout. The secret sin that blocks us from God. Instead of hope, we feel discouraged as though we are mired in last place.

But have you heard the good news? You can begin again. God promises to make everything new for all those who turn back to him, admitting their mistakes and wrongs and leaning on his strength.

When that happens, does that guarantee popularity, the teacher throwing away the bad homework, Mom and Dad forgetting the mess-ups, and the coach realizing your full potential

and making you a star? Not really. But much more important than any of those, you will be right with God.

And that's better than winning the World Series.

> Throw off your old sinful nature and your former way of life, which is corrupted by lust and deception. Instead, let the Spirit renew your thoughts and attitudes. **Ephesians 4:22-23, NLT**

FUN FACT On August 4, 1985, Tom Seaver recorded his 300th win against the New York Yankees on "Phil Rizzuto" Day— Seaver eventually broadcast games with Phil Rizzuto.

Making a **Difference**

On this day in 1947, Jackie Robinson became the first African American to play in Major League Baseball, playing with the Brooklyn Dodgers.

A t UCLA Jackie won varsity letters in four sports: baseball, basketball, football, and track (the first at that school to do so). After college, he spent a couple of years in the army and then a year as a college athletic director. He was interested in playing professional baseball, but the only option for black players was the Negro leagues—so he signed on with the Kansas City Monarchs. Branch Rickey of the Dodgers wanted to sign a black player, and in the process he spoke to Jackie. In a three hour interview, Rickey asked if Jackie could face the racial names and comments without reacting in anger. Jackie was shocked and answered, "Are you looking for a Negro who is afraid to fight back?" Rickey said no—he needed a player "with guts enough not to fight back."

After a short stint in the minor leagues, Jackie was called up to the majors and made history in the process. Because he began his major-league career at twenty-eight, Jackie played only ten years, all of them with the Dodgers. During that time, he competed in six World Series and six All-Star games. Jackie had the rare combination of hitting ability and speed. He scored more than 100 runs in six seasons and had a career .311 batting average, a .409 career on-base percentage, a .474 slugging percentage, and way more walks than strikeouts. He also stole home nineteen times! And Jackie was an outstanding fielder at every position he played, spending most of his career as a second baseman. During his whole career, Jackie had to deal with open racism and hatred, including death threats. But he continued to play at the highest level as well as speak out on racial

issues. Instead of answering hate with hate, he let his play on the field do the talking.

Jackie Robinson made a tremendous difference with his life, breaking the color barrier in baseball. He was a great example of courage and grace.

God wants you to make a difference, too. You may not make history like Jackie, but you can break the barriers of cliques at your school. You can speak up for people who are being bullied. You can reach out to those who need help. You can show people what Jesus is like.

Make a difference.

ALSO ON THIS DAY . . .
1896—Spiridon Louis won the first Olympic marathon (2:58:50).

1916—The first professional golf tournament was held.

1979—J. R. Richard threw a major league record six wild pitches in one game for the Houston Astros in the Astrodome.

2005—Sébastien Bourdais began his Champ Car title defense the right way, beating Paul Tracy to win the Toyota Grand Prix of Long Beach.

BIRTHDAYS:

1936—John Madden, Austin, MN, NFL coach (Oakland Raiders) and sports commentator

1965—Karen Booker, Franklin, TN, WNBA center (Utah Starzz and Houston Comets)

1980—Kasey Kahne, Enumclaw, WA, American NASCAR driver

But Jesus spoke to them at once. "Don't be afraid," he said. "Take courage. I am here!" Matthew 14:27, NLT

Fun Fact In Jackie's first year of eligibility for the Hall of Fame (1962), he encouraged voters to consider what he did on the field, rather than the fact that he was the first black to play. He was elected on the first ballot, becoming the first African American inducted into Cooperstown.

A Masters for **the Master**

On this day in 1993 Bernhard Langer won the fifty-seventh Golf Masters Championship, shooting a 277.

A German professional golfer, Bernhard Langer won the prestigious Masters golf tournament twice, first in 1985. He was also the first official number-one-ranked player in 1986 and was one of the world's leading golfers

throughout the 1980s and '90s. In 1993, the final day of the Masters happened to be Easter Sunday. When Langer won, he talked about the thrill of winning this great tournament. But then he said that a greater

thrill was winning it on Easter Sunday, the celebration of the resurrection of his Lord and Savior Jesus Christ. Langer had come to faith in Christ after his last Masters win and was known as a devoted Christian. He displayed that conviction with his powerful testimony on a national stage.

Many other Christian athletes have done the same, sincerely sharing their faith after stirring victories and crushing defeats. Super Bowl MVPs have boldly stated, "I give all the glory to my Lord and Savior Jesus Christ." Track stars have thanked God for giving them the strength and endurance to compete. Many athletes display Christian symbols on their clothes or equipment. And often, if you look carefully, you'll see competitors kneeling together after a contest to pray.

These men and women understand that God has given them opportunities to share the gospel, to influence sports fans, young and old. And they do it sincerely and humbly—not preaching, just sharing in their own words.

Eventually you may have a similar platform. But you don't have to wait till you're famous to share your faith. Every day, God gives you occasions to let people know of his love and of your commitment to Christ. You can do this through your actions and, when you get the chance, through your words.

Be ready.

....

ALSO ON THIS DAY . . .

1917—Babe Ruth beat the New York Yankees, pitching a three-hit, 10-3 win for the Boston Red Sox.

1921—Radio station KDKA (Pittsburgh) broadcast the first sporting event, a boxing match (Ray vs. Dundee).

1987—Zoja Ivanova won the second female world cup marathon (2:30:39).

2004—Phil Mickelson won the Masters Golf Tournament, his first win in a Major; he won it again on this day in 2010.

BIRTHDAYS:

1972—Nicole Levesque, Kingston, RI, WNBA guard (Charlotte Sting)

1978—Josh Hancock, Cleveland, MS, Major League pitcher for Red Sox, Phillies, Reds, and Cardinals (died 2007)

1980—Mark Teixiera, Annapolis, MD, Major League first baseman (Rangers, Braves, Angels, Braves, Yankees)

But in your hearts set apart Christ as Lord. Always be prepared to give an answer to everyone who asks you to give the reason for the hope that you have. But do this with gentleness and respect. **1 Peter 3:15**

Fun Fact In 2006, in recognition of his contribution to the game of golf, Bernhard Langer was appointed as an honorary officer of the Most Excellent Order of the British Empire (OBE).

Positively **Courageous**

12 APRIL

ON THIS DAY IN 1980—TERRY FOX BEGAN HIS "MARATHON OF HOPE" AT ST. JOHNS, NEWFOUNDLAND.

Terrance "Terry" Fox was a Canadian athlete, a distance runner and basketball player in high school and college. But in 1977 he was diagnosed with cancer and had his right leg amputated. Despite the handicap, Terry continued to run, wearing an artificial leg, and he played wheelchair basketball, winning three national championships. The "Marathon of Hope" was his attempt to run across Canada to raise cancer awareness and research funds. His goal was to raise one dollar for each of Canada's twenty-four million people. Terry began his journey at St. John's, Newfoundland, and ran the distance of about a marathon a day (26.2 miles). By the time he got to Ontario, he had become nationally known. Unfortunately,

he had to end his run outside of Thunder Bay, after 143 days and 3,281 miles, because the cancer had spread to his lungs. He died nine months later.

Terry Fox knew that life was short, that he had little time left on this earth. So he determined to make the most of every day, to invest his life in a cause bigger than himself. At the end of Terry's letter to the Canadian Cancer Society he wrote: "The running I can do, even if I have to crawl every last mile. We need your help. The people in cancer clinics all over the world need people who believe in miracles. I am not a dreamer, and I am not saying that this will initiate any kind of definitive answer or cure to cancer. But I believe in miracles. I have to."

Terry's courage and positive message inspired the world. Today, millions of people in over sixty countries participate in the annual Terry Fox Run, now the

world's largest one-day fundraiser for cancer research, and over C$500 million has been raised.

Actually, life is short no matter how long we live. Any eighty-year-old will say the years passed in a moment. Unlike Terry, most people don't have a clue about when they will die, but they move through life acting as though it will never happen. Don't do that. Don't think about waiting until you're older to make a difference with your life. Do it now. Like Terry, make every day, every moment count.

....

ALSO ON THIS DAY . . .

1877—A catcher's mask was first used in a baseball game.

1941—The Boston Bruins swept the Detroit Red Wings in four games to win the Stanley Cup.

1959—Betsy Rawls won the LPGA Babe Didrikson Zaharias Golf Open.

1992—Matt Young of the Boston Red Sox no-hit Cleveland but lost the game 2-1.

2009—Angel Cabrera won the Masters Golf Tournament.

BIRTHDAYS:

1917—M. Marie Widlow, St. Louis, MO, Hall-of-Fame softball pitcher

1972—Paul Lo Duca, Brooklyn, NY, Major League catcher (Dodgers, Marlins, Mets, Nationals, and Rockies)

1985—Ted Ginn Jr., Cleveland, OH, NFL wide receiver and return specialist (Miami Dolphins, San Francisco 49ers)

Why, you do not even know what will happen tomorrow. What is your life? You are a mist that appears for a little while and then vanishes. Instead, you ought to say, "If it is the Lord's will, we will live and do this or that." James 4:14–15

FUN FACT Terry Fox was named Canada's Newsmaker of the Year in both 1980 and 1981.

Fun**Quiz** • April 13 & 14

FAMOUS for what SPORT

Match the player to the SPORT he/she is famous for:

1. **Sammy Sosa**
2. Steve Young
3. **Bonnie Blair**
4. Greg Louganis
5. **Al Unser**
6. Steffi Graf
7. **Earl Anthony**
8. Rocky Marciano
9. **Tony Hawk**
10. Larry Bird
11. **Oscar de la Hoya**
12. Travis Patrana
13. **Seth Wescott**

a. Skateboarding
b. Basketball
c. Bowling
d. Motocross
e. Diving
f. Boxing
g. Car racing
h. Football
i. Boxing
j. Tennis
k. Snowboarding
l. Baseball
m. Speed skating

ANSWERS: 1.l, 2.h, 3.m, 4.e, 5.g, 6.j, 7.c, 8.f, 9.a, 10.b, 11.i, 12.d, 13.k

Looking **Ahead**

On this day in 1931, the first walk across America backward began.

This event is noted in several lists of what happened on this day in history, but no details are given. So we don't know who made this backward walk or why. Perhaps the person was trying to get in shape or to just do something different. It wasn't a sport, but he or she must have been in good shape. Since then, many have walked or run long distances backward, even across the country.

Walking backward is like driving backwards; the walkers or drivers have a difficult time seeing where they are going, but they have a pretty good idea of where they've been.

Some people live that way, always looking back. Maybe you've heard them talking about the "good old days."

Besides the fact that those days probably weren't as good as they remember, the problem with spending so much time looking backwards is that those people can't see ahead. And they can more easily stumble and fall. Or they run into walls!

People focus on the past for many reasons: they may not like the present, what's happening to them right now; they may fear the future; they may want to hold onto a person, place, or memory. Whatever the reason, it's not a good idea.

Remember the ancient Israelites in Egypt? They lived as slaves and had to work in terrible conditions under cruel masters. Then God, through Moses, led them out and away from their captivity. But when the going got tough in the wilderness, many of the former slaves began talking about the "good old days" in Egypt. Check out Numbers 11:4–6. What were they thinking?

Yes, we need to remember what God has done for us in the past and the lessons we learned. But God wants us to live in the present, while keeping an eye on the future. In fact, if we have a good idea of where we are going, we usually will do better right where we are.

Imagine your life five, ten, or fifteen years from now. What do you see yourself doing in your career? In your community? In the church? How should you be living now to get where God wants you to go?

....

ALSO ON THIS DAY . . .

1910—President Taft became the first president to throw out a first ball at a Major League Baseball game.

1989—Ninety-five people were crushed to death at Sheffield Soccer stadium in England.

1996—Moses Tanui of Kenya won the 100th Boston Marathon in 2:09:15.9.

1997—Major League Baseball honored Jackie Robinson by retiring his number (forty-two) for all teams.

BIRTHDAYS:

1875—James J. Jeffries, Carroll, OH, American heavyweight boxing champion

1967—Dara Torres, Jupiter, FL, American swimmer in five Olympics (1984, 1988, 1992, 2000, 2008) and winner of 12 Olympic medals—4 gold, 4 silver, and 4 bronze

1985—John Danks, Austin, TX, Major League Baseball pitcher (Chicago White Sox)

> Brothers, I do not consider myself yet to have taken hold of it. But one thing I do: Forgetting what is behind and straining toward what is ahead. **Philippians 3:13**

Fun Fact
Backward running, backward walking, and retropedaling are becoming more popular in all parts of the world. Many years ago great names in sports, such as William Muldoon, Gene Tunney, Bill Robinson, Ed Schultz, and others, used backward running in their training regimes.

How's That for an **Opening!**

ON THIS DAY IN 1940, CLEVELAND INDIAN'S PITCHER BOB FELLER HURLED AN OPENING-DAY NO-HITTER AGAINST THE CHICAGO WHITE SOX, WINNING 1-0.

Bob Feller spent his entire eighteen-year career with the Cleveland Indians. He earned the nickname "Rapid Robert" because of his fastball, which many say reached speeds of more than 100 mph. He won more games than any pitcher in Cleveland Indians history, and during his great career, he pitched three no-hitters, led the league in wins six times and in strikeouts seven times, and was an eight-time all-star. In 1962 he was inducted into the baseball Hall of Fame in his first year of eligibility.

In baseball, the pitcher gets credit for the "wins" and "losses," even though the whole team either won or lost the game. Suppose a pitcher had a brilliant game but "lost" 1-0, does that seem fair? Actually, that's what happened in this opening day in 1940—nobody remembers the losing pitcher, who must have pitched a great game himself. On the other hand, a pitcher could have a horrible

game, struggling through five innings, and still end up with the win.

Baseball is a team sport, and everyone on the team contributes to the win or loss. In fact, Feller's no-hitter was saved with a diving-play by the Cleveland second baseman, Ray Mack, on the final out.

Wise players are quick to credit their teammates and coaches, realizing that they couldn't be successful on their own. A quarterback wouldn't be able to even throw a pass, much less complete a bunch, without a decent offensive line (or a defense that gets him the ball). Champion cyclists draft behind team members. All athletes need competent coaches and trainers. The "star" athlete who begins to believe his or her press clippings usually begins to slip or is

traded away.

Christianity is like a team sport. Sure, some stand in the spotlight and get lots of attention, but God designed the church as a group of gifted believers who join and use their gifts together for his glory. Successful churches (youth groups, too) function that way, loving each other and worshipping, learning, and serving—together.

Opening day is over and you're into the season. How's your team doing?

....

ALSO ON THIS DAY . . .

1929—The New York Yankees became the first team to wear uniform numbers.

1940—WGN-TV televised the first baseball game, the Chicago White Sox vs. the Chicago Cubs in an exhibition game.

1972—Jane Blalock won the first Colgate Dinah Shore Golf Championship.

1980—Arthur Ashe retired from professional tennis.

NO HITTER

> The body is a unit, though it is made up of many parts; and though all its parts are many, they form one body. So it is with Christ. **1 Corinthians 12:12**

Fun Fact
In June 2009, at the age of ninety, Feller was one of the starting pitchers at the first Baseball Hall of Fame Classic at Cooperstown, New York.

BIRTHDAYS:

1928—Dick "Night Train" Lane, Austin, TX, NFL defensive back (Los Angeles Rams, Chicago Cardinals, Detroit Lions)

1947—Kareem Abdul-Jabbar, New York, NY, Hall-of-Fame NBA center (Milwaukee Bucks, Los Angeles Lakers)

1993—Mirai Nagasu, Montebello, CA, American figure skater (2008 National Champion, 2010 silver medalist)

A Great **Teammate**

On this day in 1951, Mickey Mantle made his Major League Baseball debut with the New York Yankees.

Mickey Mantle was one of the greatest players to ever play baseball. During his eighteen-year Major League career, all with the New York Yankees, he won three American League MVP titles and the A.L. Triple Crown (1956), and he played in sixteen All-Star games and on twelve pennant-winning teams and seven World Series Championship teams. He was a switch-hitter with power from both sides of the plate, the quickest batter running to first, and an outstanding center-fielder. Mantle still holds the records for most World Series home runs (18), RBIs (40), runs (42), walks (43), extra-base hits (26), and total bases (123). He retired on March 1, 1969, and in 1974, as soon as he was eligible, Mickey was inducted into the Baseball Hall of Fame.

The Yankees retired his uniform, number seven.

While Mickey played hard and had great accomplishments on the field, off the field he partied hard and wasn't so great. He drank a lot and later struggled with alcoholism, which eventually cost him his life. Mantle admitted his hard living had hurt both his playing and his family.

Unfortunately, many rich and famous athletes have followed the same path. The good news, in Mickey's case, is that one day he listened to the testimony of his former teammate, Bobby Richardson, and gave his life to Christ. He spent his remaining time trying to help others.

Everyone needs Christ—poor, rich, young, old, famous, nobodies, men, women, all races, all nationalities. Sometime we can forget that fact, or we might assume that a person is beyond hope, too much of a partier or

too self-centered to ever come to Christ. But Mickey Mantle listened to the gospel message and was born again. At that point in his life, he may have been looking for answers, realizing that all his accomplishments, fame, and fortune didn't fulfill his deepest need. And Bobby was there to tell him the truth and lead him to the Savior.

Pray for those you want to find faith: friends, family members, teachers, your favorite sports heroes. Ask God to bring someone into their path to share the good news. Maybe that will be you.

ALSO ON THIS DAY . . .

1920—The American Professional Football Association was formed (became the NFL).

1976—In one of Major League Baseball's greatest comeback games, trailing 12-1, the Phillies beat the Cubs 18-16 in ten innings; Mike Schmidt hit four consecutive home runs.

1983—Nolan Ryan struck out his 3,500th batter.

2006—Robert "Mwafrika" Kipkoech Cheruiyot of Kenya won the Boston Marathon in 2:07:14, a race record time (he also won in 2003, '07, and '08).

BIRTHDAYS:

1961—Norman "Boomer" Esiason, West Islip, NY, NFL quarterback (Cincinnati Bengals, New York Jets) and broadcaster

1966—Susie Redman, Salem, OH,

So we tell others about Christ, warning everyone and teaching everyone with all the wisdom God has given us. We want to present them to God, perfect in their relationship to Christ. That's why I work and struggle so hard, depending on Christ's mighty power that works within me. **Colossians 1:28–29, NLT**

18 Idle **Idol**

On this day in 2005, Lance Armstrong, six-time winner of the Tour de France, announced that he would retire from competition after that summer's Tour.

Probably the greatest competitive cyclist in history, Lance won the Tour de France a record-breaking seven consecutive years, from 1999 to 2004 and then in 2005, after making this announcement. The previous record was five wins. Even more amazing is the fact that he is also a cancer survivor. He had done it all and deserved to retire at the top. But then, after a few years away from the sport, Lance unretired and returned to competitive cycling in January 2009, finishing third in that year's Tour.

Lance was not the only great athlete to retire and then change his mind and begin competing again. Michael Jordan came back twice from retirement before finally giving up professional basketball for good. Ricky Henderson continued to come back, well into his forties. At forty-one, swimmer Dara Torres returned to win Olympic silver medals in Beijing. Unretired

Evander Holyfield continues to look for one last boxing title before finally calling it quits. And not even Brett Favre knows when he will leave football (he also has "retired" twice).

Why do many athletes find leaving their sport so difficult? Some may need the money. Others may miss the fun and camaraderie. A number of factors could be involved. But for some the sport and competition itself so dominated their lives that they experienced an emptiness, a hole in life, and they had to fill it. So they returned . . . with mixed results.

The Bible has much to say about idolatry. An idol is anything we put in God's place; so it could be a person, money, being popular, a job, appearance, or even a sport—something that consumes our attention and devotion. That may not be the case with these great athletes, but sometimes it looks like it. And the fact that walking away is such a

struggle should be a warning that something similar could happen to us.

So here's the big question: If God told you to give up _____ (whatever you love the most here on earth) would you? Could you? Many of those "idols" aren't bad in themselves, but nothing should take God's place as number one in our lives.

ALSO ON THIS DAY . . .

1966—Bill Russell became the first black coach in the NBA (Boston Celtics).

1984—Joan Benoit ran a world-record female marathon (2:22:43).

1995—Joe Montana announced his retirement from professional football.

2007—Mark Buehrle threw a no-hitter as the Chicago White Sox defeated the Texas Rangers, 6-0.

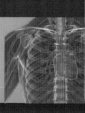

BIRTHDAYS:

1966—Michelle Chryst, WPVA volleyball player, (Santa Cruz)

1973—Derrick Brooks, Pensacola, FL, NFL linebacker (Tampa Bay Buccaneers)

1986—Maurice "Mo" Edu, Fontana, CA, American soccer player

"You shall have no other gods before me." Exodus 20:3

Fun Fact Lance Armstrong has a recorded aerobic capacity of 83.8 mL/kg/mi (VO2max), which is much higher than the average person (40-50), and has a resting heartbeat of 32-34 beats per minute.

Keep **Hustlin'**

ON THIS DAY IN 1994, MONTREAL EXPOS RIGHT FIELDER LARRY WALKER THREW OUT SAN FRANCISCO GIANTS PITCHER JOHN BURKETT AT FIRST BASE ON A GROUND BALL INTO RIGHT FIELD.

In baseball, when a ball is hit past the infield and isn't caught in the air by a fielder, it should be a base hit, especially if it's a ground ball hit to an outfielder. Yet in this instance, Larry Walker was able to field the ball and throw it to first base in time to beat the hitter. A 9-3 putout is extremely rare, especially in the major leagues. Certainly Larry Walker was quick to the ball, but still Burkett should have had a single. Instead, he was thrown out because he didn't run fast—he wasn't hustling down the line.

Pitchers aren't paid to hit, except perhaps to lay down a sacrifice bunt. In the American League they are usually replaced in the batting lineup with the "designated hitter." So most pitchers don't take hitting very seriously

or spend much time in batting practice. But John's at bat could have been the turning point in the game.

Great athletes understand the importance of hustling, of giving their all on every play. This means speeding down the court or field (even without the ball), getting back on defense, diving for fumbles, and running out every ground ball. Players who relax on a play or two every now and then or give up on a ball (or a race) usually aren't successful.

This lesson carries over to other areas in life. Successful students don't coast through a class but do their assignments on time. Successful workers don't just get by but do their jobs well (even household chores). Successful relationships come from not taking other people for granted.

In our spiritual lives, this means giving our all for Christ, trying to do what's right in

every situation, even when no one seems to be watching. This means honoring him in how we speak (no matter what anyone else is saying), reaching out to someone who is hurting (even if we're busy), and telling others about Jesus (even if we feel uncomfortable). God expects nothing less, and we never know when our actions will be the turning point in someone's life.

Keep hustlin'!

ALSO ON THIS DAY . . .

1897—The first Boston Marathon was won by John McDermott of New York in 2:55:10.

1966—Roberta Bignay became the first woman to run the Boston Marathon.

1991—Evander Holyfield beat George Foreman in twelve rounds to win the heavyweight boxing title.

2004—Ernst Van Dyk of South Africa set a new world record in the wheelchair division of the Boston Marathon (1:18:27).

BIRTHDAYS:

1981—Troy Polamalu, Garden Grove, CA, NFL strong safety (Pittsburgh Steelers)

1986—Candice Parker, St. Louis, MO, WNBA forward (Los Angeles Sparks), the first high school girl to dunk in a game, and the first woman to dunk in an NCAA tournament game

1987—Maria Sharapova, Russian tennis player

If you have raced with men on foot and they have worn you out, **how can you compete with horses? If you stumble in safe country, how will you manage in the thickets by the Jordan?** Jeremiah 12:5

FUN FACT The Montreal Expos were moved to Washington at the end of the 2004 season and renamed the Washington Nationals.

FunQuiz • April 20 & 21

Baseball Nicknames

Match the baseball player to his nickname

1. **Hank Aaron**
2. Babe Ruth
3. **Francisco Rodriguez**
4. Frank Thomas
5. **Pete Rose**
6. Dontrelle Willis
7. **Derek Jeter**
8. Alex Rodriguez
9. **Andre Dawson**
10. Ernie Banks
11. **David Ortiz**
12. Greg Maddux
13. **Ivan Rodriguez**
14. Jimmy Rollins
15. **Joe Jackson**
16. Mark McGwire
17. **Carlton Fisk**
18. Covelli Crisp
19. **Nolan Ryan**
20. Ken Griffey Jr.
21. **Ted Williams**
22. Orel Hershiser
23. **Willie Mays**
24. Reggie Jackson
25. **Randy Johnson**
26. Adam Dunn
27. **Sammy Sosa**

a. **Charlie Hustle**
b. Big Papi
c. **Mr. November**
d. J-Roll
e. **Mr. Cub**
f. Junior
g. **Shoeless**
h. Donkey
i. **The Say Hey Kid**
j. D-Train
k. **The Splendid Splinter**
l. The Ryan Express
m. **K-Rod**
n. Mr. October
o. **The Big Unit**
p. Hammerin' Hank
q. **Bulldog**
r. The Big Hurt
s. **Slammin'**
t. The Great Bambino
u. **Pudge**
v. Mad Dog
w. **Big Mac**
x. A-Rod
y. **Coco**
z. Pudge
aa. **The Hawk**

ANSWERS: 1.p, 2.t, 3.m, 4.r, 5.a, 6.j, 7.c, 8.x, 9.aa, 10.e, 11.b, 12.v, 13.u, 14.d, 15.g, 16.w, 17.z, 18.y, 19.l, 20.f, 21.k, 22.q, 23.i, 24.n, 25.o, 26.h, 27.s

Pit Crew

On this day in 2006, Kevin Harvick completed a weekend sweep of the spring NASCAR races at Phoenix International Raceway by winning the NEXTEL Cup Subway Fresh 500 after taking the Busch Series Bashas' Supermarkets 200 the night before.

Kevin Harvick had quite a NASCAR weekend, driving hundreds of miles in two races in two days and winning both of them. Although Kevin drove alone—no one else was in the cars—he didn't win the races by himself. He had a huge support team behind him. One group had to put the cars together and make sure they were mechanically sound. Others managed pre- and post-race details. During the races, Kevin's crew chief acted like a sideline coach, monitoring the car, the conditions, and the other cars and giving instruction.

During a race, the driver needs fuel, new tires, and other car adjustments. And on pit road, pit crews wait to spring into action. These people have to be good athletes because of the quick and precise work they have to do within tight regulations. And they have to work quickly; it's a race. Good pit crews can handle most pit stops in about forty seconds or less. NASCAR pit crews include a jackman, two tire changers, a gas man, catch can man, two tire carriers, and a utility man—all working together.

How many pit crews do you have? How many are you on? Everyone needs at least one. Think of your family. You walk out of the house, ready for school. But someone kept the house together; someone got your clothes; someone made breakfast . . . you get the picture. And you were part of the team that helped others get prepared for the day, especially if you did your chores the night before.

Successful individuals and teams always have a large supporting cast that's almost invisible. It's true in sports, school, home, church, and communities. This means we need each other, and we need to work together. It also means that your contribution is needed. Everyone wins this way. And remember that God is the ultimate crew chief—he's in charge, making sure that everything runs smoothly.

....

ALSO ON THIS DAY . . .

1876—The Boston Braves beat the Philadelphia Athletics 6-5 in the first National League baseball game.

1947—The Philadelphia Warriors beat the Chicago Stags four games to two in the first NBA championship series.

1988—Women were allowed to compete in the Little 500 bicycle race (Indiana).

2008—Kevin Garnett of the Boston Celtics was named the NBA Defensive Player of the Year.

BIRTHDAYS:

1961—Jeff Hostetler, Hollsopple, PA, NFL quarterback (New York Giants, Los Angeles/Oakland Raiders, Washington Redskins)

1967—Bart Bowen, Albuquerque, NM, cyclist in the 1996 Olympics

1980—Monica Flammer, Gainesville, FL, alternate gymnast for the 1996 Olympics

The Lord has assigned to each his task. I planted the seed, Apollos watered it, but God made it grow. So neither he who plants nor he who waters is anything, but only God, who makes things grow. The man who plants and the man who waters have one purpose, and each will be rewarded according to his own labor. For we are God's fellow workers. **1 Corinthians 3:5–9**

Fun Fact

During the final round of pit stops in the 1981 Daytona 500, Richard Petty's crew called off a planned tire change and only added fuel. The lightning-fast stop put Petty back in the lead, and he held off a shocked Bobby Allison to win the race for a record seventh time.

A Winner!

On this day in 1916, Hall-of-Fame football coach Charles Burnham "Bud" Wilkinson was born in Minneapolis, Minnesota.

Bud Wilkinson played football and hockey at the University of Minnesota, earned his master's degree at Syracuse University, and served in the US Navy during World War II. During his lifetime, he headed up President Kennedy's national physical fitness campaign, was a White House advisor during the Nixon administration, ran for the US Senate, coached the NFL's St. Louis Cardinals, and served as a sports analyst and broadcaster for ABC and ESPN. But Bud is most well known for his accomplishments in college football.

In 1947, Bud was only thirty-one when he became the head football coach at the University of Oklahoma, and during the next seventeen years, he created a football dynasty. His Sooners teams earned a 145-29-4 record, including five undefeated seasons, three national championships ('50, '55, and '56). From 1948 through 1950, his teams won thirty-one straight. Then from 1953 through 1957, they won a national-record forty-seven consecutive games. His teams also won fourteen conference championships and seven of nine bowl games.

Now that's a winner!

When asked the secret of his success, Bud answered that his players knew that they only had to please one person: him. He went on to explain that sometimes players play for themselves, to get glory. Others worry about their teammates. Some play to the opposition and get distracted by poor or dirty play. And, of course, some play to the fans, perhaps a favorite one or two. On his teams, however, players know that what the fans see or what the other players do is not important. All that matters is what he, the head coach, sees, how he evaluates their individual performances.

The Christian life is the same. We can become focused on personal stats or get distracted by other believers or the opposition from nonbelievers. Or we can worry about how certain people might think we're doing. But the only One who matters is God. That's who we're living for. We have an audience of One.

Learn that lesson, live that way, and you'll be a winner.

....

ALSO ON THIS DAY . . .

1954—Hammerin' Hank Aaron hit the first of his 755 home runs.

1989—Kareem Abdul-Jabbar played in his final game as a Los Angeles Laker.

1991—Bjorn Borg lost in tennis 6-2, 6-3 to Jordi Arrese after an eight-year layoff.

2005—In soccer, the LA Galaxy and Chivas USA played the first-ever Honda SuperClasico. The Galaxy scored three goals in the first half on the way to a 3-1 win. The Galaxy and Chivas USA were in the same city and shared the Home Depot Center.

BIRTHDAYS:

1921—Warren Spahn, Buffalo, NY, Hall-of-Fame left-handed pitcher for the Boston/Milwaukee Braves

1943—Tony Esposito, Sault Ste. Marie, Ontario, NHL goalie (Chicago Blackhawks)

1965—Donna Weinbrecht, West Milford, NJ—won the first gold medal awarded in the first Olympic mogul competitions in freestyle skiing in 1992

No one serving as a soldier gets involved in civilian affairs—he wants to please his commanding officer. Similarly, if anyone competes as an athlete, he does not receive the victor's crown unless he competes according to the rules. **2 Timothy 2:4–5**

FUN FACT

Wilkinson's offensive style was ball control, using the split T. His defensive style was pure dominance. During Bud's time at Oklahoma, his defense allowed an average of 10.15 points per game. And his offense averaged 28.65 points per game. In 1969, Bud Wilkinson was inducted into the College Football Hall of Fame.

Rivalries

ON THIS DAY IN 2009, THE BOSTON RED SOX BEAT THE NEW YORK YANKEES 5-4 IN ELEVEN INNINGS.

What's the big deal? That's just one game of more than 160 at the beginning of a new baseball season. Good point. But it was the Red Sox against the Yankees, one of baseball's biggest rivalries.

The game was good, too. Both teams had many chances to score (the hits ended up fourteen to thirteen), but they entered the ninth inning with the Yankees on top four to two. But with two out in the bottom of the ninth, Jason Bay sent the ball rocketing over the Green Monster for a two-run homer to tie the score (off baseball's best reliever, Mariano Rivera). Then, in the bottom of the eleventh, Kevin Youkilis sent everyone home with his towering home run that cleared the park. Evidently that was the first time the Red Sox had a game-tying home run against the Yankees in the ninth and then a walk-off home run in extra innings.

Now back to the rivalry issue. Most teams have an archrival, the team they love to beat. In high school, that's usually the school across town. In college, it's usually a team in the conference. In the pros, in addition to those factors, the teams probably also have a long history of competing against each other. That's why the Yankees–Red Sox rivalry may be the fiercest one in American professional sports, having been faught for over 100 years.

These games bring out the fans—cheering like crazy for their team. But they also bring out the worst in fans who, in addition to booing the opposing players, mock them, swear at them, and, sometimes, even try to hurt them. Fans can often be heard saying how much they hate the rival team. Yes, rivalries can get way out of control.

That's quite a contrast to how Jesus told us to act. As his followers, we're supposed to be known for our love—for fellow believers, family members, neighbors, and even those who treat us poorly, our "enemies."

So in that big game, cheer for your team . . . but don't get carried away. They're athletes, not evil people. And, after all, it's just a game.

ALSO ON THIS DAY . . .

1981—Bill Shoemaker won his 8,000th race, 2000 more than any other jockey.

1994—The New York Rangers swept the New York Islanders in the NHL playoffs.

1996—The Minnesota Twins beat the Detroit Tigers twenty-four to eleven in the highest-scoring Major League Baseball game in seventeen years.

2009—Dikembe Mutombo (Houston Rockets) received the Walter Kennedy Citizenship Award, the first player ever to win the award twice.

BIRTHDAYS:

1966—Pascale Paradis-Mangon, French tennis star

1972—Chipper Jones, DeLand, FL, Major League infielder for the Atlanta Braves

1977—Carlos Beltran, Puerto Rican Major League Baseball outfielder (Kansas City Royals, Houston Astros, New York Mets)

Therefore, as we have opportunity, let us do good to all people, especially to those who belong to the family of believers. **Galatians 6:10**

Fun Fact In September, 1990 when the Red Sox visited Yankee Stadium, the fans chanted "1918!" to remind the Red Sox of their most recent World Series championship. That became a common Yankee fan cheer. In 2004, the Red Sox finally won their first World Series championship in 86 years, beating the Yankees and then sweeping the Cardinals in the Series.

25 Spotlight

On this day in 2009, with the first pick in the NFL draft, the Detroit Lions selected University of Georgia quarterback Matthew Stafford.

The NFL draft is a big deal. New York's Radio City Music Hall was packed with potential top draft picks and their close relatives, NFL executives, the press, and fans. Just after 4:00 PM, the Detroit Lions, who had "earned" the first pick because they had ended the previous season with the league's worst record (the first NFL team ever to finish a season at 0–16), announced their selection. Then Matthew Stafford strode to centerstage, wearing a new Lions cap, and joined the commissioner. The full spotlight of the auditorium and the nation's media was on him. And he will continue to be in the glare of the spotlight for the rest of his career, with high hopes for him as the number-one pick.

Some wear that spotlight well, performing up to expectations. Some, however, do poorly and have short professional football careers. A spotlight focuses attention—all eyes are on the person in the light—and brings performance pressure. Many seek the spotlight; others can't avoid it.

The Bible uses *light* often to talk about God's truth and believers' lives. We shouldn't seek the spotlight, but we should "walk in the light" (1 John 1:7); that is, we should live God's way. Also, our lives are to shine out as lights (Matthew 5:14–16) in a dark world, helping people find God. And Jesus said that he was "the light of the world"; thus, those who follow him will not stumble around in the dark (John 8:12).

Remember this guy? "God sent a man, John the Baptist, to tell about the light so that everyone might believe because of his testimony. John himself was not the light; he was simply a witness to tell about the light. The one who is the true light, who gives light to everyone, was coming into the world" (John 1:6–9, NLT). John the Baptist was pointing people to the Light, in some ways like a "spotlight" himself.

That's what we're supposed to be, too—shining out and putting the focus on Christ. When you're in the spotlight, do people see the Savior? And like John, do you point people to him?

ALSO ON THIS DAY . . .

1901—Erve Beck hit the American League's first home run.

1974—The NFL moved the goal posts and adopted the sudden-death playoff.

1989—Mario Lemieux (Pittsburgh Penguins) tied the NHL playoff record of four goals in the first period.

2005—Jeff Gordon won the "Aaron's 499" NASCAR race at Talladega.

For you were once darkness, but now you are light in the Lord. Live as children of light.
Ephesians 5:8

Fun Fact
Six (five quarterbacks) out of all the number-one draft picks chosen between 1999 and 2009 have never been selected to the Pro Bowl.

BIRTHDAYS:

1969—Marisa Pedulla, Bellefonte, PA, half-lightweight judoka (Olympics, 1996)

1969—Joe Buck, St. Petersburg, FL, American sportscaster

1976—Tim Duncan, Christiansted, US Virgin Islands, all-star NBA forward (San Antonio Spurs)

A Good **Sport**

On this day in 1935, Frank Boucher was given the National Hockey League's Lady Byng trophy for sportsmanship permanently.

Frank Boucher was a brilliant hockey forward. His career spanned from 1921 through 1944 as he played for the Ottawa Senators, Vancouver Maroons, and New York Rangers. Frank has been listed as one of the 100 all-time greatest hockey players, and he was inducted into the Hockey Hall of Fame in 1958. In addition to Boucher's hockey skills, he was also one of the game's classiest.

Lady Byng, wife of Viscount Byng, the governor-general of Canada, donated a trophy to be awarded to the NHL's "most gentlemanly player." We may think that kind of athlete would be hard to find in such a physical sport, with fighting almost a part of the game. But as a New York Ranger, Frank won the Lady Byng Memorial Trophy seven times in eight years. For winning it so many years, he was given the trophy to keep, and Lady Byng donated another one to the league.

Imagine the discipline it must have taken Frank to not retaliate after being slammed into the boards, to not take cheap shots on a vulnerable opponent, to not verbally assault the opposition and refs, and to not fight when provoked. That's "class" and "sportsmanship"—and it's what makes a good player great.

Playing with that kind of emotional discipline doesn't make the athlete less of a competitor. In fact, Boucher scored over forty goals in eleven seasons (forty-eight four times). It definitely reveals the athlete's character.

Christians should be known for competing with class. They shouldn't be among those who throw rackets, yell at officials, mock fans and reporters, showboat after making a score, disrespect opponents, and play dirty, even in the more violent sports. Those antics may gain some headlines and perhaps even a larger contract. But the payoff will come at a price.

As you compete, think of what your attitude and actions say about you and how they reflect on Christ.

....

ALSO ON THIS DAY . . .

1931—Lou Gehrig hit a home run but was called out for passing a runner, and that mistake costs him the American League home-run crown; he and Babe Ruth tied.

1966—Arnold "Red" Auerbach retired as the Boston Celtics' head coach.

1995—The Major League Baseball season began after a lengthy strike.

2009—Scott Dixon won the IndyCar Series: Road Runner Turbo Indy 300 race in Kansas City, Kansas.

BIRTHDAYS:

Do not repay anyone evil for evil. Be careful to do what is right in the eyes of everybody. **Romans 12:17**

FUN FACT Frank Boucher was also a Royal Canadian Mounted Policeman, a "Mountie."

FunQuiz • April 27 & 28

Featured Events

1.   How many times has Lance Armstrong won the Tour de France? (April 18)
2.   What sport did Bud Wilkinson coach? (April 23)
3.   Who set an NBA record of forty-one rebounds in one game? (April 5)
4.   What years did Bernhard Langer win the Golf Masters Championship? (April 11)
5.   What year did the NHL last go on strike? (April 1)
6.   For what Major League Baseball team did David Cone pitch in 1990? (April 30)
7.   How did Terry Fox lose his leg? (April 12)
8.   Which team had the first pick in the 2009 NFL draft? (April 25)
9.   Who upset Michigan State University in the 2010 NCAA basketball semifinals? (April 3)
10. Who was the first African American baseball player in Major League Baseball? (April 10)
11. Why is someone awarded the Lady Byng trophy? (April 26)
12. What is "retropedaling"? (April 15)
13. To where did the Montreal Expos move in 2004? (April 19)
14. Babe Ruth and Lou Gehrig were struck out by what female athlete? (April 2)
15. How did Martin Luther King Jr.'s assassination affect baseball? (April 8)
16. Against what team did Cleveland Indian pitcher Bob Feller pitch an opening day no-hitter? (April 16)
17. What famous American race car driver died in a last-lap crash during the 2001 Daytona 500? (April 29)
18. Mickey Mantle started his baseball career with what Major League Baseball team? (April 17)
19. What is Tommy John surgery? (April 4)
20. How many opening games has pitcher Tom Seaver started? (April 9)
21. Before winning the 2004 World Series, how long had the Boston Red Sox gone without a championship? (April 24)
22. Who did Richard Petty beat in the 1981 Daytona 500? (April 22)

Find the correct answers on the dates in parentheses.

The Intimidator

On this day in 1951, Dale Earnhardt, American race car driver, was born in Kannapolis, North Carolina.

One of the most successful drivers in NASCAR history, "The Intimidator" won seventy-six races in his career and seven championships (tied for most all-time with Richard Petty). Because of his aggressive driving style, Earnhardt was a controversial figure, so he was also called "The Man in Black" and "Ironhead" (sounds a bit like Earnhardt). Tragically, Dale died in a last-lap crash during the Daytona 500 in 2001. Just after his death, he was named NASCAR's most popular driver in 2001, the only time he received the award, and he has been inducted into the Hall of Fame of America (2002) and the International Motorsports Hall of Fame (2006).

Although many people disliked him, Earnhardt was one of the sport's most popular drivers. So his death drew a considerable amount of reaction from NASCAR and his fans across the nation. And in the years since his death, he has retained almost a cult following. Look closely and you'll see his name or "The Intimidator" or number three (his number) on lots of cars in his honor.

The way fans have idolized Dale Earnhardt is similar to what happens with other athletes, movie stars, and popular musicians. Not only do people look up to them, appreciating their work, but many also copy how they dress and act. The way people dress, talk, and play a sport have all been influenced. People want to "be like Mike" (as in Jordan) or Dale.

But check out this note from Paul: "Be imitators of God, therefore, as dearly loved children" (Ephesians 5:1). A child who has a great relationship with his or her father and mother will usually grow up imitating those parents. The first words that babies say, for example, are the words they hear Mommy and Daddy say around the house, like "uh oh" and "no." And they may try walking around in their parents' shoes or put on their clothes. Paul is saying that in the same way, we should imitate our heavenly Father, trying to be like him in everything we do.

Having favorite athletes and actors is fine. Just don't copy them. Instead, be an "imitator of God." Hint: you can find out what he's like by reading his Word.

....

ALSO ON THIS DAY . . .

1936—Nagoya defeated Daitokyo, 8-5, in the first professional base-ball game played in Japan.

1962—Mickey Wright won the LPGA Titleholders Golf Championship.

1987—Andre Dawson of the Chicago Cubs hit for the cycle.

2007—Troy Tulowitzki of the Colorado Rockies executed an unassisted triple play in the eleven-inning 9-7 Rockies victory over the Atlanta Braves.

BIRTHDAYS:

1970—Andre Agassi, Las Vegas, NV, former number one tennis professional and winner of sixty-eight titles

1983—Jay Cutler, Santa Claus, IN, NFL quarterback (Denver Broncos, Chicago Bears)

1988—Jonathan Toews, Winnipeg, Manitoba, Canada, NHL forward, captain of the Chicago Blackhawks, Olympic gold medal winner (team Canada, 2010), Stanley Cup Champion and Conn Smythe Trophy

Dear friend, do not imitate what is evil but what is good. Anyone who does what is good is from God. Anyone who does what is evil has not seen God. **3 John 11**

FUN FACTS Movies such as *The Dale Earnhardt Story* (2004) and *Dale* (2007), tell of his life. *The Intimidator 305* is a roller coaster at Kings Dominion in Doswell, Virginia. And *Earnhardt Tower* is a seating section at Daytona International Speedway.

APRIL 30 Snapped

On this day in 1990, as New York Mets pitcher David Cone was arguing a call at first base, two Braves baserunners came around to score.

With two outs and two on, the second baseman fielded a slowly hit ground ball and tossed it to the pitcher, Cone, who was rushing toward first. Cone tried to brush the bag with his foot as he glided by, but the umpire called the runner safe. Cone was livid. Totally ignoring the base runners, he started yelling at the umpire near foul territory. While he argued and his teammates screamed at him, two runners continued around the bases and scored. The official scorer ruled the runs crossed the plate on "player indifference." When asked about the play, Cone replied, "I'm a human being, and I'm an emotional person. I snapped emotionally and I have to live with it. . . . For two minutes, I snapped. I was in my own little world."

That crazy play cost the Mets the game. Cone was a fierce competitor who didn't like to lose. In this case, his competitive nature and his emotions got the best of him. He was out of control and, as he said, in his "own little world."

Emotions are funny. Sometimes they can flare up and make us almost like a different person. We might feel sad, for example, and then suddenly start crying like a baby. At times we might be so excited and happy that we can't stop laughing and talking. In both situations, we may feel a bit embarrassed—but that's about it.

Anger is different and can be like a raging fire. People who are overcome by this feeling can do serious damage emotionally and physically to others and themselves. Out-of-control anger has destroyed friendships and families . . . and futures.

At times, anger is okay—when we get upset at our sin or see someone being wronged—and we channel that emotion into action. That's what Jesus did when he cleared out the merchants from the temple (Matthew 21:12–13). But not the destructive, out-of-control kind.

So when you feel frustrated by a competitor's play or an official's call, keep your cool. (Ask God to help; he will.) Don't go to that "little world." It could cost you more than a game.

ALSO ON THIS DAY . . .

1916—The Chicago Cubs, playing their first game at Weeghman Park (Wrigley Field), beat the Reds.

1967—Stu Miller and Steve Barber of the Baltimore Orioles lost 2-1 despite no-hitting the Detroit Tigers.

1989—The United States beat Costa Rica 1-0 in the third round of the 1990 World Soccer Cup (qualifying).

2008—The Dallas Mavericks fired head coach Avery Johnson, despite his 194-70 regular-season record over three full years, because the team lost in the first round of the playoffs the previous two years.

And "don't sin by letting anger control you." Don't let the sun go down while you are still angry, for anger gives a foothold to the devil. **Ephesians 4:26–27, NLT**

Fun Fact Interviewed after the game, Davey Johnson, the Mets' manager, said, "I've seen some strange things in my lifetime, but that's at the top of the list."

BIRTHDAYS:

1965—Daniela Costian, Australian discus/shot-putter (1996 Olympics)

1961—Isiah Thomas, Chicago, IL, NBA guard (Detroit Pistons)

1974—Cedric Jones, Houston, TX, NFL defensive end (New York Giants)

Airing **Errors**

ON THIS DAY IN 1901, THE DETROIT TIGERS COMMITTED TWELVE ERRORS IN A GAME AGAINST THE CHICAGO WHITE SOX.

That year, 1901, marked the first season for the American League and thus the first for both the Tigers and the White Sox (then called the White Stockings), so the quality of baseball and equipment was far from what we expect today. Still, twelve team errors is a lot by any standard. An error occurs when a player in the field makes a bad play trying to catch, throw, or hold onto the ball. Mental errors don't count (misjudging a flyball, throwing to the wrong base, forgetting the number of outs, etc.). Every game has possibilities for probably hundreds of errors—mental and physical. For example, a ground ball could lead to an error in fielding, throwing, or catching. But still, twelve is a ton of errors for any

professional team in one game.

Every error is embarrassing, especially if it leads to runs. The player feels like digging a hole, crawling in, and hiding but has to stand there, out in the open, for everyone to see . . . and boo.

Everyone makes errors, all the time. We drop stuff, add wrong, trip and fall, and make stupid comments. And every time we wish we could hide, especially when lots of people saw or heard us slip up. Mistakes and errors are common because no one is perfect—and we're all sinners. The Bible also says the world itself is "fallen"; that is, even nature was affected when sin entered the world. So stuff decays or breaks, natural disasters happen, and every living plant and animal eventually dies.

Years ago, the poet

Alexander Pope said, "To err is human, to forgive divine," echoing what Jesus said about not judging but being quick to forgive others for their mistakes. Jesus said, "Do not judge, and you will not be judged. Do not condemn, and you will not be condemned. Forgive, and you will be forgiven" (Luke 6:37).

Actually, isn't that just the way that you would like to be treated when you mess up? So when someone makes an error, don't criticize, ridicule, or boo. Instead, think about what Jesus said, and quickly pray for that person (even the error-prone ballplayer).

ALSO ON THIS DAY . . .

1973—Bobby Riggs beat Margaret Smith Court in a Mother's Day match in California.

1977—Chantal Langlace ran a female-world record marathon (2:35:15.4).

1991—Texas Ranger Nolan Ryan, at age forty-four, pitched a record seventh no-hitter, beating Toronto 3-0.

2008—Kevin Durant of the Seattle Super-Sonics was named NBA Rookie of the Year.

OOPS!

BIRTHDAYS:

1930—Ollie Matson, Trinity, TX, NFL halfback (Cardinals, Rams, Lions, Eagles)

1962—Paula Weishoff, Hollywood, CA, volleyball player (winner of two Olympic medals: silver in 1984 and bronze in 1992)

1981—Wes Welker, Oklahoma City, OK, NFL wide receiver (New England Patriots)

So, if you think you are standing firm, be careful that you don't fall! **1 Corinthians 10:12**

FUN FACT From 1901 to 1920, the White Sox won five out of a possible nineteen pennants, winning the World Championship in 1917. Led by Ty Cobb, the Tigers won the American League in 1907, 1908, and 1909.

GO TEAM   GO TEAM

Iron **Horse**

On this day in 1939, Lou Gehrig ended his 2,130 consecutive game streak as the Yankees beat the Tigers 22-2.

Henry Louis "Lou" Gehrig was an amazing baseball player who set several major league records, including the most career grand slam homeruns. He was elected to the Baseball Hall of Fame in 1939, was voted the greatest first baseman of all time by the Baseball Writers' Association in 1969, and was the leading vote-getter on the Major League Baseball All-Century Team chosen by fans in 1999.

But Lou is most remembered for his streak of playing in consecutive games—2,130, from 1925 through 1939—earning him the nickname "The Iron Horse." The streak ended only when Gehrig became disabled by the neuromuscular disease (now known as Lou Gehrig's disease) that claimed his life two years later. His record stood for fifty-six years, until finally broken by Cal Ripken Jr. on September 6, 1995.

More than durability, that's dependability. Every day that Lou's

manager filled in the lineup card, he didn't have to wonder who would play first base. Lou was always ready, willing, and able.

Everyone appreciates people they can count on. When dependable people promise to do something, we know they will do it. When they say they will be somewhere at a certain time, we can almost set our watch by their arrival. They don't use excuses or even reasons to get out of an assignment or responsibility. Coaches want that kind of player; teachers appreciate that kind of student; bosses like that kind of employee. And that's the kind of person God wants each of his children to be.

No matter how many abilities a person has, natural or otherwise, he or she can always have dependability. In fact, being undependable almost makes the other abilities worthless.

How dependable are you? Start your streak today.

Pay careful attention to your own work, for then you will get the satisfaction of a job well done, and you won't need to compare yourself to anyone else. **Galatians 6:4, NLT**

Fun Fact In Detroit, before the game, Lou told Joe McCarthy, his manager, "I'm benching myself, Joe," explaining that it was "for the good of the team." Gehrig himself took the lineup card to the shocked umpires before the game, ending the fourteen-year streak. The Tigers' fans gave him a standing ovation while he sat on the bench with tears in his eyes. For a few more weeks, Lou stayed with the Yankees as team captain, but he never played again.

Your **EPS**

On this day in 2000, the sport of geocaching began, with the first cache placed and the coordinates from a GPS posted on Usenet.

In geocaching, participants use a Global Positioning System (GPS) or something similar to look for special containers that have been hidden.

These containers, or caches, are usually small and waterproof, with a logbook inside. Larger ones can also contain items for trading, usually toys or trinkets of little value. Geocaching is usually described as a high-tech treasure hunt or game of hide-and-seek. Geocaches can be found in over 100 countries and on all seven continents, even Antarctica. As of April 10, 2010, there were over 1,031,429 active geocaches around the world.

In this first geocache game, Dave Ulmer of Beavercreek, Oregon posted the location of his cache on the Internet along with its latitude and longitude coordinates. By May 6, it had been found twice and logged once. The original stash was a black plastic bucket buried most of the way in the ground that contained software, videos, books, food, money, and a slingshot.

Sounds like fun, combining thinking and physical activity—but people would need money and transportation to participate. This isn't a sport you can play in the park. Well, maybe you can, if you don't use a GPS and just use clues.

Global Positioning Systems are changing our lives. We have units in our cars. We can get one to wear on a wrist to help us when jogging. And we can even get one on a smart phone. By using signals from orbiting satellites, they can tell us where we are and help us get to where we want to go. We feel lost without them.

Here's something even better—an EPS, an Eternal Positioning System. Far beyond the satellites, God sees the whole universe; he also sees the past and the future. Better yet, he wants to guide us through life and to him, in heaven at the end of life. And we don't need a hi-tech device; we just need the Bible, his Word. Read it daily and discover his will and his way. You'll head in the right direction.

....

ALSO ON THIS DAY . . .

1936—New York Yankee Joe DiMaggio made his major-league debut and got three hits.

1973—Kansas City Royals' George Brett got his first major-league hit.

1992—Gregg Olson (Baltimore Orioles) became the youngest relief pitcher to record 100 saves.

2007—The men's basketball rules committee of the NCAA voted to move the three-point line back 1 foot to 20 feet, 9 inches. Women's basketball would continue to use the 19'9" line.

Trust in the Lord with all your heart and lean not on your own understanding; in all your ways acknowledge him, and he will make your paths straight. **Proverbs 3:5–6**

[un ACT] The Oregon Public Broadcasting program *Oregon Field Guide* covered geocaching on a February, 2010, episode, visiting the original site. A metal memorial now sits on the actual site, but a functioning cache is located nearby in some bushes.

Championship Trophies

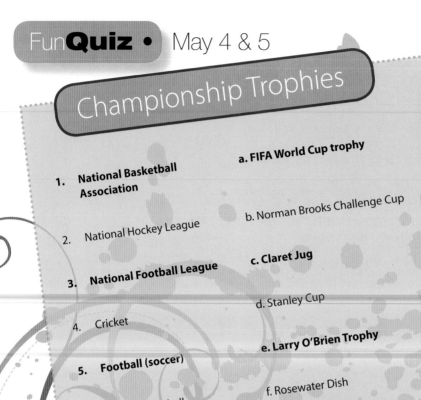

MATCH the trophy to the SPORT

1. **National Basketball Association**

2. National Hockey League

3. **National Football League**

4. Cricket

5. **Football (soccer)**

6. NCAA basketball

7. **Rugby**

8. Major League Baseball

9. **Golf—British Open**

10. Golf—The Masters

11. **Tennis—Australian Open**

12. Tennis—Wimbledon

a. **FIFA World Cup trophy**

b. Norman Brooks Challenge Cup

c. **Claret Jug**

d. Stanley Cup

e. **Larry O'Brien Trophy**

f. Rosewater Dish

g. **Vince Lombardi Trophy**

h. Green Jacket

i. **Commissioner's Trophy**

j. Bledisloe Cup

k. **NCAA Championship Trophy**

l. The Ashes

ANSWERS: 1.e, 2.d, 3.g, 4.l, 5.a, 6.k, 7.j, 8.i, 9.c, 10.h, 11.b, 12.f

Impossible?

On this day in 1954, Roger Bannister broke the 4-minute mile.

Not too long ago, everyone thought that running a mile under four minutes was impossible. No human being would ever be able to run that fast, said the experts in the scientific and athletic community. Obviously they were wrong. On this day, during a meet between the British AAA and Oxford University, 3,000 people watched Roger Bannister accomplish the "impossible." He did it! He broke the barrier! At the end of the race, the announcer said, "R. G. Bannister . . . with a time which is a new meeting and track record, and which—subject to ratification—will be a new English Native, British National, All-Comers, European, British Empire, and World Record . . . "The crowd roared, drowning out his announced time of 3 minutes 59.4 seconds.

Since then, many male runners have broken the "four minute barrier," and in the last fifty years, the record has been lowered by almost seventeen seconds. So what was thought impossible wasn't so impossible after all.

As you go through life, you will encounter many seemingly impossible situations. You may, for example, wonder how you will ever get out of a difficult situation. Or you may have a teacher who won't give you a break . . . or an illness that has knocked you down . . . or finances tight with no job or money in sight. Whatever the case, what seems impossible to us is always very possible with our eternal, almighty God. That's why we should pray and talk through everything with him. God may choose to grant our requests, but he may answer in a way we could never predict. He can do whatever he wants—everything is possible for him.

So when you hit a deadend, an impossible situation, keep praying, keep hoping, and keep trusting your Father who loves you, knows what's best for you, and can do absolutely anything. You may never run a four-minute mile, but you'll do great things for him.

ALSO ON THIS DAY . . .

1979—Nancy Lopez won the LPGA Women's International Golf Tournament.

1998—Rookie pitcher Kerry Wood of the Chicago Cubs struck out twenty Houston Astros to tie the major league record held by Roger Clemens. He threw a one-hitter and did not walk a batter in his fifth career start.

2006—Dale Earnhardt Jr. won the Crown Royal 400 at the Richmond International Raceway.

2008—Kobe Bryant of the Los Angeles Lakers won his first NBA Most Valuable Player Award.

BIRTHDAYS:

1931—Willie Mays, Westfield, AL, Hall-of-Fame MLB legend (New York/San Francisco Giants)

1972—Martin Brodeur, Montreal, Quebec, amazing NHL goalie (NJ Devils) and winner of two Olympic gold medals with Team Canada

1985—Chris Paul, Winston-Salem, NC, all-star NBA point guard (New Orleans Hornets)

[Jesus said,] "For nothing is impossible with God." **Luke 1:37**

Fun Fact The fiftieth anniversary of Sir Roger's achievement was marked by a commemorative British 50-pence coin. Bannister, the most famous mile record-setter, is also the person who held the record for the shortest period of time, as his record was broken forty-six days later by John Landy of Australia.

Security

On this day in 1966, the New York Yankees fired manager Johnny Keene.

On the last day of the season in 1964, the St. Louis Cardinals, managed by Johnny Keane, clinched the National League pennant. The Cardinals then went on to defeat the Yankees in a seven-game World Series. Shortly after all the celebrations in St. Louis, the Cards called a press conference. Most expected that a contract extension for Keane would be announced. Instead, the general manager revealed that Johnny had turned in a resignation letter in late September. Then, even more surprising, just a few days later, he became the manager of the Yankees, replacing Yogi Berra, who had been fired after the World Series. But the 1965 Yankees fell to sixth place, and Keane was fired when the 1966 version won only four of its first twenty games.

Anyone wanting job security should not become a Major League Baseball manager. In fact, most managers take the job knowing that eventually (often sooner rather than later) they will be fired.

We like security. We want to know that we can count on family, friends, and finances being there for us. And most people don't like change—they want things to stay the same, especially if they are feeling good and doing well.

But change is one of the few things we can count on. In this world, everything changes. We grow up, leave home, and begin life on our own. Friends and loved ones move away. Elections bring in different ways of governing. Natural disasters strike. Recessions hit, and people lose jobs. And, eventually, everyone dies.

So if we put our trust, our security, in this world, we'll be very disappointed.

Only God can give us the security we need. Only God never changes. And he promises to be with us now and into eternity.

When change is happening so fast you can't stand it, remember your unchanging God, and trust him—for your present and your future.

....

ALSO ON THIS DAY . . .

1925—The Philadelphia Phillies had their eighth game in a row postponed.

1951—The International Olympic Committee voted to allow Russia to participate in the 1952 Olympics.

1957—Cleveland Indians' pitcher Herb Score was hit by a line drive off Gil McDougald.

2005—At the age of forty-six years and 257 days, Julio Franco of the Atlanta Braves becomes the second-oldest player to hit a home run in Major League Baseball history.

Every good and perfect gift is from above, coming down from the Father of the heavenly lights, who does not change like shifting shadows. **James 1:17**

FUN FACT In 2007, eight MLB managers were fired. Only four lost their jobs in 2008. But in 2009 eight again bit the dust.

BIRTHDAYS:

1933—Johnny Unitas, Pittsburgh, PA, Hall-of-Fame NFL quarterback (Baltimore Colts and San Diego Chargers)

1969—Melanie Valerio, Cleveland, OH, 400 meter freestyle swimmer (1996 Olympics)

1985—Drew Neitzel, Grand Rapids, MI, American college basketball player

Playing with **Heart**

ON THIS DAY IN 1970, WILLIS REED OF THE NEW YORK KNICKS LIMPED ONTO THE COURT AND INTO LEGEND (THE KNICKS WON THE NBA TITLE AFTER THEIR CAPTAIN'S HEROIC ENTRANCE).

Willis Reed, a center/forward for the New York Knicks, had an amazing career. He was the NBA Rookie of the Year (1965), a seven-time NBA all-star (1965-1971), and a two-time NBA champion (1970, 1973). He was also the MVP of the 1970 all-star game and the MVP of the NBA finals in both championship seasons. With all of that success and reward, he is most famous for his performance in the seventh game of the 1970 NBA finals against the Los Angeles Lakers, in Madison Square Garden.

A severely torn thigh muscle had kept Willis out of game six, so he was not expected to even dress for game seven. So everyone was shocked when he walked onto the court during warm-ups. Then he started the game and scored the Knicks' first four points on his first two shot attempts. Reed's play inspired the Knicks, and Walt Frazier went on to score thirty-six points. The Knicks won the game 113–99, giving New York City its first NBA title. Willis Reed walking onto the court has been voted the greatest moment in the history of Madison Square Garden.

In obvious pain throughout the game, Willis played with great courage, almost willing his team to the championship.

Courage seems rare these days. Maybe the reason is the big contracts, but some athletes don't play with even a minor injury. That's why Reed's performance, despite his injury and pain, was such an inspiration.

When Joshua became leader of Israel, Moses told him, "Be strong and courageous" (Deuteronomy 31:7). He knew that Joshua would face many painful and difficult challenges.

Then he added, "The Lord himself goes before you and will be with you; he will never leave you nor forsake you. Do not be afraid; do not be discouraged" (vs. 8).

That's great advice for us. We can encounter any situation with the assurance that God is with us and is working in us, giving us courage and power to do what he wants. We just need to depend on him.

Be strong and courageous!

ALSO ON THIS DAY . . .

1936—Jockey Ralph Neves was unexpectedly revived after being declared dead after a fall. His wife fainted when he returned to the track.

1973—Ernie Banks filled in for Chicago Cubs manager Whitey Lockman, who had been ejected during the game, thus technically becoming baseball's first black manager.

1994—Colorado Silver Bullets (all-female pro baseball team) played their first game.

2005—The Phoenix Suns' Steve Nash was named the NBA's most valuable player, becoming the first Canadian to win the award. He had been drafted fifteenth overall in 1996 by the Suns, making him the lowest-drafted player ever to be named MVP.

BIRTHDAYS:

1959—Ronnie Lott, Albuquerque, NM, Hall-of-Fame NFL defensive back (San Francisco 49ers)

1978—Cindy Parlow, Memphis, TN, soccer forward (1996 Olympics)

1986—Marvell Wynne, Pittsburgh, PA, defender in MLS (New York Red Bulls, Toronto FC, Colorado Rapids) and on the US National Team

But we have this treasure in jars of clay to show that this all-surpassing power is from God and not from us. **2 Corinthians 4:7**

FUN FACT Willis Reed Jr. spent his entire professional playing career with the New York Knicks and was inducted into the Basketball Hall of Fame in 1982. They have retired number nineteen, his number.

Perfectionists **Beware**

On this day in 1989, in a game against the Cincinnati Reds, the New York Mets' Rick Cerone made an error after 159 errorless games as catcher; also, the Mets' Kevin Elster made an error after 88 errorless games at shortstop.

Wow—two errorless streaks broken in the same game. No wonder the Mets lost 3-1.

No one wants to make an error—we'd all like to be perfect. But errors are part of life—and baseball. It certainly isn't a game for perfectionists. Consider batting averages, for example. The player winning the batting championship in either league will probably only hit safely around one out of three times at bat, for a .333 batting average. In other words, he will make an out two-thirds of the time. That's not even close to perfection!

We know we're not perfect in any area of life—far from it. Besides the fact that we misplay the ball, strike-out, or fumble sometimes, we also sin. In other words, we do or think what we shouldn't and don't do what we should. Sinning comes naturally; we even do it without thinking.

The problem with our sinful "errors," however, is that they separate us from God and actually make us his enemies. Now, if that were the whole story, we'd lose much more than a game. We would be doomed, in this life and the next. But here's the great news: Jesus, who was and is perfect, came to earth and took the penalty for our sins (which is death, by the way). He died on the cross. Then he rose from the dead, showing his power over sin and death and the truth of his message. And he will forgive us; all we have to do is believe in him, admit that we're sinners in need of a Savior, and trust him to save us.

If you've done that, then no matter how many mistakes, errors, or sins you do today, tomorrow, or whenever, you're forgiven. God loves you that much!

Doesn't that take a load off? Do your best, of course, but you don't have to be perfect . . . because of Jesus.

....

ALSO ON THIS DAY . . .

1929—New York Giant Carl Hubbell no-hit the Pittsburgh Pirates.

1975—Brian Oldfield shot-put 22.86 m for a world record.

2001—In Ghana, 129 football fans died from a stampede (caused by the firing of tear gas by police personnel at the stadium) that followed a controversial decision by the referee.

2009—Mark Martin won the Southern 500 NASCAR Sprint Cup Series race in Darlington, South Carolina.

BIRTHDAYS:

1939—Ralph Boston, Laurel, MS, long jumper (winner of three Olympic medals: gold in 1960, silver in 1964, and bronze in 1968)

1960—Tony Gwynn, Los Angeles, CA, MLB outfielder and multiple batting average winner (San Diego Padres)

1969—Carla Overbeck, Pasadena, CA, soccer defender (1996 Olympics)

1985—Jake Long, Lapeer, MI, NFL offensive tackle (Miami Dolphins)

But God demonstrates his own love for us in this: While we were still sinners, Christ died for us. **Romans 5:8**

Fun Fact In 1998, Rick Cerone founded the Newark Bears, a minor league ball club in the independent Atlantic League. He sold it in 2003.

Using **Your Head**

On this day in 2008, Greg Maddux became just the ninth pitcher in major-league history with 350 career wins.

Most baseball experts agree that Greg Maddux is a sure first-ballot Hall of Famer. Check out this career. He pitched in the major leagues from 1986 through 2008, mostly for the Cubs and Braves, accumulating a 355-227 record and winning the NL Cy Young Award four years in a row, 1992–1995. No one else has ever done that. During those seasons, Greg's record was 75-29, with a 1.98 ERA. He also is the only pitcher in MLB history to win at least fifteen games for seventeen straight seasons, and he won Gold Gloves (to the best fielding player at each position) a record eighteen times.

Greg was a control pitcher. That is, instead of trying to overpower batters with his fastball, he would throw the ball where he wanted, nibbling on the outside corner of the plate.

Maddux was a student of the game, constantly studying hitters so he would know how to pitch to them. Bobby Cox of the Braves, Greg's former manager, said, "Was he the smartest pitcher I ever saw? The most competitive I ever saw? The best teammate I ever saw? The answer is yes to all of those."

Some athletes, especially when they're young, simply rely on the athletic ability: strength, speed, and so forth. But that only goes so far. Great athletes use their minds.

According to the Bible, God expects us to use the brains he gave us, to think things through. Sometimes, especially when we're young, we can make poor decisions, because of pressure from friends or based on how we feel instead of on the facts. We may even do what we know

is wrong. The Bible calls people who live like that "foolish." Our minds count.

Also, some people think that those who follow Christ don't think or analyze the facts; they just believe (blind faith). But God doesn't want us to check our brains at the door. The Christian faith is based on real history, facts that can be investigated.

Use your mind: ask questions, look for answers, investigate. Our faith is true and makes sense.

....

ALSO ON THIS DAY . . .

1929—Walter Hagen shot a 292 at Muirfield Gullane to win the sixty-fourth British Golf Open.

1941—Eddie Arcaro aboard Whirlaway won the sixty-seventh Preakness (horse race) in 1:58.8.

1973—The Montreal Canadians beat the Chicago Blackhawks, four games to two, to win the Stanley Cup.

2009—Ben "Elbowz" Spies won Race 2 in the Superbike World Championship in Monza, Italy.

BIRTHDAYS:

1930—Pat Summerall, Lake City, FL, NFL placekicker (Detroit Lions, Chicago Cardinals, New York Giants) and sportscaster

1960—Merlene Ottey, Jamaican/Italian running star (Olympics)

1975—Hélio Castroneves, Brazilian race car driver

1977—Amanda Borden, Cincinnati, OH, gymnast (world silver medal, 1994; Olympic gold medal, 1996)

For God did not give us a spirit of timidity, but a spirit of power, of love and of self-discipline. **2 Timothy 1:7**

Fun Fact
Maddux could outthink his opponents and anticipate results. Former teammate outfielder Marquis Grissom recalled a game in 1996 when Maddux was having trouble spotting his fastball. Between innings, Greg told Marquis, "Gary Sheffield is coming up next inning. I am going to throw him a slider and make him just miss it so he hits it to the warning track." The at-bat went as Maddux had predicted.

MLB—American League Nicknames

1. **Chicago**
2. New York
3. **Tampa Bay**
4. Minnesota
5. **Detroit**
6. Texas
7. **Oakland**
8. Cleveland
9. **Kansas City**
10. Toronto
11. **Boston**
12. Los Angeles
13. **Seattle**
14. Baltimore

a. **Tigers**
b. Indians
c. **Rangers**
d. Red Sox
e. **Royals**
f. Blue Jays
g. **Orioles**
h. Angels
i. **White Sox**
j. Rays
k. **Mariners**
l. Twins
m. **A's**
n. Yankees

Weather **or Not**

On this day in 1975, hailstones as large as tennis balls hit Wernerville, Tennessee.

Wait a minute—what's a story about weather doing in a sports book?

Good question, but you'll notice that the hailstones were as large as tennis balls. Imagine playing tennis and seeing the hail. You'd get very confused just before you got injured!

Actually, weather plays a major role in outdoor sports. Baseball games get called or postponed often because of "inclement weather," especially in the spring. A few years ago, the Cleveland Indians had to play some April home games in Chicago because of snow in Cleveland. Football games, however, are played in almost any weather: you may remember hearing about the "ice bowl," when the Packers beat the Cowboys in the 1967 League Championship Game, or the "fog bowl," when the Bears beat the Eagles in a playoff game.

Weather impacts us all the time, so we have "snow days" for school, "rain-outs" in sports, "fogged-in" airports, icy roads, wind alerts, cold fronts, and heat waves. Thus, every news outlet gives weather forecasts, and TV has a Weather Channel.

No wonder everyone talks about the weather!

Usually our weather discussions involve complaints: it's too hot or too cold or too humid or too windy or . . . But we can't control the weather; we have to live with it and deal with it.

And that brings us to the point of this devotional. Right in the middle of the Bible we find this encouragement: "This is the day the Lord has made; let us rejoice and be glad in it" (Psalm 118:24).

That verse and the surrounding ones don't say, "rejoice . . . when the temperature is eighty degrees, the sun is shining, a slight breeze is blowing, and the humidity is low." The point seems to be that we should thank God for each day, regardless of the weather—because he made it and he's in it.

So even if this day in May feels like August (or November), thank God for his goodness, for being alive, and for opportunities to serve him.

....

ALSO ON THIS DAY . . .

1905—James J. Jeffries, "The Boilermaker," retired as heavyweight boxing champion.

1995—New Zealand beat the United States to win the America's Cup.

2005—Tiger Woods missed his first cut in seven years on the PGA Tour. Before this, he had made the cut for a tour-record 142 consecutive tournaments.

2008—Annika Sörenstam, the leading money winner in the history of the LPGA, announced her retirement effective at the end of the 2008 season.

BIRTHDAYS:

1977—Sara DeCosta, Warwick, RI, ice hockey goalie (USA team—Olympics, 1998)

1978—Mike Bibby, Cherry Hill, NJ, NBA point guard (Grizzlies, Kings, Hawks)

1982—Oguchi Onyewu, Washington, DC, American soccer center back (US national team)

All the days ordained for me were written in your book before one of them came to be. **Psalm 139:16b**

FUN FACT On December 31, 1988, heavy, dense fog rolled over Soldier Field in the second quarter of the playoff game between the Bears and Eagles and stayed. Visibility dropped to 10–20 yards. Players complained that they could not see the sidelines or first-down markers. The Bears won 20-12.

14 Burned **Out**

On this day in 2008, citing burnout, Justine Henin, the number-one-ranked woman tennis player in the world, announced her retirement, effective immediately.

Burnout" just means that someone is sick and tired of doing something. An entertainer can be tired of singing, dancing, or acting every night for weeks. A worker can get sick of doing the same thing over and over. A student can feel like he or she can't study another second. And athletes can grow very weary of their sport, especially those who have been practicing and playing for years and years.

In 1984, when Justine was only two, her family moved next to a tennis club, and she began playing—and never stopped. By the end of 1998, she had won five International Tennis Federation tournaments. She turned pro in 1999 at the Belgian Open and became only the fifth player to win her first WTA Tour event. Since then, Henin has won forty-one WTA titles, four Grand Slam singles titles, and the Olympic gold

medal (2004). Tennis experts have often cited the completeness of her game, her footwork, her one-handed backhand, and her mental toughness. But she retired at the age of twenty-five.

Burnout can hit anyone, even a mentally tough adult, but kids in sports are very vulnerable. Sometimes parents will encourage children to play soccer, hit a volleyball, skate, pick up the racket, swim, throw a football or baseball, or do another sport while still very young. Soon they are playing almost year-round. The sport, even practice, can be fun at first. Parents and children imagine college scholarships and professional careers. Often, however, the child burns out way before that—sick and tired of the sport. Sports really don't perform well as the most important thing in life.

In Old Testament times, the wisest man on earth, King Solomon, wrote, "There is a time for everything, and a season for every activity under

heaven" (Ecclesiastes 3:1). Sure sounds like he was talking about sports! Elsewhere, Paul wrote, "'Everything is permissible'—but not everything is beneficial. 'Everything is permissible'—but not everything is constructive" (1 Corinthians 10:23). His point: just because we can do something, doesn't mean we should. And the most important biblical principle: we shouldn't make anything so important to us that it takes God's place in our lives. That's idolatry.

So enjoy sports—playing and watching. But don't let them consume you. Keep them in moderation, and keep focused on Christ.

....

ALSO ON THIS DAY . . .

1906—A flagpole at the White Sox ballpark broke during a pennant raising.

1975—Dynamo Kiev won the fifteenth Europe Cup II (soccer).

1989—The first Tour de Trump bicycle race was run in Atlanta.

2006—To celebrate Mother's Day, the Office of the Commissioner approved use of special pink bats in all games that were played that day. Monies raised from the auctioning of these bats was given to charities for breast-cancer research.

BIRTHDAYS:

1964—Suzy Kolber, Philadelphia, PA, American sportscaster

1967—Tony "Goose" Siragusa, Kenilworth, NJ, NFL defensive tackle (Indianapolis Colts, Baltimore Ravens) and broadcaster

1978—Heather Brink, Lincoln, NE, gymnast (1996 Olympics)

Have nothing to do with godless myths and old wives' tales; rather, train yourself to be godly. For physical training is of some value, but godliness has value for all things, holding promise for both the present life and the life to come. 1 Timothy 4:7–8

[un]ACT After a twenty-month break from the sport, in September 2009, Justine Henin announced that she would return to the WTA tour. She is now ranked in the top twenty-five.

One Day, One Game, at a Time

On this day in 1941, Joe DiMaggio began his fifty-six-game hitting streak.

One of the all-time great baseball players, Joe DiMaggio won the MVP award three times. He was the only player ever selected for the all-star game every year he played. "The Yankee Clipper" is still one of the leaders on career home runs and slugging percentage. But he is most remembered for hitting safely in fifty-six games in a row (May 15 to July 16, 1941). That means he had at least one hit in each of those games. (Errors, walks, hit by pitches, and, of course, outs don't count.)

When Joe got up on that May morning, he probably didn't say, "I think I'll hit at least fifty games in a row." Even after

collecting his first hit, that idea never crossed his mind. Great hitters don't try to have hitting streaks. They just hit, and the results take care of themselves. That's true in all areas of sports: winning streaks, errorless games, free-throw records, and so forth.

The same thing happens with other types of successful people. They want to be successful, yes, but they know that their final results happen because of what they do daily— their attitudes, decisions, and actions. Little victories add up to big ones.

That's why Jesus tells his people to be faithful in the small things (Matthew 25:21) and to live one day at a time (Matthew 6:34).

Here's how it works. When you get up tomorrow, ask God to help you listen to him and follow him closely that day. Then, during the day, when you know what he wants you to do, just do it. That may mean performing your household chores, helping a

friend at school, speaking kindly to someone who insults you, praying for a person in need, or another obvious action. At the end of the day, think back and thank God for his help and say you're sorry for when you didn't do what you should have done or did what you shouldn't have done. The next morning, repeat the process.

Before long, you'll have a "hitting streak" of your own—and you'll be developing a life of God-honoring character and faithfulness.

....

ALSO ON THIS DAY . . .

1876—Bobby Swim won the second Kentucky Derby aboard Vagrant in 2:38.25.

1953—Heavyweight champion Rocky Marciano knocked out Jersey Joe Walcott in Chicago.

1991—Manchester United won the thirty-first Europe Cup II at Rotterdam.

2005—Defending IndyCar series champion Tony Kanaan won the pole position. Danica Patrick, twenty-three years old, earned the best start for a female driver by taking the fourth position.

BIRTHDAYS:

1967—John Smoltz, Detroit, MI, pitcher (Atlanta Braves, St. Louis Cardinals), winner of the 1996 Cy Young Award

1978—Amy Chow, San Jose, CA, gymnast (gold and silver Olympic medals winner, 1996)

1987—Andy Murray, Glasgow, Scotland, professional tennis player

And now, just as you accepted Christ Jesus as your Lord, you must continue to follow him. Let your roots grow down into him, and let your lives be built on him. Then your faith will grow strong in the truth you were taught, and you will overflow with thankfulness. **Colossians 2:6–7 NLT**

Fun Fact DiMaggio was an outstanding "five-tool" player (hitting for average, hitting for power, fielding, throwing, and base-running). Hank Greenberg once said that Joe covered so much ground in center field that the only way to get a hit against the Yankees was "to hit 'em where Joe wasn't."

Dissing **Disability**

On this day in 2008, South African double-amputee sprinter Oscar Pistorius was cleared to qualify for Olympic events.

Oscar Pistorius was born with no fibula bones in both legs. So when he was just eleven months old, his legs were amputated halfway between his knees and ankles. During his early school years, he played rugby, water polo, and tennis. Eventually he tried wrestling, too. In 2004, after a serious knee injury (playing rugby), he began running while undergoing rehabilitation and decided to stick with that sport. So how does a person with no legs run at all, not to mention competitively? He has artificial legs, carbon-fiber prosthetics, each looking like a J-shaped spring.

At first, Oscar was banned from competing in Olympic events because some said his artificial legs gave him an advantage. That decision was reversed. So he tried to qualify for the 400 meters at a race in Switzerland. He finished third with a personal best time of 46.25 seconds, but this was short of the Olympic qualification time of 45.55 seconds. Also, the South African Olympic Committee did not select him for the 4 x 400 meters relay team because four other runners had better times. So he entered the 2008 Summer Paralympics, where he won the gold medals in the 100-, 200-, and 400-meter sprints.

What keeps you from doing your best, achieving your dreams? For a man with no legs to become a sprinting champion is unthinkable. Yet that's exactly what happened with Oscar. He likes to say, "You're not disabled by the disabilities you have, you are able by the abilities you have." His point is that when we focus on our limitations and what we can't do, we forget what we have and what we can do.

You don't have to be a superstar athlete to be a success. And you don't have to be the most handsome or beautiful or talented or athletic to be happy. God has made you just the way you are for a purpose. And he has given you the right personality, physical make-up, and natural abilities to make it happen. Don't let anything or anyone hold you back from reaching your potential.

....

ALSO ON THIS DAY . . .

1894—Fire in Boston destroyed the baseball stadium and 170 other buildings.

1954—Ted Williams collected eight hits in his first game back after breaking his collarbone.

1985—Michael Jordan was named the NBA Rookie of the Year.

2009—The favored horse Rachel Alexandra won the Preakness Stakes in Baltimore, the first filly to win the Preakness since 1924. Calvin Borel, who rode Mine That Bird to victory in the Kentucky Derby, became the first jockey ever to win the first two legs of the same year's Triple Crown on two different horses.

BIRTHDAYS:

1928—Billy Martin, Berkley, CA, major-league second baseman (Yankees, Athletics, Tigers, Indians, Reds, Braves, Twins) and manager (Twins, Tigers, Rangers, Yankees, Athletics)

1955—Olga Korbut, Grodno, Belorussia, Russian gymnast and winner of two Olympic gold medals (1972)

1980—Michael Ryan, Boston, MA, NHL forward (Buffalo Sabres, Carolina Hurricanes)

Whatever your hand finds to do, do it with all your might. Ecclesiastes 9:10

Fun Fact Known as "the Blade Runner" and "the fastest man on no legs," Oscar hopes to compete in the 2012 Summer Olympics in London. He said, "Sprinters usually reach their peak between twenty-six and twenty-nine. I will be twenty-five in London and I'll also have two, three years' preparation."

Sounds **Fishy**

On this day in 1985, Les Anderson caught a record 97 lb. 4 oz. Chinook salmon in the Kenai River in Alaska.

Can you believe it? That's about 100 pounds of fish on that pole. Imagine how tough it must have been to keep the fish on the line and then to land it—Les must have had some help getting the salmon into the boat. And a fish that size would have fed lots of people.

Fishing is fun, if you have the patience. But people who fish are known to tell stories and exaggerate about the fish they caught in the past and the "one that got away." Maybe that's where the expression "sounds fishy to me" came from. When we're not sure a story

is true, we might say that.

Exaggerating, stretching the truth, isn't limited to fishing. We do it in lots of areas. When asked if we finished a job, for example, we might say yes, when, actually, we weren't quite done. When we report how much time we spent working, we might add an hour or two. When telling about a past incident, we might change some of the details to make us look good. And we might give the wrong score in golf or another self-policing sport.

Lying is easy, too easy. We lie for many reasons: to protect ourselves, to make ourselves look good, to fit in, to win a contest, to get out of a situation, to get

someone to like us . . . Whatever the reason or occasion, lying is wrong. Jesus is truth (John 14:6), and God expects us to tell the truth (Exodus 20:16) and live the truth (Ephesians 4:15).

So when you're asked, "Did you step out of bounds?" or "Did you hit the ball with your hand?" or "What did you get on that hole?" or "How fast did you run?" or "How big was that fish you caught last summer?" don't lie, mumble, exaggerate, or act like you didn't hear the question. Tell the truth.

That's not fishy at all!

ALSO ON THIS DAY . . .

1875—Oliver Lewis won the first Kentucky Derby, aboard Aristides, in 2:37.75.

1915—George "Zip" Zabel (Chicago Cubs) relieved with two outs in the first inning and wound up with a 4-3 nineteen-inning win over Brooklyn in the longest relief pitching job ever.

1959—"Slammin' Sammy" Snead set a PGA record for thirty-six holes at 122.

1997—Sandra Jo Shiery-Odom won the WIBC Bowling Queens tournament.

BIRTHDAYS:

1956—Sugar Ray Charles Leonard, Willington, SC, boxing champion welterweight and middleweight and winner of Olympic gold medal (1976)

1966—Mark Schmocker, Interlaken, Switzerland, US team handball goalie, 1996 Olympics

1982—Tony Parker, Bruges, Belgium, French-American all-star NBA guard (San Antonio Spurs)

Therefore each of you must put off falsehood and speak truthfully to his neighbor, for we are all members of one body. **Ephesians 4:25**

【un】【act】 The world record for Atlantic bigeye tuna is 392 lbs. 6 oz. The world record for giant sea bass is 563 lbs. 8 oz. The world record for great white shark is 2,664 lbs. True!

College Nicknames

Match the college to its nickname

1. **University of North Carolina, Chapel Hill**
2. University of Alabama
3. **University of Illinois**
4. Purdue University
5. **University of California at Los Angeles**
6. Vanderbilt University
7. **Clemson University**
8. Duke University
9. **University of Florida**
10. University of Kansas
11. **Texas A&M University**
12. Pepperdine University
13. **University of Oregon**
14. Michigan State University
15. **University of Kentucky**
16. Tulane University
17. **Bradley University**
18. Gonzaga University
19. **University of Connecticut**
20. University of Southern California
21. **University of Tennessee**
22. Oklahoma State University
23. **Ohio State University**
24. Washington State University
25. **Old Dominion University**
26. Louisiana State University

a. Gators
b. Green Wave
c. **Volunteers**
d. Cougars
e. **Crimson Tide**
f. Cowboys
g. **Wildcats**
h. Jayhawks
i. **Braves**
j. Monarchs
k. **Boilermakers**
l. Trojans
m. **Commodores**
n. Tigers
o. **Tarheels**
p. Waves
q. **Bruins**
r. Spartans
s. **Illini**
t. Buckeyes
u. **Aggies**
v. Tigers
w. **Huskies**
x. Bulldogs
y. **Blue Devils**
z. Ducks

ANSWERS: 1.o, 2.e, 3.s, 4.k, 5.q, 6.m, 7.n, 8.y, 9.a, 10.h, 11.u, 12.p, 13.z, 14.r, 15.g, 16.b, 17.i, 18.x, 19.w, 20.l, 21.c, 22.f, 23.t, 24.d, 25.j 26.v

Don't **Bet on It**

On this day in 1920, policemen raided the Cubs' bleachers and arrested 24 fans for gambling.

Usually fans buy tickets and go to the stadium to watch the game. Evidently these fans went for other reasons. Or perhaps they were watching and gambling at the same time— maybe betting on where the next ball would be hit, how long a pitcher would last, how far the batter would toss his bat after hitting the ball, or even how many times the third base coach would touch his nose during the half inning. Whatever the case, gambling was illegal, so the police were enforcing the law.

Times sure have changed. Now, rather than gambling being illegal, the government actually sponsors gambling in most stats, especially with lotteries. And most sports sections and websites post the odds for each game.

Gambling may seem like fun, but it's a terrible idea. Someone has said that the lottery is a tax on people who are bad at math. The odds are way stacked against the bettor, yet people, lots of people, think they can beat the odds and win big. They're fooling themselves. Every year, millions of people gamble their money and their lives away and our society is poorer for it.

The important lesson here, however, is not about gambling. It's about answering to a higher calling than what is or isn't legal. It's doing what we know is right and Christ honoring, even if society has changed and says otherwise.

What if, for example, the authorities no longer arrested anyone for stealing? In other words, they said people could steal as long as they didn't get caught. Should we steal? No. Because in his Word God tells us not to steal. How about taking God's name in vain? Or taking drugs? Or having sex outside of marriage? No. No. And no. We know what God said and how he wants us to live, and we'll live his way. At times we will have to say no when the world says yes.

That will mean making tough choices. But you're strong—you can do it. It would be foolish to bet against you.

ALSO ON THIS DAY . . .

1930—University of California dedicated $1,500 to research for the prevention and cure of athlete's foot.

1959—The New York Yankees sank to last place for the first time since May 25, 1940.

2007—In the World Indoor Lacrosse Championships in Halifax, Nova Scotia, Canada, Canada defeated Iroquois for the gold medal, and the United States defeated England for the bronze medal.

2008—The Chicago Bulls drew the first pick in the draft despite having only a 1.7% chance of winning the lottery. The Miami Heat, with the league's worst record, drew the second pick. (The Bulls chose Derrick Rose.)

BIRTHDAYS:

1971—Tony Stewart, Columbus, IN, American race car driver and owner

1981—Lindsay Taylor, Poway, CA, WNBA center (Comets, Mercury, Storm, Mystics)

1993—Caroline Zhang, Boston, MA, American figure skater

Therefore, come out from among unbelievers, and separate yourselves from them, says the Lord. Don't touch their filthy things, and I will welcome you. 2 Corinthians 6:17, NLT

Fun Fact If you were playing golf with three of your friends, the chances that two of you would get a hole-in-one on the exact same hole are 17 million to 1. That's better than the chances of you winning the lottery. Here's another: you are 450,000 to 3,000,000 times more likely to die in an asteroid collision in the year 2029 than to win the lottery.

It's All **You Need**

ON THIS DAY IN 1881, THE UNITED STATES NATIONAL LAWN TENNIS ASSOCIATION WAS FORMED.

Tennis seems to have originated in England, in about 1870. Because the game was played on grass, it was called "lawn tennis." In 1881, a small group of New York tennis-club members formed the United States National Lawn Tennis Association, which eventually became the United States Tennis Association, the governing body for the sport in the US.

Tennis has become very popular internationally. Most high schools and colleges have interscholastic tennis teams, and the professional tennis circuits, both men's and women's, are doing very well. It provides great exercise, and it's a sport that people of almost any age can play.

Tennis has an unusual scoring system. Instead of saying that the first player (or team) to get to four points wins (winning by two), the scoring goes this way: love, 15, 30, 40, game. No one is quite sure why *love* is used instead of *zero*. It sure sounds better.

And, hopefully, all the games begin and end with "love"—the loser congratulating the winner afterward. But players who fail to score any points usually have a tough time staying in "love." That's a challenge.

If all our sports had "love" points (or lack of them), maybe we'd see less fighting, arguing, and cheating. Actually that's true of all of life. And, come to think of it, if we had nothing else—zero—but love, we'd have all we need. That's what the Bible says.

The apostle Paul wrote, "Three things will last forever—faith, hope, and love—and the greatest of these is love" (1 Corinthians 13:13, NLT). So love is the "greatest" and will "last forever"—pretty good deal!

Love means treating other people the way we would like to be treated. Love involves meeting other people's needs. Love means listening, serving, and giving our lives. Love means living like Jesus. Everyone wants to be loved!

Be a lover. That'll be a point for God in your life.

....

ALSO ON THIS DAY . . .

1819—The first bicycles (called "swift walkers") were intro- duced in the United States (New York City).

1952—The Brooklyn Dodgers scored fifteen runs in the first inning and beat the Cincinnati Reds, 19-1.

1979—The Montreal Canadiens beat the New York Rangers four games to one to win the Stanley Cup.

2005—Mark Martin won the 2005 NEXTEL All-Star Challenge.

BIRTHDAYS:

1957—Sue Woodstra, Colton, CA, volleyball player and winner of the Olympic silver medal in 1984

1977—Ricky Williams, San Diego, CA, NFL running back (New Orleans Saints, Miami Dolphins)

1981—Josh Hamilton, Raleigh, NC, Major League Baseball outfielder (Cincinnati Reds, Texas Rangers)

Dear friends, let us love one another, for love comes from God. Everyone who loves has been born of God and knows God. **1 John 4:7**

Fun Fact
The longest men's tennis match is now John Isner versus Nicolas Mahut at Wimbledon. The match lasted 11 hours and 5 minutes and was played over three days (June 22, 23, 24, 2010). In the longest women's match, Vicki Nelson took 6 hours, 31 minutes to defeat Jean Hepner in 1984. That match had a 29-minute, 643-shot rally, the longest in professional tennis history.

Rough **Going**

On this day in 2003, Annika Sörenstam became the first woman to play the PGA Tour in 58 years.

Annika Sörenstam played in the Bank of America Colonial Golf Tournament in Fort Worth, Texas, making her the first woman to play in a PGA Tour event since Babe Zaharias in 1945, who qualified for the Los Angeles Open.

One of the most successful golfers in history, Annika has won seventy-two LPGA tournaments, including ten majors and eighteen international ones. Yet in 2008 she announced that she was "stepping away" from golf at the end of that season to start a family.

Golf takes skill, concentration, and consistency. A good golfer, such as Annika, knows how to control the direction and distance of the ball. Every stroke has unique challenges because of where the ball lies (length of grass, bunker, trees, etc.), the distance from the pin, and other conditions (wet or dry green, wind, etc.). Off the tee, the goal usually is to hit the ball long and straight, ending up in the middle of the fairway or on the green (on par three holes). Those who spray the ball around get into trouble in hazards, the rough, or two fairways away. The idea is to mentally bring in the edges of the fairway and then drive the ball in that narrow corridor, if possible. Straight and narrow will help the golfer get to the green in good shape.

Jesus said something similar, although he didn't have golf courses in mind. He said, "Enter through the narrow gate. For wide is the gate and broad is the road that leads to destruction, and many enter through it. But small is the gate and narrow the road that leads to life, and only a few find it" (Matthew 7:13–14). Again the message is "straight and narrow."

The world offers many ways to "life." The message is that God's way is broad and so wide that anyone can get to heaven.

A person only has to believe in something. No wonder so many people are traveling that road—it seems so easy. But they are being misled. The way is narrow and the gate is small because God has provided only one way—through Jesus.

Don't be fooled. Heading in those other directions will be rough going indeed. Choose God's way, the only way.

······································

ALSO ON THIS DAY . . .

1966—Shirley Englehorn won the LPGA Babe Didrikson-Zaharias Golf Open.

1990—Andre Dawson of the Chicago Cubs set a MLB record by being intentionally walked five times in one game.

2005—Paula Creamer, just eighteen, became the LPGA's second-youngest first-time winner ever, and the tour's youngest in fifty years, winning the Sybase Classic in New Rochelle, New York.

2007 Steven López of the US won the welterweight title at the World Taekwondo Championships in Beijing, China

Jesus answered, "I am the way and the truth and the life. No one comes to the Father except through me." John 14:6

[UN][FACT] Since 2006 Sörenstam has held dual American and Swedish citizenship. She and her husband welcomed their first child, Ava Madelyn McGee, on September 1, 2009.

Pedalin' **Through**

On this day in 2004, Jens Voigt of Germany won the Tour of Bavaria bicycle race.

Jens navigated the 894.5-km (about 556 miles) course over six stages around Bavaria, the largest German state, in 22 hr. 23 min. 54 sec. He has won this race more times than anyone else. This is one example of many similar races held annually around the world. Bicycling is one of those sports that a person can enjoy most of his or her life. And most communities have competitions for those who take it more seriously.

Hills are tough on cyclists, especially in a race. With gravity working against them, they push and strain and feel the burn in muscles and lungs. Riding downhill is much easier, of course, but those stretches of the course can be the most dangerous. That's because the temptation is to glide downhill, to coast. But doing that can throw cyclists off rhythm and even cause them to lose focus and to relax too much. Then when the next hill comes, they find it difficult to regain that push and rhythm to carry them to the top. It's almost as though the coasting gave them a false sense of accomplishment, as though they were doing well when it was just gravity working in their favor.

This is a good lesson about life. Often, when life is tough, when we're "peddling uphill," we become determined, work hard, and stay focused on our goal. Spiritually we pray, read the Bible, consider what God wants us to do, and look to other Christians for support. But when life is going well, almost too easy, we can coast, become complacent, and even lose our way. That's when we're most vulnerable to temptation. When we relax, let down our guard, we're more open to doing something wrong—we're "coasting."

So we need to learn to pedal through life's downhill stretches—continuing to take our nourishment (God's Word), stay in communication with our leader (prayer), keep our eyes on our goal (living for Christ), and stay in touch with our support team (church). Don't coast through any stretch of life. Keep pedalin'!

ALSO ON THIS DAY . . .

1883—A baseball game was played between one-armed and one-legged players.

1982—Colin Wilson rode a surfboard 294 miles.

1991—The San Diego Sockers won their fourth consecutive Major Soccer League championship.

2003—The New Jersey Devils beat the Ottawa Senators four games to three to win the Stanley Cup.

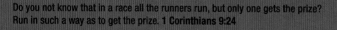

Do you not know that in a race all the runners run, but only one gets the prize? Run in such a way as to get the prize. 1 Corinthians 9:24

Fun Fact
The most expensive bicycle in the world is Aurumania's Gold Bike Crystal edition. It is almost entirely plated with twenty-four karat gold, even the spokes. The seat is made of the finest leather while the handlebar grips are made with hand-sewn, chocolate-brown leather. It's also decorated with over 600 Swarovski crystals. Cost? $114,464. Sweet—but where would you ride it?

BIRTHDAYS:

1943—John Newcombe, great Australian tennis pro (Wimbledon champion, 1967, 1970, 1971)

1969—Pat Hurst, San Leandro, CA, LPGA golfer (1995 Rookie of the Year)

1979—Brian Campbell, Strathroy, Ontario, NHL defenseman (Sharks, Sabres, Blackhawks)

Cheers and **Boos**

On this day in 1991, Gregg Jefferies wrote an open letter to the Mets' fans that was read on sports-talk radio station WFAN.

Gregg Jefferies was a solid baseball player. He had a good career in the major leagues, playing from 1987 to 2000 with the Mets, Royals, Cardinals, Phillies, Angels, and Tigers. He even made two all-star teams. Through those fourteen years, Gregg was often cheered when he made great plays in the field or came through at the plate. Yet in 1991 he was booed so much and criticized by his teammates that he wrote this letter to the radio station: "I can only hope that one day those teammates who have found it convenient to criticize me will realize that we are all in this together. If only we can concentrate more on the games than complaining and bickering and pointing fingers, we would all be better off." He had gone from hero to enemy, from being idolized to being hated.

Most professional athletes have learned how easily the cheers can turn into jeers. And some fans can get very abusive toward players, with their words and actions. Great players learn to tune out the boos, and they understand that they have to do what they are paid to do, to the best of their ability, and not worry about what the crowd thinks or does.

Jesus saw the crowds turn on him. Remember Palm Sunday? During what we know as the triumphal entry, Jesus rode into Jerusalem on the back of a donkey as people lined the road, waving palm branches, cheering, and treating him like royalty (John 12:12–15).

But just a few days later, the crowds were screaming at him and calling for his death (Mark 15:13–15).

During your life, you will experience success and failure. You'll hear people cheering and saying great things about you. At other times, you'll feel the sting of insults, and you'll be misunderstood and unfairly criticized. Just remember that regardless of what your "fans" think on any given day, what God thinks is all that counts. And you're one of his all-stars. Just keep doing what you have been called to do to the best of your ability—to glorify God. That's all that matters.

ALSO ON THIS DAY . . .

1935—In the first major league night baseball game in Cincinnati, the Reds beat the Phillies 2-1.

1987—Al Unser Sr., forty-seven, won his fourth Indianapolis 500 race.

2009—Michael Allen won the Senior PGA Championship in Beachwood, Ohio. He became only the fourth golfer ever, and the first since Jack Nicklaus in 1990, to win a major on his Champions Tour debut.

2010—The Elephant Polo Tournament began in Thailand.

BIRTHDAYS:

1975—Katie King, USA ice hockey forward (Olympics, 1998)

1982—DaMarcus Beasley, Ft. Wayne, IN, soccer forward US national team

1990—Joey Logano, Middletown, CT, NASCAR driver

Let us fix our eyes on Jesus, the author and perfecter of our faith, who for the joy set before him endured the cross, scorning its shame, and sat down at the right hand of the throne of God. **Hebrews 12:2**

Fun Fact
Greg Jefferies was the Minor League Player of the Year for both 1986 and 1987, hitting .367 with 20 home runs, 48 doubles, and 101 RBIs, earning Jefferies a call-up by the New York Mets at the end of the 1987 season. At the age of nineteen, he was the youngest player in the major leagues that season.

What sport did they play?

Match the President to his favorite sport(s)

1. Grover Cleveland

a. Cyclist

2. George H. W. Bush

b. Football, track, and swimming

3. Gerald Ford

c. Walking and jogging

4. Jimmy Carter

d. Basketball

5. George W. Bush

e. Baseball, soccer, and basketball

6. Ronald Reagan

f. Football

7. Theodore Roosevelt

g. Fishing

8. Barack Obama

h. Football and sailing

9. John F. Kennedy

i. Track and cross country

10. Dwight D. Eisenhower

j. Riding

11. Ulysses S. Grant

k. Football, swimming, and skiing

12. Bill Clinton

l. Boxing and tennis

ANSWERS: 1.g, 2.e, 3.k, 4.i, 5.a, 6.b, 7.l, 8.d, 9.h, 10.f, 11.j, 12.c

Playing for **Kicks**

On this day in 2009, Barcelona beat Manchester United 2–0 to win their third European Cup.

Soccer (or football as they call it in Europe) is huge, worldwide, and Manchester United is one of the most popular teams. Although compared to sports like baseball, football, and basketball, scoring is very limited, the sport takes great skill and endurance, with many players running almost continually during each forty-five-minute half. People who don't know much about the sport may consider it "boring" because of the lack of offense. But fans appreciate the plays, pinpoint passing, ball control, and dramatic goalkeeping saves.

One joke or comment that most soccer players are probably sick of hearing goes something like this: "I'll bet you get a kick out of playing soccer!"

That's because soccer players, except the goalies, cannot use their hands; thus most of the plays are made with their feet—and that involves lots of kicking.

Getting a "kick" out of soccer is more than a play on words. Playing a sport (and watching, too) should be fun. But too often we take these games much too seriously. For some, winning and losing is like life and death. Some players are so driven that they will do almost anything to win: bend the rules, break the rules, fight, try to intimidate the officials, and so forth. Some coaches, fans, and team owners have the same attitude.

Parents can be guilty, too, when their kids are playing youth soccer (or another sport). Even with children of six or seven, when no one is supposed to be keeping score, they do and then announce who won. And they can pressure their kids so much that they take all the fun out of it.

We need to remember that these are games, not life. Sure we play to win, but in elementary, middle, and high school sports, especially, where big bucks aren't involved, winning is not everything. Christians certainly should know this and remember that our main purpose should be to glorify God in all we do. He's way more important than any earthly competition.

Play the game. Do your best. Have fun!

ALSO ON THIS DAY . . .

1961—Ralph Boston of the United States set the long jump record at 27'½".

1984—Joanne Carner won the LPGA Corning Golf Classic.

1992—The last-place Braves beat the Phillies at Veterans Stadium, 9-3, beginning a 78-37 run that would propel Atlanta to its second straight West Division title.

2008—In the ICC World Cricket League Division Five, the United States 107/4 (28.1/33 ov.) beat Germany 104 (32.4/33 ov.) by 6 wickets.

BIRTHDAYS:

1954—Catherine Carr, Albuquerque, NM, American breaststroke swimmer and winner of two Olympic gold medals, 1972

1974—Danny Wuerffel, Ft. Walton Beach, FL, NFL quarterback (Saints, Packers, Bears, Redskins) and Heisman Trophy winner in 1996 (University of Florida)

1983—Bobby Convey, Philadelphia, PA, American soccer winger on the US National team and MLS (San Jose Earthquakes)

Not that I have already obtained all this, or have already been made perfect, but I press on to take hold of that for which Christ Jesus took hold of me. **Philippians 3:12**

FUN FACT Manchester United is one of the most successful clubs in the history of English football, having won a record 18 league titles and a record 11 Football Association Challenge Cups. The club is one of the wealthiest and most widely supported football teams in the world.

28 Blindsided

On this day in 1986, Michael Oher, NFL offensive tackle (Baltimore Ravens), was born in Memphis, Tennessee.

Michael Oher's story is told in the book by Michael Lewis, *The Blind Side: Evolution of a Game* (2006), and in the 2009 film, *The Blind Side*.

One of twelve children, Michael was born into poverty and to a cocaine-addicted mother. During his childhood, he attended eleven different schools during his first nine years as a student. Often during that time he was homeless when he wasn't being shuttled between foster homes. Eventually, through an adult friend, he was able to enroll in Briarcrest Christian School.

The film about Michael centers on Leigh Anne and Sean Tuohy and their children. After learning of Michael's situation, they reached out to him, bringing him into their home. As strong Christians, the Tuohys felt compelled to show Christ's love to this teenage boy. And despite differences in background, culture, and race, they welcomed him and became his family.

After high school, Michael enrolled at the University of Mississippi, where he played football for the Ole Miss Rebels all four years, earning all-American honors at left tackle. He graduated in 2009 with a degree in criminal justice and was drafted by the Ravens in the first round.

Although "Big Mike" was huge by any standard (now 6'4" and 310 lbs), most looked right past him—to them he was invisible. But not to the Tuohys. They saw Michael and his need, and they did what they thought God was telling them to do, reaching out with love, the love of Christ.

You don't have your own home, money, job, and car—you're not old enough to be able to do that. But you can see the "invisible" kids in your school and neighborhood and reach out to them. Maybe they just need a listening ear, a friend, or an invitation to a party or to church. Maybe they need someone to help with tough homework, or maybe they'd appreciate a ride instead of having to walk everywhere. Other people may be blind to these kids, but not you. The people you touch probably won't ever play NFL football, but your influence could make a big difference, now and in the years to come.

ALSO ON THIS DAY . . .

1951—After going 0-for-12, Willie Mays connected for his first home run.

1958—Marlene Hagge won the LPGA Land of Sky Golf Open.

1980—Joe Darby did a standing long jump of 12'5".

2006—Sam Hornish Jr. won his first Indianapolis 500, beating Marco Andretti by just six feet, despite having to serve a drive-through penalty thirty laps from the end after leaving the pits with his fuel hose still attached.

> Carry each other's burdens, and in this way you will fulfill the law of Christ.
> Galatians 6:2

FUN FACT *The Blind Side* stars Quinton Aaron as Michael Oher alongside Sandra Bullock and Tim McGraw as the Tuohys. Nominated for Academy Awards for both Best Picture and Best Actress, it lost best picture to *The Hurt Locker*. But Sandra Bullock won the Oscar for Best Actress.

BIRTHDAYS:

1968—Sandra Bacher, Long Island, NY, half-heavyweight judoka (Olympics, 1992, 1996)

1973—Todd Sweeris, Grand Rapids, MI, table tennis player (Olympics, 1996)

1975—Mike Fisher, Naperville, IL, soccer midfielder (Olympics gold medal winner, 1996)

1983—Steve Cronin, Sacramento, CA, American soccer goalkeeper (MLS Earthquakes, Galaxie, Timbers, United)

SANDRA BULLOCK

Casey's Case

On this day in 2001, the US Supreme Court ruled that disabled golfer Casey Martin could use a cart to ride in tournaments.

An all-American golfer at Stanford University, Casey Martin won the Sahalee Players Championship in 1993 and the NCAA Championship (his team) in 1994. He turned professional in 1995. He did this without veins that carry blood from his right leg back to his heart, a painful disability known as Klippel-Tranauney-Weber Syndrome. The blood goes down the leg but doesn't come back, causing great pain and swelling, and it makes the bones brittle, getting worse every year. Casey has to wear a support stocking on that leg to be able to walk at all. The stocking helps push the blood back up his leg, and he has to keep the leg elevated as much as possible. The disease has no cure.

Imagine Casey's pain in walking a golf course. Casey knew that he couldn't continue competitive golf unless he could use a cart. The NCAA permitted it for his junior and senior seasons. But the PGA said no. They thought that riding would give him an unfair advantage over all the other golfers who had to walk. The Supreme Court overruled them, and Casey was allowed to use the cart.

The media reported all this, but they didn't report Casey's strong Christian faith. Casey has used his success in golf as a platform for telling others about Christ. Although he would love God to heal him, he understands the truth of James 1:2–4 (NLT): "Dear brothers and sisters, when troubles come your way, consider it an opportunity for great joy. For you know that when your faith is tested, your endurance has a chance to grow. So let it grow, for when your endurance is fully developed, you will be perfect and complete, needing nothing."

Casey knows that God has been teaching him lessons through this trial, and that he has grown and matured through it.

What a great lesson. When we have problems, conflicts, and setbacks, we can ask God to remove them—that's fine. But we also should be asking, "What is God doing in me in this trial?" and then look for how we can give glory to God.

Remember, God is using your troubles to make you "perfect and complete, needing nothing"!

ALSO ON THIS DAY . . .

1911—The first Indianapolis 500 race was run.

1953—Sir Edmund Hillary (from New Zeland) and Tenzing Norgay (Nepal) were the first to ascend to the summit of Mt. Everest (the highest point on earth).

1977—Sue Press became the first woman golfer to hit consecutive holes-in-one.

1980—Larry Bird beat out Magic Johnson for the NBA rookie of the year.

BIRTHDAYS:

1961—Todd Boonstra, Minneapolis, MN, cross country skier, 1994 Olympics

1975—Bianca Langham, Australian field hockey fullback/halfback, 1996 Olympics

1984—Carmelo Anthony, Brooklyn, NY, all-star NBA small forward (Denver Nuggets)

No discipline seems pleasant at the time, but painful. Later on, however, it produces a harvest of righteousness and peace for those who have been trained by it.
Hebrews 12:11

Fun Fact
Casey Martin was a straight-A student growing up. He can also play the piano.

Balance

On this day in 1958, Ty Scott Page, known as one of the most innovative skateboarders in the world, was born in Hermosa Beach, California.

Ty entered his first skateboarding competition in 1973. Later, at the Santa Barbara Skateboard Championships, he won first with long-nose wheelies, headstands, and 360s. Ty ("Mr. Incredible") was a leader in the 1970s skateboard world and was always trying new moves, going bigger and faster each time. He would do four new tricks per show and invented over fifty moves. Ty was inducted into the Thrasher Skateboard Hall of Fame in 1998.

Riding a skateboard is tricky—just standing on one can be a challenge because it's wobbly and can shift abruptly on those wheels. So imagine the difficulty of moving fast, turning quickly, shifting weight, jumping, and landing while absorbing the shock, all without falling. Certainly this takes great skill and agility. But of utmost importance is balance. Lose your balance and you crash.

Have you ever heard of "the balanced life"? It stresses the importance of living with balance in all the areas of life: physical, social, mental, and spiritual. If we're overloaded in one area, we can be thrown off course. For example, someone could focus almost totally on the physical area, working out, playing sports, and so forth . . . and watch their grades go down the tubes. A person could concentrate almost 100 percent on the mental area, hitting the books, obsessing on grades, and so forth . . . and have no friends and poor health. Or someone could be a social animal, spending every spare moment with friends, at parties, and so forth . . . and fail in school. And usually the spiritual area is the most neglected of all.

Luke 2:52 describes Jesus' growing-up years and says that he grew in all four areas. God created us as spiritual, mental, social, and physical beings, and he wants us to be like Jesus and to develop in all those areas and not exclude any of them. Here's the most important point: Christ should be at the center of it all. God has something to say about all of life, not just what we do at church, and we'll do great in all areas if we listen to him and do what he says.

Stay on board—stay balanced.

ALSO ON THIS DAY . . .

1937—The second-largest crowd in Polo Grounds history, 61,756, saw the Dodgers end Carl Hubbell's consecutive-game winning streak at twenty-four.

1953—Maureen Connolly beat Doris Hart to win the twenty-third French Women's Tennis tournament.

1991—Arturo Barrios ran a world record one-hour distance, 21,096 meters (13.11 miles).

2009—The University of Texas defeated Boston College in the longest NCAA baseball game played in terms of innings played, 3–2 in 25 innings.

Jesus grew in wisdom and in stature and in favor with God and all the people.
Luke 2:52, NLT

Fun Fact Ty had incredible multi-faceted, rapid-fire technique and footwork. In order to photograph his footwork, *SkateBoarder* magazine had to buy a new high-speed camera to catch him on film for their August and September 1977 issues.

BIRTHDAYS:

1968—Amy Fuller, Westlake, CA, rower (Olympics, 1992, 1996)

1972—Manny Ramirez, Santo Domingo, Dominican Republic, All-Star major league outfielder (Cleveland Indians, Boston Red Sox, Los Angeles Dodgers)

1984—Jordan Palmer, Westlake Village, CA, NFL quarterback (Washington Redskins, Cincinnati Bengals)

A Higher **Calling**

On this day in 2002, Pat Tillman enlisted in the US Army Rangers.

Pat Tillman began his college football career at Arizona State University as a linebacker in 1994. Although he was small for that position (5'11"), he excelled and as a senior was named Pac-10 Conference Player of the Year. He was also a good student, graduating in three and a half years with a 3.84 GPA. The Arizona Cardinals chose Pat in the 1998 NFL Draft and moved him to safety, where he started ten games as a rookie. He loved playing in Arizona and at one point turned down a five-year, $9 million contract offer from the St. Louis Rams out of loyalty to the Cardinals. The events of September 11, 2001, affected Pat deeply, so he and his brother,

Kevin, gave up their athletic careers to enlist in the US Army. Pat, in fact, rejected a contract offer of $3.6 million over three years from the Cardinals to enlist. After completing the Ranger Indoctrination Program, Pat and Kevin were assigned to the seventy-fifth Ranger Regiment in Fort Lewis, Washington. Pat graduated from that program after participating in Operation Iraqi Freedom and later was deployed to Afghanistan. On April 22, 2004, he was killed in a friendly-fire incident while on patrol.

What would cause this gifted young man with such a lucrative and productive NFL career to give it up and join the Army? His sense of patriotism and duty. He left everything to do what he felt was right.

One day a rich young man came to Jesus and asked what he could do to gain eternal life. Jesus said, "Sell everything you have and give to the poor, and you will have treasure in heaven. Then come, follow me" (Luke 18:22). Jesus was saying, "give it

up and join me." In this case the man walked away, unwilling to turn his back on what he had to turn toward Christ.

That's what God wants—our complete devotion. Nothing should stand between us and Jesus, not friends, sports, possessions, or future plans. He wants all of us, sold out for him.

Pat Tillman gave up money and fame to serve his country. What will you give up to serve your Lord, an even greater calling?

ALSO ON THIS DAY . . .

1859—The Philadelphia Athletics organized to play "town ball," which became baseball twenty years later.

1990—Dana Miller-Mackie won the BPAA US Women's Bowling Open.

2009—Ben Spies won both races in the Miller Superbike World Championship round in Tooele, Utah.

2009—The United States beat Ireland in the mid-year test series in Rugby in Santa Clara, California.

BIRTHDAYS:

1943—Joe Namath, Beaver Falls, PA, Hall-of-Fame NFL quarterback (New York Jets)

1955—Laura Baugh, Gainesville, FL, LPGA golfer

1981—Jake Peavy, Mobile, AL, Cy Young Award winning major-league pitcher (San Diego Padres, Chicago White Sox)

Whoever finds his life will lose it, and whoever loses his life for my sake will find it. **Matthew 10:39**

Fun Fact After his death, the Pat Tillman Foundation was established to carry forward Tillman's legacy by inspiring and supporting those striving for positive change in themselves and the world around them. In September 2008, Rory Fanning, a fellow Army Ranger, began his "Walk for Pat" to raise money and awareness for the foundation. The stated fundraising goal was $3.6 million—the value of the contract Tillman turned down when he decided to enlist in the military.

Featured Events in *May*

Find the correct answers on the days in parentheses.

1. What year did Greg Maddox pitch his 350th career win? (May 10)

2. **What is geocaching? (May 3)**

3. When did fisherman Les Anderson catch his record 97 lb. 4 oz. chinook salmon? (May 17)

4. **For what professional football team did Pat Tillman play? (May 31)**

5. What is the most expensive bicycle in the world? (May 23)

6. **How many league titles has Manchester United won? (May 27)**

7. How many errors did the Detroit Tigers commit in a 1901 game vs. the Chicago White Sox? (May 1)

8. **In 2008, why did number one women's tennis star Justine Henin retire? (May 14)**

9. What tennis match was the longest ever played? (May 21)

10. **In what sport did Ty Scott Page compete? (May 30)**

11. What Major League Baseball player was selected for the all-star game every year he played? (May 15)

12. **How long was Lou Gehrig's** consecutive game streak? (May 2)

13. What position did the Mets' Kevin Elster play? (May 9)

14. **Other than playing golf, what is another of Casey Martin's talents? (May 30)**

15. Who first broke the four-minute mile? (May 6)

16. **Where was Baltimore Ravens' Michael Oher born? (May 28)**

17. In 2005, who was the second-oldest player to hit a home run in Major League Baseball history? (May 7)

18. **In what sport does South African double-amputee Oscar Pistorius compete? (May 16)**

19. For what Major League Baseball team did Gregg Jefferies play in 1991? (May 24)

20. **With what team did Willis Reed play in the NBA? (May 8)**

21. How many LPGA tournaments has Annika Sörenstam won? (May 22)

22. **On December 31, 1988, what weather condition affected the Bears-versus-Eagles game? (May 13)**

23. Why did policemen raid the Cubs' bleachers in 1920? (May 20)

First-Round **Draft Choice**

ON THIS DAY IN 1991, THE NEW YORK YANKEES SELECTED NINETEEN-YEAR-OLD BRIEN TAYLOR NUMBER ONE IN THE AMATEUR DRAFT.

Getting chosen number one in the draft is a big deal. It means the team choosing thought the athlete was the best available player. And that's what the Yankees thought about Brien Taylor in 1991. He had a 99 mph fast ball, and in his senior year of high school, he struck out 213 hitters while walking only 28 in 88 innings. One agent remarked that Taylor was the best high school pitcher he had ever seen. So Brien was drafted and then signed for $1.55 million. Yet because of injuries, just a few years later he was out of baseball. The money was spent, and he was struggling to make ends meet, living with his parents, working as a bricklayer, and trying to pay child support as the father of five daughters.

That story is often repeated with other highly prized athletes—so much promise that for any variety of reasons goes unfulfilled. Being chosen number one is one thing; living it out is another.

All who believe in Christ have been chosen, too—by God. The apostle Paul writes, "He chose us in him before the creation of the world" (Ephesians 1:4). Peter adds that we are "chosen people" (1 Peter 1:9).

Here's the deal—God didn't choose us because of how we looked or how smart we were or how fast we could run or throw a ball or anything like that. He just chose us because he decided to. He loves us and has great plans for us. And here's more good news: he is working in us to help us achieve our full potential, to be all that he wants us to be.

So whenever you're feeling down, just think, "I was chosen in the first round of the heavenly draft, by God himself." That's pretty special.

....

ALSO ON THIS DAY . . .

1851—The first baseball uniforms were worn, with the New York Knickerbockers wearing straw hats, white shirts, and blue long trousers.

1989—The Houston Astros beat the Los Angeles Dodgers 5-4 in twenty-two innings, with the game lasting more than seven hours.

1995—Montreal Expos pitcher Pedro Martinez's perfect game was broken up in the tenth inning as San Diego's Bip Roberts led off with a double (Montreal won 1-0).

2006—The Chicago Rush beat the San Jose Saber Cats 59-56 in the Arena Football League American Conference Championship Game.

And I am certain that God, who began the good work within you, will continue his work until it is finally finished on the day when Christ Jesus returns. **Philippians 1:6, NLT**

FUN FACT Yankees owner George Steinbrenner was suspended from baseball at the time of the 1991 amateur draft. Through the media, he said that if the Yankees let Taylor get away, they should be "shot."

BIRTHDAYS:

1962—Connie Price-Smith, St. Charles, IL, shot-putter and discus thrower (1988 and 1996 Olympics)

1970—Andrea Congreaves, English WNBA forward/center (Charlotte Sting, Orlando Miracle)

1986—Rafael Nadal, Spanish professional tennis player, winner of eight Grand Slam events and the Olympic gold medal, 2008

4 Keep Your Eye **on the Ball**

On this day in 1927, the United States beat England 9½-2½ at Worcester Country Club (Massachusetts) to win the first Ryder Cup.

The Ryder Cup is a trophy awarded to the winner of matches played between teams from the United States and Europe. These matches, jointly administered by the PGA of America and the PGA European Tour, take place every other year, over three days. Although all the players are professionals, they take this competition very seriously, almost as through they were on a college team.

Golf may seem simple—just hit a small white ball and chase it down the fairway—but playing golf well takes coordination, skill, and lots and lots of practice. One common mistake made by non-professionals is to lift one's head too soon when swinging the club, almost like trying to see where the ball is going before it has been hit.

That's why golf coaches and instructors often remind their players, "Keep your head down. Keep your eye on the ball."

Actually, the coach's reminder is good advice in lots of sports. A kicker in football and soccer needs to keep his or her eye on the ball and follow through. On defense, a basketball player has to always know where the ball is. A football receiver needs to watch the ball, looking it into his or her hands. And certainly all baseball players, whether hitting or fielding, need to follow that advice.

That's why the phrase "keep your eye on the ball" has been used in many areas of life. It simply means concentrate on the task at hand, keep your focus, watch what you are doing. If you look away, you'll top it, miss it, drop it, or strike out.

In the Christian life, this means keeping focused on Christ. We shouldn't let anything distract us from following him. Not turning to the right or to the left, we keep going straight for the goal.

Keep your eye on the ball!

ALSO ON THIS DAY . . .

1964—Los Angeles Dodger Sandy Koufax pitched his third no-hitter to beat the Philadelphia Phillies, 3-0.

1974—On ten-cent beer night in Cleveland, unruly fans stumbled onto the field and caused the Indians to forfeit the game to the Rangers with the score tied 5-5 in the ninth.

1988—Kay Cottee sailed into Sydney Harbor as the first woman to circle the globe alone.

2005—Justine Henin-Hardenne won her second French Open title in three years, defeating 2000 champion and French citizen Mary Pierce 6-1, 6-1.

BIRTHDAYS:

1965—Andrea Jaeger, Chicago, IL, professional tennis player (retired as a teenager)

1975—Betty Okino, Uganda, US gymnast (1992 Olympics)

1985—Evan Lysacek, Naperville, IL, American figure skater and gold medal winner at the 2010 Winter Olympics

Let your eyes look straight ahead, fix your gaze directly before you. Make level paths for your feet and take only ways that are firm. Do not swerve to the right or the left; keep your foot from evil. Proverbs 4:25–27

Fun Fact
In the 1999 Ryder Cup, a great comeback helped the US to a 14.5-13.5 victory after trailing 10-6 heading into the final day. When Justin Leonard holed the deciding forty-five-foot putt, a wild celebration broke out, with other US players, their wives, and some fans running onto the green—very inappropriate behavior. Later, many US team members apologized.

A Student of **the Game**

On this day in 1977, the Los Angeles Dodgers retired Walter Alston's number 24.

Although Walter Alston played in the big leagues (briefly), he made his mark in baseball as a manager. The amazing fact about his time in that role is that he was able to manage one team, the Dodgers, his whole career—twenty-three years, beginning in 1954. Team owners tend to replace their managers fairly quickly; these days, some only last a year or two on the job. And during this time, Alston never had a multi-year contract, signing them one year at a time.

Alston's teams won seven National League pennants, and this was before the days of "wild cards" and playoffs. In 1955 he led Brooklyn to the pennant and its only World Series championship. After the Dodgers moved to Los Angeles, they won the National League in 1959, 1963, 1965, 1966, and 1974 and the championship in 1959, 1963, and 1965. He was the first Dodger manager to win a World Series. Alston won Manager of the Year six times, and he managed the NL All-Star squad a

record seven times, all victories. His career record stands at 2,063 wins (2,040 in the regular season and 23 in the postseason). He was elected to the Hall of Fame in 1983.

Walter Alston was known for his scholarly approach—he was a student of the game. This was way before computer analyses and printouts. He listened to his scouts and knew his players as well as the opposition. His teams played together and played solid, fundamental baseball . . . and they won, again and again.

Are you a student of the game? Life is much more important than an athletic contest, so we should be even more careful about finding the truth and making right choices. This is serious business. Teams and individuals who rush onto the field of play without thinking through their offensive or defensive moves lose.

Our opposition is Satan, who the Bible says prowls around like a lion (1 Peter 5:8), so we should know his tactics, where he might strike, and be ready. Personal Bible

study is important. So are worship services, Sunday school classes, and Christian mentors.

Don't be casual about your faith. Be a student of the game.

....

ALSO ON THIS DAY . . .

1952—In the first sporting event televised nationally, Jersey Joe Walcott beat Ezzard Charles in fifteen rounds for the heavyweight boxing title.

1981—Astros' Nolan Ryan passed Early Wynn as the all-time walks leader (1,777).

1993—Julie Krone won the 125th Belmont Stakes horse race aboard Colonial Affair, in 2:29.8.

2005—Rafael Nadal beat Mariano Puerta for the men's singles title in the French Open tennis tournament.

[FUN FACT] A reporter once asked Alston about his playing record; he said, "Well, I came up to bat for the Cards back in '36, and Lon Warneke struck me out. That's it." He also played first base—two fielding chances, one error.

BIRTHDAYS:

1945—John Carlos, Harlem, NY, track star (Olympic bronze medal winner in 1968, where he gave the black power salute on the medal stand)

1964—Laura Charameda, Marshall, MI, cyclist (1996 Olympics)

1983—Marques Colston, Harrisburg, PA, NFL wide receiver (New Orleans Saints)

Risky **Business**

On this day in 1966, the National Football League and the American Football League announced their merger.

In 1920, the National Football League was formed, originally called the American Professional Football Association. The league grew in size and popularity through the years and had virtually no competition until 1959, when the American Football League burst onto the scene. With creative changes to the game (for example, the two-point conversion) and broadcasting and a nice television contract, this rival league was highly successful, forcing the merger of the two leagues. A new NFL was formed, with two conferences—the AFC and the NFC—greatly expanding the league and beginning the annual championship game, the Super Bowl.

One reason for the success of the AFL was their wide-open offensive style, featuring passing and big plays, while the NFL was much more conservative on offense and, thus, boring. These days, a team's style mostly depends on the coach's philosophy.

Sometimes the defensive strategy can become quite conservative as well, especially when a team has a lead near the end of the game. Not wanting to risk giving up a big play, the coaches often revert to a "prevent defense." This involves the defensive backs playing off the receivers to make sure that no one gets behind them. Of course that leaves the middle of the field wide open. People critical of this strategy say that the only thing the "prevent defense" prevents is victory.

Successful teams play to win. Those who play not to lose usually do. It happens in all sports. Athletes who play "not to lose" become tentative, less aggressive, and allow the opposition to take the game to them. Winning coaches, athletes, and teams understand that they will need to take risks; they can't just play it safe and be successful.

That's a great lesson for life, and it's one that Jesus made several times. In his parable about the talents, the servant called "wicked and lazy" is the one who buried the talent—he played it safe. Jesus expects us to take action for him and his cause, and that will involve risk. But people who lose everything here gain everything there. With the risks come the rewards.

Be a risk-taker for Christ.

ALSO ON THIS DAY . . .

1937—Trailing St. Louis 8-2, the Phillies forfeited the game.

1985—Chris Evert beat Martina Navratilova to win the fifty-fifth French Open Women's Championship.

1986—Jurgen Schull set the world discus record (74.04m).

2007—The Anaheim Ducks beat the Ottawa Senators four games to one to win the Stanley Cup. Scott Niedermayer won the Conn Smythe Trophy as MVP of the playoffs.

BIRTHDAYS:

1907—Bill Dickey, Bastrop, LA, New York Yankee Hall-of-Fame catcher and manager

1963—Dannette Leininger, Kailua, HI, team handball wing (1992 and 1996 Olympics)

1974—Brooke Wilkins, Australian softball pitcher (Olympics bronze medal winner, 1996)

> Whoever tries to keep his life will lose it, and whoever loses his life will preserve it. **Luke 17:33**

Fun Fact
After the merger, during the first four Super Bowls, the fans stayed loyal to their former leagues. For example, hundreds of Buffalo Bills fans met the New York Jets at the Buffalo airport for their post–Super Bowl III visit to play the Bills. The Jets also received standing ovations in opponents' stadiums in other former AFL cities.

Last and **First**

On this day in 2008, 38-1 long shot De'Tara won the Belmont Stakes horse race.

This was a huge upset. Big Brown had already won the Kentucky Derby and the Preakness Stakes and was favored to win the third jewel in racing's Triple Crown, the Belmont Stakes. He would have been the first Triple

Crown winner since Affirmed, thirty years ago to the day. Instead, Big Brown finished dead last as Da'Tara had a huge upset victory.

From first to last, and from last to first—if that sounds familiar, it should. Jesus said, "But many who are first will be last, and many who are last will be first" (Matthew 19:30). Jesus was always catching people by surprise, turning their expectations upside down—like the reverse roles of the winner and loser of the Belmont Stakes.

Jesus said that the "greatest" person would be a "servant" (Matthew 23:11), that those who "exalt" themselves will be "humbled" and vice versa (Matthew 23:12), and the only way to gain life is to lose it (John 12:25).

Those statements are the exact opposite of what we hear from voices in our society. They say that we need to assert ourselves, grasp all we can, push to get ahead, and get everything we "deserve." But that's because most people live as though this world is all there is. So, they say, we may as well "eat, drink, and be merry," for we'll soon be dead—

and that's it (Ecclesiastes 8:15).

God knows otherwise. He says that what we do on earth is important, but it's only a prelude to what comes after death. Heaven, eternal life with God, is all that truly counts. And there the "last will be first"!

Praise God.

....

ALSO ON THIS DAY . . .

1989—Zola Budd, the twenty-three-year-old Olympic barefoot South African runner, retired.

1994—Rickey Henderson (Oakland Athletics) stole his 1,100th base.

2007—Billy Donovan changed his mind about coaching the Orlando Magic and returned to the University of Florida.

2009—Roger Federer won the French Open for the first time and equaled Pete Sampras' record of fourteen Grand Slam men's singles title. He also becomes the sixth man in history to win all four Grand Slam tournaments.

BIRTHDAYS:

1970—Mike Modano, Livonia, MI, NHL forward (Team USA, Dallas Stars)

1975—Allen Iverson, Hampton, VA, NBA guard (Philadelphia 76ers)

1981—Anna Kournikova, Russian professional tennis player

Therefore, since we are surrounded by such a great cloud of witnesses, let us throw off everything that hinders and the sin that so easily entangles, and let us run with perseverance the race marked out for us. Hebrews 12:1

Fun Fact The American Triple Crown races are the Kentucky Derby (1¼ miles at Churchill Downs in Louisville, KY), the Preakness Stakes (1³/₁₆ miles at Pimlico Race Course in Baltimore, MD), and the Belmont Stakes (1½ miles at Belmont Park in Elmont, NY).

NBA Finals **History**

1. Who was the first team to win three consecutive NBA titles?
   a. Hawks
   b. Jazz
   c. Lakers
   d. Bobcats

2. Which former ABA team, by name, was the first to win an NBA championship?
   a. Houston Rockets
   b. San Antonio Spurs
   c. Detroit Pistons
   d. Washington Wizards

3. Who was the first team to lose three consecutive NBA championships?
   a. Charlotte Bobcats
   b. Orlando Magic
   c. Philadelphia/San Francisco Warriors
   d. New York Knicks

4. Who was the first player to receive the NBA Finals MVP award?
   a. Sam Jones
   b. Chet Walker
   c. Oscar Robertson
   d. Jerry West

5. How many times was Wilt Chamberlain the NBA Finals MVP in his career?
   a. 1
   b. 5
   c. 3
   d. 7

6. The Boston Celtics ran off eight consecutive NBA championships until which team in the 1966-67 season stopped their streak?
   a. Philadelphia 76ers
   b. Los Angeles Clippers
   c. Cincinnati Royals
   d. Chicago Storm

7. The Milwaukee Bucks went to their first Finals in franchise history in the 1970-71 season. They skunked the Baltimore Bullets four games to none. Who was the MVP of the series?
   a. Allen Iverson
   b. Oscar Robertson
   c. Kareem Abdul-Jabbar
   d. Steve Nash

8. How many three-point field goals did Michael Jordan score in the first half in the first game of the 1991-92 season NBA Finals?
   a. 4
   b. 5
   c. 6
   d. 7

9. What basketball legend played in his first NBA championship when the Miami Heat defeated the Dallas Mavericks in 2006?
   a. Alonzo Mourning
   b. Shaquille O'Neal
   c. Pat Riley
   d. LeBron James

10. What basketball team dominated the NBA in the 90s?
    a. Cleveland Cavaliers
    b. Chicago Bulls
    c. Orlando Magic
    d. Phoenix Suns

ANSWERS: 1.c, 2.b, 3.d, 4.d, 5.a, 6.a, 7.c, 8.c, 9.a, 10.b

Youth is **Served**

On this day in 1944, Joe Nuxhall, fifteen, of the Cincinnati Reds, became the youngest player ever to appear in a modern-era Major League Baseball game.

Fifteen years old—now that's quite young to pitch in a big-league game! The team was short of players because of World War II, so Joe got the chance. Nuxhall went on to have a good career in Major League Baseball, mostly with the Reds. He was a two time all-star, and in his sixteen years in the majors, he compiled a 3.90 earned run average and a record of 135-117. Then he was a broadcaster for the Reds from 1967 through 2004.

Many young people are pressured to perform way too early. And, certainly, fifteen is much too young to be called up to play big-time baseball under normal circumstances. But sometimes people look down on kids and don't think they can do much of anything just because of their age. Then those people are surprised when a fourth grader begins collecting coats for the homeless, a fifth grader raises thousands of dollars for relief in Haiti, and a sixth grader leads a friend to Christ.

The Bible has several examples of young people who made a difference. When Jesus fed the more than 5,000 people, he used the lunch of a boy who volunteered his bread and fish (John 6:9). When Timothy was just a young man he became pastor of a church founded by his mentor, the apostle Paul. And the most dramatic case is Josiah, who was only eight years old when he was crowned king of Israel (2 Kings 22:1).

Obviously God can use people of any age to serve him, to do his work in the world. He just needs those who are willing to go where he leads and do what he says. This begins with doing what we already know he wants: keeping him at the center of our lives, loving others, honoring our parents, and sharing the good news. But he also may ask us to do something extraordinary. Are we ready?

Don't let your age hold you back from serving God. He wants to use you, big time.

....

ALSO ON THIS DAY . . .

1921—Babe Ruth became the all-time home run leader with number 120.

1973—Secretariat won the Triple Crown and became King of Horses.

2000—The New Jersey Devils beat the Dallas Stars four games to two to win the Stanley Cup.

2007—Jeff Gordon won the Pocono 500 (NASCAR) in Long Pond, PA.

BIRTHDAYS:

1976—Freddy Garcia, Caracas, Venezuela, Major League pitcher (Mariners, White Sox, Phillies, Tigers)

1977—Mike Rosenthal, Pittsburgh, PA, NFL offensive tackle (Giants, Vikings, Dolphins) and sports radio talk show host

1982—Tara Lipinski, Philadelphia, PA, figure skater (1998 Olympic gold medal winner)

Don't let anyone look down on you because you are young, but set an example for the believers in speech, in life, in love, in faith and in purity. 1 Timothy 4:12

Fun Fact Nuxhall is still the youngest person to play in a major-league game in the modern era (since 1901). In 1887, fourteen-year-old Fred Chapman pitched five innings in one game and is the youngest-ever participant in major-league history. Joe said, "I was pitching against kids thirteen and fourteen years old . . . All of a sudden, I look up and there's Stan Musial and the likes. It was a very scary situation."

JUNE

11 Bigger Than **Life**

On this day in 1955, a Le Mans race car accident killed eighty-four spectators, but the race continued.

This horrific crash occurred a couple of hours into the "24 Hours of Le Mans" race when one of the cars hit another car, flipped, flew into the air, broke apart, and burst into flames, killing the driver, Pierre Levegh, and 84 spectators, and injuring another 100. This was and is the worst accident in the history of motorsports. The race continued with officials saying that they wanted to prevent departing spectators (fleeing the scene or just going home if the race had been cancelled) from jamming the roads and slowing ambulances from getting to the crash site.

That explanation seems rather lame. Think about it—eighty-five people died and many more were injured, and race officials knew this, at the most, just a few hours later. Yet the race continued another twenty hours or

so. Was the race that important? More important than the tremendous human tragedy? Evidently so.

Actually we shouldn't be too surprised. These days, values seem to be twisted every which way except right. For many people, especially those with lots of money at stake, a game, tournament, race, or other competition becomes more important than anything, even life. In addition, some businesspeople put work ahead of their families. Certain politicians put personal ambitions before their duty to serve the people who elected them. And many men and women choose their own freedom and convenience over unborn and newly born children.

Certainly that's not what God wants—his Word makes that clear. The Great Commandment, which actually summarizes the Ten Commandments, says that we should love God with our "heart, soul, mind, and strength" (that

covers everything) and then our "neighbors as ourselves" (Mark 12:30–31). This means that nothing should come before him, and that the needs of others take precedence as well. No game, match, or race (or business deal, career path, advancement opportunity) is more important than human beings. Only God is bigger than life.

As you go through this day, think of how your priorities and values line up with God's.

ALSO ON THIS DAY . . .

1990—Nolan Ryan pitched his sixth no-hitter, beating Oakland.

1992—Tracy Austin, twenty-nine, became the youngest inductee into the International Tennis Hall of Fame.

2005—Former heavyweight champion Mike Tyson quit his fight with little-regarded Kevin McBride after six rounds, giving the large Irishman an unexpected victory.

2006—The Chicago Rush won the AFL Championship, beating the Orlando Predators 65-61 in Arena Bowl XX. The Rush became the first team with a sub-.500 regular season record (7–9) to win four games on the road and win the championship.

BIRTHDAYS:

1913—Vince Lombardi, Brooklyn, NY, legendary Hall-of-Fame NFL head coach (Green Bay Packers, Washington Redskins)

1956—Joe Montana, New Eagle, PA, one of the all-time great NFL quarterbacks (San Francisco 49ers, Kansas City Chiefs)

1964—Kim Gallagher, Philadelphia, PA, 800m runner (winner of Olympic silver medal, 1984)

1982—Diana Taurasi, Chino, CA, WNBA shooting guard/small forward (Phoenix Mercury)

If you think you are too important to help someone, you are only fooling yourself. You are not that important. Galatians 6:3, NLT

Fun Fact An official inquiry ruled that the car company was not responsible for the crash, that it was a racing incident. The spectators' deaths were blamed on inadequate safety standards for the track design. This led France, Spain, Switzerland, Germany, and other nations to ban motorsports until the tracks could meet a higher safety standard.

Three **Strikes**

ON THIS DAY IN 1981, MAJOR LEAGUE BASEBALL PLAYERS BEGAN A FIFTY-DAY STRIKE, THEIR THIRD STRIKE.

For baseball to have a third strike seems funny, since in the game of baseball, at each at bat the batter gets just three strikes. So we might think that would be it—no more strikes in baseball. That would be wishful thinking. In 1994, the players struck again, the eighth work stoppage in baseball history and the fourth in just twenty-three years. This strike led to the cancellation of about 940 games, including all the playoff games and the World Series. Thus Major League Baseball became the first professional sport to lose its entire postseason due to a labor dispute.

"Three strikes and you're out" is a very familiar baseball phrase. Why three—why not one? Who knows, but that's a rule of the game. Actually, batters are thankful that they get that many strikes (more, actually, since foul balls that hit the ground don't count). This way they can get their timing down as they swing, and maybe on the third swing they will connect. And with called strikes they can get an idea of the umpire's strike zone that day.

We use that expression in relationships, too. Someone hurts us once, and we let it slide. Even twice. But the third time is one too many, and the person is ruled "out" as far as we're concerned. With certain friends, we may stretch that beyond three, but, eventually, we reach the end of our forgiveness.

That's probably what was behind Peter's question when he asked Jesus how many times he should forgive someone. We'd probably say, "Three strikes and they're out, right?" Peter asked, "Lord, how often should I forgive someone who sins against me? Seven times?" Peter simply wanted to know the limit, and seven seemed generous enough. But Jesus answered, "No, not seven times but seventy times seven!" (Matthew 18:21–22, NLT). Jesus was saying, in effect, don't keep track—just keep forgiving.

Instead of counting and looking for a way to stop forgiving, we should be extending grace, trying to forgive. So when someone slights you, just write it off to that person having a bad day. Instead of being like an umpire, ready to "ring 'em up," be like a loving parent tossing the ball to a child, giving another chance to hit.

....

ALSO ON THIS DAY . . .

1839—The first baseball game was played in America.

2002—The Los Angeles Lakers beat the New Jersey Nets four games to zero to win the NBA Championship.

2005—Annika Sörenstam became the first woman since 1986 to win the first two majors of the year, winning the LPGA Championship. Second place went to fifteen-year-old Michelle Wie, the highest finish by an amateur in a major since 1998.

2007—Justin Verlander of the Detroit Tigers pitched a no-hitter against the Milwaukee Brewers, winning 4-0.

Make allowance for each other's faults, and forgive anyone who offends you. Remember, the Lord forgave you, so you must forgive others. **Colossians 3:13, NLT**

FUN FACT In the 1994 strike, before the season was officially canceled, Minnesota traded Dave Winfield to Cleveland for a "player to be named later," so no player was named. To settle the deal, the executives of the teams went to dinner, and Cleveland picked up the tab, meaning Winfield had been dealt for dinner.

BIRTHDAYS:

1941—Marv Albert, Brooklyn, NY, Basketball Hall-of-Fame sportscaster

1974—Hideki Matsui, Japanese Major League outfielder and designated hitter (New York Yankees, Anaheim Angels)

1979—Dallas Clark, Sioux Falls, SD, NFL tight end (Indianapolis Colts)

13 Integrity

On this day in 1994, Chicago Cub Ryne Sandberg retired due to his poor play, forfeiting $15.7 million of his $25 million contract.

Can you imagine walking away from 15.7 million dollars? Most of us would hobble onto the field if we could collect that much money for just showing up. But not Ryne Sandberg.

"Ryno" played nearly his entire career with the Chicago Cubs, playing second base as well as anyone in baseball history. He was selected to the National League All-Star team ten years in a row and won the Gold Glove (for fielding) at second base nine times, from 1983 through 1991. He holds the major-league record for fielding percentage at second base. He could hit, too, both for power and for average. Sandberg was elected to the Hall of Fame in 2005.

When Ryne retired, he didn't have to. His contract hadn't expired, and no one was pressuring him to leave. He just felt as though he wasn't playing up to his own standards. He had too much respect for the game to just take his paycheck. He didn't believe he should be paid if he couldn't perform well.

That's integrity—and, unfortunately, it is becoming increasingly rare in our world. Many people seem to put in their time on a job, and don't care much about how well they're doing. That's like cheating—it's dishonest.

Integrity means putting in an honest day's work for a day's pay. Integrity means living up to a contract or agreement— doing what we promised to do. Integrity means working hard, doing our best. And a true measure of a person's integrity is how he or she acts when no one is looking. Other words for *integrity* are *honesty*, *truthfulness*, *honor*, and *reliability*. God wants his people to be boys, girls, men, and women of their word.

The best word for *integrity* is *Christlike*. May that be said about you.

....

ALSO ON THIS DAY . . .

1914— Mary K. Browne beat Marie Wagner to win the twenty-eighth US Women's Tennis Championship.

1997— The Red Wings Vladmir Konstantinov and Slava Fetisov were seriously injured in an automobile accident.

2002— The Detroit Red Wings beat the Carolina Hurricanes four games to one to win the Stanley Cup.

2008— In the NASCAR Nationwide Series, Joey Logano won the Meijer 300 at Kentucky Speedway, becoming the youngest driver to win an event in the series' history (eighteen years, twenty-one days).

BIRTHDAYS:

1962—Hannah Storm, Oak Park, IL, sports journalist and commentator

1964—Jennifer Gillom, Abbeville, MS, WNBA center/forward (Phoenix Mercury), winner of the Olympic gold medal (1988), and coach (Minnesota Lynx and Los Angeles Sparks)

1973—Sam Adams, Houston, TX, NFL defensive tackle (Seahawks, Ravens, Raiders, Bills, Bengals, Broncos)

People with integrity walk safely, but those who follow crooked paths will slip and fall. **Proverbs 10:9, NLT**

Fun Fact Sandberg was drafted in the twentieth round of the 1978 amateur draft by the Philadelphia Phillies, and he began as a shortstop. Ryne is one of two Hall of Famers who came up through the Phillies farm system and earned their Hall-of-Fame credentials primarily as Cubs, the other being Ferguson Jenkins.

God's **People**

On this day in 1963, Eric Rupe, "old school" professional bicycle motocross (BMX) racer, was born in Reseda, California.

Eric has been called one of the most underrated professional BMX racers in history, with a long list of wins and achievements after his name. And he is admired by his peers and younger racers. He was inducted into the American Bicycle Association Hall of Fame in 1980. Although his prime competitive years were from 1978 to 1990, Eric continued to race into his forties. He won the USA Cycling BMX National Championship in the ABA Veteran pro class in 2009, at age forty-six.

Nicknamed "Big Daddy" because he's a family man, Eric is a dedicated father of three boys. He also is known for his faith. According to one description, "his clean-cut born-again Christian lifestyle and philosophy lent greatly to the family-man image."

That's quite a combination: world-class BMX racer, family man, born-again Christian. Those three descriptions aren't usually combined, especially with the wild image projected by many extreme sports enthusiasts. Knowing that God is using this man on this stage with this crowd encourages people of faith.

God has his people everywhere—on fields, courts, fairways, and tracks, in boats, starting blocks, huddles, and scrums, flipping on boards, twisting on ice, moving on snow, hitting targets, scoring goals, and riding bikes. Outstanding athletes are living for Christ and telling others about him.

This goes way beyond sports. We can find Christians in every part of society: business owners, elected officials, teachers, doctors, clerks, toll booth collectors, lawyers, machinists, farmers, executives, actors, cashiers, referees, writers, entertainers, plumbers, filmmakers, technicians, mechanics, landscapers . . . you name it. And God has strategically placed his people in homes, schools, and neighborhoods—all kinds of people, including you. Ask God to show you how you can be his person in your place.

ALSO ON THIS DAY . . .

1922—Gene Sarazen won the fifth PGA Championship at Oakmont CC, Oakmont, PA.

1989—Nolan Ryan became the second pitcher in Major League history to defeat all twenty-six teams.

1992—The Chicago Bulls won the forty-sixth NBA Championship, beating the Portland Trailblazers four games to two.

2007—Sidney Crosby of the Pittsburgh Penguins won the Hart Memorial Trophy as the most valuable player in the 2006-07 National Hockey League season.

BIRTHDAYS:

1958—Eric Heiden, Madison, WI, US speed skater (winner of five Olympic gold medals in 1980)

1967—Wendy Lian Williams, St Louis, MO, US diver (winner of two Olympic bronze medals, 1988, 1992)

1969—Steffi Graf, Bruhl, West Germany, former world number-one professional tennis player, winner of twenty-two Grand Slam titles, and the only tennis player (male or female) to achieve the Calendar Year Golden Slam by winning all four Grand Slam singles titles and the Olympic gold medal in the same calendar year

There are different kinds of spiritual gifts, but the same Spirit is the source of them all. There are different kinds of service, but we serve the same Lord. God works in different ways, but it is the same God who does the work in all of us. **1 Corinthians 12:4–6, NLT**

Fun Fact
Eric turned professional when he was fourteen years old. He retired from active competition when he was twenty-six.

Extreme Sport Scramble

1. romtsosoc _____

2. boangniwodrs _____

3. xbm _____

4. cclbiye ttnus _____

5. fsrkgnryius _____

6. cei libmincg _____

7. badnsaeorigkt _____

8. iinnel kagsntgi _____

9. terest geul _____

10. rtmbngspiiclo _____

Unscramble the letters in each word to determine the sport.

ANSWERS: 1. motocross, 2. snowboarding, 3. BMX, 4. bicycle stunt, 5. skysurfing, 6. ice climbing, 7. skateboarding, 8. inline skating, 9. street luge, 10. sportclimbing

150

Determined Love

ON THIS DAY IN 1965, DAN JANSEN, OLYMPIC SPEEDSKATER, WAS BORN IN WEST ALLIS, WISCONSIN.

West Allis is a speedskating center and location of the Petit National Ice Center. Dan was close to his sister, Jane, and followed her into the sport, where he excelled. In fact, at sixteen, he set a junior world record in the 500 meters, and, at eighteen, finished sixteenth in the 1000 meters and fourth in the 500 meters at the 1984 Winter Olympics.

Four years later, at the 1988 Olympics, Dan was favored to win both the 500- and 1000-meter races, having become world sprint champion one week before. But early on the day of the 500, he heard that Jane wasn't doing well (she was battling leukemia). Later that morning, Jane died. Dan competed in the 500 but fell. A few days later, in the 1000 meters, he started strong but fell again. So he left with no medals.

Determined to try another time, Dan entered the 1992 Olympics as the favorite again, especially since he held the world record in the 500 meters. But he finished out of the medals in both races.

Dan didn't give up and continued skating, winning his second World Sprint Championship in 1994. The Olympics would be held later that year, and he would give it one last shot. Then, in the 500 meters he finished eighth, and everyone assumed he would end his career medal-less. But he skated the 1000 meters in world-record time and won! Dedicating that gold medal to his beloved sister, he took an emotional victory lap around the rink, holding his one-year-old daughter, Jane.

What a great example of courage, persistence, and endurance! But Dan Jansen's story is primarily about love and family. Most people will never win an Olympic medal, but we all can learn from Dan's example, especially his love for his sister.

God gives us families and other special people for his reasons. We don't know how long we'll get to enjoy each other because life is so tenuous and short. So we need to value each relationship and each moment together.

Thank you, Lord, for moms, dads, sisters, and brothers—for all those we love and who love us. They are precious gifts.

....

ALSO ON THIS DAY . . .

1976—ABA teams (Nets, Pacers, Nuggets, and Spurs) merge into the NBA.

1994—O. J. Simpson didn't turn himself in on murder charges, and the Los Angeles police chased his white Ford Bronco for an hour before he surrendered.

1997—The NHL announced that it would add four new teams: Nashville in 1998, Atlanta in 1999, and Minneapolis-St. Paul and Columbus in 2000.

2007—Ángel Cabrera of Argentina, who had never won a PGA Tour event, won the US Open by one stroke over Tiger Woods and Jim Furyk.

BIRTHDAYS:

1923—Elroy "Crazylegs" Hirsch, Wausau, WI, NFL running back and wide receiver (Los Angeles Rams and Chicago Rockets)

1980—Venus Williams, Palm Beach Gardens, FL, professional tennis player, ranked as high as number one in the world (winner of seven Grand Slam singles titles)

1983—Donald Robinson, Napa, CA, American professional "New/Current School" Bicycle Motocross (BMX) racer

Consider it pure joy, my brothers, whenever you face trials of many kinds, because you know that the testing of your faith develops perseverance. **James 1:2–3**

Fun Fact Dan received the 1994 James E. Sullivan Award and was chosen by his fellow Olympians to carry the US flag at the closing ceremony. In 2004, Jansen was inducted into the United States Olympic Hall of Fame. He has also set up the Dan Jansen Foundation (to fight leukemia) in memory of his sister.

18 Dave's **Choice**

On this day in 1991, San Francisco Giant pitcher Dave Dravecky's cancerous left arm was amputated.

Dave Dravecky was enjoying a good career in Major League Baseball. In 1983, just his second season in the majors, this left-hander won fourteen games and represented the San Diego Padres in the all-star game. Then he helped the Padres win their first division pennant the next year. In 1987, Dave was traded to the Giants, and he pitched brilliantly, winning a shutout against the Cardinals in the playoffs, losing another game 1-0.

The next year doctors discovered a cancerous tumor in Dave's pitching arm. After surgery (October, 1988) and rehab, he began pitching again, and on August 10, 1989, he made his dramatic return to the major leagues, pitching eight innings and defeating the Reds 4-3. The next start began great,

with Dave pitching three no-hit innings. But he felt a tingling in his left arm two innings later. He kept pitching, but on his first pitch to the third batter of the sixth inning, his humerus bone snapped, and he collapsed in agony on the mound.

The Giants won the National League championship that summer, but in the post-game celebration, Dave's arm was broken again. When the doctor checked him out, he found a mass—the cancer had returned. Eighteen days later, he retired from baseball. Even after two more surgeries, his left arm continued to deteriorate, so, less than two years after his comeback with the Giants, Dave Dravecky's left arm and shoulder were amputated.

Imagine the pain, frustration, disappointment . . . and questioning of God and his plan. But Dave didn't sit and feel sorry for himself or give up. Instead, he turned his attention and energies toward helping others

and spreading the good news about Christ. Dave has written three books— *Comeback*, *When You Can't Come Back*, and *Called Up*—and he travels the country with the theme "Don't waste your life," telling about his experiences and pointing people to Christ.

When confronted with a serious issue or crisis, we have a choice. We can give up and become isolated and bitter. Or we can give in, submitting to God's will and leading and using our personal disaster for his glory.

What will you choose?

ALSO ON THIS DAY . . .

1960—Arnold Palmer shot 280 to win the sixtieth US Golf Open at Cherry Hills in Denver.

1972—The US Supreme Court, 5-3, confirmed lower-court rulings in the *Curt Flood* case, upholding baseball's exemption from antitrust laws.

1973—NCAA made urine testing mandatory for participants.

2006—In Major League Baseball, the "Seventh Inning Stretch" was moved to the sixth inning (that day only) to draw awareness to the fact that one in every six men get prostate cancer.

BIRTHDAYS:

1939—Lou Brock, El Dorado, AK, all-star leftfielder and one-time baseball stolen-base leader (Chicago Cubs, St. Louis Cardinals)

1966—Robert Kempainen, Minneapolis, MN, marathoner (1992 and 1996 Olympics)

1980—Antonio Gates, Detroit, MI, NFL tight end (San Diego Chargers)

We are hard pressed on every side, but not crushed; perplexed, but not in despair; persecuted, but not abandoned; struck down, but not destroyed. We always carry around in our body the death of Jesus, so that the life of Jesus may also be revealed in our body. **2 Corinthians 4:8–10**

Fun Fact Dave retired with a 64-57 record, 558 strikeouts, and a 3.13 ERA in 1,062.2 innings. In 1991, Dave and his wife, Jan, established Dave Dravecky's Outreach of Hope. The mission of the ministry is to offer comfort, encouragement, and hope through Jesus Christ to those who suffer from cancer, amputation, or serious illness.

Feeling **the Draft**

On this day in 1984, the Chicago Bulls drafted Michael Jordan, the third player chosen overall.

The 1984 National Basketball Association draft was held at Madison Square Garden in New York City. This group of drafted players is one of the best in NBA history, producing seven all-stars and four Hall of Famers. But it also had one of the biggest draft mistakes. Houston had chosen Hakeem Olajuwon as the draft's first pick, and Portland had the next choice. Instead of drafting Michael Jordan, they took Sam Bowie. Although Bowie was a fine player and might have enjoyed a good NBA career, his career was cut short by five leg surgeries, and he ended up playing only 139 games in five years with the Trailblazers.

Michael Jordan, on the other hand, became the greatest player in NBA history. During his brilliant career, mostly with the Bulls, Jordan won Rookie of the Year, ten All-NBA First Team designations, five MVP awards, nine All-Defensive First Team honors, fourteen NBA all-star teams (three-time MVP of the game), ten scoring titles, three steals titles, and NBA Defensive Player of the Year. His Bulls teams won six championships, and he won the MVP for the finals in all of them. He also won Olympic gold medals in 1984 and 1992.

What a difference a choice can make. Portland's took them in one direction, while the Bull's choice took them in quite another.

Our choices are important, and even little ones can make a huge difference. Someone chooses to do something wrong with a friend and begins a life in the wrong direction. Another chooses to study hard and moves toward a successful career. Bad choices can lead to hurt, sorrow, sin, and guilt. Good choices can lead to healing, joy, forgiveness, and life. The most important choice, of course, is what a person will do with Jesus. Only he offers eternal life, and God gives us the choice of following him or rejecting him. In the world's eyes, the Bulls made one of the all-time great choices. But choosing Christ means so much more.

Every day, think carefully about your choices, and honor God with them. By the way, he drafted you in the first round!

....

ALSO ON THIS DAY . . .

1936—German boxer Max Schmeling, World Champion, knocked out Joe Louis.

1977—The Boston Red Sox hit sixteen home runs, setting a three-game record against the New York Yankees.

1988—Thirty-two divers finished cycling underwater on a standard tricycle to complete 116.66 miles in seventy-five hours twenty minutes.

2000—Tiger Woods won golf's US Open by fifteen shots, a record for all majors, with a record score of twelve under par.

BIRTHDAYS:

1903—Lou Gehrig, New York City, NY, Hall-of-Fame MLB legend first baseman (New York Yankees)

1960—Patti Rizzo, Hollywood, FL, professional golfer and golf instructor and LPGA Rookie of the Year in 1982

1978—Dirk Nowitzki, Wursburg, Germany, all-star NBA power forward (Dallas Mavericks)

1987—Rashard Mendenhall, Skokie, IL, NFL running back (Pittsburgh

But if serving the Lord seems undesirable to you, then choose for yourselves this day whom you will serve, whether the gods your forefathers served beyond the River, or the gods of the Amorites, in whose land you are living. But as for me and my household, we will serve the Lord. **Joshua 24:15**

FUN FACT During his sophomore year in high school, Michael tried out for the varsity basketball squad, but the coach thought he was too short (5'11") to play at that level. His taller friend, Harvest Leroy Smith, was the only sophomore to make the team. That slight motivated Jordan, and he became the star of the junior varsity squad, with several forty-point games.

20 Touching All **the Bases**

On this day in 2007, Texas Ranger Sammy Sosa hit the 600th home run of his career in a game against the Chicago Cubs, with whom he had hit 545 home runs in thirteen seasons.

Sammy Sosa was a hero in Chicago, with his tape-measure home runs, little hop after hitting one, and interaction with the fans. In 1998, he and Mark McGwire were the talk of the nation with their home-run race, chasing Roger Maris' record. But Sammy was caught using a corked bat in a 2003 game, and then he had some strange injuries that kept him out of the lineup. When his home runs and clutch hits stopped, the fans soured on him. His last season as a Cub was 2004.

Sosa became only the fifth player in Major League Baseball history to hit 600 home runs. He is one of only two National League Players to ever reach 160 RBI, which he did in 2001. Also, in 1998, Sosa's 416 total bases were the most in a single season since Stan Musial's 429 in 1948. Sammy hit sixty plus home runs three years in a row. And he is the all-time home-run leader among foreign-born big league players.

With all that success, however, Sammy's image has been tarnished, as he has been accused of taking steroids to improve his performance. He denies this.

Anyone who hits a home run knows the importance of touching all the bases. Even if the ball goes out of the park, the hitter must touch them all. If one is missed, the run doesn't count. Can you imagine the batter saying, "I hit it far enough, so I think I'll just go back to the dugout!"? No good.

So people use that expression when they mean "make sure you do everything right" or "be sure to do what you have to, in the right order—don't forget anything." You need to "touch all the bases." Evidently Sammy missed a few of those in his career.

Touching all the bases in school means listening in class, doing homework, and studying for tests. At home it means taking care of your clothes and other things, doing your chores, and having a good attitude. Doing this spiritually means talking with God and reading his Word regularly, worshipping, being with Christians, and reaching out to others.

No shortcuts allowed—touch all the bases.

....

ALSO ON THIS DAY . . .

1968—Jim Hines became the first person to run 100 meters in under ten seconds.

1986—Jim Fregosi replaced Tony LaRussa as the Chicago White Sox manager.

1992—Kelly Saunders became the second female baseball announcer (Baltimore Orioles).

2006—Miami Heat won its first NBA championship in franchise history in six games, with Dwayne Wade named Finals MVP.

BIRTHDAYS:

1960—Donna Mayhew, DuPont, PA, javelin thrower (Olympics, 1988 and 1992)

1978—Bobby Seay, Sarasota, FL, MLB pitcher (Detroit Tigers, Tampa Bay Devil Rays, Colorado Rockies)

1983—Darren Sproles, Waterloo, IA, NFL running back (San Diego Chargers)

But if you look carefully into the perfect law that sets you free, and if you do what it says and don't forget what you heard, then God will bless you for doing it. **James 1:25, NLT**

Fun Fact When Sammy Sosa hit his 600th home run against the Cubs, it meant he had hit a home run against every active MLB team. With 545 home runs as a Cub, Sosa is the all-time home-run leader for that team.

Only a **Game**

On this day in 1947, Duane Thomas was born in Dallas, Texas.

You probably have never heard of Duane Thomas, but he was a good NFL running back, playing from 1970 to 1974 for the Dallas Cowboys and San Diego Chargers. Actually, the Cowboys tried to trade him to the Patriots before the 1971 season. But after a problem with the coach, the Patriots sent him back (the NFL allowed it). Evidently Duane wasn't the easiest player to get along with. As we might imagine, Duane wasn't happy with his old team for trying to get rid of him, so he didn't talk with any of the Cowboys personnel all season. He let his play on the field speak for him, and he helped lead the Cowboys to their first championship (Super Bowl VI), rushing for ninety-five yards and one touchdown and catching three passes.

Most experts assumed Duane Thomas had won the Super Bowl MVP, but Roger Staubach was announced as the winner, perhaps because Duane hadn't treated the media very well during the season, and he continued that routine before and after the big game. On Media Day, he had refused to answer any questions, sitting quietly until his required time had passed. After the game, a reporter asked him a long question that basically asked, "You're fast, aren't you?" Duane answered, "Evidently." But the reason he's featured here is his answer to another question. A reporter commented on how well Duane had performed in "the big game." Duane simply replied, "If it's so big, why do we play it every year?"

Good point. And his statement is true about every annual championship. We make a huge deal about the NCAA championships, the NFL, NBA, NHL, and MLB championships, and the various golf and tennis tournament winners. But almost as soon as each champion has been crowned, talk begins about the next year (Will they repeat? Who's favored to win?), and the media turn to the next big event.

Winning a title is great, especially something with "state," "national," or "world" in it. But that victory should not be the ultimate goal of anyone's life, because ultimately it will be unsatisfying.

Don't get caught up in the hype by friends, fans, and media. Remember, it's only a game—not life. Pretty soon someone will be playing the next "game of the century."

....

ALSO ON THIS DAY . . .

1939—The New York Yankees announced Lou Gehrig's retirement.

1994—Steffi Graf became the first defending tennis champion to lose in the first round of a major tournament (Wimbledon, to Lorrie McNeal).

1997—The Women's National Basketball Association began, with the New York Liberty beating the Los Angeles Sparks.

2005—The NBA and NBA Player's Association agreed that all American NBA players must be at least nineteen years old on draft day.

2009—St. Louis Cardinals manager Tony LaRussa won his 2,500th game as a baseball field manager.

...do not consider myself yet to have taken hold of it. But one thing I do: Forgetting what is behind and straining toward what is ahead, I press on toward the goal to win the prize for which God has called me heavenward in Christ Jesus. **Philippians 3:13–14**

!UN!FACT According to one sports reporter: "All [Duane] did was take the ball and run every time they called his number—which came to be more and more often, and in the Super Bowl Thomas was the whole show." During training camp in 1972, Dallas successfully traded Thomas to San Diego.

BIRTHDAYS:

1956—Rick Sutcliffe, Independence, MO, Major League pitcher (Dodgers, Indians, Cubs, Orioles, Cardinals)

1973—Merlakia Jones, Montgomery, AL, WNBA guard/forward (Cleveland Rockers)

1980—Richard Jefferson, Los Angeles, CA, NBA small forward (Nets, Bucks, Spurs)

Rules of Major League Baseball

1. What are the only two defensive players allowed (but not required) to wear a "mitt"?
   a. Right fielder and catcher
   b. Pitcher and catcher
   c. Catcher and first baseman
   d. First baseman and pitcher

2. With runners on first and third, a batter hits a ball that hits an umpire who is standing behind the pitcher but in front of the fielder. What is the ruling?
   a. The man on first is out.
   b. The batter is out.
   c. The play is dead.
   d. The ball is live.

3. The first base umpire incorrectly calls a runner out at first base. A different umpire sees the incorrect call and overrules the first base umpire. Is this allowed?
   a. Yes
   b. No

4. What happens if a batter swings and foul tips the ball into the catcher's glove and the catcher hangs onto it?
   a. The batter is automatically out.
   b. The batter is out only if there are two strikes on him.
   c. The batter is out if the catcher tags him.

5. If a fielder catches a fly ball in foul territory, can a runner on base tag up?
   a. Yes
   b. No

6. How many umpires are on the field during a World Series game?
   a. 4
   b. 5
   c. 6
   d. 7

7. If the right fielder makes an error, how is it scored (written in the record book)?
   a. E9
   b. RFE
   c. Duh'oh!
   d. ERF

8. What is the play called when a pitcher steps toward home plate then moves his foot and throws to first base to try to pick off the runner?
   a. False move
   b. Gotcha
   c. Ball
   d. Balk

9. What happens when a batted ball hits the outfield grass and bounces over the wall in fair territory without a fielder touching it?
   a. Home run
   b. Double
   c. Player is out
   d. No hit—called strike

10. If a player catches a fly ball and then jumps over the fence in fair territory, it is a home run?
    a. Yes
    b. No

ANSWERS: 1.c, 2.d, 3.b, 4.b, 5.a, 6.c, 7.a, 8.d, 9.b, 10.b

You've Got **a Prayer**

On this day in 2009, LSU defeated Texas 11-4 to win the College Baseball World Series.

Do you play baseball or follow your favorite teams? If you watch it very long, even the College Baseball World Series, you are sure to see a player make the sign of the cross just after entering the batter's box. The player is asking for God's help in hitting. You may witness similar actions in other sports, athletes who are religious hoping that God will help them do their best or thanking him for success on the field of play.

Prayer happens before and after games, too. In the locker room, often a player will lead the team in a prayer. Sometimes players from both teams will gather and pray briefly together, after, on the field.

Some have made fun of these public displays, saying that God isn't interested in the outcome of a game. Others say these athletes are using prayer as a type of good-luck charm, in the same way that a player might always eat the same meal before a contest or wear a special T-shirt.

So does prayer help in sports or not? Well, that depends on the player and his or her attitude and purpose for praying.

God wants to be involved in every part of our lives. That includes home, school, friendships, entertainment, and activities, including sports. And he's told us to pray everywhere (1 Timothy 2:8), about everything (Philippians 4:6), and at all times (1 Thessalonians 5:17).

So how does that affect sports? First, we should thank God for the opportunity to be in this situation and express our desire to do everything to glorify him. Second, we shouldn't ask for a victory but for God to help us do our best, to remember what we've learned in all our preparation. Third, we should ask him to help us clear our minds of distractions and focus on the task at hand. Then, afterward, we should be sure to thank God for his work in our lives and look for any lessons he might be teaching us, whether we hit a home run or strike out, win or lose.

Keep playing and praying.

....

ALSO ON THIS DAY . . .

1894—It was decided to hold the summer Olympics every four years.

1979—Ricky Henderson debuted for the Oakland Athletics and stole his first base.

2006—Erik Johnson (American defenseman) was chosen first overall in the NHL draft by the St. Louis Blues.

2007—The United States defeated Mexico 2-1 to win the CONCACAF Gold Cup (soccer).

BIRTHDAYS:

1960—Juli Inkster, Santa Cruz, CA, LPGA golfer

1974—Carrie Zarse, Chicago, IL, diver (1996 Olympics)

1984—J. J. Redick, Cookeville, TN, NBA guard (Orlando Magic)

Fun Fact The LSU baseball program is considered one of the elite programs in the nation (Texas, too). Teams have been in fifteen College World Series, they've won six national championships (1991, 1993, 1996, 1997, 2000, and 2009), and they've sent many players to the Majors.

JUNE 25 Decision **Time**

On this day in 1903, the New York Yankees and Chicago White Sox ended their baseball game after eighteen innings, deadlocked at 6-6.

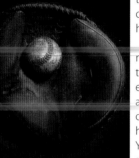

Imagine the feeling after that game. They played for eighteen innings, but nothing was decided—no winner. Someone has said that a tie is like "kissing your sister (or brother)." Pretty blah—very unappealing. We want each competition to come to a satisfying conclusion, and usually that means having a winner and a loser. It's why we play the games, why we compete against others. Otherwise, the effort would just be practice. Even losing, if we've done our best, is easier to take than a tie, a no decision.

Some people live that way—in the world of the "tie." Not that everything is a contest with

a winner and loser, but in the sense that they can't make a decision. Instead, they don't take a stand; they ride the fence and put off saying yes or no, right or left, up or down. Life happens to them instead of them making it happen.

Usually to not decide is to decide. For example, suppose a friend's mom offers you a ride home after school. You stand there for a while, thinking, but can't make up your mind. The car will leave without you. Your not deciding will be saying no. Or suppose you're on your bike and heading for a pond, and you can't decide what to do. If you don't take action, the decision will be made for you—you'll be soaked and covered in pond scum.

Those may be silly examples, but the point is

deadly serious. Jesus said that people are lost without him and heading for disaster—in this life and the next (much worse than a scummy pond). They need to stop, turn around, and go to him, putting their faith in Christ as their Savior. If they put off making that decision—they wait too long—their destination is clear.

If you haven't made the decision to follow Christ, do it today. If you have, pray for your friends that they would see the importance of deciding. Not making this decision is much worse than a tie, it's an eternal loss.

....

ALSO ON THIS DAY . . .

1948—Joe Louis knocked out Jersey Joe Walcott in the eleventh round to win the heavyweight boxing title.

1968—Bobby Bonds hit a grand slam home run in his first major league game (San Francisco Giants).

1991—Martina Navratilova won a record 100th singles match at Wimbledon.

2009—Chaunte Howard won the women's high jump in the US Track and Field Championships, clearing 6.4 feet.

BIRTHDAYS:

1966—Dikembe Mutombo, Kinshasa, DR Congo, NBA center (Nuggets, Hawks, 76ers, Nets, Knicks, Rockets)

1967—Joan Smith, Rochester, NY, biathlete (1994 Olympics)

1986—Charlie Davies, Manchester, NH, American soccer player (US National Team)

For he says, "In the time of my favor I heard you, and in the day of salvation I helped you." I tell you, now is the time of God's favor, now is the day of salvation. 2 Corinthians 6:2

FUN FACT A tie in baseball used to be possible if the game was called because of weather or other conditions after the fifth inning. But in 2007, the Major League Baseball Rules Committee eliminated tie games. Instead, if games are called with the score tied, they will be replayed from the start, but statistics from the "tie" game will still count.

To **Represent**

ON THIS DAY IN 1994, THE UNITED STATES LOST TO ROMANIA 1-0 IN THE WORLD CUP SOCCER TOURNAMENT.

Although soccer is very popular in the United States, with millions of kids playing in youth leagues and just about every high school, college, and university fielding teams, the country hasn't done very well internationally in men's competitions. Every four years when the World Cup comes around, we get our hopes up, thinking that this may be the breakthrough year—and every now and then we do fairly well—but teams from countries like Brazil, Italy, and Germany usually dominate.

Win or lose, the athletes competing for the USA are proud to wear the uniform, proud to represent their country. It's a great honor and privilege.

In all sports, wearing a specific uniform represents a certain school, club, professional franchise, city, or nation. That's why on draft days, the chosen players will put on the cap or jersey of their new team. Then they'll say how much they appreciate the opportunity to be part of the team's tradition. Wearing the uniform identifies the athlete with the team, the city, and all the past great players on that team.

Some players and coaches become so identified with a team that we automatically think of the team when we hear their names: Babe Ruth, Vince Lombardi, Mia Hamm, Michael Jordan, Roberto Clemente, Pat Summit . . . .

And an athlete who behaves poorly, on the field or off, disrespects the team and can bring disgrace to its name.

So what does it mean to be on Christ's team, to represent him? We don't have a special uniform to wear, complete with team colors and logo. But the Bible is pretty clear that people should know we belong to him by our attitudes and actions. It's also clear that when we're known as being on Christ's team, we honor or disgrace his name by our actions.

So the big questions are these: Do your friends know you're on Christ's team? If so, what do they know about Christ and think about him from watching you?

You are Christ's representative—represent well.

....

ALSO ON THIS DAY . . .

1959—Sweden's Ingemar Johansson beat Floyd Patterson on a technical knockout in the third round to win the heavyweight boxing title.

1970—Frank Robinson hits two grand slams as the Baltimore Orioles beat the Washington Senators 12-2.

1991—The Charlotte Hornets made Larry Johnson of UNLV NBA's number one draft pick.

2005—South Korea's Birdie Kim won the US Women's Open (LPGA) championship.

We are therefore Christ's ambassadors, as though God were making his appeal through us. We implore you on Christ's behalf: Be reconciled to God. **2 Corinthians 5:20**

Fun Fact

Seven different nations have won the World Cup in the eighteen tournaments. Brazil, the only team to have played in every tournament, has won five times. Italy, the current champion, has won four titles, and Germany has won three. The most widely viewed sporting event in the world, an estimated 715.1 million people watched the 2006 final match.

BIRTHDAYS:

1911—Mildred Ella "Babe" Didrikson Zaharias, Port Arthur, TX, golf, basketball, and track legend

1968—Shannon Sharpe, Chicago, IL, all-pro NFL tight end (Denver Broncos, Baltimore Ravens)

1976—Chad Pennington, Knoxville, TN, NFL quarterback (New York Jets, Miami Dolphins)

May I Have Your Attention Please

On this day in 1988, the Cincinnati Reds batted out of order against the San Diego Padres in the first inning.

Before every game, baseball managers make up the lineup and batting order. They meet at home plate with the head umpire and exchange copies of those items. Teams are required to bat in the designated order, one through nine. Otherwise, a team could simply bat the best hitter in every scoring opportunity. Any player hitting out of order is "out." Every person who has ever played baseball knows this rule. So how did professionals who have been playing baseball most of their lives make such a foolish mistake, especially in the very first inning, before any lineup changes?

They weren't paying attention. Maybe the manager had switched the order of a couple of batters. Perhaps a player just acquired in a been inserted into the lineup. Or maybe the batters were distracted. Whatever the case, they looked pretty silly and took themselves out of an inning.

Paying attention is vital in many areas. A surgeon needs to focus on the operation, not watch TV in the operating room. A pilot needs to listen to the control tower and check the instruments, not daydream about a vacation. A driver needs to keep eyes on the road and other cars, not talk to friends or text message.

Paying attention also means seeing obvious signs. If we're aware of dark clouds moving in, we'll prepare for rain. If we hear the teacher announce a test, we'll study and be ready. If a friend begins acting strangely, we will know something is wrong and get help.

Since creation, God has been sending signals, giving signs about his nature and his plan. He revealed himself in nature, performed miracles, sent prophets to give his messages, provided his written Word, and sent his Son. But many people weren't paying attention and missed God entirely. Some even met Jesus face-to-face, watched him heal, heard him teach, touched him, and saw how others were changed by him; yet they missed the Savior. Often Jesus would say, "Those who have ears, let them hear" (Matthew 13:9). In other words, if you're paying attention, really listening to me, you'll understand what I am saying.

Have you heard Jesus lately? Have you been paying attention?

ALSO ON THIS DAY . . .

1979—Muhammad Ali confirmed that his third retirement was final (it wasn't).

1986—Anne White shocked Wimbledon by wearing only a body stocking.

1992—American Dan O'Brien, an Olympic favorite, failed on pole vault and was eliminated from the Olympic decathlon.

2007—Philadelphia Phillies first baseman Ryan Howard hit his 100th career home run, becoming the fastest player to reach that milestone (325 games).

BIRTHDAYS:

1943—Rico Petrocelli, Brooklyn, NY, major league shortstop/third baseman (Boston Red Sox)

1973—Jennifer Brundage, Irvine, CA, US softball pitcher (winner of Olympic gold medal in 1996)

1985—Svetlana Kuznetsova, St. Petersburg, Russia, professional tennis player and winner of the US Open (2004) and the French Open (2009) singles titles

While he was still speaking, a bright cloud enveloped them, and a voice from the cloud said, "This is my Son, whom I love; with him I am well pleased. Listen to him!" Matthew 17:5

Fun Fact
According to the rules of baseball, when the batting-order mistake is discovered right after the wrong batter hits, then the umpire will consider that batter and the previous one improper, nullifying any advances or scores as a result of the wrong batters' actions. That batter is removed from th bases reached, and the proper batter is called "out."

Come Out **Swinging**

On this day in 2007, Craig Biggio of the Houston Astros became the twenty-seventh member of the 3,000-hit club, going five for five against the Colorado Rockies.

Craig Biggio was a Houston Astro his entire major-league career. A seven-time all-star, he played three positions well: catcher, second base, and outfielder, winning the Gold Glove four times. But he's probably known most for his hitting, ranking twentieth all-time with 3,060 career hits. He ended his career with 668 doubles, fifth all-time, and he holds the record for the most doubles by a right-handed hitter. He is the only player in baseball history with 3,000 hits, 600 doubles, 400 stolen bases, and 250 home runs. When Craig went to the plate, he took his cuts.

While hitting a home run is an exciting experience for a hitter, striking out can be frustrating. But hitting a baseball is one of the most difficult tasks in sports, especially when trying to hit a ninty-eight-mph fastball or a slider diving down and away. So strikeouts are part of the game. Worse than striking out is the way the batter strikes out—some, for example, get fooled by a pitch and take a weak swing. Some batters don't swing at all and are called out by the umpire. Now that's embarrassing. Craig Biggio had his share of strikeouts, but he usually went down swinging.

That expression could also refer to someone in a boxing match. Either way, it means not giving up, taking a shot, trying, giving 100 percent. A batter can't get a base hit without swinging. Just standing at the plate may result in a walk or a hit-by-pitch but usually will end in an embarrassing called strike out.

In life, some people don't "swing" (take a chance) because they're afraid of failing, of missing the ball. Some may even fear hitting it in the wrong place. But doing nothing isn't the answer. God expects his people to make a difference in this world. That takes courage and commitment. It involves hard work and taking risks. God isn't concerned about the strikeouts; he's concerned about the effort.

You know that God would like you to do something for him—what's holding you back? You have a dream that you want to pursue—what's stopping you? Take a swing. You just might connect.

....

ALSO ON THIS DAY . . .

1973—The Black Sports Hall of Fame was formed, with Paul Robeson, Elgin Baylor, Jesse Owens, Jim Brown, Wilma Rudolph, Joe Louis, and Althea Gibson the first athletes elected.

1992—The US Dream Team beat Cuba in their first exhibition basketball game, 133-57.

1997—Mike Tyson took a bite out of Evander Holyfield's ear in their fight.

2008—The Los Angeles Dodgers defeated the Anaheim Angels, 1-0, despite not getting a hit. The Dodgers scored on an error, a stolen base, another error, and a sacrifice fly in the fifth inning.

And without faith it is impossible to please God, because anyone who comes to him must believe that he exists and that he rewards those who earnestly seek him. **Hebrews 11:6**

Fun Fact Biggio was called the "king of hit batsmen" for being hit by pitches. On June 29, 2005, he broke the modern-era career hit-by-pitch record with 267, second to only Hughie Jennings on the all-time list with 287. Despite being hit so often, Biggio received no serious injuries and never charged the mound.

BIRTHDAYS:

1937—Ron Luciano, Endicott, NY, Major League Baseball umpire (American League)

1974—Joshua Crosby, Manchester, MA, rower (1996 Olympics)

1976—Seth Benjamin Wescott, Durham, NC, American snowboarder and two-time Olympic champion in the snowboard cross (2006 and 2010)

1977—Lindsay Lee-Water, Oklahoma City, OK, professional tennis player

Featured Events in *June*

1. **When did the National Football League and American Football League merge? (June 6)**

2. In what sport did Dan Jansen compete? (June 17)

3. **What year did Chicago Cubs player Ryne Sandberg retire? (June 13)**

4. How many hits did baseball player Craig Biggio have in his career? (June 28)

5. **What featured college baseball team is considered one of the elite programs in the nation? (June 24)**

6. In 1991, who did the New York Yankees select number one in the amateur draft? (June 3)

7. **What basketball star did the Chicago Bulls draft in 1984? (June 19)**

8. Currently, can Major League Baseball games end in a tie? (June 25)

9. **Who was the youngest player ever to play in a Major League Baseball game? (June 10)**

10. In what year did a Le Mans race car accident kill eighty-four spectators? (June 11)

11. **How many home runs did Sammy Sosa hit with the Chicago Cubs? (June 20)**

12. Who has won the most World Cup soccer tournaments? (June 26)

13. **Who won the first Ryder Cup golf tournament? (June 4)**

14. How long did the 1984 Major League Baseball strike last? (June 12)

15. **For what NFL team did Duane Thomas play in the Super Bowl? (June 21)**

16. In 2008, who upset Big Brown at the Belmont Stakes horse race? (June 7)

17. **In what sport does Eric Rupe compete? (June 14)**

18. What jersey number did Los Angeles Dodgers's Walter Alston wear? (June 5)

19. **What happened to Dave Dravecky's left arm? (June 18)**

20. In Major League Baseball, what happens if a player bats out of order? (June 27)

Find the correct answers on the dates in parentheses.

Sacrifice

On this day in 1990, despite Andy Hawkins no-hitting the White Sox, the Yankees lost 4-0.

Every now and then a pitcher throws a brilliant game, a no-hitter even, but loses. Usually the score is something like 1-0. So how did the White Sox get four runs on no hits? By taking advantage of poor fielding in the eighth inning when the Yankees made three errors.

People may think that the only way to score runs is by hitting home runs or stringing together hits. That works, of course. But teams can also "manufacture runs." Let's say the leadoff hitter gets a walk. Then he steals second. The next batter bunts and sacrifices him to third. And the next batter hits a fly ball, allowing the runner to tag up after the catch and

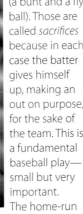

race home (a sacrifice fly). The team would have "manufactured" a run, scoring one without a hit.

Successful teams know how to score this way. It's a team effort and usually involves a sacrifice. In our example, the team used two (a bunt and a fly ball). Those are called *sacrifices* because in each case the batter gives himself up, making an out on purpose, for the sake of the team. This is a fundamental baseball play—small but very important. The home-run hitter may get the headlines, but players who do the little things, like sacrifice, are just as important.

We need to learn this lesson and apply it to other areas of life. It's a principle found in Scripture. Think of all the sacrifices made by parents for their kids to help them grow strong and wise and to get them through high school and college. Then there's the spouse who sacrifices and makes possible a husband or wife's success in a career. Some people sacrifice by supporting others financially—the church, missions, ministry organizations, or people in need. A self-centered person doesn't want to give anything. But an other-centered person looks for ways to help . . . and sacrifices.

What can you give to help others? What do you think God might be asking you to sacrifice? You don't need to hit a home run to make a difference for Christ.

....

ALSO ON THIS DAY . . .

1961—Mickey Wright won the sixteenth US Women's Open Golf Championship.

1977—Virginia Wade beat B. Stove to win the eighty-fourth Wimbledon Women's Tennis Championship.

2005—Kenny Rogers was suspended for twenty games and fined an undisclosed amount for his tirade that sent a cameraman to the hospital.

2007—Cristie Kerr won her first major championship with a two-stroke victory in the US Women's Open (LPGA).

BIRTHDAYS:

1941—Rod Gilbert, Canada, NHL wing for the New York Rangers

1958—Nancy Lieberman Cline, Brooklyn, NY, WNBA guard (Phoenix Mercury) and winner of the Olympic silver medal, 1976

1961—Carl Lewis, Birmingham, AL, world-class track athlete and winner of nine Olympic gold medals in four Olympics (1984, 1988, 1992, and 1996)

Now that I, your Lord and Teacher, have washed your feet, you also should do as I have done for you. John 13:14–15

Fun Fact

Chicago was the home team, so the game ended after the Yankees batted in the ninth. So Hawkins only pitched eight innings. The next year baseball changed the rule and took away his no-hitter because he hadn't pitched nine innings, but he was credited with a complete game. In his next start, after the White Sox game, Hawkins took a shutout into the twelfth inning but lost to Minnesota, 2-0.

Timing is **Everything**

On this day in 1970, Horace Clarke of the New York Yankees broke up a no-hitter in the ninth inning for third time in twenty-eight days.

How's that for dramatic timing? And to do this three times—even twice in a career would be significant, but three times within a month—wow! On June 4 the pitcher was Jim Rooker; on June 19, Sonny Seibert; on July 2, Joe Niekro.

You've probably never heard of Horace Clarke until now, but he played Major League Baseball from 1965 through 1974, mostly with the Yankees. Born in the Virgin Islands (1940), Horace signed to the Yankees in 1958 and made his big-league debut in 1965, replacing retired Bobby Richardson at second base. Besides breaking up no-hitters, he also led the American League in singles in 1967 and 1969. He timed three of those singles perfectly, at almost the last moment to break through for his team.

Timing is crucial. A good sales person knows exactly when to say what to a customer. A comedian understands when to give the punch line. And you certainly know that when you want to discuss an issue with Mom or Dad, you had better choose the right time. You don't want to approach them when they're busy or in a bad mood!

Centuries ago, Queen Esther faced a dilemma. She was queen and, thus, in the perfect spot to influence the king. She had learned that her people, the Jews, were being threatened by a royal decree. She knew she could ask the king to reverse his decree, but that would be a risky move, especially if he was in a foul mood. The king held all the power—life and death. Then Esther's uncle, Mordecai, said this: "Who knows but that you have come to royal position for such a time as this?" (Esther 4:14). Esther realized that God had given her this opportunity ("such a time as this") to act for him and her people, so she responded: "Though it is against the law, I will go in to see the king. If I must die, I must die" (Esther 4:16, NLT).

She took the risk and saved her people.

Timing is everything. Where has God placed you, at this time, so that you can make a difference for him?

You intended to harm me, but God intended it for good to accomplish what is now being done, the saving of many lives. **Genesis 50:20**

[UN] [ACT In May of 1974, the Yankees sold Clarke to the San Diego Padres. He retired after that season. Then he worked as an assistant scout for the Kansas City Royals and a baseball instructor in the Virgin Islands.

BIRTHDAYS:

1937—Richard Petty, Level Cross, NC, NASCAR racing legend with 200 career wins, including the Daytona 500 in 1979 and 1981

1964—DeAnne Hemmens, San Francisco, CA, sprint kayak (1996 Olympics)

1984—Johnny Weir, Coatesville, PA, American figure skater, three-time National Champion (2004-2006) and

Personal **Best**

On this day in 1983, Calvin Smith of the US became the fastest man alive, running the 100 meters in 9.93 seconds.

Calvin Smith had a brilliant career at the University of Alabama. Then, in 1983, he set the world record in the 100 meters, breaking the record set by Jim Himes that had lasted almost fifteen years. Although Calvin won a gold medal in the 4x100 at the 1984 Olympics, he never won an Olympic individual gold. He won bronze four years later in Seoul.

Since Calvin ran 9.93 in 1983, the record has been broken several times. In fact, he doesn't even appear in the list of the top thirteen runners with the best times. The current world record is 9.58, set by Usain Bolt in August of 2009. How low

can the time go? Certainly not too much lower.

A problem that many runners and swimmers face is trying to keep improving their times when their only true competition is the stopwatch. A child can run (or swim) a good race and then beat his or her time every year as he or she grows and gains in strength and experience. But eventually the new times decrease less and less until they stop, with the athlete reaching his or her limit. The race for serious competitors isn't just against other competitors; they race against the clock. This pushes many into eating disorders and using performance-enhancing drugs. Many also struggle with depression because they can't go faster.

While their drive is commendable, their values are misplaced. Setting records and winning shouldn't be everything in life. Much more important should be simply doing your

best. For a short time Calvin Smith was on top of the world, but soon someone else had taken that spot. But that's okay. What's important is that he worked hard, competed well, and ran as fast as he could.

That's what God expects of us in every area—to do our best for his glory. You don't have to win the MVP trophy to be valuable in his sight. And you don't have to be the best student, artist, singer, writer, soccer player, runner, swimmer, or dancer in the world or even in your school. Those awards are nice, but they'll fade quickly. Instead, work for your personal best . . . and give God the glory.

ALSO ON THIS DAY . . .

1954—Babe Didrikson-Zaharias won the ninth US Women's Open Golf Championship.

1989—Peter Koech of Kenya set a 3k steeplechase record (8:05.39) in Stockholm.

2005—Roger Federer won his third successive Wimbledon Gentlemen's Singles championship, defeating second-seeded American Andy Roddick.

2006—Annika Sörenstam won the eighteen-hole playoff for the 2006 US Women's Open, her third US Women's Open title and her tenth major title overall.

BIRTHDAYS:

1957—Orel Hershiser, Buffalo, NY, outstanding major-league pitcher (Dodgers, Indians, Giants, Mets) and broadcaster

1970—Teemu Selanne, Helsinki, Finland, NHL right wing (Ducks, Sharks, Avalanche, Jets) and member of the Finnish Olympic team (1998, 2006, 2010)

1975—John Hargis, Little Rock, AK, 100-meter butterfly (1996 Olympics)

Listen, my son, accept what I say, and the years of your life will be many. I guide you in the way of wisdom and lead you along straight paths. When you walk, your steps will not be hampered; when you run, you will not stumble. **Proverbs 4:10–12**

FUN FACT In the 1988 Summer Olympics, Smith finished fourth, behind Ben Johnson, Carl Lewis, and Linford Christie. When Johnson was disqualified after testing positive for steroids, Calvin got the bronze. Later, both Lewis and Christie admitted to having had some steroid involvement. Of the top five runners in that race, Smith is the only one who never failed a drug test, and he probably should have been given the gold medal.

The **Luckiest Man**

On this day in 1939, the New York Yankees had a day to honor Lou Gehrig.

One of the all-time great Yankees and Major League Baseball players Lou Gehrig was dying. He had been losing power at the plate and had stumbled a time or two while running, so he knew something was wrong. The doctors at Mayo Clinic gave him the bad news that he had "amyotrophic lateral sclerosis" (ALS) disease, with no known cure. Lou would never play baseball again. On June 21, 1939, the New York Yankees announced his retirement and proclaimed July 4 as "Lou Gehrig Appreciation Day" at Yankee Stadium.

That day, between games of the doubleheader against the Washington Senators, the ceremonies were held on the diamond, and 62,000 fans heard Lou say these immortal words:

"Fans, for the last two weeks you've been reading about the bad break I got. Yet today I consider myself to be the luckiest man on the face of the earth. I have been in ballparks for seventeen years and have never received anything but kindness and encouragement from you fans. . . . When you have a father and a mother who work all their lives so you can have an education and build your body—it's a blessing. When you have a wife who has been a tower of strength and shown more courage than you dreamed existed— that's the finest I know. So I close in saying that I may have had a tough break, but I have an awful lot to live for."

With his career ending at its peak and with no hope for a cure in sight, Lou Gehrig knew what was important, and he spoke from the heart. Two years later he was gone.

Lou Gehrig's death reminds us that life is short, so we should live for what is truly important. And we should have a grateful attitude, appreciating everything that God has given to us: parents, siblings, friends, teachers, and, most of all, his Son. As recipients of God's kindness, we truly are most fortunate.

Regardless of your "tough breaks," you, too, have an awful lot to live for.

ALSO ON THIS DAY . . .

1973—Meeting with Italian cyclists, Pope Paul VI praises athletes who "offer the magnificent show of a healthy, strong, generous youth."

2007—In the ninety-second Nathan's Hot Dog Eating Contest at Coney Island, NY, Joey Chestnut upset six-time champion Takeru Kobayashi by downing a record sixty-six hotdogs and buns in twelve minutes.

2009—Serena Williams defeated her sister Venus to win the Ladies' Singles Championship at Wimbledon for the third time and her eleventh Grand Slam tournament.

2009—The United States defeated Canada 12-6 in the Americas qualification playoff for Rugby World Cup qualifying.

For to me, to live is Christ and to die is gain. Philippians 1:21

Fun Fact When actor Edward Hermann was hired to play Lou Gehrig in a made-for-TV movie, he had trouble capturing the personality of the quiet and reserved baseball hero. He said, "What made it so tough is I could find no 'key' to his character. There was no strangeness, nothing spectacular about him. As [his wife] told me, he was just a square, honest guy."

BIRTHDAYS:

1929—Al Davis, Brocton, MA, NFL team owner (Oakland Raiders)

1962—Pam Shriver, Baltimore, MD, professional tennis player and winner of four Olympic gold medals in 1988 and 1992

1970—Louise Van Voorhis, Rochester, NY, 470 yachter (Olympics 1992 and 1996)

Noticed and **Known**

On this day in 1980, Bjorn Borg beat John McEnroe to win the Wimbledon championship.

If you were living in 1980, you would know all about Bjorn Borg and John McEnroe. Tennis personalities were in the news. And if you were a tennis fan, you would be glued to your TV set to watch their championship match at Wimbledon. The Championships at Wimbledon is the oldest and most prestigious tennis tournament in the world. It is the only Grand Slam event still played on grass. Bjorn Borg is a former number one tennis player in the world from Sweden, considered to be one of the greatest tennis players of all time. He won a record five consecutive Wimbledon singles titles, 1976 through 1980. American John McEnroe, also once rated number one in the world, won three Wimbledon singles titles—1981, 1983, and 1984.

In this 1980 match, McEnroe had reached the men's singles final for the first time, while Borg was going for his fifth Wimbledon championship in a row. In a fourth-set tiebreaker that lasted twenty minutes, McEnroe saved five match-points and eventually won 18-16. McEnroe, however, could not break Borg's serve in the fifth set, which the Swede won 8–6. This match has been named the best Wimbledon final and one of the greatest sporting events in history.

Those athletes were international stars and would be recognized anywhere. But others have taken their place on the stage, names like Sampras, Federer, Roddick, and Nadal. And except for an occasional look back at Wimbledon history during a broadcast, little mention is made of this famous match.

That's the nature of fame in this world. Today's hero is tomorrow's goat. Today's celebrity is tomorrow's has-been. And just think of the countless thousands of young men and women who sacrificed everything and never came close to stardom. Yet that's most people's goal—to be known and noticed, to be on top of the world. We find that push in sports and entertainment, of course, but also in business, politics, and even the ministry.

If that's where hard work and dedication take you, great. But don't make being a star your goal. Rather, remember that what God thinks about you is infinitely more important, and you have a starring role in his kingdom.

....

ALSO ON THIS DAY . . .

1947—Larry Doby signed with the Cleveland Indians, the first black player in the American League.

1968—The Philadelphia 76ers traded Wilt Chamberlain to the Los Angeles Lakers.

2008—Venus Williams defeated her sister Serena to win the Ladies' Singles Championship at Wimbledon.

2009—Dani Pedrosa of Spain won the United States motorcycle Grand Prix in Laguna Seca, California.

BIRTHDAYS:

1923—John McKay, Everettville, WV, football coach (USC, Tampa Bay) and five-time Rose Bowl champion.

1969—John Oostendorp, Iowa City, IA, 220-lb. Greco-Roman wrestler (1996 Olympics)

1973—Christy Rowe, St. Paul, MN, soccer defender (1996 Olympics)

But seek first his kingdom and his righteousness, and all these things will be given to you as well. **Matthew 6:33**

Fun Fact
"Johnny Mac" was known for his outbursts on the tennis court. In 2007, he appeared on the *30 Rock* TV show as the host of a game show called "Gold Case," in which he uttered his famous line, "You cannot be serious!" when things went wrong. In 2009, he appeared on *30 Rock*, invited to dinner because he was of the world of "art critique and yelling."

1. Which player ran through the streets of Atlanta after winning the gold at the 1996 Olympics?
   a. Kristine Lilly
   b. Brandi Chastain
   c. Briana Scurry
   d. Julie Foudy

2. Which player attended Stanford University?
   a. Tiffanie Roberts
   b. Lorrie Fair
   c. Michelle Akers
   d. Julie Foudy

3. What US women's soccer player has scored the most goals in World Cup matches?
   a. Mia Hamm
   b. Brianna Scurry
   c. Michelle Akers
   d. Kristine Lilly

4. Which player got off the bus (while in New York traffic) and ran to a nearby coffee shop just to get a Tall Iced Double Latte?
   a. Julie Foudy
   b. Mia Hamm
   c. Tiffeny Milbrett
   d. Kristine Lilly

5. Which player got married to a US Marine in 1999?
   a. Tisha Venturini
   b. Mia Hamm
   c. Shannon MacMillan
   d. Tiffeny Milbrett

6. Who was the first-ever (played in 1985) US Women's National Team game played against?
   a. England
   b. Germany
   c. Brazil
   d. Italy

7. What college did Mia Hamm attend?
   a. University of North Carolina at Chapel Hill
   b. UCLA
   c. Berkeley
   d. Notre Dame

8. Which of these is not a former player?
   a. Robin Confer
   b. Jessica Hanks
   c. Lorrie Schwoy
   d. Debbie Keller

9. Who has a twin sister?
   a. Christie Pearce
   b. Tiffany Roberts
   c. Lorrie Fair
   d. Cindy Parlow

10. What was the final score of the 1999 Women's World Cup championship match when the US defeated China?
    a. 1-0
    b. 0-0
    c. 3-2
    d. 2-0

ANSWERS: 1.c, 2.d, 3.c (12), 4.c, 5.b, 6.d, 7.a, 8.b, 9.c, 10.b (the US won on penalty kicks, 5-4)

All **Stars**

ON THIS DAY IN 1935, THE AMERICAN LEAGUE WON THE THIRD ALL-STAR BASEBALL GAME 4-1 AT MUNICIPAL STADIUM IN CLEVELAND.

Every sport at almost every level has designated all stars. In professional sports, these athletes are chosen by fans, players, or coaches—or a combination of those. Then they usually compete in an annual all-star game, sometimes after the season, as with the NFL's Pro Bowl, but often about halfway through the season, as with the MLB, NHL, and NBA's all-star games. These games are mostly for the fans—exhibitions—with participants not taking them too seriously. But all athletes would like to be chosen, to be recognized as one of the great players of their sports.

So in America, where we almost worship celebrities, we have all-conference, all-state, all-American, and all-pro designations. Being named to one of those lists or being labeled all-star feels great, affirming one's skill, performance, and even value as a human being.

Did you know that the Bible talks about "all stars"? It does—well sort of—but not an annual list of athletes in a small portion of planet Earth. The geographical area is much greater—the universe. Now that's an all-star team—"all-universe"! In his letter to believers in the city of Philippi, Paul told them that they "shine like stars in the universe" (Philippians 2:15). He was saying that because of the way they were living ("blameless and pure" as "children of God"), their actions caused them to stand out and shine bright. Like a dominating performance by a superior athlete, everyone could see and be dazzled. They were, in fact, God's all-stars. That's God's message to us, too.

So here's the question of the day: To whose all-star team would you rather belong—one that only lasts till the next season or God's, that lasts forever? Think of it this way: God is the team owner, the general manager, and the coach. Because you're on his team, you are already an all-star, an elite group of people who belong to him and play for him. So remember that fact when you feel like a benchwarmer . . . and shine!

ALSO ON THIS DAY . . .

1980—The National League won the fifty-first all-star game, 4-2, at Dodger Stadium, with Ken Griffey named game MVP.

1990—Greg Lemond won his third Tour de France bicycle race.

2001—Lisa Raymond and Rennae Stubbs beat Kim Clijsters and Ai Sugiyama to win the Wimbledon Women's Doubles Championship.

2005—The International Olympic Committee announced that baseball and softball would be dropped from the Olympic docket of sports for the 2012 Summer Olympics in London.

So that you may become blameless and pure, children of God without fault in a crooked and depraved generation, in which you shine like stars in the universe. **Philippians 2:15**

CONTACT In voting for the 1957 baseball All-Star Game, Cincinnati Reds' fans stuffed the ballot box and elected seven Reds players to the starting lineup. The Reds were known to be a great offensive team with many outstanding position players, but most baseball experts agreed that they did not deserve seven starters. An investigation showed that over half of the ballots cast came from Cincinnati.

Sisters

On this day in 2000, in the Wimbledon Women's Doubles Finals, Venus Williams and Serena Williams defeated Julie Halard-Decugis and Ai Sugiyama.

This was the first Wimbledon Women's Doubles Championship for the team of Venus and Serena Williams. They also won in 2002, 2008, and 2009. These sisters have dominated the sport of tennis (when playing seriously) since 1997. Venus, the older sister, reached the U.S. Open finals at the age of 17 as an unseeded player. Not long after, in 1998, after winning the Lipton Championships, she was ranked in the top ten in the World Tennis Association rankings. So far, she has been ranked number one three times. To this point in her career, Venus has won forty-three singles titles, sixteen doubles titles, and three Olympic gold medals (the most of female tennis players of all time),

one in singles (2000) and two in doubles (2000 and 2008).

Serena is the younger sister (by about a year) and has been ranked number one in the world five times. She has won 36 singles and 18 doubles titles, of which 25 are Grand Slams: 12 in singles, 11 in women's doubles, and 2 in mixed doubles, more Grand Slam titles than any other active female player. She has won two Olympic gold medals in women's doubles.

The Williams sisters are great athletes for sure, but they are great friends as well. Although they often have to face each other in tournament finals (Serena holds the edge, thirteen to ten), they have a friendly rivalry, each doing her best to win but gracious in defeat. They are as close as sisters can be and support each other on and off the court.

Families face daily stresses and pressures, so brothers and sisters often bicker and fight. Big brothers and sisters can get on our nerves when they boss us

around and act like they know everything. Little brothers and sisters can be annoying with their pestering and whining. That's normal. But God gives us family members for a reason—to love and encourage each other and to learn from each other.

How are you and your siblings getting along? Instead of focusing on their issues and habits, recognize the positives in their personality and talents. Thank God for the gift of family and work to be a peacemaker in your home.

....

ALSO ON THIS DAY . . .

1955—D. L. Hayes caught the world-record smallmouth bass, weighing eleven pounds and fifteen ounces, in Dale Hollow Lake, along

the Tennessee-Kentucky boundary.

1966—Jack Nicklaus shot 282 to win the ninety-fifth British Golf Open at Muirfield Gullane.

2005—Danny Way jumped over the Great Wall of China on a skateboard.

2007—Vladimir Guerrero of the Los Angeles Angels won the All-Star Home Run Derby, defeating Alex Rios of the Toronto Blue Jays in the final round.

How good and pleasant it is when brothers live together in unity! **Psalm 133:1**

[unFACT] The Williams sisters are the only women to have played each other in four consecutive Grand Slam singles finals. They have met a total of eight times in the finals, just behind the record of fourteen set by Chris Evert and Martina Navrátilová.

BIRTHDAYS:

1952—Rod Boll, Fillmore, Saskatchwan, trap shooter (1996 Olympics)

1970—Trent Green, Cedar Rapids, IA, NFL quarterback (Chargers, Redskins, Rams, Chiefs, Dolphins)

1971—Danalee Bragado, Honolulu, HI, WPVA volleyball player

Great **Expectations**

10 JULY

On this day in 2005, Dale Earnhardt Jr. won the USG Sheetrock 400 at Chicagoland Speedway.

Dale Earnhardt Jr. may be the most popular driver in NASCAR, probably because of his father, "The Intimidator." Dale Jr. began his racing in 1991, at the age of seventeen. In the years following, he has performed well, with eighteen Sprint Cup wins and twenty-two Nationwide wins. His greatest victory came in 2004 when he won the Daytona 500, the "Great American Race," six years to the day after his father had won his only title there and three years after Dale, Sr. had been killed in the same race. In 2007, Junior said he would be leaving Dale Earnhardt, Inc. (founded by his father) to drive for another team. And a month later, he announced his signing of a five-year contract with Hendrick Motorsports.

To many, the career of Dale Earnhardt, Jr. has been disappointing. His fans expected him to follow his father's legacy and dominate on the track. While Junior has been competitive and done well, he hasn't come close to fulfilling those expectations.

The burden of great expectations can be heavy. As with Junior, a parent may be the one people assume we will be like. Often an older brother or sister has set a high standard—in grades, sports, spiritual walk, and so forth—that we are trying to match. Sometimes the expectations come from what we did when we were younger. For example, we may have shown promise on the piano, on the swim team, in writing, or at some other endeavor, and adults just assume we will keep improving and be terrific in that area. That weight gets heavy, and we just want to throw it off, quit, and do something else.

God has made each person unique and uniquely gifted. Yes, he has expectations for us, but he doesn't expect us to be more than we are, to do more than we can. And, by the way, his opinion is the only one that ultimately counts (even more than that of friends, coaches, teachers, pastors, or parents). And here's what he expects: to use our gift well, to do our best, and to rely totally on him. When we understand that, we can live free.

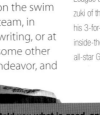

ALSO ON THIS DAY . . .

1914—The Boston Red Sox purchased Babe Ruth from the Baltimore Orioles.

1934—Carl Hubbell struck out Ruth, Gehrig, and Foxx in the all-star game.

1989—Paula Ivan ran a female world record for the mile (4:15.61).

2007—The American League won the Major League Baseball All-Star Game 5-4, with Ichiro Suzuki of the Seattle Mariners earning MVP honors for his 3-for-3 performance, capped off with the first inside-the-park home run in all-star Game history.

BIRTHDAYS:

1921—Jake LaMotta, Bronx, NY, middleweight boxing champ, 1949-51, and the subject of the movie *Raging Bull*

1933—Chuan-Kwang Yang, Taiwanese decathlete and winner of the silver medal in the 1960 Olympics

1945—Virginia Wade, English tennis star, winner of Wimbledon (singles) in 1977

1954—Andre Dawson, Miami, FL, Hall-of-Fame outfielder (Montreal Expos, Chicago Cubs, and Florida Marlins) and winner of the 1987 NL MVP

O people, the Lord has told you what is good, and this is what he requires of you: to do what is right, to love mercy, and to walk humbly with your God. **Micah 6:8, NLT**

Fun Fact
Dale appeared in *Talladega Nights: The Ballad of Ricky Bobby*. In the movie, he walks up and asks Ricky Bobby for his autograph but says, "Don't tell any of the other drivers." The number eight car (his original number) also appears in *Herbie: Fully Loaded* in the final race, where Herbie overtakes him.

Follow-**Through**

On this day in 1993, Jack Nicklaus won the fourteenth US Seniors Golf Open.

Jack Nicklaus is one of the all-time great golfers. Known as "The Golden Bear," this Hall of Famer was continuously ranked number one in the world at the peak of his career and still holds the record for winning the most major championships (eighteen). Jack played in 100 majors during his twenty-five years as a professional, finishing either first or second 36 times, in the top three 45 times, the top five 54 times, and the top ten 67 times. When Nicklaus turned fifty in January of 1990, he became eligible to join the Senior PGA Tour (the Champions Tour), and he proceeded to win there, too, taking all of the Champions Tour majors with the exception of the Senior British Open. His last competitive US tournament was in Overland Park, Kansas, on June 13, 2005.

A precision sport, golf takes considerable skill, attention, and technique. To send a golf ball flying 300 yards straight down the middle of a fairway, a golfer doesn't need size and muscles. It's much more about physics and involves the right stance and placement of the golfer to the ball, a slow backswing with weight moving to the back leg, a good forward swing with the arms in the correct position, weight shifting from the back leg to the front at the right time and eyes on the ball, and good follow-through. Every part of the swing is important. Try to muscle the ball, and you'll be in trouble.

One of the most important but often overlooked aspects of the golf swing is the follow-through. That's also true with bowling, baseball, basketball, tennis, badminton, horseshoes, darts, even shuffleboard. With poor follow-through, the ball (birdie, horseshoe, puck, dart, etc.) usually will go awry.

Follow-through means completing the task, carrying some project or promise to full completion. So it's involved in carrying out an assignment, meeting responsibilities. And it means keeping our word. Someone can easily promise to do something, but without follow-through, the talk is hollow, meaningless. God wants us to be people of our word and people of action. We need to do what we promise and do it right.

How's your follow-through?

ALSO ON THIS DAY . . .

1914—Babe Ruth debuted as a pitcher for the Boston Red Sox and beat the Cleveland Indians 4–3.

1976—JoAnne Carner won the thirty-first US Women's Open Golf Championship.

2004—Philip Rabinowitz, a centenarian sprinter from South Africa, made it into the *Guinness Book of World Records* as the fastest one hundred-year-old to run 100 meters, in 30.86 seconds.

2009—Brock Lesnar (USA) defeated Interim Heavyweight Champion Frank Mir (USA) by TKO in the second round to win the Ultimate Fighting Championship unification bout.

So then, just as you received Christ Jesus as Lord, continue to live in him, rooted and built up in him, strengthened in the faith as you were taught, and overflowing with thankfulness. **Colossians 2:6–7**

BIRTHDAYS:

1965—Ernesto Hoost, Heemsherk, Netherlands, kickboxer, four-time K-1 World Champion

1981—Mary Beth Arnold, Reno, NV, gymnast

1990—Caroline Wozniacki, Odense, Denmark, professional tennis player

Fun Fact
When Jack Nicholas joined the Senior Tour, he declared, "I'm never satisfied. Trouble is, I want to play like me—and I can't play like me anymore." Then he won his first start on the tour, The Tradition, a major championship. He went on to win another three Traditions—the final two in succession. No one else has won more than two.

Watch **Out!**

ON THIS DAY IN 1949, BASEBALL OWNERS AGREED TO ERECT WARNING PATHS BEFORE EACH FENCE.

Every sport has dangerous moments: blindside hits, screaming pucks, airborne flips, collisions, smashes . . . especially contact sports. Baseball is usually considered relatively safe, with players spread over the field. But tell that to the batter who has to face a pitcher throwing a 100-mph fastball, or the second baseman who has to avoid the raised spikes of a runner trying to break up a double play or the pitcher knowing that a batted ball could be blasted back toward his face or the outfielder crashing into a brick wall attempting to snag the long drive. Pretty dangerous. So we have batting helmets and arm pads, catcher's masks and protectors, and padding on walls.

In Major League Baseball, the warning path or track was another early attempt to make the game safer. The goal is to let the outfielder know when the wall is close. As the speeding outfielder looks up and follows the flight of a ball, the wall is out of sight—and out of mind until too late. But when spikes move from grass to dirt, the outfielder knows the wall is just a few feet away and can make a safe decision.

Warnings are important; their purpose is to keep us safe from harm. Flashing lights, railroad crossing signals, sirens, medicine bottle labels, signs on fences, and other warnings scream "watch out," "be careful," "stay away," "danger ahead." Wise people see the signs and take action to avoid the trouble. Foolish people barge ahead, either taking no notice of the signal or thinking it doesn't apply to them.

The Bible has numerous warnings. Like the baseball owners trying to protect players, these warnings are for our good, not to keep us from having fun. Here are a few: "Be careful, and watch yourselves closely" (Deuteronomy 4:9); "Watch out for false prophets" (Matthew 7:15); "Watch out that no one deceives you" (Mark 13:5).

God wants only the best for us, so he gives us plenty of warnings to help us be alert and make the right choices. Sometimes the warning is a sensitive conscience and the Holy Spirit whispering, "This is wrong. Don't do it."

Are you paying attention? You're on the warning track.

ALSO ON THIS DAY . . .

1926—Paavo Nurmi speed-walked a world-record 4x1500m (16:26.2).

1979—At "Disco Demolition Night" at Comiskey Park in Chicago (baseball promotion), fans go wild and cause the White Sox to forfeit the second game of a doubleheader to the Tigers.

1996—The first "Super 8s" cricket tournament began in Kuala Lumpur.

2009—Kelly Sutherland of the Kay Dee Ranching team won the Chuckwagon Race at the Calgary Stampede.

BIRTHDAYS:

1949—Rick Hendrick, Warrenton, NC, NASCAR team owner

1980—Tina Tharp, Jacksonville, FL, rhythmic gymnast (1996 Olympics)

1988—Inbee Park, Seoul, South Korea, LPGA golfer

Stay alert! Watch out for your great enemy, the devil. He prowls around like a roaring lion, looking for someone to devour. 1 Peter 5:8, NLT

FUN FACT
Some baseball historians say the term *warning track* comes from Old Yankee Stadium, where an actual running track was built for use in track meets.

Match the sport with the surface it is played on.

1. Football

2. Curling

3. Basketball

4. Motocross

5. Tennis

6. Skateboarding

7. Skysurfing

8. Boardercross

9. Flowboarding

10. Climbing

a. Clay

b. Snow

c. Rock

d. Turf

e. Air

f. Dirt

g. Ice

h. Water

i. Cement

j. Wood

No Alibis, **No Regrets**

On this day in 1912, Jim Thorpe won two gold medals and became recognized as the world's greatest athlete.

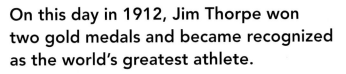

Jim Thorpe's gold medals came at the Olympic Games in Stockholm, Sweden, in the pentathlon and decathlon. The pentathlon consisted of these events: long jump, javelin throw, 200-meter dash, discus throw, and 1,500-meter run. For the decathlon (ten events), athletes had to compete in the 100-meter dash, long jump, shot put, high jump, 400 meter run, 110 meter hurdles, discus, pole vault, javelin, and 1,500-meter run. Thorpe defeated local favorite Hugo Wieslander in the decathlon by 700 points, placing in the top four of all ten events. Overall, he won eight of the fifteen individual events in the two competitions. No wonder the king of Sweden proclaimed him "the greatest athlete in the world." With

his versatility and all-around athletic ability, Jim Thorpe went on to play professional football, basketball, and baseball.

Making Thorpe's accomplishments even more amazing is his background. A Native American, he was born in Indian Territory near Prague, Oklahoma, in 1888 and reared in the Sac and Fox nation. Money and other resources were meager, so he had no weight training, personal coaching, or equipment available to athletes today. Both of his parents died during his youth, so he had to take several jobs to support himself. Blessed with natural ability, he worked hard to develop his athletic skills and to perform at the highest level.

Times have changed dramatically since the days of Jim Thorpe, but hard work and dedication still pay off. Some people use their background—broken family, poverty, poor education, and so forth—as

an excuse for not performing. But everyone has something to overcome, even those raised by loving parents with no financial worries and given the best education. So a person looking for excuses can find them.

Instead of listing what we don't have and feeling sorry for ourselves, we should look at what we have—God's gifts of abilities, relationships, and opportunities—and maximize those, doing the best we can for his glory.

You may not win a decathlon, but you can be God's winner in other areas. Don't make excuses. Use who you are and what you have for him.

BIRTHDAYS:

1935—Alex Karras, Gary, IN, all-pro NFL defensive tackle (Detroit Lions) and actor

1956—Kathy Kreiner, Timmins, Ontario, Canadian skier and winner of the gold medal in the giant slalom in the 1976 Olympics

1976—Rebecca Snyder, Grand Junction, CO, air pistol (1996 Olympics)

Do you see a man skilled in his work? He will serve before kings; he will not serve before obscure men. **Proverbs 22:29**

Fun Fact Jim Thorpe led Carlisle College to the national championship in 1912, scoring twenty-five touchdowns and 198 points. The team's record included a 27–6 victory over Army and future president Dwight Eisenhower. In a speech in 1961, Eisenhower recalled of Thorpe, "My memory goes back to Jim Thorpe. He never practiced in his life, and he could do anything better than any other football player I ever saw." Thorpe was named all-American in 1911 and 1912.

JULY 16 Seed **Planting**

On this day in 1995, Betsy King won the forty-fourth US Women's Open Golf Championship.

From 1984 through 1989, Betsy King won a total of twenty LPGA events, more wins during that time period than any other golfer in the world, male or female. During her career, Betsy was named player of the year three times and won two scoring titles and three money titles. The last of her thirty-four LPGA wins came in 2001. With her thirtieth win in 1995, she gained entry into the World Golf Hall of Fame. Taking her Christian faith seriously, she also organized for Habitat for Humanity and worked with orphan relief agencies in former Soviet bloc countries.

If you watch much golf, you'll see many approaches to putting, different club heads, grips, and stances. Some golfers have regular routines that they follow before striking the ball. Putting is an extremely important part of the game. Par golfers are expected to putt just twice; thus, on a par-four hole, half of the strokes would be putts. An old golf expression states, "You drive for show but putt for dough."

It starts by lining up the putt, looking carefully at the surface of the green between the ball and the hole, considering the slopes and the texture of the grass. Quality golf courses spend lots of money and time in making this grass almost like carpet. This involves locating the greens for plenty of sun and watering, fertilizing, and mowing them at just the right times. Greenskeepers choose high-quality seed, usually a heavy layer of velvet-bent grass seed—spread evenly and then raked into the surface of the soil. The goal is a thick layer of grass—green and cut low, with no bare spots.

Obviously the seeds are important—no grass, no green.

Our hearts are God's ground, hopefully fertile and receptive to his seeds, his Word. He wants lush growth with no bare spots. This happens when we read the Bible and memorize passages. As we plant those seeds, they can grow and become part of us, helping us live the way God wants us to live.

Memorized verses will spring to mind when we need them, as this one reminds us: "How can a young person stay pure? By obeying your word" (Psalm 119:9, NLT).

May your life be God's "green." Plant his Word—here's a good verse to start with.

ALSO ON THIS DAY . . .

1950—Uruguay beat Brazil 2-1 in Rio de Janeiro to win soccer's fourth World Cup.

1988—Jackie Joyner-Kersee set a women's heptathlete record of 7,215 points.

1993—San Francisco Giants outfielder Darren Lewis set a record of 267 consecutive errorless games.

2009—The Old School beat the Young Guns 22-21 (OT) in the Major League Lacrosse All-Star Game in Denver, Colorado.

I have hidden your word in my heart that I might not sin against you. Psalm 119:11

Fun Fact "A lot of people are scared to say, 'Hey, I gave it my best and it wasn't good enough.' As a Christian you can say, 'Hey, I gave it my best and if it's not good enough, that's fine. And if it is, that's good too—because my relationship with the Lord isn't going to change whether I win a tournament or don't win a tournament."—Betsy King

BIRTHDAYS:

1943—Jimmy Johnson, NFL coach (Dallas Cowboys, Miami Dolphins) and broadcaster

1968—Barry Sanders, NFL running back (Detroit Lions) and winner of the 1988 Heisman Trophy

1979—Kim Rhode, Whittier, CA, double trap shooter and winner of four Olympic medals (gold in 1996 and 2000, silver in 2008, bronze in 2004)

What a **Relief!**

ON THIS DAY IN 1989, CINCINNATI REDS RELIEF PITCHER KENT TEKULVE RETIRED AFTER 1,050 APPEARANCES.

Relief pitchers are valuable in baseball, and Kent Tekulve was one of the best and most durable. He began in the majors in 1974, but his best seasons were 1978 and 1979—he saved thirty-one games in both with ERAs of 2.33 and 2.75. When the Pirates defeated the Orioles in the World Series, Kent saved three of the games. He holds the National League record for career innings pitched in relief, as he pitched effectively into his forties. With the Phillies, in 1987 at the age of forty, he led the National League in games pitched (ninety) for the fourth time. Before the 1989 season, Tekulve signed with the Cincinnati Reds and pitched in thirty-seven games before retiring.

In modern baseball, an effective starting pitcher is expected to pitch at least five innings before giving way to the set-up relief pitcher. The job of this player is to protect a lead or keep the score close until handing the ball to the closer relief pitcher. Managers and players want relief pitchers they can depend on—to throw strikes (no walks) and get outs. These athletes must be consistent and reliable.

What kind of relief pitcher would you be—not at throwing a baseball but at being consistent and reliable? Those are valued character traits, important in lots of areas in addition to baseball.

Consistency means performing at a certain level every time. A consistent student always does the homework assignments. A consistent musician pays attention to the director or conductor. A consistent employee puts in the required hours. A consistent athlete keeps the workout schedule and always shows up on time to practice.

Reliability means doing what we say, following through. When Dad says he will pick you up after school at a certain time, you know he'll be there—you can count on him. When Mom says she will do something, you know she will keep her word—she's reliable. What other "reliable" people do you know?

God is perfectly consistent and reliable. That's a relief!

....

ALSO ON THIS DAY . . .

1979—Sebastian Coe ran a world-record mile (3:49) in Oslo.

1990—The Minnesota Twins became the first team to turn two triple plays in a game, but they still lost to the Boston Red Sox 1-0.

2004—Laila Ali retained her Women's Boxing world title, knocking out Nikki Eplion in four rounds.

2007—A federal grand jury indicted Atlanta Falcons quarterback Michael Vick and three other men on charges of running a dog-fighting operation.

BIRTHDAYS:

1941—Daryle Lamonica, Fresno, CA, AFL and NFL quarterback (Buffalo Bills and Oakland Raiders)

1962—Jay Barrs, Jacksonville, FL, archer and winner of an Olympic gold medal in 1988

1972—Melissa Schwen, Bloomington, IN, rower and winner of an Olympic silver medal (coxless pairs) in 1996

For the word of the Lord is right and true; he is faithful in all he does. Psalm 33:4

[un][ACT] Kent Tekulve ended his career having pitched in 1,050 games with a win-loss record of 94-90, an earned run average of 2.85, and 184 saves.

18 A Winner **and a Loser**

On this day in 1994, the Houston Astros tied a National League comeback record, beating the St. Louis Cardinals 15-12 after trailing 10-0.

Imagine you're playing baseball and early in the game the other team hits well and gets every break, and before you can say "relief pitcher," you're down ten to zero. How do you feel? How will you react? Lots of players would figure the game was over and then just play out the innings. We can see it in their body language—head down and shoulders stooped, kicking at the dirt, shuffling instead of running. That's not how the Astros responded in this game. They kept battling and eventually scored fifteen runs while holding the Cardinals to just two more—and they won!

Now imagine you're on the other team, the one that scored the quick ten runs. How do you feel? How will you react? Some teams relax in that situation, thinking the game is already won, even though they have several innings left. They may even joke around at the other team's expense. Maybe that's what happened to the Cardinals; and before they knew it, they had lost.

Every game has a winner and a loser—in this case, the Astros won and the Cardinals lost. But the real winners are those who never give up and keep doing their best, regardless of the situation and outlook. Even if they come out on the losing end of the score, they've won. But the opposite is also true. Losers are those athletes who don't give their best, who slide through the game. Even if they get a trophy for their efforts, they haven't really won; they've just beaten another team.

In life you'll encounter many situations where the outcome seems hopeless. You know that God wants you in a certain place at a certain time, but you can't see any way out, any solution to the problem. You may feel like a loser. That's when you need to remember this lesson: God has a purpose for you being there, and he is with you. He will see you through. Keep your head up and keep doing your best for him.

Be a winner!

....

ALSO ON THIS DAY . . .

1959—William Wright became the first black person to win a major golf tournament.

1976—At the 1976 Summer Olympics, Nadia Comaneci became the first person in Olympic Games history to score a perfect ten in gymnastics.

1993—Hiromi Kobayash won the LPGA JAL Big Apple Golf Classic.

2009—Italy beat Germany 42-30 to win the rugby RLEF European Shield for the second consecutive year.

BIRTHDAYS:

1935—Tenley Albright, Boston, MA, figure skater and Olympic gold medal winner in 1952 and 1956

1943—Calvin Peete, Detroit, MI, PGA golfer

1978—Ben Sheets, Baton Rouge, LA, four-time all-star major-league pitcher (Milwaukee Brewers, Oakland Athletics)

> For everyone born of God overcomes the world. This is the victory that has overcome the world, even our faith. 1 John 5:4

Fun Fact In 2004, the Houston Astros started the season 44-44, but went 48-26 in the second half of the season to make it to the postseason.

Putting in **the Miles**

On this day in 1900, Michel Théato won the second Olympics marathon in Paris.

Very little is known about Michel, except that he was from Luxembourg, a cabinetmaker in Paris, and a member of the St-Mandé Athletic Club. He won the marathon race in very hot temperatures in just under three hours. Through the years the times have dropped significantly, with much more sophisticated training routines and coaching.

The men's marathon record currently stands at 2.03:59, set in Berlin by Haile Gebrselassie of Ethiopia on September 28, 2008.

A marathon is 26.2 miles. Supposedly that distance was chosen to match how far the fabled Greek soldier-messenger Pheidippides ran from the Battle of Marathon to Athens in 490 B.C. Whatever—it's a long race, the longest in the Olympics, and anyone who even finishes one should celebrate. To some, especially those who can hardly jog around the block without getting winded, that distance may seem way too long for anyone to run. But here's a startling truth: except for those with physical limitations, just about anyone can do it. The next time a marathon is on TV (like the big ones in Boston, New York, and Chicago), take a close look at the runners. You'll see men and women of all shapes, sizes, and ages. They just have to have the discipline to prepare, to put in the miles.

Preparation means at least three months of training to build endurance in legs and lungs, running on a schedule of gradually increasing distances. Most marathon training schedules feature a long run or two of twenty miles. Running that far isn't so long that it depletes the runners but long enough to give them confidence that they can actually make it the whole 26.2 miles—they can finish.

Endurance is a familiar word in Scripture. God wants his people to run the race of life his way, to run it well, without getting sidetracked, and to finish strong. To accomplish this, we must prepare—do what is necessary. This involves diet ("feeding" on God's Word) and exercise ("building" faith muscles by depending on him). It also involves pushing through the daily frustrations and problems that come our way, all of which will help us in the long run.

You're at the start of God's marathon. Are you ready? You can do it!

....

ALSO ON THIS DAY . . .

1877—Spencer W. Gore beat Marshall in the first Wimbledon Men's Tennis championship.

1980—The twenty-second modern Olympic games opened in Moscow with the United States and other nations boycotting.

2009—Argentina beat Australia, 4-3, by penalty strokes to take the Women's Champions Trophy for field hockey in Sydney, Australia.

2009—Russia won the synchronized swimming competition at the World Aquatics Championships in Rome, Italy.

BIRTHDAYS:

1964—Teresa Edwards, Cairo, GA, basketball forward (Minnesota Lynx) and winner of five Olympic medals (bronze in 1992 and gold in 1984, 1988, 1996, and 2000)

1979—Rick Ankiel, Ft. Pierce, FL, major-league pitcher/outfielder (St. Louis Cardinals and Kansas City Royals)

1981—Naomi Grabow, Arrowhead, CA, pairs skater with Benjamin Oberman

Dear brothers and sisters, when troubles come your way, consider it an opportunity for great joy. For you know that when your faith is tested, your endurance has a chance to grow. So let it grow, for when your endurance is fully developed, you will be perfect and complete, needing nothing. **James 1:2–4, NLT**

FUN FACT Fauja Singh from India holds the world record for the marathon for runners over ninety. At ninety-two, he finished in 5 hours 40 minutes. He's ninety-nine and still running.

MLB—National League Mascots

Match the location to the mascot.

1. New York
2. Philadelphia
3. St. Louis
4. Chicago
5. San Diego
6. San Francisco
7. Florida
8. Washington
9. Cincinnati
10. Milwaukee
11. Colorado
12. Arizona
13. Atlanta
14. Houston
15. Los Angeles

a. Giants
b. Cardinals
c. Reds
d. Marlins
e. Braves
f. Diamondbacks
g. Mets
h. Rockies
i. Padres
j. Dodgers
k. Astros
l. Brewers
m. Phillies
n. Nationals
o. Cubs

ANSWERS: 1.g, 2.m, 3.b, 4.o, 5.i, 6.a, 7.d, 8.n, 9.c, 10.l, 11.h, 12.f, 13.e, 14.k, 15.j

Mr. **Irrelevant**

On this day in 2008, David Vobora agreed to a three-year, $1.24 million contract with the St. Louis Rams.

When David Vobora was selected in the NFL draft in 2008, he was labeled "Mr. Irrelevant." That's because he was the final pick, way behind all the guys getting the big headlines and signing bonuses. The person is given that label because no one really cares about the player chosen last and because that player probably won't make it in pro football anyway.

Every now and then, however, a player like David Vobora comes along and surprises the "experts" by making an NFL team and doing well. At first, he was on the Rams' practice squad. But on November 4th he was promoted to the active roster when a couple of wide receivers were placed on injured reserve. Then, on November 30, David made his first career start. According to those who keep track of such things, that was the first time a "Mr. Irrelevant" had started in a game during his rookie season since 1994, when Marty Moore started four games for the New England Patriots. David performed well in the game, with five tackles, the second best on the team.

Sports journalists like to have fun with this and mean no harm, nothing personal, but how would you like to wear that label? Maybe you feel that way from time to time—not important, unnoticed, irrelevant, and unnecessary.

Here's the truth, straight from God—no one is irrelevant. Every person is important in his sight. He created us, loves us, chose us, sent Jesus to die for us, is with us, and sent the Holy Spirit to be in us. He forgives, guides, protects, and heals. And we don't have to earn all this through our performance or go through a "draft." God freely gives himself to us; that's called *grace*.

Regardless of where you stand in the popularity rankings or how you have done in the class, in the gym, or on the field, you matter to God. You're one of his first-round picks and he has great plans for you.

....

ALSO ON THIS DAY . . .

1963—Sonny Liston knocked out Floyd Patterson in the first round to win the heavyweight boxing title.

1973—Susie Maxwell Berning won the twenty-eighth US Women's Open Golf Championship.

2005—The National Hockey League board of governors unanimously ratified the new NHL Collective Bargaining Agreement, formally ending the lockout that cancelled the 2004–2005 NLH season.

2007—Mike Coolbaugh, first-base coach with the Tulsa Drillers of the Double-A Texas League, died after getting hit in the head with a line drive at a game in North Little Rock, Arkansas.

BIRTHDAYS:

1949—Lasse Viren, Finnish 5K/10K runner, winner of Olympic gold medals in 1972 and 1976

1971—Kristine Marie Lilly, New York, NY, soccer midfielder, 1996 Olympics

1983—Steven Jackson, Las Vegas, NV, NFL running back (St. Louis Rams)

But God chose the foolish things of the world to shame the wise; God chose the weak things of the world to shame the strong. **1 Corinthians 1:27**

FUN FACT Of 45 games at the University of Idaho, Vobora started 33 and ranks sixth in school history with 341 tackles (209 solo), including 3 sacks, 28 stops for losses. As a senior he led the school in tackles with 148 (59 solo) and had a sack, an interception, and a fumble recovery and was All-WAC for the second consecutive season.

Standing **Strong**

On this day in 1996, Kerri Strug completed her second and final vault to secure the first-ever Olympic gold medal for the United States' women's gymnastic team.

Kerri Strug had competed in gymnastics for most of her life, beginning at eight years old. At fourteen, she was the youngest Olympian in 1992, and at eighteen she made the Olympic team again (Atlanta). In the team competition, the Russians had dominated for decades, and they came into that event with a narrow lead. It came down to the final rotation—the Russians on floor exercise and the Americans on vault. At first the outlook was good for the US, but then one of Kerri's teammates fell twice on her landings, registering poor scores. Kerri was the last to vault for the United States.

On Kerri's first attempt, she landed awkwardly and felt a pop in her ankle. Her scores reflected the poor landing. Because a Russian would be performing after her, Kerri needed to land a second vault on her feet to clinch the victory. Kerri's coach, Bela Karolyi, urged her, saying, "Kerri, we need you to go one more

time. We need you one more time for the gold. You can do it!" Kerri could barely walk, let alone sprint down the runway and fling herself up and over the horse to land with great purpose onto only one good leg. But in obvious pain, she did, landing her second vault perfectly . . . on one foot . . . and for victory. Then she collapsed in agony and was carried off the mat. With two torn ligaments in her ankle, she couldn't compete in any individual events.

Imagine the pressure in front of that vast worldwide audience, with your team and nation riding on you. Yet she performed with courage and came through.

At times we are called to take a stand, to work through pressure and pain and do what we know is right, what God wants us to do. We can sense the Holy Spirit whispering, "You can do it!" It may

mean standing up for truth in a conversation, standing up for a classmate who is being bullied, standing up for God with friends, or standing up to resist temptation. God knows we can do it, and he promises to give us the strength.

So run, vault, and stand strong. "You can do it!"

....

ALSO ON THIS DAY . . .

1987—Petra Felke of East Germany threw a javelin 78.89 meters, setting a women's world record.

1993—Chris Board-man from England bicycled a world-record one-hour distance (32.48 miles).

2005—Eighteen-year-old LPGA rookie Paula Creamer won the Evian Masters golf tournament in France, cruising to an eight-stroke victory over Michelle Wie and Lorena Ochoa.

2009—Mark Buehrle of the Chicago White Sox threw the eighteenth perfect game in the history of Major League Baseball and became the sixth pitcher in the history of the game to hurl both a no-hitter and a perfect game, beating the Rays, 5-0.

> Be strong and courageous. Do not be afraid or terrified because of them, for the Lord your God goes with you; he will never leave you nor forsake you. **Deuteronomy 31:6**

Fun Fact
Kerri Strug became a national sports hero for her final vault, visiting the president, appearing on television talk shows, making the cover of *Sports Illustrated*, and appearing on a Wheaties cereal box with other team members. Today Kerri lives and works in Washington, DC. In her free time she enjoys running marathons, working with charities, traveling the world for special events, and cheering on young athletes as they pursue their own dreams.

BIRTHDAYS:

1936—Don Drysdale, Van Nuys, CA, Hall-of-Fame pitcher (Los Angeles Dodgers) and winner of the Cy Young Award in 1962

1974—Tara Williams, WNBA guard (Phoenix Mercury)

1984—Brandon Roy, Seattle, WA, NBA shooting guard (Portland Trailblazers)

Losing **Streak**

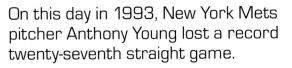

On this day in 1993, New York Mets pitcher Anthony Young lost a record twenty-seventh straight game.

Twenty-seven losses in a row—how does someone handle that? Actually, Anthony Young was a decent pitcher. Remember, only accomplished athletes with a record of successes make it to the major leagues. Anthony did, and he pitched six years in the big leagues—for the Mets, Cubs, and Astros. And despite the win-loss record (15-48), his lifetime earned run average is a respectable 3.89. So Anthony Young wasn't a "loser." But taking that ball every four or five days and climbing the mound, he must have felt like it when the losses began mounting. Couldn't just one of those

games have been a "laugher," with the Mets bats coming alive and pounding out a bunch of runs? Evidently not.

Sometimes setbacks seem to come like that—in bunches. Remember Job in the Bible? That's what happened to him . . . only much worse. He had lost everything—money, livelihood, family, and health. Then his buddies came to cheer him up, but all they did was lecture him, saying that he must have brought all these calamities on himself; God was punishing him for doing something terribly wrong.

Job was struggling in every way. But hear what he said about God to these so-called friends: "Though he slay me, yet will I hope in him" (Job 13:15).

Job could have packed it in, given up, and turned bitter.

He could have said, "You're right—all the evidence seems to indicate that I am a certified loser. And I certainly deserve everything I've received." But he didn't. Instead, Job kept trusting in God, even through he felt terrible and certainly didn't know why all the terrible stuff had happened to him.

Are you on a losing streak? Just because you've had a few setbacks doesn't make you a loser. Remember that God has a much different way of measuring success—faith in him and his promises. And he says you're a winner. So keep your head up, and keep trusting him!

ALSO ON THIS DAY . . .

1929—The New York to San Francisco foot-race ("Bunion Derby") ended (after two months); a sixty-year-old from Monteverde won.

1976—John Naber was the first to swim the 200-meter backstroke in under two minutes.

2005—The USA beat Panama 3-1 (on penalties) in the CONCACF Gold Cup Final (soccer).

2005—Lance Armstrong won his seventh straight Tour de France and then retired from racing.

What, then, shall we say in response to this? If God is for us, who can be against us? He who did not spare his own Son, but gave him up for us all—how will he not also, along with him, graciously give us all things? **Romans 8:31–32**

Fun Fact
Anthony Young's losing streak ended four days later when the Mets scored twice in the bottom of the ninth against the Marlins. A few weeks after, he flew to Los Angeles to be on *The Tonight Show*. While mired in the streak, he had been prime monologue material for Leno, so when they met, Jay offered Anthony the chance to get back at him, saying, "You can make fun of my chin if you want to."

183

Sweetness

On this day in 1954, Hall-of-Fame NFL running back Walter Payton was born in Columbia, Mississippi.

Growing up in modest surroundings in the racially charged South, Walter Payton followed his brother Eddie to Jackson State University, in Mississippi near his home, where he achieved all-American. In 1975, the Chicago Bears chose Walter in the first round of the draft, the fourth player selected overall. He spent the next thirteen seasons with the Bears, where he developed into a superstar and set just about every record for a running back. At his retirement, Walter's records included total yards, seasons with 1,000 or more yards rushing (ten), yards rushing in one game, games with more than 100 yards rushing (seventy-seven), and rushing touchdowns (110). He also won the NFC rushing title five straight years, from 1976 to 1980, led the NFC in scoring

in 1977, and won the NFL kickoff return championship in his rookie year. Walter was selected as the NFL's MVP and offensive player of the year in 1977 and 1985 and the NFC Most Valuable Player in 1977, and he played in nine Pro Bowl games. He won Super Bowl XX with the 1985 Chicago Bears. Extremely durable, Walter missed one game in his rookie campaign and then played in 186 consecutive games, sometimes with injuries, including cracked ribs.

Hall-of-Fame NFL player and coach Mike Ditka described Walter Payton as the greatest football player he had ever seen—but even greater as a human being. Nicknamed "Sweetness" for his personality and playing style, Walter was a leader and role model for teammates, kids, and other running backs, unusual in these days of ego, greed, and

immorality by many pro athletes. Walter was a solid citizen, a faithful husband, and a good father. He was also a man of faith.

His life leads us to the question of how we are living. Walter only lived to forty-five, dying in 1999 from a rare liver disease. But he influenced so many for good.

People, especially those who are younger, look to us for leadership and example. We need to show them what a follower of Christ looks like in our attitudes and actions. God may not use us to set NFL rushing records or win games, but he can use us to win others to him. May our lives be filled with his sweetness and light.

....

ALSO ON THIS DAY . . .

1940—John Sigmund began his swim of eighty-nine hours forty-six minutes in the Mississippi River.

1976—East German Annegret Richter ran the 100 meters in 11.01.

1997—NFL quarterback Brett Favre re-signed with the Green Bay Packers for $50 million for seven years.

2004—Michael Schumacher (Ferrari) won the German Grand Prix, equaling his own record of eleven victories in one season and closing in on his seventh Formula One championship. It was also his sixth consecutive victory.

For we are to God the aroma of Christ among those who are being saved and those who are perishing. 2 Corinthians 2:15

Fun Fact
Walter wouldn't celebrate after scoring touchdowns; instead, he would often hand the ball to his teammates or the official. He specialized in pranks, particularly during training camp. He would set off fireworks in the middle of the night, rearrange papers on the coaches' desks and "borrow" their phones. Payton insisted his pranks were his way of staying young. "Life is too short, you better enjoy it while you can," he said.

BIRTHDAYS:

1964—Tony Granato, Broadview, IL, NHL left wing (Rangers, Kings, Sharks)

1971—Billy Wagner, Marion, VA, major-league relief pitcher (Astros, Phillies, Mets, Red Sox, Braves)

1981—Conor Casey, Dover, NH, MLS forward (Colorado Rapids)

Sudden **Shock**

On this day in 2007, Skip Prosser, Wake Forest basketball coach, died suddenly of an apparent heart attack.

Prosser collapsed in his office around noon after jogging at the track adjacent to his office on campus. He was rushed to Wake Forest University Baptist Medical Center, where he was pronounced dead from an apparent sudden massive heart attack. He was fifty-six years old.

Skip Prosser coached basketball at Wake Forest University (Winston-Salem, North Carolina) for six seasons, compiling a 126-86 record. His career record was 291-146 in fourteen seasons, including six as the head coach at Xavier and one at Loyola (MD). Prosser's Wake Forest teams averaged twenty-one wins per season while playing in the Atlantic Coast Conference, probably the most difficult league in the country. Even more important than a win-loss record, every senior that Prosser coached earned his degree in four years. Skip Prosser was successful as a coach and mentor. And his death shocked everyone who knew and loved him.

When someone dies like this, in the prime of life, we are shocked into reality. Everyone, especially young people, act as though they will live forever. We know that's not true, that eventually every person has to die. But we'd rather not think about it while we're feeling good, having fun, and enjoying life. Then tragedy strikes, and we remember the truth.

No one is guaranteed a long life, and certainly no one can be sure of taking even one more breath. So making the most of the time God has given us on earth only makes sense.

First Peter 1:24-25 reminds us, "People are like grass; their beauty is like a flower in the field. The grass withers and the flower fades. But the word of the Lord remains forever" (NLT). Grass and flowers don't last very long—neither do we. God doesn't want us to be fearful or morbid, thinking about death all the time; we should enjoy his gifts of laughter, friends, rest, and food. But he wants us to take seriously the time and opportunities he gives, living moment by moment and day by day for him.

Knowing that this day could be your last on earth, how should you live?

ALSO ON THIS DAY . . .

1970—Johnny Bench of the Cincinnati Reds hit three consecutive home runs off the Phillies' Steve Carlton.

1990—The US beat the Soviet Union 17-0 in baseball at the Goodwill Games.

2004—The Netherlands defeated Germany 5-4 in the final of the canoe polo 2004 world championships held in Miyoshi, Japan.

2009—In the FIVB World League Final (volleyball), Brazil beat Serbia, winning the league for the eighth time and equaling Italy's record.

Be very careful, then, how you live—not as unwise but as wise, making the most of every opportunity, because the days are evil. **Ephesians 5:15–16**

FUN FACT In 2008, the Skip Prosser Award was established to honor coaches who not only achieve success on the basketball court but who display moral integrity off of it as well.

1. Who was the first person in Olympic Games history to score a perfect ten in gymnastics? (July 18)
2. How did Skip Prosser, Wake Forest basketball coach, die? (July 26)
3. In 1983, who became the fastest man alive? (July 3)
4. What was the first year Venus and Serena Williams won the Wimbledon Women's Doubles Final? (July 9)
5. In order to warn outfielders of an oncoming wall, what did baseball owners do? (July 12)
6. To what team did the New York Yankees lose when the Yankees pitcher Andy Hawkins threw a no-hitter? (July 1)
7. Who won two gold medals at the 1912 Olympics in Stockholm, Sweden, and became recognized as the world's greatest athlete? (July 15)
8. With what NFL team did David Vobora sign a three-year contract in 2008? (July 22)
9. Who is one of the top bass fishermen in the world? (July 31)
10. What sport did Betsy King play? (July 16)
11. For what team did Horace Clarke play? (July 2)
12. How old was Dale Earnhardt Jr. when he began his racing in 1991? (July 10)
13. How many games did New York Mets pitcher Anthony Young lose in his streak? (July 24)
14. How many relief appearances did Kent Tekulve of the Cincinnati Reds make before he retired? (July 17)
15. How many years has Tommy Lasorda served with the Dodgers? (July 30)
16. What match has been named the best Wimbledon final and one of the greatest sporting events in history? (July 5)
17. What Hall-of-Fame golfer is known as "The Golden Bear?" (July 11)
18. What year did Lou Gehrig retire? (July 4)
19. What was Walter Payton's nickname? (July 25)
20. For what NFL team did Brett Farve play soon after his 2008 retirement? (July 29)
21. How many Cincinnati Reds players were elected to the 1957 all-star team? (July 8)
22. On which gymnastics event did Kerri Strug win the gold medal for the US team at the 1996 Olympics in Atlanta? (July 23)
23. Who won the second Olympics marathon in Paris? (July 19)

Decision **Time**

On this day in 2008, former Green Bay Packers quarterback Brett Favre, who had announced his retirement after the 2008 season, faxed a letter seeking reinstatement to the NFL.

Brett Favre was a Packer legend, but he had decided to retire after fifteen years with the team, at almost forty years of age. So the Packers celebrated Favre, invested in their new quarterback, and moved on. But then Brett changed his mind and sent this letter. Eventually he played the 2008 season with the New York Jets. Then he retired again. But he changed his mind again and played the 2009 season as a Minnesota Viking. Obviously Brett Favre has trouble making up his mind about football. Although his body takes much longer to recuperate these days and the season feels very long by the time December rolls around, he can't stay away—it's just too much a part of his life, of who he is.

We really can't blame Brett too much for his flip-flopping. Making a decision can be tough, especially when two appealing options are involved. Question: "Do you want strawberry or chocolate?" Answer: "I like them both. I can't make up my mind." If we wait too long, however, we may miss out on both (the ice cream will melt).

Some decisions aren't very important, so changing our minds in those cases won't matter very much. But others are extremely important. When you read the story of Israel in the Old Testament, you'll find several times when the people had to make life-and-death decisions. They had to decide if they would listen to Moses, Joshua, and other godly leaders and go God's way, or just live their own way. Pretty important, right? These decisions were turning points in their lives and the life of the nation.

One day, Joshua stood before them and put it on the line. He said, "But if serving the Lord seems undesirable to you, then choose for yourselves this day whom you will serve, whether the gods your forefathers served beyond the River, or the gods of the Amorites, in whose land you are living. But as for me and my household, we will serve the Lord" (Joshua 24:15).

We face the same choice today. So what's your decision? Who will you serve?

ALSO ON THIS DAY . . .

1957—Kathy Cornelius won the eleventh US Women's Open Golf Championship.

1965—The Phillies (16) and the Pirates (10) set a Major League record for strikeouts in one game (26).

1978—Penny Dean swam the English Channel in a record seven hours and forty minutes.

2007—Timmy M. Ferry won the AMA Toyota Motocross Championship at Washougal Motocross Park, Washougal, Washington.

BIRTHDAYS:

1969—Alison Dunlap, Denver, CO, cyclist (1996 Olympics)

1981—Jennie Thompson, Wichita Falls, TX, gymnast (1996 Olympics)

1984—Chad Billingsley, Defiance, OH, major-league pitcher (Los Angeles Dodgers)

Elijah went before the people and said, "How long will you waver between two opinions? If the Lord is God, follow him; but if Baal is God, follow him" But the people said nothing. 1 Kings 18:21

FUN FACT One day after his father died, Favre decided to play in a Monday night game against the Oakland Raiders. He passed for four touchdowns in the first half and 399 total yards in a 41–7 victory. Afterwards, Favre said, "I knew that my dad would have wanted me to play. I love him so much and I love this game. It's meant a great deal to me, to my dad, to my family, and I didn't expect this kind of performance. But I know he was watching tonight."

Teachers

On this day in 1996, Tommy Lasorda retired as the Los Angeles Dodgers' manager.

Tommy Lasorda became the Los Angeles Dodgers' field manager on September 29, 1976, after the retirement of long-time manager Walter Alston. Tommy managed two decades and continued to work for the Dodgers organization after he retired. He now has served more than sixty years with them. During his twenty years as the Dodgers' skipper, Tommy compiled a 1,599-1,439 record, won two World Series championships in (1981 and 1988), four National League pennants, and eight division titles. Tommy managed in four all-star games, and he ranks fourth all-time in postseason games managed (sixty-one), behind Bobby Cox, Casey Stengel, and Joe Torre. That's great company—those are great managers.

Great managers understand that they do more than manage and strategize. They also teach. Usually they bring in other "teachers"—pitching, hitting, conditioning, position, and other coaches.

Gifted athletes usually find that sports come easy to them—their natural talent takes over, so they can feel self-reliant. Then, when they become pros, they suddenly have lots of money and even more independence. But just as coaches and managers need to teach, great players understand that they must continue to learn and develop. And that means listening to their coaches and following their instructions. Athletes who think they know better than their coaches are sure to struggle.

Learning begins with the right attitude—submitting to the coaches' directions and doing what they say. The Bible talks a lot about this—not about coaches and athletes, but about submitting and learning from our teachers, including parents, pastors, and other church leaders. Also, husbands and wives are supposed to learn from each other. And everyone needs to submit to God and be taught by the Holy Spirit.

Who are your teachers: Mom, Dad, pastor, school teachers, Sunday school teacher, choir director, coach, grandparent? God uses them to build skills, to inform, and to prepare you for life.

Submit, listen, and learn.

ALSO ON THIS DAY . . .

1908—The Around the World Automobile Race ended in Paris.

1930—Uruguay beat Argentina 4-2 for soccer's first World Cup, in Montevideo.

1988—Harry Drake shot an arrow record for distance—1,873 meters (1.16 miles).

2005—The Pittsburgh Penguins selected superstar prospect Sidney Crosby as the first overall pick in the NHL Entry Draft.

Let us fix our eyes on Jesus, the author and perfecter of our faith, who for the joy set before him endured the cross, scorning its shame, and sat down at the right hand of the throne of God. **Hebrews 12:2**

BIRTHDAYS:

1963—Ingrid Butts, Denver, CO, cross country skier (1994 Olympics)

1963—Chris Mullin, Brooklyn, NY, NBA forward (Golden State Warriors, Indiana Pacers) and winner of Olympic gold medals in 1984 and 1992

1984—Kevin Pittsnogle, Martinsburg, WV, outstanding college basketball player (University of West Virginia)

Fun Fact
Lasorda and his wife, Jo, have been married 60 years. They named a gymnasium and youth center in memory of their son, Tom Jr., in Yorba Linda, California, on September 7, 1997. They have a daughter, Laura, and a granddaughter, Emily. In June 2005, President George W. Bush asked Lasorda to serve as a delegate to the US National Day at the World Exposition in Aichi, Japan.

Re-Creation

On this day in 2005, Kevin VanDam won his second Bassmaster Classic championship in Pittsburgh, Pennsylvania.

Often called KVD, Kevin VanDam is one of the top bass fishermen in the world. He has won the Bassmaster Classic tournament three times, the most recent in 2010. So he is the current world champion. Bass fishing is huge. In fact, Lake Norman in North Carolina hosts a fishing tournament almost every week of the year. The most popular of these are bass tournaments, which range in size from ten boats to a couple hundred in the large events. The biggest and the one with the most prize money was the Wal-Mart FLW Tour National Guard Open. Held in April, 2008, 400 men and women fished for a purse of $1.5 million.

Fishing is big business; it's also fun. Most fishermen and fisherwomen aren't trying to win trophies or big bucks. They just enjoy the challenge of finding, hooking, and landing an elusive fish while experiencing nature firsthand. Freshwater fishing happens on a lake, river, bayou, pond, or stream, from the shore, dock, boat (large or small), or canoe. Some anglers stand in the water. Usually the only sound is the line leaving the reel, paddles in the water or the low purr of the motor, the hooked fish splashing to the surface, and low conversation among fishing buddies. The occasion is peaceful, serene. Fishing often involves standing or sitting with line in the water, surrounded by quiet that is broken only by the occasional cry of a loon.

Those who practice their sports, such as fishing, in nature enjoy creation, seeing God's beauty at every turn of the river: deer splashing downstream, eagles soaring above, evidence of raccoons and other animals on the shoreline, and so many trees and wildflowers. God's fingerprints are obvious to those who are looking.

Life gets busy, and we spend much of each day caught in traffic, sitting in classes or meetings, and hanging out inside. In all this we miss the natural display of God's handiwork.

Reconnect with creation. Take a walk in a forest preserve or park. Spend time looking for God's fingerprints, listening to his whisper, and talking to him about life.

ALSO ON THIS DAY . . .

1984—The US men's gymnastics team won the team gold medal at the Los Angeles Olympics.

1997—The Oakland Athletics traded Mark McGwire to the St. Louis Cardinals.

2007—The Boston Celtics traded seven players to the Minnesota Timberwolves for ten-time all-star Kevin Garnett, the first time in NBA history so many players had been traded for a single player.

2009—The United States won the women's water polo championship at the World Aquatics Championships in Rome, beating Canada 7-6.

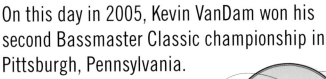

BIRTHDAYS:

1916—Louise Smith, Barnesville, GA, the second woman to race in NASCAR at the top level and known as "the first lady of racing"

1951—Evonne Goolagong Cawley, Australian professional tennis player, winner of Wimbledon in 1971

1958—Mark Cuban, Pittsburgh, PA, owner of the NBA Dallas Mavericks

1987—Michael Bradley, Princeton, NJ, soccer player and member of the US National Team

The heavens declare the glory of God; the skies proclaim the work of his hands. **Psalm 19:1**

FUN FACT All of the fishing tournaments promote "catch and release," which does not deplete the fishery. About 98 percent of the fish weighed are returned to the lake. The world record for large mouth bass belongs to Manabu Kurita (Japan) and George Perry (USA)—22 lb. 4 oz. and caught seventy-seven years apart.

1 The Real **Race**

On this day in 1992, Gail Devers won the 100-meter dash at the Olympic Games in Barcelona, Spain.

Winning the Olympic gold medal is a huge accomplishment in itself. But for Gail Devers this victory was even more remarkable.

Gail was a world-class sprinter and hurdler, so she was expected to do well in the Seoul Olympics. While training, however, she began to struggle physically with migraine headaches, sleeplessness, fainting spells, and frequent loss of vision. Instead of hitting her peak performance, she was constantly exhausted. At first she thought the cause to be her tough training regimen, and for a while doctors dismissed her problems as being "all in her head." But then they discovered she had Grave's disease, a crippling thyroid disorder. Eventually Gail's feet were blistered and swollen, the skin cracked, and the pain excruciating, so she could hardly walk, let alone run. As her condition worsened, the doctors said that they probably would have to amputate both of her legs.

Gail was devastated, as you might imagine, but she didn't give up. In her words: "The word *quit* has never been part of my vocabulary. With lots of hard work, determination, perseverance, and faith in God, I was able to resume training and regain my health." Then, less than seventeen months after the doctors had suggested amputation, Gail won the gold medal in the 100-meter dash at the Barcelona Olympics and was named "world's fastest woman." Four years later, she won two gold medals in Atlanta, adding the 4x100 relay to the 100-meter race.

To all who wonder about her miraculous recovery, Gail quotes her favorite Bible verse: "Faith is the substance of things hoped for the evidence of things not seen" (Hebrews 11:1, KJV). Gail prays all the time and credits her comeback to faith plus hard work. Her philosophy is that God gives us opportunities and strength, but he expects us to do our part. She says, "God gave me a box of potential, and all he asks is that I keep reaching into that box, and he'll keep blessing it."

God has filled you with potential. Do you believe he can use you? Trust him to do miracles in you.

....

ALSO ON THIS DAY . . .

1957—Glen Gorbous, Canadian major-league outfielder (Philadelphia Phillies, Cincinnati Redlegs) threw a baseball a record 135.89 m (445' 10").

1983—New Zealand scored their first Test Cricket match victory in England.

1992—The USA/USSR Around World Air Race began at Santa Monica.

2009—Michael Phelps (USA) set a world record in the men's 100m butterfly (49.82 seconds) at the World Aquatic Championships in Rome, Italy.

BIRTHDAYS:

1962—Joetta Clark, East Orange, NJ, 800 meter runner (Olympics, 1988, 1992, 1996, 2000)

1976—Nwankwo Kanu, Owerri, Nigeria, professional soccer player, member of the Igbo, UNICEF ambassador, most decorated soccer player in history

1978—Edgerrin James, Immokalee, FL, NFL all-pro running back (Colts, Cardinals, Seahawks)

Everyone who competes in the games goes into strict training. They do it to get a crown that will not last; but we do it to get a crown that will last forever. 1 Corinthians 9:25

FUN FACT Gail Devers left competition in 2005 to give birth to a c with her husband and returned in 2006. On February 2, 2007, at the age of fort Devers edged 2004 Olympic champion Joanna Hayes to win the sixty-meter hurdles event at the Millrose Games in 7.86 seconds—the best time in the wor that season and just 0.12 off the record she set in 2003. The time was also sev tenths of a second faster than the listed world record for a forty-year-old.

He Is **For You**

ON THIS DAY IN 2005, MIAMI HEAT CENTER SHAQUILLE O'NEAL SIGED A FIVE-YEAR, $100-MILLION CONTRACT EXTENSION.

At 7 ft. 1 in. and 325 pounds, Shaquille O'Neil is a mountain of a man, one of the biggest NBA players ever. Not only is Shaq big, he's also good, using his size and strength to overpower his opponents for points and rebounds. After an all-American career at Louisiana State University, Shaq was chosen by the Orlando Magic as the first pick in the 1992 draft. He played four years for the Magic and then eight years for the Los Angeles Lakers, where he won three consecutive NBA championships (2000, 2001, and 2002). He was traded to the Miami Heat in 2004 and won another NBA championship there in 2006. Since then, he has also played for the Phoenix Suns (2008–9) and the Cleveland Cavaliers (2009–present). Shaq has won many individual awards, including the 1992–93 Rookie of the Year, 1999–2000 MVP, fifteen all-star teams, three all-star game MVPs, three Finals MVPs, two scoring titles, fourteen all-NBA teams, and three NBA all-Defensive teams. Not bad at all!

So imagine that you sign up for a two-on-two basketball tournament, and your teammate is Shaquille O'Neil? How do you think you would do, especially if all the other teams only had players of your age, ability, and experience? No contest, right? With Shaq on your team, how could you lose?

Well, get this—someone lots bigger and way more powerful than Shaq stands with you, on your team, ready to help you win. In writing to the Romans, Paul listed all kinds of ways that God had shown that he was on the side of all believers. Then Paul wrote, "What, then, shall we say in response to this? If God is for us, who can be against us? (Romans 8:31). The answer: No one, of course. Not even close.

So here's the point. When you're facing a problem, conflict, or struggle, remember who's on your team. God is for you, cheering you on, supporting you, and giving you power.

ALSO ON THIS DAY . . .

1979—All-Star Yankees catcher Thurman Munson died in a plane crash, trying to land his personal jet.

1986—Jackie Joyner-Kersee (US) set a world record for heptathlon (7161 points).

1987—Michael Andretti ran the fastest Indy car race in history (171.49 mph).

2007—The game between the Minnesota Twins and the Kansas City Royals to be played at the Hubert H. Humphrey Metrodome in Minneapolis was postponed due to the collapse of the I-35W Mississippi River Bridge. The game the day before began less than an hour after the collapse but proceeded because cancelling would have sent thousands of vehicles onto the roads and hindered rescue efforts.

BIRTHDAYS:

1960—Linda Fratianne, Los Angeles-Northridge, CA, figure skater, four-time US Champion (1977-1980) and winner of the Olympic silver medal (1980)

1966—Tim Wakefield, Melbourne, FL, major-league pitcher (Boston Red Sox)

1970—Tony Amonte, Hingham, MA, NHL right wing (Rangers, Blackhawks, Coyotes, Flyers, Flames) and Team USA

1976—Michael Weiss, Washington DC, figure skater, three-time national champion (1999, 2000, 2003) and Olympic team member (1998, 2002)

> No, in all these things we are more than conquerors through him who loved us. **Romans 8:37**

un Fact Most of the sports media like Shaq for his playful tone in [inte]rviews. He called himself "The Big Aristotle" for insights during these interviews. [In a]ddition to "Shaq," O'Neal has several nicknames, many given by the media. Some [of th]e most common ones are "The Diesel," "Shaq Fu," "The Big Daddy," "Superman," ["Th]e Big Cactus," "The Big Shaqtus," "The Big Galactus," "Wilt Chamberneezy," "The Baryshnikov," "Dr. Shaq" (after earning his MBA), and, recently, "Shaqovic."

If You Heard...

1. Infield fly
2. Double dribble
3. Horse collar
4. Icing
5. Flip turn
6. Bicycle kick
7. Bump and run
8. Passing shots
9. Back-to-back
10. Side-out

a. Football
b. Soccer
c. Gymnastics
d. Baseball
e. Auto racing
f. Volleyball
g. Ice hockey
h. Swimming
i. Basketball
j. Tennis

ANSWERS: 1.d, 2.i, 3.a, 4.g, 5.h, 6.b, 7.e, 8.j, 9.c, 10.f

Climb

On this day in 1858, Julia Archibald Holmes became the first woman on record to reach the summit of Pikes Peak.

Married just a year, Julia Holmes and her husband, James, headed west in a wagon train, hoping to find gold at Pikes Peak. On August first, they and two miners began to climb the Colorado mountain. After four days they had scaled all 14,110 feet. Here's what she said: "I have accomplished the task which I marked out for myself. . . . Nearly everyone tried to discourage me from attempting it, but I believed that I should succeed." Not only was Julia the first woman to climb Pikes Peak, but she also was the first known woman to climb any of the 14,000-foot mountains in Colorado.

Mountaineering has many challenges, including terrain, altitude, and weather. Mountain climbers need the right skills and equipment. They must endure the climb, too. It isn't like walking to the top row in a stadium. The climb won't be straight up, and a mountain has no steps. Climbers should be strong, able to pull up themselves and their partners. They should be wise, too, making the right choices for routes and techniques and trusting those who know better.

The Christian life is like climbing a mountain, with the goal to be more like Christ and to live with him forever in heaven. We need to be prepared for the journey, building endurance and skill and carrying the right equipment. We can't be carried but must walk on our own. At first, the climb may seem easy, with a gradual slope. Soon, however, the landscape will change and the journey will become more difficult, not smooth and straight but with numerous ups and downs. Along the way, we'll encounter huge boulders or outcroppings, so we'll have to figure out a way around or over.

We certainly need to help our fellow climbers—and be helped by them. And we'll need to follow our guide and listen to the wise advice of others who are more experienced. On some days, we may feel as though we're not making progress, just going sideways or switching back. We can't get discouraged but must keep pushing forward. The climb is not all work, of course. We will enjoy the beauty, the fun, and the friendship along the way. But we're always straining to reach the goal.

Keep climbing.

ALSO ON THIS DAY . . .

1961—The Chicago Bears (NFL) beat the Montreal Alouettes (Canadian Football League) 34-16 in Montreal.

1984—Joan Benoit (US) won the first Olympic marathon for women (2:24:52).

2005—The National Collegiate Athletic Association announced a ban on American Indian mascots in NCAA playoff tournaments as of 2008.

2007—Lorena Ochoa won the Women's British Open at the Old Course at St. Andrews for her first major championship.

BIRTHDAYS:

1962—Patrick Ewing, Kingston, Jamaica, Hall-of-Fame NBA center (Knicks, SuperSonics, Magic), winner of the Olympic gold medal, 1992, and assistant coach for the Orlando Magic

1981—Carl Crawford, Houston, TX, major-league outfielder (Tampa Bay Rays)

1986—Paula Creamer, Mountain View, CA, LPGA golfer and Rookie of the Year in 2005

lift up my eyes to the hills—where does my help come from? My help comes from the ord, the Maker of heaven and earth. Psalm 121:1–2

Fun Fact Holmes wore a short skirt, moccasins, and a hat for her climb, her "American costume." At the peak, she wrote several letters. To her mother Julia said: "Extending as far as the eye can reach, lie the great level plains, stretched out in all their verdure and beauty, while the winding of the grand Arkansas is visible for many miles. . . . Here I am, and feel that I would not have missed this glorious sight for anything at all."

The Courage **to Create**

On this day in 2005, Bob Burnquist won the gold medal for best trick at X Games 11 in Los Angeles.

Titles like "Blunt to Fakie," "900," "ollie to fakie," "Nollie Heel Flip 540 across channel," "540 McTwist to tail," and "Switch Big Flip" won't mean much to most people, but they're names of competitive skateboard moves. In fact, the winning trick for Bob Burnquist was the "Frontside 540 Nar-Jar." To translate, "frontside" means that while airborne, the competitor grabs the skateboard with the back hand between the toes on the front rail of the board. "Five hundred forty" refers to the number of degrees in the turn (360 + 180 = 540). The "Nar-Jar" part of the move just means grabbing the nose of the board while doing the 540. Anyway, Bob Burnquist beat out Colin McKay, Pierre-Luc Gagnon, Shawn White (of snowboarding fame), and others to win the gold.

Burnquist was born in Rio de Janeiro (1976) and began skateboarding seriously at age eleven. He turned pro at fourteen. As an adult he moved to America and holds dual citizenship in Brazil and the US. This medal in 2005 was his tenth. His specialty is switch-stance skateboarding, and his signature trick is called "one-footed smith grind." Bob continually tries to find new ways to make his tricks more creative and more difficult.

Creativity is definitely the best word to describe these skateboarding competitions, with the athletes trying new ways to hold, spin, twist, and ride their boards. Human creativity can be seen in many areas, of course, and it's one of the ways that we reflect the image of God.

Way back in Genesis we read about God creating men and women "in his image" (Genesis 1:27–27). That special creation makes humans different from other animals. We can think conceptually and creatively, and we can relate to God spiritually. Creativity is a gift that we can use in the arts and sciences, in our relationships, in sports, and even in worship. Being creative can be risky—people may resist doing things differently; others may not understand. (Skateboarders can get injured.) But creative risk-takers invent life-saving machines, make breakthroughs in medicine, push performances to new levels, and bring people closer to God. As long as we're not doing something that God has told us is wrong, we should feel free to express our (his) creativity.

Look at you—you're a marvelous creation of a creative God. Now live that way.

....

ALSO ON THIS DAY . . .

1890—Cy Young pitched and won his first game; he still holds the records for most career innings pitched, most career games started, and most complete games.

1926—Gertrude Ederle became the first woman to swim the English Channel.

1953—Ted Williams returned to the Red Sox after serving in the military.

2008—Quarterback Brett Favre was traded from the Green Bay Packers to the New York Jets for a draft pick that would increase in value depending on the Jets' results in 2008.

BIRTHDAYS:

1961—Bruce Matthews, Raleigh, NC, NFL center/guard (Tennessee Titans), considered one of the best offensive linemen in NFL history

1961—Mary Lou Piatek-Daniels, Whiting, IN, professional tennis player

1965—David Robinson, Key West, FL, Hall-of-Fame NBA center (San Antonio Spurs) and Olympic gold medal winner, 1992

I praise you because I am fearfully and wonderfully made; your works are wonderful, I know that full well. Psalm 139:14

FUN FACT Bob Burnquist has been featured in the video game "Tony Hawk's Pro Skater" and most of its sequels and "X Games Skateboarding." He lives in Vista, California, where he has a world-renowned vert ramp in his backyard.

Power-up

ON THIS DAY IN 2007, BARRY BONDS OF THE SAN FRANCISCO GIANTS BROKE BASEBALL GREAT HANK AARON'S RECORD BY HITTING HIS 756TH HOME RUN.

In 1986, Barry Bonds was a "five-tool" player—he could hit for average, hit for power, field well, run fast, and throw strong and accurately. A gifted athlete and skilled ballplayer, he had six outstanding seasons with the Pittsburgh Pirates, winning two National League MVPs (1990, 1992) and other awards. In 1993, he signed a huge contract with San Francisco, where he continued his outstanding play. Over his career, Bonds was named MVP seven times, won twelve Silver Slugger and eight Gold Glove awards, and was named to the all-star Team fourteen times—quite the list of achievements.

Barry Bonds' career, however, has been tainted with controversy. In the late 90s, his power numbers increased dramatically, along with his muscles. He, Sammy Sosa, and Mark McGuire began hitting the ball out of the park at amazing rates. People began to wonder if these men, and others, had been using steroids and other drugs to bulk up, and investigations ensued. Eventually, evidence was produced that several big-league players, including many stars, had, in fact, used performance-enhancing drugs. Bonds is always mentioned in this discussion.

It's all about power. Baseball sluggers want to hit with more power, and pitchers want to throw with power. Weightlifters and shot-putters want more strength, and runners want more speed. Boxers want to punch with power, and even golfers want to swing with power. Many will do almost anything to enhance their strength, speed, and endurance, even, perhaps, forfeiting their future health. But this power urge isn't limited to professional athletes or to banned substances. We can go into any store and buy "power" bars or drinks. Obviously the world's values are upside down.

Instead of more physical strength, our real need is power for living—the ability to change and to become, to fulfill God's purpose for us. We can only have that power through God's Spirit in us. When we submit to God, he promises to give us power to change, to achieve, to love, to forgive, to spread his word, and to make a difference in the world. Real power, supernatural power, comes from him.

Don't fall for phony promises or quick fixes. Tap into the real deal—God's power source. Power up!

....

ALSO ON THIS DAY . . .

1907—Walter Johnson ("Big Train") of the Washington Senators won the first of his 416 wins, 7-2 over Cleveland.

1986—Daniel Buettner, Bret Anderson, Martin Engel, and Anne Knabe began their cycling journey of 15,266 miles from Prudhoe Bay, Alaska to Argentina.

1987—Lynne Cox swam 2.67 miles from the US to the USSR in the 39° F Bering Sea.

1991—Charles Austin broke the US high-jump record at 7'10".

2004—Dallas Friday won the women's wakeboarding competition at the X Games at Huntington Beach, California (74.05).

> ...ut he said to me, "My grace is sufficient for you, for my power is made ...rfect in weakness." Therefore I will boast all the more gladly about my ...eaknesses, so that Christ's power may rest on me. **2 Corinthians 12:9**

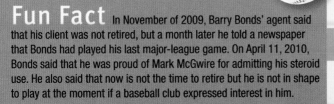

Fun Fact In November of 2009, Barry Bonds' agent said that his client was not retired, but a month later he told a newspaper that Bonds had played his last major-league game. On April 11, 2010, Bonds said that he was proud of Mark McGwire for admitting his steroid use. He also said that now is not the time to retire but he is not in shape to play at the moment if a baseball club expressed interest in him.

8 Seeing **the Light**

On this day in 1988, the lights were turned on in Wrigley Field.

So the lights were turned on—what's the big deal? This event was huge because Wrigley Field was the last major-league ballpark to install lights. Until that day in 1988, all of the Chicago Cubs

home games were played in daylight—no night games at all. Built in 1914 and located in the residential Lakeview neighborhood of Chicago, Wrigley Field is almost a national monument because of its age, ivy-covered walls, hand-operated scoreboard, and other unique features. They only agreed to install the lights

after baseball officials said no postseason games would be played there unless they did. So the lights were put in and turned on with much fanfare. Ironically, the first game to be played (against the Phillies) was rained out in the fourth inning.

Usually lights aren't so controversial. We appreciate electricity and light bulbs, allowing us to play (including baseball games), study, travel, and be entertained during the nighttime hours. Imagine what life would be like without headlights, lamps, streetlights, lit screens, flashlights, warning lights, lit signs, stoplights, and many other lights.

In Bible times, people didn't have any of the electrically powered fixtures, but lights still were very important—lamps, lanterns, torches, and candles illuminated homes and paths. The Old Testament uses light to represent hope, truth, victory, and forgiveness. In speaking of the coming Messiah, Isaiah

wrote, "The people walking in darkness have seen a great light; on those living in the land of the shadow of death a light has dawned" (Isaiah 9:2). So people in Jesus' day understood his claim to be "the light of the world" (John 8:12). Jesus also warned, "The judgment is based on this fact: God's light came into the world, but people loved the darkness more than the light, for their actions were evil" (John 3:19, NLT). Later, Jesus urged his followers to live in the light and to let their lights shine out to the world.

Have you seen the light? Look to Jesus. If you know him, shine out so that others can see the truth and know the way.

ALSO ON THIS DAY . . .

1900—The first Davis Cup tennis competition, named after Dwight Filley Davis, began at Longwood Cricket Club in Massachusettes and was won by the US two days later.

1976—The Chicago White Sox wore shorts as part of their uniforms.

1988—Matt Biondi swam a US record in the 200-meter freestyle (1:47.72).

2004—Danny Way won the Big Air skateboard competition at the X Games in Los Angeles, California (91.66).

BIRTHDAYS:

1968—Suzy Hamilton, Stevens Point, WI, middle-distance runner (1992, 1996, 2000 Olympics)

1981—Roger Federer, Basel, Switzerland, professional tennis player (perhaps the greatest player of all time), currently number one in the world and winner of sixteen Grand Slam titles, and counting

1984—Devon McTavish, Winchester, VA, MLS midfielder (Boulder Rapids, DC United)

When Jesus spoke again to the people, he said, "I am the light of the world. Whoever follows me will never walk in darkness, but will have the light of life." John 8:12

IUNI ACT Night games at Wrigley Field are still limited in number by agreement with the city council. Wrigley Field has served as the home baseball park for the Cubs since 1916. From 1921 to 1970, the Chicago Bears also played their games there before moving to Soldier Field.

The Race **Race**

On this day in 1936, Jesse Owens won his fourth gold medal at the Berlin Olympics.

The grandson of a slave and the son of a sharecropper, Jesse Owens achieved great success despite his humble beginnings. His four gold medals at the 1936 Olympics have made him the best remembered of all Olympic athletes.

While at Ohio State University, Jesse set three world records (long jump, 220-yard sprint, 220-yard low hurdles) and tied for a fourth (100-yard sprint) in about forty-five minutes at the Big Ten Track meet in 1935. So the world knew he could run before he arrived in Berlin.

Holding the Olympics in Germany was controversial because the Nazis' racist views were well known. The US Olympic Committee opposed a boycott, explaining that the games shouldn't be political. But Hitler tried to use the games to promote the idea of white racial supremacy, assuming that his German athletes would dominate the games. And he only congratulated the winners who fit his profile.

So imagine Hitler's disgust with this black athlete from America winning four gold medals: one each in the 100 meters, the 200 meters, the long jump, and member of the 4x100 meter relay team. Later Hitler explained that people whose ancestors came from the jungles were primitive, with stronger physiques than those of civilized whites and, thus, shouldn't be allowed to compete. Despite these feelings, the 110,000 spectators in the Olympic stadium wildly cheered Jesse after his victories.

Ironically, at that time blacks in the United States were being denied equal rights. In fact, after a ticker-tape parade in his honor in New York City, Jesse had to ride a freight elevator to attend his reception at a prestigious downtown hotel.

Some people today continue to hold racist views. The Bible clearly teaches that all people of all races and nations are created by God and loved by him. We see Jesus reaching out to those excluded by society, such as the hated Samaritans, unclean lepers, and little children. Paul teaches that the Christian community is for everyone—Jews, Gentiles, men, women, slaves, and free. We need to see people as God sees them: valuable, loved, and worth dying for.

Whatever your race (black, Hispanic, white, Asian, other), don't discriminate against those who are different. Don't give in to racism.

....

ALSO ON THIS DAY . . .

1925—The only time Babe Ruth was pinch-hit for; Bobby Veach flied out.

1981—Six English lifeguards set a relay-swim record for swimming across the English Channel (7:17).

1988—The Cubs beat the Mets 6-4 in their first official night game at Wrigley Field.

2009—Whitney McClintock (Cambridge, Ontario) won the tricks competition at the World Water Ski Championships, making her the triple championship winner.

In this new life, it doesn't matter if you are a Jew or a Gentile, circumcised or uncircumcised, barbaric, uncivilized, slave, or free. Christ is all that matters, and he lives in all of us.
Colossians 3:11, NLT

Fun Fact "After I came home from the 1936 Olympics with my four medals, it became increasingly apparent that everyone was going to slap me on the back, want to shake my hand, or have me up to their suite. But no one was going to offer me a job."—Jesse Owens

BIRTHDAYS:

1967—Deion Sanders, Fort Myers, FL, NFL cornerback/wide receiver (Falcons, 49ers, Cowboys, Redskins, Ravens) and MLB outfielder (Yankees, Braves, Reds, Giants)

1974—Derek Fisher, Little Rock, AR, NBA point guard (Lakers, Warriors, Jazz)

1977—Chamique Holdsclaw, Queens, NY, WNBA forward (Mystics, Sparks, Dream) and Olympic gold medal winner, 2000

1982—Danieal Manning, Corsicana, TX, NFL defensive back and return specialist (Chicago Bears)

Summer **X Games**

1. Ryan Sheckler
2. Tommy Clowers
3. Danny Harf
4. Mike Metzger
5. Simon Tabron
6. Andy Macdonald
7. Anthony Napolitan
8. Ashley Fiolek
9. Jeremy Lrisk
10. Tarah Gieger

a. Wakeboarding
b. FMX
c. Skateboarding
d. Skateboard Streetpark
e. Moto-X Super-X
f. Moto-X Freestyle
g. Supercross
h. BMX Vert
i. Moto-X Step-up
j. Bicycle

Match the *athlete* with his/her sport

ANSWERS: 1.d, 2.i, 3.a, 4.f, 5.h, 6.c, 7.j, 8.e, 9.b, 10.g

Ready to Serve

On this day in 1986, Red Sox pitcher Tim Lollar got a pinch-hit single.

Why is this event featured? Getting a pinch-hit single doesn't seem like a big deal, especially in light of all the events that have occurred on this day. But this event is significant because, first, a pitcher getting a hit, especially in the American League, is highly unusual; second, in the AL, teams can use a "designated hitter" in the pitcher's spot, so why would Lollar be hitting at all; third, the pitcher was pinch-hitting, meaning that the manager chose him to come off the bench and bat.

Speaking of pinch-hitting, on October 6, 2001, Mets' utility infielder Lenny Harris lined a single into right. Play was stopped, and Harris' teammates rushed the field to greet him at first base. The reason? Leonard Anthony Harris had just etched his name into the record books. Under the category "Most pinch hits, career," we'll now find, "Harris, Lenny—151."

Pinch-hitters, like Lenny, are a special breed. They have to wait for their chances. That's not easy, especially when we are confident that we can do well and want to prove it. But the coach or teacher or director keeps us sitting there . . . just waiting.

In that role, some players develop bad attitudes, whispering put-downs of the coach and teammates who have been chosen to play instead. Others harbor bitterness and can't wait for someone to fail so they can be put in the lineup. Some just sort of give up, resigning themselves to the fate of not being good enough. If you've been there, you know the feeling and the temptation to react in one of those ways.

But some players choose a positive attitude and cheer for their teammates, hoping for their success. Though disappointed at not playing, they support the coach's decision and work even harder. And they pay attention to the game, always ready to go in and contribute.

Athletic teams have bench-warmers, but so do clubs, churches, music groups, and others. To succeed, all teams need everyone doing his or her part. That's the picture that God, through the apostle Paul, gives of how Christians should work together. Everyone is needed and has a vital role to play.

Wherever you are, be willing to be used, ready to serve. Your pinch hit could make the difference in the game!

ALSO ON THIS DAY . . .

1891—Jon Erikson (US) became the first person to triple-cross swim the English Channel (thirty-eight hours, twenty-seven minutes).

1994—The Major League Baseball Players Association went on strike.

2004—French soccer player Zinedine Zidane, one of the most celebrated players of all time, announced his international retirement.

2008—Michael Phelps set a swimming world record in winning the 200-meter freestyle race at the Beijing Olympics (1.42.96).

BIRTHDAYS:

1929—Charles Moore, Coatsville, PA, 400-meter hurdler, winner of a gold and a silver medal at the 1952 Olympics

1959—Lynette Woodard, Wichita, KS, Hall-of-Fame WNBA forward (Cleveland Rockers, Detroit Shock), Olympic gold medal winner (1984), and first female member of the Harlem Globetrotters

1976—Antoine Walker, Chicago, IL, all-star NBA forward (Celtics, Mavericks, Heat, Timberwolves, Grizzlies)

Just as each of us has one body with many members, and these members do not all have the same function, so in Christ we who are many form one body, and each member belongs to all the others. **Romans 12:4–5**

Fun Fact
Actually, Tim Lollar, who pitched in the majors from 1980–1986, was a decent hitter with a career average of .238 with eight home-runs and thirty-eight runs-batted-in in 231 at-bats. In his career, he hit home runs against Hall-of-Fame pitchers Phil Niekro and Tom Seaver.

Truth and Consequences

On this day in 2004, two Greek sprinters were suspended from the Greek Olympic team.

This caused quite a stir because the athletes Konstantinos Kenteris and Ekaterini Thanou were outstanding sprinters and expected to do well in the games. Konstantinos had won gold medals in the 200 meters at the 2000 Olympics, the 2001 World Championships, and the 2002 European Championships, so he was a favorite to medal. Ekaterini had won the silver medal in the women's 100 meters at the 2000 Olympics team. To make matters worse, Athens, in their home country, was hosting the games, so you can imagine the disappointment of the Greek fans.

The two sprinters were suspended because they missed a compulsory doping test. They were dropped from the Greek team and didn't compete.

These athletes were punished

because they broke the rules. This wasn't a mistake or accident; they missed the test, probably because they knew what the result would be. So they had to suffer the consequences.

Our actions have consequences. Some are obvious because of natural laws. If we fall out of a second-story window, we'll get hurt because of gravity. If we miss lunch, we'll be hungry. We also make choices; for example, we may choose to do something wrong. At those times, we may think we can get away with it. But that action will have a consequence just as sure as gravity pulled us to the ground.

The Bible says a lot about sinful choices—attitudes, thoughts, actions, and inactions. We (every human being ever born) do these all the time—it's in our nature. And the Bible calls it sin. The bad news is that our sin has terrible consequences— separation from God, eternal death. We can try to hide, cover up, or escape, but God sees and knows—and we're guilty. Like

being thrown off the team, we're done.

But here's the good news. God sent Jesus to die on the cross to pay the penalty for our sins. So we can be forgiven, our slate wiped clean. All we have to do is admit our sin, that we have done terribly wrong, thank God for sending his Son for us, and trust in Christ to forgive us, make us right with God, and put us on his team, headed for victory—eternal life.

Have you trusted him? Who can you tell about this amazing news?

ALSO ON THIS DAY . . .
1950—Babe Didrikson Zaharias won the LPGA World Golf Championship.
1962—Bert Campaneris, while playing for Daytona Beach (Florida State League), pitched ambidextrously (right and left arms).
1988—Ronald J. Dossenbach set the world record for pedaling across Canada from Vancouver, BC, to Halifax, NS, in thirteen days, fifteen hours, four minutes.
2008—Michael Phelps won the 200-meter butterfly in world-record time, touching out László Cseh of Hungary by .67 second. During the race, his goggles filled with water, preventing him from seeing anything while he was finishing the second lap. This was his tenth overall Olympic gold medal; he would go on to win another one in the 4x200 meter freestyle relay later that day.

BIRTHDAYS:

1860—Annie Oakley (born Phoebe Ann Mosey), Willowdell, OH, sharpshooter and exhibition shooter

1960—Joe Simpson, Kuala Lumpur, Federation of Malaysia, English mountaineer

1962—Turner Gill, Ft. Worth, TX, all-American quarterback for the University of Nebraska and current head football coach at the University of Kansas

1982—Shanti Davis, Chicago, IL, world-class speed skater and winner of two Olympic gold medals (2006, 2010)

For the wages of sin is death, but the gift of God is eternal life in Christ Jesus our Lord. **Romans 6:23**

Fun Fact The opening ceremony for the Athens Olympics culminated in the lighting of the Olympic Cauldron by 1996 Gold Medalist Windsurfer Nikolaos Kaklamanakis. The gigantic cauldron, styled after the 2004 Olympic Torch, pivoted down to be lit by the thirty-five-year-old before slowly swinging up and lifting the flame high above the stadium. Kaklamanakis would later win his silver medal in the men's mistral.

Special

ON THIS DAY IN 1953, LORETTA CLAIBORNE WAS BORN IN YORK, PENNSYLVANIA.

ieve....

I will succeed !!

Loretta Claiborne grew up in a single-parent family of six children. Born partially blind and mildly retarded, she did not walk or talk until she was four years old. Social services advised Loretta's mother to put her daughter in an institution for the mentally retarded; instead, she enrolled Loretta in public school. There, kids were pretty tough on Loretta with their teasing. When the taunts got worse, she began to run from her tormentors and became a good runner. Over the years, Loretta began to enjoy running and wanted to be an athlete and on the school teams, but she wasn't allowed because she was in special education classes. When her anger got the best of her and she began to fight those who were making fun of her, she was expelled from high school. Eventually Loretta met social worker Janet McFarland. Janet saw that Loretta could run

and introduced her to the Special Olympics in 1971. This was a defining moment for Loretta.

Since then, Loretta has competed in six Special Olympics world games, winning gold medals in the mile run (1983), the thirteen-mile half marathon (1991, 1999), singles bowling and mixed doubles bowling (1995), and the 3,000 meters (2003). She also won silver in the 3k run (1999) and figure skating (2005). Loretta has completed over twenty-five marathons, placing in the top 100-finishes twice at Boston and the top 25 in Pittsburgh. She is also a black belt in karate and continues to train in running, figure skating, soccer, skiing, golf, basketball, softball, swimming, and bowling. Loretta has won many awards, and a movie was made of her life.

Looking back, Loretta says her relationship with Janet McFarland and her involvement with Special Olympics turned her life around. Janet reached out to this angry teenager and pointed her in the right direction.

We can easily ignore people with physical and mental disabilities, as though they aren't good enough to get to know or to join in our activities. That's not how Jesus acted. He made a special point of seeing people's needs—those with physical problems, social outcasts, and misfits—drawing them close, healing them, and changing their lives. And he expects us to do the same.

How many people like Loretta do you know?

....

ALSO ON THIS DAY . . .

1873—*Field and Stream* magazine began publishing.

1959—The American Football League was organized with teams in New York, Dallas, Los Angeles, Minneapolis, Denver, and Houston.

1977—A crowd of 77,691 saw the New York Cosmos beat the Ft. Lauderdale Strikers 8-3 at Giant Stadium (soccer).

2007—Atlanta Braves manager Bobby Cox was ejected in the fifth inning of the Braves' 5-4 win over the Giants, the 132nd ejection of Cox's career, breaking the record set by John McGraw more than seventy years earlier.

2009—The Philadelphia Eagles signed quarterback Michael Vick, recently released from federal prison after serving over two years for his dogfighting activities.

BIRTHDAYS:

1959—Magic Johnson, Lansing, MI, Hall-of-Fame point guard (Los Angeles Lakers)

1970—Trise Jackson, WNBA guard (Los Angeles Sparks)

1975—Mike Vrabel, Akron, OH, all-pro NFL outside linebacker (Steelers, Patriots, Chiefs) and three-time Super Bowl champion

[Jesus is speaking] "'For I was hungry, and you fed me. I was thirsty, and you gave me a drink. I was a stranger, and you invited me into your home. I was naked, and you gave me clothing. I was sick, and you cared for me. I was in prison, and you visited me.' . . . And the King will say, 'I tell you the truth, when you did it to one of the least of these my brothers and sisters, you were doing it to me!'" **Matthew 25:35–36, 40, NLT**

Fun Fact Loretta Claiborne was honored in 1996 with the Arthur Ashe Award for Courage. Her life is recounted in *The Loretta Claiborne Story* (Walt Disney Productions) and in the biography *In Her Stride*. Loretta says, "I figured if my story could change a person's mind about another person, or especially a child's mind about another child, then it was the right thing to do."

15 Final **Victory**

On this day in 1993, Nolan Ryan pitched his 324th and final victory, Rangers 4, Indians 1.

Nolan Ryan was inducted into the Baseball Hall of Fame in 1999 because of his outstanding career in the major-leagues. Ryan pitched in a record twenty-seven seasons for the New York Mets, California Angels, Houston Astros, and Texas Rangers, from 1966 to 1993. During those years, he pitched seven no-hitters, three more than anyone else, and he is tied with Bob Feller for the most one-hitters, with twelve. He also pitched eighteen two-hit games. Ryan was selected to eight all-star teams, his number was retired by three major-league teams (Angels, Astros, and Rangers), and he was named to the major-league all-century Team.

Before the 1993 season, Ryan announced that he would be retiring at the end of that season. A month after his final victory, Ryan's very durable arm finally gave out in Seattle, when he tore a ligament, ending his career

a bit earlier than planned. Attempting to pitch through the injury, he threw one more pitch with his injured arm; this final pitch was clocked at ninety-eight miles per hour.

What a career! That's the way most people would like to have their lives play out—record-setting performances, big contracts, winning teams, and national reputation, capped off with the Hall of Fame.

God's plan for our lives follows a different trajectory. Whether or not we gain recognition as a world champion in a sport or other field, he wants us to focus first on doing his will. This means faithfully doing what he wants us to do, regardless of conditions, hardships, or rate of worldly success. And we shouldn't be surprised if we don't get notoriety in this life for our accomplishments. In fact,

Jesus told his disciples that instead of honoring them, people would persecute and even hate them for being his followers. But when that happens, we should "bless those who curse [us], pray for those who mistreat [us]" (Luke 6:28). Our goal should be that at the end we will hear our Savior say, "Well done, good and faithful servant" (Matthew 25:23).

What a final victory that will be!

....

ALSO ON THIS DAY . . .

1970—Patricia Palinkas became the first woman pro football player (Orlando).

1989—In his second start since finishing cancer treatment, Giants pitcher Dave Dravecky broke his pitching arm while throwing to Tim Raines.

2007—Referee Tim Donaghy pleaded guilty to two federal charges related to the investigation regarding betting on NBA games.

2009—Christian Cantwell (USA) won the men's shot put at the World Championships in Berlin (22.03 ft.).

BIRTHDAYS:

1950—Anne Elizabeth Alice Louise Windsor, English Princess and Olympic equestrian (1976)

1979—Carl Edwards, Columbia, MO, NASCAR driver

1982—Casey Burgener, American weightlifter

I have fought the good fight, I have finished the race, I have kept the faith. Now there is in store for me the crown of righteousness, which the Lord, the righteous Judge, will award to me on that day—and not only to me, but also to all who have longed for his appearing. 2 Timothy 4:7–8

[un][act] In February 2008 Nolan Ryan was hired as team president for the Texas Rangers. After the 2009 season Ryan partnered with another man to purchase the team.

Translation **Please**

On this day in 1981, New Zealand defeated Fiji 13-0, the highest winning score ever in a World Cup soccer match.

Soccer (called *football* in many regions) is huge, probably the most popular sport on the planet, and the biggest soccer tournament is the FIFA (Fédération Internationale de Football Association) World Cup. Held every four years, this men's competition features thirty-two national teams, with qualifying matches held the preceding three years, all over the world. An estimated 715.1 million people watched the final match of the 2006 World Cup, held in Germany. South Africa hosted the 2010 World Cup, and the 2014 host will be Brazil.

Surfing TV channels, we can usually find a soccer match. Because of the international nature of the sport, many of the broadcasts will be in a different language—except, of course, when a goal is "S C O O O O O O R E D!" Regardless of the language, we can always appreciate the quality of play.

Language is interesting— signs, symbols, and sounds formed into words and strung together in sentences to communicate information. Depending on what is considered a language and not just a dialect, the world has between 5,000 and 10,000 languages. Going from one country or culture to another makes communication interesting. We need interpreters. If we don't know the language, we can easily misunderstand what someone is saying.

Sometimes people who share a language still can't understand each other. That's what often happened to Jesus as Pharisees and others tried to figure him out. At times even his disciples got confused: "But they did not understand what he meant and were afraid to ask him about it" (Mark 9:32). Later he opened their minds "so they could understand the Scriptures" (Luke 24:45). The apostle Paul warned believers that most people won't figure out God's message because only those "who are spiritual" will be able to understand (1 Corinthians 2:14).

Does this mean we should stop sharing God's good news? No. We should take every opportunity to tell people about Jesus. But we must pray and ask God to open their minds and hearts to his Word. And all the while, we should let our lives do the talking too. Like watching international soccer on TV, our friends may not know the language, but they know the plays.

····································

ALSO ON THIS DAY . . .

1954—*Sports Illustrated* magazine began publishing.

2008—Usain Bolt set a new 100-meters dash world record of 9.69 seconds at the Beijing 2008 Olympics.

2009—Vincent Hancock (USA) won the men's skeet in the World Shotgun Championships in Maribor, Slovenia. 149 (124).

2009—Tyler Farrar (USA) (Garmin-Slipstream) won cycling's UCI Pro Tour Vattenfall Cyclassics: 5:30:38".

BIRTHDAYS:

1966—Ed Olczyk, Palos Heights, IL, NHL center (Blackhawks, Leafs, Jets, Rangers, Kings, Penguins), head coach (Penguins), and broadcaster

1970—Bonnie Bernstein, Brooklyn, NY, radio and television sportscaster

1971—Rulon Gardner, Afton, WY, heavyweight Greco-Roman wrestler and winner of the gold medal in the 2000 Olympics

1983—Colt Brennan, Laguna Beach, CA, NFL quarterback (Washington Redskins)

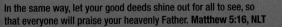

In the same way, let your good deeds shine out for all to see, so that everyone will praise your heavenly Father. Matthew 5:16, NLT

Fun Fact
According to one source, these are the top ten languages, according to the number of people who speak them as their first language: 1. Mandarin Chinese (1.1 billion); 2. English (330 million); 3. Spanish (300 million); 4. Hindi/Urdu (250 million); 5. Arabic (200 million); 6. Bengali (185 million); 7. Portuguese and Russian (160 million each); 9. Japanese (125 million); 10. German (100 million).

Not Like the Others

1. Net, birdie, racket, ball
2. Paddle, water, table, net
3. Sand, glove, ring, hook
4. Post, net, down, safety
5. Post, pick, roll, diamond
6. Swimming, rowing, ice skating, diving
7. Jordan, Zambrano, Ewing, Barkley
8. Goalie, striker, forward, guard
9. Golf, basketball, soccer, football
10. Hook, net, line, jab

Which of these don't belong?

ANSWERS: 1. Ball (badminton), 2. Water (table tennis), 3. Sand (boxing), 4. Net (football), 5. Diamond (basketball), 6. Ice skating (water sports), 7. Zambrano (basketball players), 8. Guard (soccer), 9. Basketball (played on grass), 10. Jab (fishing)

Don't Lose **the Victory**

ON THIS DAY IN 1985, LINDSEY JACOBELLIS WAS BORN IN DANBURY, CONNECTICUT.

Lindsey Jacobellis is an amazing snowboarder, having won six X Game gold medals and two in the FIS Snowboarding world championships. Instead of those victories, however, she may be known for one she didn't win, for not winning in the last couple of winter Olympics. During the final race of the Snowboard Cross at the 2006 Winter Olympics in Turin (February 17), Lindsey was approaching the finish line with a 140-foot, three-second lead—substantial for that point in the race. Victory was so close, and it was hers. She had just one more jump and then the finish line. But she decided to show off a bit and tried a "method grab." This is a complex trick where the rider rotates the board ninety degrees, facing the opposite direction of travel, and then grabs the center of the board.

Instead of moving back smoothly, she landed on the edge of her snowboard and fell. The next racer passed her. Lindsey recovered enough to win silver, but she could have won gold.

A well-known verse in Proverbs states, "Pride goes before destruction, a haughty spirit before a fall" (16:18). While Lindsey wasn't haughty or destroyed, her pride was showing, and she certainly took a fall. Through those words in Proverbs, God is warning against an attitude that basically says, "I'm doing fine. I'm cool. I've got it made." When we think that way, we can become complacent, lose focus, and "fall" into bad habits, or become vulnerable to temptation. It's like walking down a sidewalk in the winter that looks clear of ice and snow. We still need to be careful because if we're not paying attention and hit an icy patch—whoop, splat!

Being alert spiritually means staying close to God, talking with him about everything, depending on him, and relying on his strength. It also means knowing our weaknesses and using our minds to avoid tempting situations. Every person is a sinner, with sinful tendencies. So instead of thinking we're above temptation and would never give in, we need to have a more realistic view of ourselves and our situation.

You're approaching the finish line. Stay alert and focused.

....

ALSO ON THIS DAY . . .

1941—Umpire Jocko Conlan ejected Pittsburgh Pirates manager Frankie Frisch for coming out on the field holding an umbrella, implying that the game should be rained out.

1951—Bill Veeck, Major League Baseball owner and promoter, sent Eddie Gaedel, a 3'7" midget, to pinch-hit in a game for the St. Louis Browns.

2004—Aaron Peirsol (USA) won the men's 200-meter backstroke at the Athens Olympics.

2008—Dawn Harper (USA) won the women's 100-meter hurdles at the Beijing Olympics.

BIRTHDAYS:

1935—Bobby Richardson, Sumpter, SC, great major-league second baseman (New York Yankees)

1960—Morten Andersen, Copenhagen, Denmark, NFL kicker (Saints, Falcons, Giants, Chiefs, Vikings)

1971—Mary Joe Fernandez, Dominican Republic, US tennis star and winner of two Olympic gold medals, 1992, 1996

So, if you think you are standing firm, be careful that you don't fall! **1 Corinthians 10:12**

[un][ACT Lindsey started racing snowboardcross at age eleven and was invited to compete in the X Games at fifteen.

20 Dream **Runner**

On this day in 2004, Hikmat Alaa Jassim ran the 100-meter dash at the Athens Olympics.

Hikmat Alaa Jassim was the only female competitor at the 2004 Olympics from Iraq. The United States and allies had liberated her country from the dictator Saddam Hussein, but the conflict was continuing against Saddam loyalists, insurgents, and other forces. At the time, Jassim was an eighteen-year-old student from Baghdad. Her father had died a few years before of a heart attack, so she was living with her mother, in a house with a corrugated iron roof and limited water supply. At times she had to dodge gun battles and bombings in the streets nearby, often on her way to train at al-Kishafa Stadium.

There her starting "blocks" were holes carved into the dirt, and she trained by running around the rubbish-strewn dirt track, wearing secondhand running shoes given to her on a training trip to Jordan. Despite these difficult conditions and obstacles, she ran . . . and she made it to the Olympics. In Athens, Jassim ran her own race in her qualifying heat, not concerned that her competition was ahead of her. The fact that she was there, competing, was a victory.

Jassim should bring hope to all who wonder how they can accomplish anything in life with their humble surroundings and meager resources. This dedicated young athlete didn't allow poverty, destruction, or even bullets to keep her from achieving her goal.

Many young people from much more economically stable environments and with a wide variety of quality resources at their disposal don't even push back from the video consoles or slide off their couches to go outside and walk to a nearby park. They need their sports well funded and organized and may even complain that "there's nothing to do in this town." This example could be extended beyond sports—to school, neighborhood, and church.

What resources are at your disposal: sports centers, youth groups, recreation halls, libraries, church gyms, tutors, personal trainers/coaches, park districts, home work-out equipment, neighborhood schools and parks, . . . ? Be a doer, not a complainer. Hikmat Alaa Jassim knew what she had to do to achieve her dream—and she did it. What's stopping you?

....

ALSO ON THIS DAY . . .

1920—Allen Woodring won the Olympic 200-meter dash wearing borrowed shoes.

1978—Mark Vinchesi of Amherst, Massachusetts, kept a Frisbee aloft 15.2 seconds.

1980—Reinhold Messner, Italian mountaineer, made the first successful solo ascent on Mt. Everest.

1985—Hanspeter Beck of South Australia, finished a 3,875-mile, fifty-one-day trip from Western Australia to Melbourne on a unicycle.

2008—Usain Bolt (Jamaica) set a new world record in the men's 200-meter race (19.30).

BIRTHDAYS:

1931—Don King, Cleveland, OH, boxing promoter best known for his association with Mike Tyson and for his unusual hairstyles

1954—William Quinn Buckner, Phoenix, IL, NBA guard (Milwaukee Bucks and Boston Celtics), winner of the Olympic gold medal in 1976, and broadcaster

1991—Marko Djokovic, Serbian tennis player

Therefore, since we are surrounded by such a great cloud of witnesses, let us throw off everything that hinders and the sin that so easily entangles, and let us run with perseverance the race marked out for us. Let us fix our eyes on Jesus, the author and perfecter of our faith, who for the joy set before him endured the cross, scorning its shame, and sat down at the right hand of the throne of God. **Hebrews 12:1–2**

FUN FACT "I feel I am representing all of the Iraqi people, not just the women. I started training for these Olympics in March, but because of the situation there, I couldn't train as well as I wanted to. If it was possible, I would have trained five to six times a week, but because of the bombs and explosions I often could not."—Hikmat Alaa Jassim

Redemption

On this day in 2000, Tiger Woods won the PGA Championship to become the first golfer since Ben Hogan in 1953 to win three majors in a calendar year. He tied the strokes-to-par record for the PGA (-18) with Bob May and won in a playoff.

Eldrick Tont "Tiger" Woods is arguably the best professional golfer of all time; at least his golfing achievements seem to place him there. For most of his fourteen-year professional career, he has been ranked at or near the top in the world of golf. He has won fourteen major golf championships, the second highest of any male player (Jack Nicklaus has eighteen) and seventy-one PGA Tour wins.

The list of Woods' achievements and records (and winnings and endorsements) goes on and on. But in December of 2009, Tiger's world came crashing down when his numerous extramarital affairs came to light. In trying to pull his life back together, especially in his marriage and family, Woods took an indefinite leave from professional golf. After a few months away from the spotlight, personal counseling, and a few public apologies, Tiger Woods returned to competition for the 2010 Masters tournament on April 8, 2010.

Whenever a public figure is disgraced through scandals of one type or another, eventually the person attempts a comeback. This happens often in sports, where victories seem to measure a person's worth. At those times, we see the word *redemption* in headlines. Whether the athlete is a former steroid user, gambler, dog-fighter, or whatever, he or she expresses remorse for the past and pledges to never do that again and to be a better person. The person asks for forgiveness and, then, hopes to once again hear the cheers from fans as achievements and victories pile up.

True forgiveness is available. Any person can begin again—be born again—but real redemption can only come from God through Christ. The sins of some people are obvious and public, but all people are sinners (check out Romans 3:23), guilty and separated from God and deserving of his punishment. But Jesus paid the price—redeemed us (that's what *redeem* means), so anyone who turns from sin and turns to him can be totally forgiven—past, present, and future. Regardless of what reporters, commentators, or fans say, the person has been redeemed (bought back, made right with God).

Hopefully Tiger Woods is sincere about changing his values and lifestyle. We certainly can pray for him and other fallen stars. And we can continue to share the good news about redemption in Christ.

....

ALSO ON THIS DAY . . .

1887— "Mighty" Dan Casey struck out in a game with the New York Giants!

1947—The Maynard Midgets of Williamsport, PA, won the first Little League World Series.

2004—Paul Foerster and Kevin Burnham (USA) won the men's sailing 470 at the Athens Olympics.

2008—American men swept the medals in the 400-meter run at the Beijing Olympics: gold, La Shawn Merrit (43.75); silver, Jeremy Wariner; bronze, David Neville.

BIRTHDAYS:

1936—Wilt Chamberlain, Philadelphia, PA, Hall-of-Fame NBA center (Warriors, 76ers, Lakers) and four-time league MVP and two-time NBA champion

1983—Josh Harrington, Greenville, NC, professional BMX rider

1984—B.J. Upton, Norfolk, VA, major-league centerfielder (Tampa Bay Rays)

1986—Usain Bolt, Jamaican sprinter, winner of three Olympic gold medals in Beijing and world record holder for the 100 meters, 200 meters, and 4x100 meters relay

But God demonstrates his own love for us in this: While we were still sinners, Christ died for us. **Romans 5:8**

Fun Fact In a televised speech on February 19, 2010, Woods admitted that he had been unfaithful to his wife. He said he used to believe he was entitled, that he could do whatever he wanted to do, and because of his success, the normal rules didn't apply to him. He said he was wrong and apologized for the hurt he had caused his family, friends, fans, and business partners.

Passing **the Baton**

On this day in 2009, Jamaica won the men's 4x100 meters relay at the World Championships in Berlin, Germany. Usain Bolt won his third world title, this time without a world record.

Running a relay around the track can be tricky because several runners are involved for each team and because a baton must be passed runner to runner within a certain space. There's little room for error. The "4x100" race means that the competing teams have four runners each, with each one running 100 meters. The relay baton must be passed within a 20-meter changeover box, usually marked by yellow lines on the track. This box extends 10 meters on each side of each 100-meter mark. Another line is 10 meters further back, and the new runner must begin in front of that line before accelerating and getting the stick. If the baton handoff occurs outside of the allotted space, the team is disqualified.

Because this race is so fast, the outgoing runner has to reach back with open hand without turning and looking. Then the incoming runner must thrust the baton into the teammate's hand and not let go until he or she has it. If a runner drops the baton, that team will probably end up last because of the time needed to recover. In the last few Olympics, American teams have dropped batons.

The picture of passing a baton has been used to describe those occasions when responsibilities and knowledge are transferred from one person to another. Outgoing pastors, elected officials, coaches, business leaders, and others "pass the baton" to their successors. They need to make sure that those who come after them have the knowledge and skills to take over and, then, move the enterprise along. In each case, a smooth handoff depends on both people, so these leaders usually look for young people who can be trusted to take the baton and run well.

This principle holds for faith as well. When Paul was passing his baton to young Timothy, he counseled him to do the same with others: one teacher teaching another who would teach another, and so on. If Timothy and others hadn't done this, the Church would have died long ago.

You're probably too young to have someone to whom you can hand the faith baton. But you probably have an older teacher (parent, pastor, or mentor) who wants to pass his or her wisdom to you. That's a great privilege and responsibility. Grasp that baton and run!

································

ALSO ON THIS DAY . . .

1950—Althea Gibson became the first black competitor in the national tennis competition.

2007—The Texas Rangers routed the Baltimore Orioles 30-3, the most runs scored by a team in modern MLB history.

2008—Juli Furtado (USA) won the World Mountainbike Championship, XC, Elite (F), 1990.

2008—The US Women's team won the gold medal in the WFDF 2008 World Ultimate & Guts Championships (Ultimate Frisbee) in Vancouver, Canada.

BIRTHDAYS:

1939—Carl Yastrzemski, Southampton, NY, Hall-of-Fame left fielder/first baseman (Boston Red Sox), eighteen-time all-star selection,

You have heard me teach things that have been confirmed by many reliable witnesses. Now teach these truths to other trustworthy people who will be able to pass them on to others. 2 Timothy 2:2, NLT

Perfect Timing

On this day in 2009, Eric Bruntlett of the Philadelphia Phillies had an unassisted triple play.

Baseball triple plays are very unusual and unassisted ones extremely rare, with only fifteen in major-league history. Everything has to come together just right, with two base runners and a fielder in perfect position. In Eric's case, the runners were on first and second in the ninth inning, and a run was already in. The batter hit a line drive up the middle that seemed to be headed toward center field for a single. But because both runners were stealing on the pitch, Bruntlett was moving over to cover second base and was in perfect position. He caught the line drive (out one) and stepped on second (out two) to double up the runner who had been running toward third. Then he tagged the other runner who was trying to get back to first (out three). Eric became the second player in major-league history to get the final three outs on his own, preserving his team's 9-7 victory over the New York Mets.

For someone to get an unassisted triple play, the circumstances have to be just right, and the timing has to be perfect.

In so many sports, timing is everything: the start in swimming and track, the blocking in football, the liftoff in ski jumping and snowboarding, goalies' reactions, and on and on. Often a split second can make the difference between success and disaster, victory and defeat.

Timing is crucial in other areas of life as well. Here's a comforting truth: God's timing is always perfect. Every time he's on time, never early or late. When praying, we may want God to answer now, but he may want us to wait. His later answer will be right and the best for us, even though we may not realize that right away. Eventually, looking back at our life events, we will see that God worked everything together for our good, according to his timetable. He sent Jesus at just the right time, and he called us at just the right time.

Do you wonder about the future? Are you concerned about God's actions? Trust him and his timing. It's perfect, and even better than a triple play.

....

ALSO ON THIS DAY . . .

1883—The Philadelphia Phillies made twenty-seven errors against Providence (wild pitches, walks, and passed balls counted as errors prior to 1888).

1969—Audrey McElmory (US) won the World Cycling Championships.

1992—Dennis Eckersley, who previously had set the record for most consecutive saves (forty), became the first pitcher to record forty saves in four different seasons.

2008—The US men's and women's teams both won the 4x400 meter relay at the Beijing Olympics; the men's team—LaShawn Merritt, Angelo Taylor, David Neville, Jeremy Wariner; the women's team—Mary Wineberg, Allyson Felix, Monique Henderson, Sanya Richards.

BIRTHDAYS:

1911—Elizabeth "Betty" Robinson, American sprinter and winner of two Olympic gold medals, the first Olympic 100 meters for women in 1928 and the 4x100 meter relay in 1936

1969—Jeremy Schaap, New York City, NY, sportswriter, television reporter, and author

1977—Nicole Bobeck, Chicago, IL, figure skater, US Champion in 1995

1978—Kobe Bryant, Philadelphia, PA

You see, at just the right time, when we were still powerless, Christ died for the ungodly. Romans 5:6

[UN][ACT] Bruntlett was playing second because all-star Chase Utley was being rested, and he had made one of two Phillies errors earlier in the inning.

Summer Olympics **Champions**

1. In which sport did Mary Lou Retton win the gold medal at the 1984 Olympics?
   a. Vault
   b. Floor exercise
   c. Uneven bars
   d. All-around

2. In which event at the 1992 Olympics did Carl Lewis win a gold medal?
   a. 400-meter sprint
   b. Long jump
   c. Pole vault
   d. Discus throw

3. In which sport did Andre Agassi win a gold medal at the 1996 Olympics?
   a. Swimming
   b. Baseball
   c. Water polo
   d. Tennis

4. In which event at the 1996 Olympics did Shannon Miller win a gold medal?
   a. Balance beam
   b. Vault
   c. Floor exercise
   d. Uneven bars

5. In which sport did Tiffany Roberts win a gold medal at the 1996 Olympics?
   a. Volleyball
   b. Fencing
   c. Soccer
   d. Track and Field

6. In which sport at the 2000 Olympics did Steven Lopez win the gold medal?
   a. Taekwondo
   b. Boxing
   c. Fencing
   d. Cycling

7. In which sport at the 2004 Olympics did Matthew Emmons win the gold medal?
   a. Fencing
   b. Shooting
   c. Dodge ball
   d. Gymnastics

8. In which event at the 2004 Olympics did Paul Hamm win the gold medal?
   a. All around
   b. Horizontal bar
   c. Pommel Horse
   d. Parallel bars

9. In which sport at the 2000 Olympics did Lisa Leslie win the gold medal?
   a. Soccer
   b. Basketball
   c. Softball
   d. Gymnastics

10. At the 2000 Olympics, in which event did Nancy Johnson win a gold medal?
    a. Bicycle
    b. Boxing
    c. Ping pong
    d. Air rifle women

11. In which event did Janet Evans win a gold medal at the 1992 Olympics?
    a. 400-meter freestyle
    b. 400-meter individual medley
    c. 800-meter freestyle
    d. 800-meter backstroke

12. In which sport at the 1996 Olympics did Karch Kiraly win a gold medal?
    a. Beach volleyball
    b. Tennis
    c. Gymnastics
    d. Basketball

13. In which event at the 1992 Olympics did Summer Saunders take home the gold medal?
    a. 200-meter butterfly
    b. 400-meter butterfly
    c. 800-meter butterfly
    d. 200-meter breaststroke

14. At the 2004 Olympics, in which sport did Tyler Hamilton win the gold medal?
    a. Wrestling
    b. Cycling
    c. Shooting
    d. Yelling

15. In which sport at the 2004 Olympics did Mariel Zagunis win a gold medal?
    a. Sleeping
    b. Writing
    c. Fencing
    d. Yodeling

16. At the 2008 Olympics, in which event did Michael Phelps win a gold medal?
    a. 400-meter individual medley
    b. 200-meter freestyle
    c. 200-meter butterfly
    d. 200-meter individual medley
    e. 100-meter butterfly
    f. All of the above

ANSWERS: 1.d, 2.b, 3.d, 4.a, 5.c, 6.a, 7.b, 8.a, 9.b, 10.d, 11.c, 12.a, 13.a, 14.b, 15.c, 16.f

A Matter of **Control**

On this day in 1903, the Phillies walked seventeen Dodger hitters in a game.

The one aspect of baseball that drives managers crazy has to be the walk, bases on balls, giving the batter a free pass to first base. All managers will say that usually those walks come around to score—they almost always hurt. The pitcher needs to trust the rest of the team to field the ball and make plays; that's why they're there. Outside of the "intentional walk," pitchers try hard to not walk anyone, especially not seventeen in one game. The problem: they can't control where the ball is going. Throwing a ball at a high speed to a precise location isn't easy, especially when trying to fool professional batters. The great pitchers have mastered this skill and keep the walks to a minimum. But pitchers

without control end up beating themselves and don't last long in the game or on the team.

Control, self-control especially, is important in many areas. Sometimes a teacher will send a disruptive student to the office because the student was out of control. In other words, he or she refused to cooperate, settle down, and do the work. At times disagreements can heat up and get out of control, even leading to violence. Or we may hear of out-of-control spending. Successful people understand the importance of self-control, of not beating themselves.

God wants us to be self-controlled, disciplined. Paul listed self-control as a "fruit of the Spirit" (Galatians 5:22–23), and Peter wrote that we should add "self-control" to our faith (2 Peter 1:6). The key to having this discipline, however, is submission. That sounds strange, but it's true—the way to

gain control is to give it up . . . to God. When we yield to his control, he releases the Holy Spirit's power in us, helping us want to obey him and do what he wants (Philippians 2:13). The Holy Spirit produces the fruit and empowers us to make the right choices, to speak or stay silent when we should, to help those in need, to share the good news about Jesus, and to resist temptation—in short, to have self-control.

True self-control is really Spirit-control. Let God do his work in you. Don't beat yourself.

ALSO ON THIS DAY . . .

1973—Ten-year-old Mary Boitano was the first woman to finish the 6.8-mile Dipsea Race in Marin County, California, beating a field of 1,500 runners.

1896—Rosa Mota won the Stuttgart female marathon (2:28:38).

2000—The Houston Comets beat the New York Liberty two games to zero to win the WNBA Championship.

2004—The US Women's soccer team won the gold medal at the Athens Olympics.

For God did not give us a spirit of timidity, but a spirit of power, of love and of self-discipline. **2 Timothy 1:7**

FUN FACT The record for most walks given up in a nine-inning game is sixteen, shared by three pitchers: Bruno Haas for Philadelphia (6/23/1915), Bill George for New York (5/30/1887), and George Van Haltren for Chicago (6/27/1887). The bases sure were clogged in 1887!

BIRTHDAYS:

1954—Sarah Lundy, first female trainer to saddle a horse in the Belmont Stakes

1979—Jamal Lewis, Atlanta, GA, NFL running back (Baltimore Ravens, Cleveland Browns)

1968—Christopher Boardman, English racing cyclist, winner of the Olympic gold medal in individual pursuit (1992); broke the world hour record three times

Toughest **Ticket**

On this day in 1921, Curly Lambeau and the Green Bay Football Club were granted an NFL franchise.

The Green Bay Packers professional football team is one of the oldest and most successful in NFL history. Since joining the league in 1921, the Packers have won twelve league championships (more than any other team), including nine NFL Championships before the Super Bowl era and three Super Bowls (1967, 1968, and 1996). The Packers are also unique in that they are the only non-profit, community-owned major league professional sports team in the United States. And they represent a small town, not a major metropolis with a huge population base. The population of Green Bay, Wisconsin, is about 100,000, with a median annual household income at about

$42,000. The fact that the team can survive, let alone thrive in this area of big salaries and major-market media is amazing.

Yet season tickets for Packer games are almost impossible to get. Despite having by far the smallest local TV market, the Packers have one of the largest fan bases in the country, so they also have one of the longest waiting lists for season tickets. In 2008, 78,000 people were on that list. The average wait time for season tickets is said to be over thirty years. That's why some fans will name a recipient of their season tickets in their wills or place newborns on the waiting list after receiving birth certificates.

Many want to get in but can't. The stadium can only hold so many.

Heaven's like that . . . well sort of. Everyone wants to go there, but not everyone will get in. Unlike Lambeau Field, however, heaven has plenty of room. And get this—the ticket is free, with no waiting list. But

still, many will be left out by their own choosing.

God wants everyone to be there; in fact, he's paid the price of admission through Christ's death on the cross. But he won't force us. He lets us make that choice. Some people miss out because they think they have to work hard to earn their way in. Others are standing in the wrong line and think God should let them in anyway. And a few others say they aren't sure that God and his heaven even exist. But if you think a Packers-Bears game is exciting, heaven will be infinitely better—a party with no end!

ALSO ON THIS DAY . . .

1918—Christy Mathewson resigned as Reds manager to accept a commission as a captain in the chemical warfare branch of the Army.

1985—Mary Joe Fernandez, fourteen years and eight days old, became the youngest to win a US Tennis Open match, beating Sara Gomer in the first round.

1990—In Major League Baseball, the Brewers–Blue Jays game was delayed thirty-five minutes because of gnats.

2006—In billiards, the Philippine team defeated the American team at the World Cup of Pool held at Newport, Wales.

BIRTHDAYS:

1968—Christine Schaefer, Florence, KY, WPVA volleyball player

1970—Jim Thome, Peoria, IL, outstanding major-league infielder/designated hitter (Indians, Phillies, White Sox, Twins)

1972—Chris Imes, South Paris, ME, US hockey defenseman, 1994 Olympics

For it is by grace you have been saved, through faith—and this not from yourselves, it is the gift of God—not by works, so that no one can boast. Ephesians 2:8–9

Fun Fact Packers fans are often called "cheeseheads" because of all the cheese produced in Wisconsin. Originally the name was used as in insult, but now Packer fans love it and even wear hats that look like huge slices of cheese.

Strength **Renewed**

On this day in 1926, Emil "Dutch" Levsen of the Cleveland Indians pitched complete doubleheader victories over the Boston Red Sox.

Can you imagine pitching eighteen innings (two full baseball games) and winning both? That seems impossible, but Dutch Levsen did it. But that feat probably shortened his career. After that game, he won only three more games in his final two seasons and was out of baseball at the age of thirty. No one knows for sure if pitching the doubleheader ruined Dutch's arm, but it sure didn't help. In that era, teams had no pitching coaches, radar guns to check a pitcher's velocity, or ice packs for tired arms after the games. These days, major-league teams have all that and much more, including as many as twenty-four coaches in spring training, including a core of relief pitchers and a relief-pitching coach.

At times, every athlete wishes for increased strength, to lift more weight, to run, throw, ski, or pedal faster and further, to swing or kick harder, to hold on longer, or to jump higher.

World-class athletes spend hours each day conditioning, with the express purpose of building their strength. But regardless of how much a person trains, that athlete, even the best in the world, has a limit. We're human and can only do so much. At some point, we reach the end of our strength, our endurance. We can't continue.

Tucked away in the book of Isaiah is a startling statement from God about strength: "Even youths grow tired and weary, and young men stumble and fall; but those who hope in the Lord will renew their strength. They will soar on wings like eagles; they will run and not grow weary, they will walk and not be faint" (40:30–31). At first this sounds like a recipe for athletic victory, but God is talking about strength for living.

Just like in sports, we can reach the end of our emotional and spiritual strength—feeling exhausted, spent, and tempted to give up and quit. But God is all-

powerful. We just need to put our hope in him, to give him our hopeless situation and ask for his help. When we rely on his strength, he will renew us and give us the power to live his way.

Walk . . . run . . . soar, in his strength.

....

ALSO ON THIS DAY . . .

1989—In the first regular-season matchup of defending Cy Young Award winners, Frank Viola of the Mets outdueled Orel Hershiser of the Dodgers, 1-0.

2005—West Oahu from Ewa Beach, Hawaii, came from behind with a three-run sixth inning and then won the first extra-inning game since 1971, defeating Willemstead, Curaçao, 7-6 in seven innings to win the Little League World Series.

2009—Sanya Richards (USA) won the 400-meter race at the Golden League Championships in Zurich, Switzerland (48.94).

BIRTHDAYS:

1950—Ron "Louisiana Lightning" Guidry, Lafayette, LA, major-league pitcher (New York Yankees), Cy Young Award winner (1978) and four-time all-star

1958—Scott Scovell Hamilton, Toledo, OH, figure skater and winner of the Olympic gold medal (1984)

1971—Janet Evans, Fullerton, CA, 400-meter/800-meter swimmer and

---

He gives strength to the weary and increases the power of the weak. **Isaiah 40:29**

Fun Fact The Major League Baseball record for the most innings pitched in a season is held by Will White of Cincinnati, who pitched 680 innings in 1879. The career record is held by Walter Johnson of Washington, who pitched 5,914.1 innings (1907 to 1927). Now that's endurance.

AUGUST 29 Above **the Storm**

On this day in 2005, Hurricane Katrina battered the Gulf Coast, killing 1,836.

With wind and water damage from the hurricane and from the subsequent floods, this was the deadliest US hurricane since the 1928 Okeechobee hurricane and was the largest natural disaster in US history, causing $81 billion in damage. Even the Superdome was ruined, forcing the New Orleans Saints to play all their "home" games in the Alamodome in San Antonio or LSU's Tiger Stadium in Baton Rouge. Because Katrina caused extensive damage to the New Orleans Arena, the city's NBA team, the Hornets, had to move out, too, and played most of their home games for both that season and the next in Oklahoma City, Oklahoma.

When a natural disaster such as a hurricane strikes, we realize how weak and powerless we are, totally subject to these natural forces. Most of the time, we live as though we are in control of our lives, that we can control our destiny. . . until we're blindsided by sudden tragedy and shocked into reality. We can't be sure about any moment of the future.

Imagine that you're in a stadium, like the Superdome, playing or watching a game. Your team is winning by a wide margin and the time is running out on the game clock. You begin to celebrate because you are sure, absolutely sure, that your team will win—just a couple of minutes to go. But outside the stadium, above and beyond the roof and our sight, a terrible tornado is closing in. You and no one else inside the stadium realizes it, but that game will be terribly interrupted before the end. You thought you and your team had everything under control—not even close.

We need to remember, in times of sun or storm, good days and bad, that God is above and beyond everything that is happening in our world, in the whole universe for that matter. We do not control events, but he does. And he is working everything in our lives together for our good and his glory (Romans 8:28). Then, when our time on earth is over, he will bring us safely home. That he has promised.

We can have hope in the storm, relying on our powerful and loving Father.

....

ALSO ON THIS DAY . . .

1885—Boxing's first heavyweight title fight with three-oz. gloves and three-minute rounds was fought between John L. Sullivan and Dominick McCaffrey.

1968—In the first US Open tennis match, Billie Jean King beat Dr. Vija Vuskains.

1992—The Braves' Charlie Leibrandt recorded his 1,000th career strikeout and decided to keep the ball, rolling it to the dugout and allowing Ricky Jordan to take second base on an error.

2009—Travis Pastrana claimed the overall victory at the Ojibwa Forests Rally, his fifth win of the season, sealing his fourth consecutive Rally America driver's title, the most in series history.

BIRTHDAYS:

1946—Bob Beamon, Jamaica, NY, long jumper (world-record holder for twenty-three years) and winner of the Olympic gold medal in 1968

1977—Roy Oswalt, Weir, MS, all-star major-league pitcher (Houston Astros)

1980—David West, Teaneck, NJ, NBA power forward (New Orleans Hornets)

He replied, "You of little faith, why are you so afraid?" Then he got up and rebuked the winds and the waves, and it was completely calm. The men were amazed and asked, "What kind of man is this? Even the winds and the waves obey him!" Matthew 8:26–27

Fun Fact In the fall of 2006, the Saints returned to play all of their regular home games in the Superdome. The Hornets made their permanent return to New Orleans on October 31, 2007, when they opened the 2007–08 season. During the 2008 all-star game, the NBA donated $5 million towards relief work and staged an NBA Cares program throughout New Orleans to help the rebuilding efforts.

Pulling **Together**

On this day in 2009, the United States won the women's eight at the world championships in rowing in Lake Malta, Poznań, Poland (6:05:34).

In rowing competitions, a boat is propelled by one or more rowers (also called *scullers*), each of whom operates two oars, one in each hand. Even if the boat (scull) has only one rower, the process can be tricky because the oar handles overlap when pulled at the same time. So the rower has to hold one hand in front of or higher than the other. Boats with more than one rower also have to make sure that all the rowers are pulling together. Competitions are held with single sculls (one rower), double sculls (two rowers), quad sculls (four rowers), and eights. In these championships, the American women won the eights race—eight rowers with a coxswain (the person who sits in the back and steers the boat, encourages the crew, and controls the rowing rate).

Success in any rowing competition requires efficient strokes, with the scullers working together, keeping time. This takes hours and hours of practice, with all the rowers pulling at the same time and the same depth. Imagine the coordination necessary for a scull of eight, especially in the pressure of a race when they are trying to go as fast as possible.

What would happen if one rower decided to rest awhile? Or what if another rower decided to pull harder that the others? Or if another took short, choppy strokes instead of the longer ones like everyone else? Chaos. Oars would clash, the boat would veer, and the team would lose. This sport has no place for freelancing or hot-dogging. Everyone must submit his or her ego to the group and to the coxswain, who is calling the shots. Win or lose, they must be together.

If you've been on a team—at school, in sports, or at church— you know the importance of working together, with everyone playing his or her appointed role and pulling together. And you probably know what happens when someone refuses to submit—the team falls apart. Putting pride and ego aside for the good of the team isn't easy, but it's necessary. And come to think about it, that's the way Christians are always supposed to work together.

ALSO ON THIS DAY . . .

1979—In a wild US Tennis Open match, John McEnroe defeated Ilie Nastase 6-4, 4-6, 6-3, 6-2; Nastase was defaulted by the umpire but then reinstated.

1990—Ken Griffey and Ken Griffey Jr. became the first father and son to play on the same team (Seattle Mariners); they both singled in the first inning.

1997—Greg Rudaski became the first person to serve two 141 mph serves in a match (US Open).

2006—Eric Malone won the APBA Watercross Nationals Jet Ski championship.

BIRTHDAYS:

1942—Jean-Claude Killy, French champion alpine ski racer who won three gold medals at the 1968 Olympics (giant slalom, slalom, and downhill)

1978—Cliff Lee, Benton, AR, all-star major-league pitcher (Indians, Phillies, Mariners) and AL Cy Young Award winner (2008)

1982—Andy Roddick, Omaha, NE, outstanding professional tennis player (former number one, US Davis Cup team several years)

What, after all, is Apollos? And what is Paul? Only servants, through whom you came to believe—as the Lord has assigned to each his task. I planted the seed, Apollos watered it, but God made it grow. So neither he who plants nor he who waters is anything, but only God, who makes things grow. **1 Corinthians 3:5–7**

Fun Fact In the 2004 Olympic Games in Athens, in the middle of the women's eights final, Australian rower Sally Robbins suddenly stopped rowing, put down her oars, and fell back in the boat, even though her team was in second place at the time. No one was quite sure what happened, but the story is told in a book, *Don't Rock the Boat* by Wilkins Peter.

Featured Events in **August**

1. Which league in Major League Baseball uses the designated hitter? (August 12)
2. What country did Hikmat Alaa Jassim represent in the 2004 Olympics? (August 20)
3. When did the New Orleans Saints return to the Superdome after Hurricane Katrina? (August 29)
4. How high is Pikes Peak in Colorado? (August 5)
5. What year did Wrigley Field start using lights? (August 8)
6. As a boy, what was Usain Bolt's first sport interest? (August 22)
7. What year did Green Bay join the NFL? (August 27)
8. How many victories did Nolan Ryan have in his career? (August 15)
9. What did Australian rower Sally Robbins do during the finals at the 2004 Olympic Games in Athens? (August 30)
10. Who won the gold medal for Best Trick at X Game II in 2005? (August 6)
11. Where were the 1992 Summer Olympics held? (August 1)
12. Why was Loretta Claiborne not allowed to play on her school teams? (August 14)
13. Who holds the record for the most innings pitched in a season? (August 28)
14. What is the highest winning score ever in a World Cup soccer match? (August 16)
15. With what team did NBA player Shaquille O'Neal sign in 2005? (August 2)
16. In what year did Tiger Woods win three Majors? (August 21)
17. What is the record for most walks given up in a nine-inning baseball game? (August 26)
18. How many medals did Jesse Owens win at the Berlin Olympics? (August 9)
19. On what MLB teams did Barry Bonds play? (August 7)
20. For what sport is Lindsey Jacobellis known? (August 19)
21. Why were two Greek sprinters suspended from the 2004 Greek Olympic team? (August 13)
22. How many unassisted triple plays have occurred in MLB history? (August 23)

Stepping In and Stepping **Up**

On this day in 2006, filling in for injured Cleveland Indians designated hitter Travis Hafner, Kevin Kousmanoff became the first American League player to hit a grand-slam home run in his first career at bat.

Selected as the 216th player in the 2003 MLB Draft, Kevin Kousmanoff began his professional career on a short-season-A minor league team in Ohio. Then he went to Virginia, where he continued to do well. The next year, he played in the South Atlantic League, where he had sixteen home runs, eighty-seven RBI, and a .330 average. His next minor-league stop was in North Carolina. Starting the 2006 season with Double-A Akron, Kousmanoff hit close to a .400 average and finished at .389 before being promoted to the Buffalo Bisons in July. He had done well in the minors and was ready for the big leagues, so on September 2, Cleveland called him up . . . and he got his opportunity. Then he hit the first pitch he saw out of the park for a grand-slam home run!

Talk about seizing the moment—he stepped in, and he stepped up . . . big time!

Have you ever heard of Wally Pipp? He was playing for the Yankees and when the manager decided to bench him for a game and give a new, young player a chance, Lou Gehrig stepped in and began his streak of 2,130 consecutive games. He took advantage of the opportunity and came through, again and again.

These athletes were ready, willing, able, and eager. Centuries ago, God asked Isaiah, "Whom should I send? And who will go for us?" And Isaiah answered, "Here am I. Send me!" (Isaiah 6:8) When the Lord told Ananias to help a former enemy, he did (Acts 9:10–18). And a small boy gave his lunch to the disciples and watched Jesus feed thousands (John 6:9).

You may say that you'd go if God asked. But he does. He gives us opportunities every day to serve him, to make a difference, not just in a game like baseball, but in lives. And not just for an earthly victory, but for eternity. When Mom tells about a neighbor in need; when you see a new kid at school who seems confused, lost; when the pastor asks for volunteers; when you read about suffering people in another country; when a friend says, "How can I be sure about going to heaven"?—that's when God is whispering, "Who will go for me?" How about you?

Step in and step up!

ALSO ON THIS DAY . . .

1919—The National Commission recommended a best-of-nine World Series.

1966—Mickey Wright won the LPGA World Series of Golf.

1989—Eric Robert Carter, BMX racer, turned professional at nineteen years of age at the National Bicycle League Grand National in Louisville, Kentucky.

2006—Kimberly Zenz led the American team to compete in the Kings Cup Elephant Polo Championships in Thailand.

BIRTHDAYS:

1948—Terry Bradshaw, Shreveport, LA, Hall-of-Fame quarterback (Pittsburgh Steelers; four-time Super Bowl winner and two-time Super Bowl MVP) and broadcaster

1952—Jimmy Connors, East St. Louis, IL, one of the all-time great tennis players (winner of the US Open in 1978, 1982, and 1983 and Wimbledon in 1974 and 1982)

1982—Jason Hammel, Greenville, SC, major-league pitcher (Colorado Rockies)

In Damascus there was a disciple named Ananias. The Lord called to him in a vision, "Ananias!" "Yes, Lord," he answered. Acts 9:10

FUN FACT It's too early to tell, but so far Kevin Kousmanoff hasn't been Lou Gehrig. In 2006, the Indians traded him to San Diego. In 2010, the Padres traded him to the Athletics.

217

3 Coming **Alongside**

On this day in 1965, Derek Anthony Redmond was born in Bletchley, Buckinghamshire, England.

Derek grew up in England and became one of the country's premier sprinters. He held the British record for the 400-meter sprint, and at the 1991 World Championships he was a member of the British team, which shocked the athletics world by beating the much-favored American team to win the gold medal in the 4x400 meters relay. In the months before the 1992 Olympic Games in Barcelona, Derek fought through several injuries, but he was ready and was expected to win a medal.

Running the fastest time of the first round of the 400 meters, Derek went on to win his quarterfinal. In the semifinal he started well, but while sprinting around a turn about 250 meters from the finish, his hamstring snapped, and he hobbled to a halt and then fell to the track in terrible pain. Then, as the crowd watched in stunned silence, with grim determination, Derek waved away the stretcher-carriers, struggled to his feet, and began to limp down the track. Suddenly a man came out of the stands, pushed past security, and came to Derek's side—Derek's father, Jim. He put his arm around his son and together they completed the race and crossed the finish line as the 65,000-person crowd rose and gave a standing ovation.

Jim Redmond demonstrated his love for his son by going to him, coming alongside, comforting him, and helping him to the finish line. It's a beautiful picture of what God does for us. Our Father loves us so much that he comes to us.

Jesus called the Holy Spirit "the comforter," and the word literally means, "one who comes alongside." God is with us in our struggles, empowering, encouraging, and helping us on the way. And that's what he wants us to do for others as well.

Do you see someone "limping down the track"? Maybe a friend has problems at home. Perhaps you know of a classmate who has missed lots of school because of sickness or injury. Or you may just know someone who needs a friend.

Get out of the stands. Come alongside and run the race together.

....

ALSO ON THIS DAY . . .

1903—Reliance (USA) beat Shamrock III (England) in the thirteenth America's Cup.

1986—The Houston Astros and Chicago Cubs used a record fifty-three players in an eighteen-inning game.

1989—Chris Evert defeated fifteen-year-old Monica Seles for her one hundred and first, and last, US Tennis Open singles victory.

2009—NFL commissioner Roger Goodell ruled that Philadelphia Eagles quarterback Michael Vick would be eligible to play in the third game of the regular season.

BIRTHDAYS:

1968—Dawn Allinger, Salt Lake City, UT, team handball back court (1996 Olympics)

1980—Jennie Lynn Finch, La Mirada, CA, professional softball pitcher (Chicago Bandits), winner of Olympic gold and silver medals (2004 and 2008)

1986—Shaun White, San Diego, CA, snowboarder and skateboarder, winner of two Olympic gold medals (2006 and 2010)

Carry each other's burdens, and in this way you will fulfill the law of Christ. **Galatians 6:2**

Fun Fact The official Olympic records state that Derek Redmond did not finish the race (because he had help), but in the public's eyes, he had finished and done so heroically. This incident has become one of the great moments in Olympic history and has been used in of one of the International Olympic Committee's *Celebrate Humanity* videos. In 2008, Nike featured this incident in their *Courage* commercials.

Shock **the World**

On this day in 2007, after their shocking upset by Appalachian State University, the University of Michigan dropped from number five to completely out of the top twenty-five in both polls.

No Division I college football team has dropped farther in the AP Poll in one week since the poll was expanded to twenty-five teams in 1989. Here's why.

With a strong team of returning starters, Michigan was seen as one of the best football teams in the country, favored to win the Big Ten Championship. And while Appalachian State (Boone, NC) had an excellent team, as a Division I-AA school, most experts believed they didn't stand a chance, especially since the game would be on Michigan's home turf—"the Big House" in Ann Arbor. Michigan was installed as a twenty-seven-point favorite. But in one of the biggest upsets in the history of American sports, on September 1, 2007, the Mountaineers shocked the fifth-ranked Wolverines 34-32. One sportswriter called this the "Miracle in Michigan."

It has happened before, of course—underdogs overcoming odds to beat the highly favored individual or team. In sports we remember Cassius Clay knocking out Sonny Liston to win the boxing heavyweight championship in 1964, the Jets humbling the Colts in Super Bowl III in 1969, UConn overcoming powerful Duke to win the 1999 Men's NCAA Basketball Championship, the Boston Red Sox beating the Yankees four games straight after being down three games to none to win the ALCS in 2004, number twelve-seed Ball State knocking off number five-seed Tennessee in the NCAA Women's Basketball tournament in 2009, and so many others. Every year seems to bring memorable upsets.

If you really want to read about world-shocking upsets, however, open your Bible. During the long journey to the Promised Land, Israel left Egypt against the Pharoah's will and proceeded to defeat numerous powerful armies on. Gideon and a handful of men conquered the mighty Midianites (Judges 7). A small shepherd boy named David downed mighty Goliath with just a slingshot and a stone. All these amazing upsets and many more had one fact in common: God was with them and led them to victory. And in the greatest upset of all, Jesus came back to life and walked out of the grave. Eventually the world will be shocked to see him again—in all his power and glory.

God is still working, and he wants to work in and through you. You'll be amazed at what you can do through his power. Shock the world!

....

ALSO ON THIS DAY . . .

1972—US swimmer Mark Spitz became the first athlete to win seven Olympic gold medals.

2005—Kyle Busch became the youngest driver to win a NASCAR Nextel Cup race, at twenty years, four months, and two days, winning the Sony HD 500 at California Speedway.

2008—The NFL announced it would allow the pro bowl receiver formerly known as Chad Johnson to use his new legal name, Chad Ocho Cinco, on his uniform.

2009—Caroline Buchanan (Australia) beat Jill Kintner (USA) and Melissa Buhl (USA) to win the four-cross women competition in the Mountain Bike World Championships in Canberra, Australia.

BIRTHDAYS:

1949—Tom Watson, Kansas City, MO, one of the all-time great golfers, winner of eight major championships

1968—Mike Piazza, Norristown, PA, all-star major-league catcher (Dodgers, Marlins, Mets, Padres, Athletics)

1970—Janae Lautenschlager, Canoga Park, CA, diver, 1996 Olympics

For everyone born of God overcomes the world. This is the victory that has overcome the world, even our faith. 1 John 5:4

Fun Fact
In describing the upset win, ESPN's Pat Forde wrote: "We'll still be talking about it a few decades from now. Especially in the locker rooms of every huge underdog, where they'll say, 'If Appalachian State can beat Michigan, why can't we shock the world, too?'"

5 No Cause **for Course**

On this day in 1987, John McEnroe was fined $17,500 for his tirades at the US Tennis Open.

John McEnroe, "Johnny Mac," was a great tennis player, but he was known for his explosive temper, especially for berating officials. So this incident was more the rule than the exception with him. McEnroe wasn't and isn't alone with these kinds of actions. We find bad examples in every sport.

Besides yelling at officials and getting technical fouls, ejections, red cards, penalties, or fines, many athletes are known for their words to their opponents. Sometimes it's just playful gamesmanship—"talkin' smack." But often it becomes mean-spirited trash talking and personal. And if you can read lips, watch out, because you'll see a steady stream of curse words that have to be bleeped on television.

Anger needs to be controlled. An out-of-control athlete can hurt an opponent, himself or herself, and the team. After some notorious hockey incidents, players have been convicted of assault and even manslaughter. But what is said causes problems, too. Usually how people speak reveals what they are like on the inside, their character. They can hold it in for a while, being nice and polite, but under pressure and angry, suddenly they can erupt, spewing venom.

Of all people, Christians should be known for their positive and gracious speech. This means not taking God's name in vain (even using the expression OMG or "my God!"), using other swear words, telling dirty jokes, or putting people down. The Bible makes this very clear: "Nor should there be obscenity, foolish talk or coarse joking, which are out of place, but rather thanksgiving" (Ephesians 5:4). We will get angry—that's only natural—but we must control our anger, with God's help, and refuse to engage in name-calling and making insulting remarks. Remember, we represent Christ, and people learn what his followers are like by watching and listening to us.

In the heat of an argument or competition, watch what you say. In an effort to win a contest, control the trash talk. When friends begin to slam others or share dirty jokes, walk away. Watch your words.

....

ALSO ON THIS DAY . . .

1960—Cassius Clay captured the Olympic light heavyweight gold medal.

1972—Terrorists murdered eleven Israeli athletes at Munich Olympics.

1979—Roscoe Tanner fired eleven aces, broke the net with his bullet serve, and upset top-seeded Bjorn Borg in the US Tennis Open quarterfinals.

2005—Forty-two-year-old Jerry Rice announced his retirement from football, declining a role with the Denver Broncos as their fourth wide receiver. He retires holding most of the NFL's career records in receiving.

In the same way, the tongue is a small thing that makes grand speeches. But a tiny spark can set a great forest on fire. . . . People can tame all kinds of animals, birds, reptiles, and fish, but no one can tame the tongue. It is restless and evil, full of deadly poison. Sometimes it praises our Lord and Father, and sometimes it curses those who have been made in the image of God. And so blessing and cursing come pouring out of the same mouth. Surely, my brothers and sisters, this is not right! James 3:5, 7–10, NLT

BIRTHDAYS:

1936—Bill Mazeroski, Wheeling, WV, Hall-of-Fame major-league second baseman (Pittsburgh Pirates)

1960—Willie Gault, Griffin, GA, NFL wide receiver (Chicago Bears, Los Angeles Raiders), bobsled racer, and actor

1972—Dirk Copeland, Los Angeles, CA, pursuit cyclist, 1992 and 1996 Olympics

Fun Fact According to Jason Silverman at PsychologyToday.com, trash talking is "one of our culture's most beloved, and most reviled, phenomena . . . Commercials from athletic companies . . . often glorify trash talking, suggesting that bad manners are essential to good basketball. But critics see in trash talk the decline of sportsmanship and consider it yet another sign of society's general loss of civility."

Road **Trip**

On this day in 2004, the New York Yankees asked for a forfeit in the first game of a doubleheader against the Tampa Bay Rays because the Rays were late getting to Yankee Stadium after delays caused by Hurricane Frances.

This seems rather cold-hearted, don't you think? Evidently the baseball commissioner, Bud Selig, agreed. He denied the request and said a make-up game would be held on October 4 if required. The Yankees won the only game played, 7-4.

Even with great weather conditions, playing on the road can be difficult. Players are away from their own beds and other comforts of home; sometimes they have brutal travel schedules, flying back and forth over time zones. Then they have to contend with stadiums and gymnasiums filled with fans cheering for their defeat. Baseball experts say that successful teams need to win at home and just break even on the road.

Do you ever feel as though your life is like a "road game"—you're not really at home? Actually, for all Christians, that's true. The first line of a song sung years ago in many churches (your parents may remember it—ask them to sing it for you) says, "This world is not my home, I'm just a passin' through . . ." You see, when we trust Christ as Savior, the Bible says that we are "born again" (John 3:3) into God's family. In other verses we learn that we are also "adopted" (Ephesians 1:5). This means that we are God's children, in his family. It also means that we are destined for our heavenly home in heaven (John 14:1–3).

The main reason that we can feel out of place in this world, however, is because we have been changed on the inside. The Holy Spirit has made and is making us different from the rest of the world, in our outlook on life, our values, our desires, and our way of thinking. He's left us here for a reason, of course—to do his work, to spread his truth, and to help others become his kids, too. In all of this, in every part of our lives, we are to be in this world but not of it. We are in a different family, on the visiting team.

So when you feel a bit out of place and long for home, thank God that you belong for him and that one day you'll truly be home.

....

ALSO ON THIS DAY . . .

1954—The Yankees used a record ten pinch hitters in one game.

1988—Thomas Gregory (eleven years old) swam across the English Canal (twenty-two miles).

1995—Cal Ripken Jr. broke Lou Gehrig's record, playing in his 2,131st consecutive game (eventually 2,632).

2009—Emily Jackson (USA) won the K-1 championship at the Kayak ICF Freestyle World Championships in Thun, Switzerland.

2009—Ben Spies (USA) won the Nürburgring Superbike World Championships (Yamaha—39:04.818).

BIRTHDAYS:

1955—Anne Henning, Raleigh, NC, US, 500 meter speed skater, winner of Olympic gold medal (1972)

1956—Pam Allen, Billings, MT, LPGA golfer

1975—Derrek Lee, Sacramento, CA, all-star major-league first baseman (San Diego Padres, Florida Marlins, Chicago Cubs)

[Jesus prayed for his disciples] "My prayer is not that you take them out of the world but that you protect them from the evil one. They are not of the world, even as I am not of it. Sanctify them by the truth; your word is truth. **John 17:15–17**

FUN FACT During the 2009–10 season, the Vancouver Canucks had the longest road trip in National Hockey League history, playing fourteen games over six weeks. That's because Vancouver was preparing to host and then was hosting the 2010 Winter Olympics.

U.S. Open—Tennis

1. Who is the winner of the most Men's singles titles after 1967?
   a. Jimmy Connors
   b. Pete Sampras
   c. Roger Federer
   d. All of the above

2. Who is the winner of the most Women's singles titles after 1967?
   a. Serena Williams
   b. Steffi Graf
   c. Chris Evert
   d. Martina Navrátilová

3. Who is the winner of the most men's championships (singles, doubles, mixed doubles) after 1967?
   a. John McEnroe
   b. Pete Sampras
   c. Andre Agassi
   d. Bob Lutz

4. Who won the most women's championships (singles, doubles, mixed doubles) after 1967?
   a. Venus Williams
   b. Serena Williams
   c. Martina Navrátilová
   d. Chris Evert

5. Who is the youngest male winner of the US Open?
   a. Roger Federer
   b. Pete Sampras
   c. Andy Roddick
   d. Rafael Nadal

6. Who is the youngest female winner of the US Open?
   a. Kim Clijsters
   b. Tracy Austin
   c. Lindsey Davenport
   d. Caroline Wozniacki

7. After Roger Federer won five years in a row, who defeated him in the 2009 finals?
   a. Novak Djokovik
   b. Andre Agassi
   c. Rafael Nadal
   d. Juan Martin del Potro

8. The US Open is the only Grand Slam that continues to use the tiebreak in the fifth set.
   a. True
   b. False

9. Where is the US Open played?
   a. Chicago
   b. Boston
   c. New York
   d. Los Angeles

10. On what type of surface do they currently play?
    a. Har-Tru Clay
    b. DecoTurf
    c. Grass
    d. Asphalt

ANSWERS: 1.d, 2.c, 3.a, 4.c, 5.b, 6.b, 7.d, 8.a, 9.c, 10.b

Everyone's **Watching**

On this day in 1926, the National Broadcasting Company was created by the Radio Corporation of America.

Less than a hundred years ago, broadcasting wasn't very advanced or widespread. In fact, although radio stations were around, NBC was the first major broadcast network in the United States. In 1928, William S. Paley bought the United Independent Broadcasters' sixteen radio stations, renaming the company the Columbia Broadcasting System, and CBS was born. Even before these two pioneer networks, the first radio broadcast of a baseball game occurred on August 5, 1921, over KDKA in Pittsburgh. Two months later, they had the first live broadcast of a college football game. On May 17, 1939, the first-ever televised sporting event was a college baseball game between Columbia and Princeton, on NBC.

Things sure have changed since those early days in broadcasting. Now we can watch just about any sport at any time on television over one of the hundreds of cable or satellite channels on a computer, or even with a smart-phone (can you spell ESPN?). And the visuals are spectacular, in high-definition, with numerous camera angles, featuring replays and players or coach/manager interviews, even during the contest.

These days, nothing escapes notice and the video camera—professional or amateur. If an event didn't make the news, we probably can find it on YouTube. Someone always seems to be watching—and videotaping.

This poses a challenge and an opportunity for Christ-followers, not just athletes. People are supposed to learn what Jesus is like by watching us, by how we live; after all, the word *Christian* means "Christ-one," one like Christ. Jesus told the disciples that all people would know they were his disciples by seeing how they loved one another (John 13:35). Elsewhere he said the disciples' good deeds should shine like lights, encouraging those who see to praise to God (Matthew 5:16). So the big question is this: By watching us, what are people learning about Jesus and the difference he makes in lives?

So watch out—everyone's watching.

ALSO ON THIS DAY . . .

1968—Arthur Ashe defeated Tom Okker to win the US Men's Tennis Open.

1983—Vitas Gerulatis (Lithuanian-American professional tennis player) bet his house that Martina Navratilova couldn't beat the one hundredth ranked male tennis player.

2002—Pitcher Randy Johnson reached 300 strikeouts for the fifth consecutive season, extending his major-league record.

2004—Lisa Leslie of the Los Angeles Sparks recorded the WNBA's third triple-double in history, scoring twenty-nine points, grabbing fifteen rebounds, and tying the WNBA's record of ten blocked shots in one game, as the Sparks defeated the defending champion Detroit Shock, 81-63, in Los Angeles.

BIRTHDAYS:

1949—Joe Theismann, New Brunswick, NJ, all-pro NFL quarterback (Washington Redskins) and sportscaster

1985—J.R. Smith, Freehold, NJ, NBA shooting guard (New Orleans Hornets, Denver Nuggets)

1986—Michael Bowden, Winfield, IL, major-league pitcher (Boston Red Sox)

We are therefore Christ's ambassadors, as though God were making his appeal through us. We implore you on Christ's behalf: Be reconciled to God. **2 Corinthians 5:20**

Fun Fact
The sporting event with the largest worldwide audience is the FIFA World Cup. Other events with huge international audiences include the Summer Olympic Games, Cricket World Cup, UEFA Champions League, Tour de France, Rugby World Cup (rugby union), Super Bowl, and the FIA Formula One World Championship.

Not **De-feeted**

On this day in 1960, Abebe Bikila won the Olympic marathon, setting an Olympic and world record (2:15:16.2).

A two-time Olympic marathon champion from Ethiopia, Abebe Bikila was the first black African in history to win a gold medal in the Olympics. Abebe was born on August 7, 1932, ironically, the day of the Los Angeles Olympic Marathon. His father was a shepherd. To support his family Abebe decided to join the Imperial Bodyguard, so he walked to Addis Ababa, about sixty miles from his home, where he began as a private. When a coach was hired by the government to train athletes, he soon spotted Abebe and began to work with him. Heading into the 1960 Olympic Games, Abebe was added to the Ethiopian team at the last moment, as a replacement for an injured runner, just before the plane was scheduled to leave for Rome.

Abebe ran a great race, winning and setting the Olympic and world record in the process. And get this—he wore no shoes! That's right—he ran barefoot. After, when asked why, Abebe answered, "I wanted the world to know that my country, Ethiopia, has always won with determination and heroism."

All serious athletes, especially runners, take good care of their feet; a blister or other problem could destroy any chance of doing well. So athletic shoes have become big business, and companies pay millions for athletes and teams to wear their gear. Obviously Abebe had no commercial arrangement with a shoe company.

Feet and shoes are mentioned in the Bible in reference to spreading God's good news. No shoe deals here, but the right footwear is vital. When talking about putting on armor for the spiritual battle, Paul wrote, "For shoes, put on the peace that comes from the Good News so that you will be fully prepared" (Ephesians 6:15, NLT). The image is that in a battle, a spiritual war, we are to be spreading peace, God's peace. This means that we need to take seriously the task of living out our faith in the world; it won't be easy, because we'll meet much opposition. But we need to be prepared, like an athlete, and run into the battle fully protected but telling everyone about God and his salvation.

Put on those shoes!

ALSO ON THIS DAY . . .

1954—Attempting to catch Hoyt Wilhelm's knuckleballs, catcher Ray Katt of the Giants had four passed balls, setting a major-league record.

1972—The Soviets beat the USA basketball team for the Olympic gold medal on a controversial third try after the Americans had "won" it twice; the Americans refused to accept their silver medals.

2006—Peyton Manning outdueled his brother Eli in their first meeting, with the Indianapolis Colts beating the New York Giants 26-21.

2009—Carly Gullickson (USA)/Travis Parrott (USA) defeated Cara Black (ZIM)/Leander Paes (IND) in the mixed doubles final of the US Tennis Open, both winning their first Grand Slam title.

> How beautiful on the mountains are the feet of those who bring good news, who proclaim peace, who bring good tidings, who proclaim salvation, who say to Zion, "Your God reigns!" Isaiah 52:7

FUN FACT
In 1964, Abebe Bikila traveled to Tokyo but was not expected to compete, but he did enter the marathon, this time wearing Puma shoes. He entered the Olympic stadium alone to the cheers of 70,000 spectators and finished in a new world-record time of 2:12:11:2. He was the first athlete in history to win the Olympic marathon twice. Right after the race, he didn't seem to be exhausted and started a routine of stretching exercises. He said later that he could have run another ten kilometers.

BIRTHDAYS:

1929—Arnold Palmer, Latrobe, PA, Hall-of-Fame professional golfer, winner of ten Majors

1955—Charlotte Lewis, Peoria, IL, basketball player, winner of the Olympic silver medal in 1976

1974—Ben Wallace, Whitehall, AL, all-star NBA forward (Wizards, Pistons, Bulls, Cavaliers)

Character, Conviction, **and Courage**

On this day in 2001, former college athlete Todd Beamer and others thwarted terrorists who had hijacked their plane.

As Todd and other passengers spoke with friends and family via in-plane and cell phones, in the chaos of their flight, they learned that the World Trade Center had been hit by hijacked airplanes. Todd tried to place a call from the plane and was routed to a GTE supervisor. He told her one passenger had been killed and a flight attendant had said that the pilot and copilot had been forced out of the cockpit. Later, he said some of the passengers were planning to jump the hijackers. Todd and the supervisor prayed together; then, according to the woman, Todd's last audible words were, "Are you guys ready? Okay. Let's roll." They stopped the terrorists, but the plane crashed in Pennsylvania.

Todd was an athlete, having played varsity baseball and basketball at Wheaton College. He was also a committed Christian and, obviously, a man of great character, conviction, and courage. He left behind his wife, Lisa, two sons, David and

At the entrance to the Beamer Center, Wheaton College

Drew, and an unborn daughter, Morgan Kay, born four months after his death. Todd and the other heroes on United Airlines Flight 93 were pretty sure that the hijackers were planning to crash the plane into the Capitol Building or White House. They knew they had to act. And they gave their lives for others and for their country.

Since that day, life hasn't been easy for Todd's family. They grieve as you might imagine. And they miss their husband and dad. Morgan, now about nine, has never met her father. But they have hope and strength because of their Christian faith. They know that one day their little family will be together again, reunited in heaven. That's God's promise. Todd lived it, and they believe it.

You probably won't be confronted by terrorists in the near future. But you will be tested and tried, confronted with situations that demand action. Will you have the character, conviction, and courage to do what God wants? Will you be able to sacrifice for others? Let's roll.

....

ALSO ON THIS DAY . . .

1983—Franco Harris of the Pittsburgh Steelers became the third NFL running back to rush 11,000 yards in a career (he ended with 12,120).

1985—Pete Rose of the Cincinnati Reds got career hit 4,192 off Eric Show of the San Diego Padres, passing Ty Cobb's record.

2004—The University of South Florida announced that female basketball player Andrea Armstrong would be allowed to play wearing her Muslim attire.

2005—The United States Solheim Cup team, captained by legend Nancy Lopez, won the event at the Crooked Stick Golf Club in Carmel, Indiana, defeating Europe 15½ points to 12½ points.

BIRTHDAYS:

1924—Tom Landry, Mission, TX, NFL all-pro player, legendary coach of the Dallas Cowboys, and two-time winner of the Super Bowl

1951—Patty Wagstaff, St. Louis, MO, aerobatic pilot

1985—Shaun Livingston, Peoria, IL, NBA point guard (Clippers, Heat, Thunder, Wizards)

1986—Dwayne Jarrett, New Brunswick, NJ, NFL wide receiver (Carolina Panthers)

For to me, to live is Christ and to die is gain. Philippians 1:21

TODD BEAMER
XXL
TITANS

Fun Fact
Todd's phrase, "Let's roll," became a battle cry for those fighting Al-Qaeda in Afghanistan. At least four facilities have been named for Todd: a post office in Cranbury, New Jersey, Todd Beamer High School in Federal Way, Washington, the Todd M. Beamer Student Center at Wheaton College, and a neighborhood park in Fresno, California.

12 A Weigh **to Go**

On this day in 2009, Allyson Felix won the 200-meter sprint at the World Athletics Final in Thessaloniki, Greece.

Allyson Felix is a champion sprinter. She has won the Olympic silver medal twice in the 200-meter race (2004, 2008), and she won Olympic gold in 2008 as a member of the US Women's 4x400 meter relay team.

She is the only woman ever to win the gold medal three times for that distance at the Athletics World Championships.

Allyson is also a devout Christian, and she sees her running ability as God's gift. "My faith is the reason I run," she says. "It calms my heart and makes everything feel like a lift. My speed is definitely a gift from [God], and I run for his glory. Whatever I do, he allows me to do it."

When you watch world-class runners like Allyson in races of all distances, you'll see that they wear the absolute lightest clothing—even their running shoes are light. They want to run as fast as possible and don't want anything to slow them down. They have very little body fat, too. Extra weight of any kind slows us down. That's why in "handicap" horse races, horses are required to carry varying amounts of weight. The amount depends on how well the horse has done in other races. Theoretically, then, all horses would have a winning chance in a race that was correctly handicapped.

Weight—extra, unnecessary weight—is a burden that slows us down and keeps us from performing well. These weights aren't limited to clothing, racing weights, or body fat. Other things can weigh us down . . . like sin, guilt, worry, fear, and despair. And trying to live with those weights is more difficult than a sprinter trying to run around the track under a fifty-pound pack. Every step can be agonizingly slow and even painful.

But we don't have to live that way. When we turn away from our sin and turn to God, asking him to forgive us, he removes the weight of our guilt and sin and frees us to walk and run unencumbered. Isaiah tells us that Jesus now carries our sorrows because God has placed our sins on him (Isaiah 53:4, 6).

Take a load off. Give it to Jesus . . . and run your race.

ALSO ON THIS DAY . . .

1930—Brooklyn catcher Al Lopez hit the major leagues' last recorded bounce home run.

1979—The Indiana Pacers cut Ann Meyers, the first woman on an NBA basketball team.

1992—Stefan Edberg beat Michael Chang in the longest match in US Men's Tennis Open history (five hr. twenty-six min.).

2009—Christian Cantwell (USA) won the shot put at the World Athletics Final in Thessaloniki, Greece (22.07).

"Son of man, say to the house of Israel, 'This is what you are saying: "Our offenses and sins weigh us down, and we are wasting away because of them. How then can we live?"' Say to them, 'As surely as I live, declares the Sovereign Lord, I take no pleasure in the death of the wicked, but rather that they turn from their ways and live. Turn! Turn from your evil ways! Why will you die, O house of Israel?'" Ezekiel 33:10–11

BIRTHDAYS:

1913—Jesse Owens, Oakville, AL, track star and winner of four Olympic gold medals in 1936

1953—John Williams, American archer and winner of the Olympic gold medal in 1972

1980—Yao Ming, Chinese all-star NBA center (Houston Rockets)

Fun Fact Allyson Felix was born and raised in Southern California. Her father, Paul, is an ordained minister and professor of New Testament at the Master's Seminary in Sun Valley, California. Her mother, Marlean, is an elementary school teacher.

You Are What **You Eat**

On this day in 1991, Kim Zmeskal became the first American to win a medal at the World Gymnastics Championships; she won the gold medal in the all-around, with 39.848 points.

In 1989, at thirteen, Kim became the US Junior National Champion. She continued to work hard and won a gold, a silver, and a bronze at the World Gymnastics Championships in 1991 in Indianapolis. Then, although competing on a stress fracture in her ankle, she managed to win a team bronze medal at the 1992 Olympics in Barcelona.

Like most female gymnasts, Kim was petite. All gymnasts need to be strong and flexible, but being light also helps as they bounce, balance, and spin. A typical diet for a gymnast would include these weekly minimums: grain products—5–7 servings; vegetables and fruit—5–7 servings; milk products—3–4 servings; meat and other alternatives—2 servings. The suggested diet would differ for other sports. Football players, for example, try to bulk up, building muscular weight. They want to run over people, not twirl on a bar or tumble in floor exercise. Just looking at the differences in body types for the high performers in each sport reveals a lot. In all cases, however, eating right is important—for health and performance.

Spiritual food is a necessary part of life as well. Even if we are physically fit, we can be out of shape spiritually. We need nourishment, the right kind and amount of food. As new believers, that means "milk," the simple truths about God, Jesus, and the Bible. But older, growing believers need the fruits, vegetables, and meat (no junk food allowed). The apostle Peter wrote to believers, "Like newborn babies, crave pure spiritual milk, so that by it you may grow up in your salvation" (1 Peter 2:2). And Paul told the Corinthian believers who were still immature in their faith, "I gave you milk, not solid food, for you were not yet ready for it. Indeed, you are still not ready" (1 Corinthians 3:2).

What does your spiritual diet look like? Good, healthy food includes generous servings of Bible study and teaching, along with worship and interaction with people who can give us counsel.

Eat well to get in shape!

ALSO ON THIS DAY . . .

1909—Ty Cobb clinched the American League home-run title with his ninth home run (all inside-the-park).

2007—The New England Patriots, confirmed to have spied on the Jets with a secret video camera in their season opener, were fined $250,000, with their coach, Bill Belichick, fined $500,000.

2008—Los Angeles Angels closer Francisco Rodriguez set a Major League Baseball record with his fifty-eighth save of the season.

2009—Team USA beat Team Great Britain and Ireland, 16½–9½, to win the Walker Cup for the third consecutive time.

BIRTHDAYS:

1980—Daisuke Matsuzaka, Japanese major-league pitcher (Boston Red Sox)

1982—Rickie Weeks, Daytona Beach, FL, major-league second baseman (Milwaukee Brewers)

1986—Sean Williams, Houston, TX, NBA forward/center (New Jersey Nets)

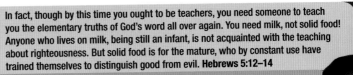

In fact, though by this time you ought to be teachers, you need someone to teach you the elementary truths of God's word all over again. You need milk, not solid food! Anyone who lives on milk, being still an infant, is not acquainted with the teaching about righteousness. But solid food is for the mature, who by constant use have trained themselves to distinguish good from evil. **Hebrews 5:12–14**

Fun Fact
Kim Zmeskal was recognized for her middle-tumbling pass on floor. It involved a round-off, three consecutive whip-backs, a back-handspring into a double-back in the tucked position (sometimes with four whips into double-back). Another trademark was the way she would flare her arms out during full-twisting elements, most notably on her full-twisting Yurchenko vault.

1. I played at the University of Oklahoma and finished as the school's third all-time leading rusher. I was named NFL rookie of the year and am only the fifth player in NFL history to have more than 3,000 yards in my first two seasons. Who am I?
   a. LaDanian Tomlison
   b. Adrian Peterson
   c. Walter Payton
   d. Peyton Manning

2. I was the first quarterback to start more than 200 consecutive games. I was drafted by the Falcons in 1991. I was the first player to win three NFL MVP awards. Who am I?
   a. Steve Young
   b. Brett Favre
   c. Troy Aikman
   d. Jim Kelly

3. In my fifteen seasons with the NFL, I was a two-time NFL Defensive Player of the Year, a thirteen-time pro-bowl selection, and a twelve-time all-pro selection. I hold second-place all-time amongst career-sack leaders with 198.5. Because of my Christian beliefs, I was nicknamed the "Minister of Defense." Who am I?
   a. Devin Hester
   b. William Perry
   c. Jason Taylor
   d. Reggie White

4. I was the New Orleans Saints quarterback for most of the 1970s. I am a graduate of the University of Mississippi and currently have two sons playing quarterback in the NFL. Who am I?
   a. Archie Manning
   b. Jim McMahon
   c. Tony Romo
   d. Lou Holt

5. I led the NFL in interceptions my rookie year. I later led my team to four Super Bowls. Who am I?
   a. Frank Tarkenton
   b. Troy Aikman
   c. Joe Montana
   d. Terry Bradshaw

6. I am the NFL's all-time leading rusher. I played on the same team as Troy Aikman and Michael Irvin, and together we led our team to three Super Bowl championships during the 1990s. I was the winner of *Dancing with the Stars* in 2006 and inducted into the pro-football Hall of Fame in 2010. Who am I?
   a. Emmitt Smith
   b. Walter Payton
   c. Adrian Peterson
   d. Johnny Knox

7. I played college quarterback at Eastern Illinois University. Our team was nicknamed Eastern Airlines because of our passing game. I had limited time as a NFL player but recently coached my team to a Super Bowl championship. Who am I?
   a. Mike Tomlin
   b. Lovie Smith
   c. Sean Payton
   d. Tony Dungy

8. I attended Indiana University and graduated with thirty-four sacks. I signed with the Miami Dolphins in 2000 and three years later lead the AFC in sacks. Miami traded me to Chicago the following year, where I continued to scare quarterbacks with my playing and broadcasters with my name. Who am I?
   a. Julius Peppers
   b. Mike Singletary
   c. Adewale Ogunleye
   d. Troy Polamalu

9. I played college football at the University of Tennessee. Although I finished my degree in three years, I chose to stay for my senior year of college instead of entering the draft. I have only played with one NFL team. I'm in numerous commercials and am considered one of the best quarterbacks of all time. Who am I?
   a. Tony Romo
   b. Peyton Manning
   c. Steve Young
   d. Dan Marino

10. I excelled at baseball, basketball, and football in high school. I was drafted by the New York Yankees and played nine years in Major League Baseball. I played eleven years in the National Football League as cornerback, wide receiver, kick returner, and punt returner. I came out of retirement in 2004 to play two more seasons. One of my nicknames is "Prime Time." Who am I?
   a. Deion Sanders
   b. Michael Irvin
   c. Jerry Rice
   d. Kevin Smith

ANSWERS: 1.b, 2.b, 3.d, 4.a, 5.d, 6.a, 7.c, 8.c, 9.b, 10.a

Hitting **the Mark**

On this day in 2000, Nancy Johnson of the United States won the ten-meter air rifle Olympic gold medal.

This was the first medal awarded in the Sydney Olympics and the first gold medal ever awarded in the women's ten-meter air rifle.

Nancy was in the US Army at the time. Her husband, Ken, also in the Army, was an Olympian, too, competing in the men's air-rifle event. After serving in the military, Nancy enrolled at Florida State University, where she earned her degree in nursing as a Cum Laude Graduate.

In Nancy's Olympic event, she had to shoot 10 meters, from a standing position, with a 0.177-in. caliber air rifle weighing no more than 12.1 lbs. She took 40 shots within 75 minutes, with a maximum of 10 points awarded for each shot.

Then the top eight shooters followed with a final 10 shots, each scored to a maximum of 10.9, with the cumulative score determining the winner. Nancy Johnson won the gold medal by .2 points!

Competitive shooters of all kinds know the importance of hitting their targets, the closer to the center, the better. Those who miss the mark miss out. It doesn't take much to lose: in this contest, the athlete who missed by just a smidgen lost the gold to Nancy Johnson.

One of the words used in the Bible for *sin* means "missing the mark." Just like that sounds, the picture is of someone aiming for a target but not hitting it. In our case, the target is perfection—that's what it takes to get into heaven; thus, even just one small sin will destroy our chances. When we do or think what we shouldn't, we miss the mark. When we don't do what we should, we miss the mark. And the Bible says that "everyone has sinned; we all fall short of God's glorious standard" (Romans 3:23, NLT). So we're all in serious trouble.

But that's where God's love and kindness come in—he sent his Son, Jesus, who was and is perfect—totally righteous. Now, because of his life, death, and resurrection, we can have his righteousness (we can be perfect in God's eyes) by trusting in him as Savior. And eventually we'll have much more than a gold medal; we'll dance on the streets of gold!

ALSO ON THIS DAY . . .

1960—Amos Alonzo Stagg retired as a football coach at ninety-eight.

1975—Rennie Stennett went seven for seven as the Pittsburgh Pirates beat the Chicago Cubs, 22-0.

1987—The California Angels' Bob Boone played catcher in a record 1,919 Major League Baseball games.

2006—The United States beat New Zealand 34-30 to win the Wheelchair Rugby World Championships.

BIRTHDAYS:

1955—Robin Yount, Danville, IL, Hall-of-Fame major-league shortstop/center fielder (Milwaukee Brewers), NL MVP 1982 and 1989

1968—Tara Cross-Battle, Houston, TX, volleyball hitter, winner of the Olympic bronze medal in 1992

1973—Clint Peay, Columbia, MD, soccer defender, winner of the Olympic gold medal in 1996

For God so loved the world that he gave his one and only Son, that whoever believes in him shall not perish but have eternal life. **John 3:16**

[un]ACT After Nancy Johnson's win, the highlight quote came not from Nancy but her husband, Ken, who was slated to compete in the men's air rifle event: "Now I'll have to win a medal, or I'll be doing the washing up for the next four years!"

17 Down the River

On this day in 2007, Clay Wright (USA) won the World Cup Freestyle Kayak Championship on the Ottawa River (Canada).

Competitive kayaking takes great skill, maneuvering the small watercraft through heavy rapids and doing flips and turns along the way. One of the world's best professional whitewater kayakers, Clay Wright pioneered "creekboating" (descending very steep low-volume whitewater, such as waterfalls and slides) and "playboating" (performing technical moves in one place). He has won numerous freestyle events and extreme races throughout the world, including the one on this day and the gold medal at the 1997 World Freestyle Championships for squirt kayaking (a very small and flat kayak).

If you've ever tried this sport, you know how unstable a kayak is—hit the current the wrong way, and you're over. Canoes are a bit more stable, but paddlers in both watercrafts have to be careful about their weight and go with the current, which can be challenging. Water flows downhill, often at a rapid rate causing whitewater, and it takes many twists and turns. And unlike still water in lakes and ponds, the depth can vary greatly along the way. If the paddler isn't paying attention, he or she may miss a turn and run into branches or worse on the bank, scrape bottom, or crash into a boulder. But the ride is exciting and fun, if you know what you're doing and stay alert.

Life is much like a kayak or canoe journey down a river or stream. As we paddle along, the water can be smooth, especially at the beginning, so we glide effortlessly and enjoy the view. We encounter turns, some rather abrupt, and have to navigate those with skill, making sure to move to the deeper water. (This may be where you are in life.) Eventually, we will encounter sudden drops and boulders. They cause the most concern, and we may scrape a few on the trip. Unfortunately, some friends and others bottom out or capsize at these rough places.

Successful navigation on life's journey means being prepared, being alert, and responding quickly to the turns (changes in life), drops (temptations), shallow water (tough times), and boulders (conflicts and problems). But here's the best part—it's not a solo journey. God is with us, and he knows the stream. We need to rely on him to get us through.

Have a great trip!

....

ALSO ON THIS DAY . . .

1947—Jackie Robinson was named Rookie of the Year by *The Sporting News*.

1959—Jack Nicklaus won the fifty-ninth US Golf Amateur Championship.

1961—The Minnesota Vikings played their first NFL game, beating the Bears 37-13.

2004—Ichiro Suzuki of the Seattle Mariners broke the Major League Baseball record for most singles in a season by hitting his 199th of the year, breaking the record of 198 set by Lloyd Waner in 1927.

> There is a river whose streams make glad the city of God, the holy place where the Most High dwells. **Psalm 46:4**

BIRTHDAYS:

1934—Maureen "Little Mo" Connolly, San Diego, CA, great tennis pro, winner of nine Grand Slam titles and the first woman to win all four Grand Slam tournaments in a year, 1953

1945—Phil Jackson, Deer Lodge, MT, NBA star (New York Knicks, New Jersey Nets), head coach (Chicago Bulls, Los Angeles Lakers), and winner of twelve NBA Championships (two as a player and ten as a coach)

1975—Jimmie Johnson, El Cajon, CA, NASCAR driver, four-time Sprint Cup Series Champion (2006, 2007,

FUN FACT Clay Wright has appeared in more than fifty extreme or instructional kayak videos. In addition to whitewater kayaking professionally, he designs kayaks. Clay lives in Rock Island, Tennessee, and paddles for Jackson Kayak, a company started by and named after one of the most successful freestyle kayakers, Eric Jackson.

Chasing **the Dream**

On this day in 1999, thirty-five-year-old Jim Morris made his major-league debut for the Tampa Bay Devil Rays as the second oldest rookie in MLB history.

Jim Morris began playing baseball at the age of three, but he moved around a lot as a child because his father was in the Navy. In every new town Jim made friends through baseball, his passion. Eventually his family settled in Texas. In 1982, at age eighteen, the Yankees selected him in the first round of the Major League Baseball draft. But he chose to continue his education and enrolled at Angelo State University on an academic scholarship. They had no baseball program, so he played football instead and did very well—but he still dreamed of pitching in the major leagues. In 1984 Morris attended major-league tryouts again and was recruited by the Brewers. He signed but suffered several arm injuries in the minor leagues and was released. He tried again with the White Sox but couldn't overcome the arm problems; so he retired from baseball and taught and coached at a high school in Texas.

While coaching baseball in the late 1990s, his players convinced him to try out one more time for the majors. He promised he would if they won the district championship, something the team had never accomplished. They did! And Coach Morris kept his end of the bargain by trying out for the Tampa Bay Devil Rays. Surprisingly, Jim discovered that despite his age and past arm surgeries, he was able to throw twelve consecutive ninety-eight-mph fastballs. After talking it over with his family, Morris signed a professional contract with the Rays. He began with the minor-league Double-A Orlando Rays but soon moved up to a spot with the Triple-A Durham Bulls. He did well there, too, and was called up and given a chance to pitch with the big club when the rosters expanded. And on September 18, 1999, the thirty-five-year-old pitcher made his debut in Arlington, Texas, against the Rangers. With most of his players and his hometown watching, relying on his fastball, he struck out the first batter he faced on four pitches. Jim Morris's goal of pitching in the majors was finally realized, and he made four more appearances later that year. He had fulfilled his dream.

What's your dream? What do you think God wants you to do? Keep praying, working, and trusting God—don't give up.

ALSO ON THIS DAY . . .

1848—Baseball ruled that a baseman can tag the base for the putout instead of the runner.

1919—Eight Chicago White Sox agreed to throw the 1919 World Series.

1938—The Chicago Bears beat the Green Bay Packers 2-0.

1977—Joanne Carner and Judy Rankin won the LPGA National Team Golf Championship.

2004—Bernard Hopkins retained his IBF, WBA, and WBC world middleweight titles, while adding the WBO one, knocking out Oscar de la Hoya in nine rounds at Las Vegas, Nevada.

BIRTHDAYS:

1961—Sharon Barrett, San Diego, CA, LPGA golfer

1971—Lance Armstrong, Plano, TX, road cyclist, possibly the best in history, seven-time winner of the Tour de France, and a cancer survivor

1984—Anthony Gonzalez, Cleveland, OH, NFL wide-receiver (Indianapolis Colts)

And afterward, I will pour out my Spirit on all people. Your sons and daughters will prophesy, your old men will dream dreams, your young men will see visions. Joel 2:28

FUN FACT *The Rookie,* released in 2002, tells Jim Morris's story. Jim's sports agent convinced the pitcher that his story could make a Hollywood movie. Walt Disney picked up the project, casting actor Dennis Quaid in the starring role.

19 **Milestones**

On this day in 1968, Denny McLain won his thirty-first game of the season, and Mickey Mantle hit his 535th career home run.

Winning thirty games in a season is almost impossible—only thirteen players have accomplished this feat in MLB history. Winning twenty games is seen as the mark of a great season for a pitcher. Yet, in 1968, Denny McLain won thirty-one for the Detroit Tigers, on their way to capturing the American League pennant and World Series. Near the end of this game, with the Tigers leading the Yankees 6-1, McLain faced Mickey Mantle again. McLain had idolized Mantle while growing up and knew he would be retiring soon. So he grooved a pitch, allowing Mickey to hit his 535th home run and pass Jimmie Foxx on the all-time home-run list.

Major League Baseball is known for keeping statistics about every aspect of the game. We probably can find something about how many triples left-handed outfielders have hit off left-handed relief pitchers in the eigth inning in April! But wins and losses for a pitcher and home runs for a hitter are two of the biggest

stats. And both of these athletes reached a significant number in this game—milestones.

We use *milestones* to indicate important events in life. Originally, this word referred to actual stones that were placed along a road, a mile apart. Today our highways have "mileposts" or "mile markers" that do the same. Their purpose is to indicate the distance travelled or the remaining distance to a destination.

In every career, people can set markers, preliminary goals, or steps to help them reach their ultimate goal. Marking these milestones can help motivate a person to work hard and achieve. We can have milestones in playing sports, getting good grades, learning a skill, developing a talent, and even growing spiritually.

God expects us to grow in our faith. Young believers won't instantly be masters of Bible knowledge and theology, but they can take steps in that direction. One milestone might be reading the whole Bible through. Another

could be memorizing a verse a month. Others could include reading books about missionaries and martyrs in church history, finding an older Christian to talk with, tithing at least ten percent, perhaps supporting a child through a relief agency, and, of course, having a daily time of Bible reading and prayer.

What are your spiritual milestones?

....

ALSO ON THIS DAY . . .

1879—At age seventeen years and one hundred ninety-eight days, Thomas Ray became the youngest person to break a world track-and-field record—polevaulting 11'2".

1988—While competing in the Olympics springboard diving competition, US diver Greg Louganis hit his head on the diving board— he went on to win the gold medal.

2000—Ken Griffey Jr. pinch-hit his 400th home run, becoming the first major leaguer to reach the mark as a pinch hitter.

2004—The Arizona Cardinals retired the number forty of Pat Tillman during halftime of their game against the New England Patriots in Tempe, Arizona.

BIRTHDAYS:

1936—Al Oerter, Astoria, NY, discus thrower, winner of four Olympic gold medals (1956, 1960, 1964, 1968)

1957—Dan Hampton, Oklahoma City, OK, Hall-of-Fame defensive tackle (Chicago Bears)

1971—Colleen Coyne, East Falmouth, MA, ice hockey defenseman for the US Women's Hockey Team, winner of the Olympic gold medal, 1998

1986—Ryan Barrow Succop, Hickory, NC, NFL placekicker (Kansas City Chiefs) and the 2009 "Mr. Irrelevant" after being selected with the final pick of the 2009 NFL Draft

For this very reason, make every effort to add to your faith goodness; and to goodness, knowledge; and to knowledge, self-control; and to self-control, perseverance; and to perseverance, godliness; and to godliness, brotherly kindness; and to brotherly kindness, love. For if you possess these qualities in increasing measure, they will keep you from being ineffective and unproductive in your knowledge of our Lord Jesus Christ. **2 Peter 1:5–8**

Fun Fact After Mickey Mantle hit his home run, the next batter McLain faced, Joe Pepitone, waved his bat over the plate, as if asking for an easy pitch of his own. McLain responded by knocking Pepitone down with his next delivery.

Hurting **and Healing**

On this day in 2009, the New Orleans Saints beat the Philadelphia Eagles 48-22. Kevin Kolb, starting for the injured Donovan McNabb, threw for 391 yards in a losing effort.

Injuries are part of the game—true in every sport. Blisters, bruises, pulled muscles, dislocated fingers, hyperextended joints, sprains, and worse occur all the time and force athletes to miss events, seasons, or years in order to heal and rehab. In this football game, starting, all-pro quarterback Donovan McNabb couldn't perform, but his replacement, only in the league a couple of years and seldom used, did very well in his place. One man's injury turned out to be another man's opportunity.

Depending on the severity of the injury, an athlete's feelings can range from irritation and disgust to despair and desperation. Certain athletes seem to get hurt every year and spend much of the season on the disabled list. That has to be frustrating. Even worse, severe knee injuries and concussions have ended several careers. Some athletes try to play through the pain or just keep coming back after each surgery (Dan Hampton had ten knee surgeries in his eleven-year professional football career).

Injuries also are a part of life—every life. That's because we're human, mortal. From our skinned knees and colds to much more serious illnesses and physical problems, every person who has ever lived has suffered. Career-ending and life-threatening diseases and injuries are also possible for each of us.

So how do you respond when you are hit by hurt? Do you feel sorry for yourself? Do you question or blame God? That's how many people react. Or do you determine to fight even harder, to come back even stronger? And do you thank God for his love and ask for his healing, if that's in his will? That's how believers should react.

Jesus is called the Great Physician, the healer of our bodies and souls. So if you're on the "injured reserve" or "disabled list" these days, go to him. Ask for his healing—physically and emotionally. Also ask him to guide you through this time and to give you his peace and hope. And if you know others who are hurting, pray for them, encourage them, and help them focus on God and hope.

Jesus cares.

....

ALSO ON THIS DAY . . .

1970—Billie Jean King defeated Bobby Riggs in the Astrodome in the Battle of the Sexes tennis match.

1973—Willie Mays announced that he would be retiring from baseball at the end of the season.

1987—Alain Prost, French racing driver, won a record twenty-eighth Formula One auto race.

2009—Lin Dan (CHN) won the men's singles badminton championship in the WF Super Series: China Masters Super Series in Changzhou.

BIRTHDAYS:

1950—Rudy Jaramillo, Beeville, TX, major-league hitting coach (Texas Rangers, Chicago Cubs)

1960—Alice Regina Brown, Jackson, MS, 4x100 meter relay runner, winner of two Olympic gold medals, 1984, and 1988

1981—Jordan Tata, Plano, TX, major-league pitcher (Detroit Tigers)

Heal me, O Lord, and I will be healed; save me and I will be saved, for you are the one I praise. **Jeremiah 17:14**

[UN ACT So far in his NFL career, Donovan McNabb has suffered forty-seven injuries forcing him to miss playing time. Most of these occurred to his ribs (nine), abdomen/legs (twelve), and ankles (fourteen).

NFC Football Teams

Match the team name to the description.

1. Army insects
2. Seven square
3. Streakers are this
4. Helpers to relocate
5. Trained to kill
6. Six rulers
7. Opposite ewes
8. Class of boy scouts
9. American gauchos
10. Fundamental rules
11. King of beasts
12. A dollar of corn
13. Louis Armstrong song
14. Hop epidermis
15. Ocean-going birds
16. Black cat

a. Packers
b. Eagles
c. Seahawks
d. Rams
e. Lions
f. 49ers
g. Redskins
h. Cardinals
i. Buccaneers
j. Giants
k. Falcons
l. Panthers
m. Bears
n. Saints
o. Cowboys
p. Vikings

ANSWERS: 1.j, 2.f, 3.m, 4.a, 5.k, 6.p, 7.d, 8.b, 9.o, 10.h, 11.e, 12.i, 13.n, 14.g, 15.c, 16.l

Bonehead?

ON THIS DAY IN 1908, NEW YORK GIANT FRED MERKLE FAILED TO TOUCH SECOND BASE, CAUSING THE THIRD OUT IN THE NINTH INNING AND DISALLOWING THE WINNING RUN.

Called the most controversial game in baseball history, for most of the nine innings it was a pitcher's duel, and both teams entered the bottom of the ninth with one point. With one out and a man on first, Fred Merkle singled down the right field line, pushing the potential winning run to third. The next batter drilled a single to center, and fans poured onto the field, thinking their team had won. In the chaos, however, Fred Merkle stopped running; and when the Cubs' shortstop Johnny Evers eventually retrieved the ball and touched second base, he was out on a force, so the run didn't count. After conferring, that's what the umpires ruled, and they stopped the game because of darkness and called it a tie. Later the Cubs won the make-up game,

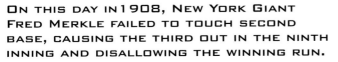

which proved decisive as they edged out the Giants by just one game to win the National League pennant. The Cubs went on to win the World Series that year—the last championship in the team's history.

In 1908, Fred Merkle was just nineteen and the youngest player in the National League. Put into the lineup because the regular first baseman was ill, this was his first major-league start. After, the *New York Times* blamed the loss on "Censurable stupidity on the part of player Merkle," and for the rest of his life his nickname was "Bonehead" because of that one play.

Sometimes we let one incident or poor decision define a person's character or reputation. Then we might make assumptions about what that person can do and not give him or her a chance. We also can often judge a person's actions and condemn

him or her without knowing the whole story. In Fred Merkle's case, everyone thought the game was over, and he said that's what the umpire had told him—but he was blamed for the result. Instead, we should be quick to forgive—Jesus made this very clear with his disciples (see Matthew 6:12–15). And we certainly shouldn't label a person with a hurtful nickname.

Are you holding a grudge because of what someone did to you in the past? Let it go. Forgive and allow that person to outlive the mistake. Give another chance.

ALSO ON THIS DAY . . .

1952—Rocky Marciano knocked out Jersey Joe Walcott in the thirteenth round to win the heavyweight boxing title.

1970—Gary Muhrcke won the first New York Marathon.

1992—Manon Rheaume, goalie, the first female to play in a NHL exhibition game (Tampa Bay Lightning) gave up two goals on nine attempts in one period.

2004—Baltimore Orioles' second baseman Brian Roberts hit his forty-eigth double of the season, breaking the franchise record set by Cal Ripkin Jr. in 1983.

BIRTHDAYS:

1964—Diane Dixon, Brooklyn, NY, 4x400 meter runner, winner of the Olympic silver medal, 1988

1985—Joba Chamberlain, Lincoln, NE, major-league pitcher (New York Yankees)

1989—Brandon Jennings, Compton, CA, NBA point guard (Milwaukee Bucks)

[Jesus said], "Do not judge, and you will not be judged. Do not condemn, and you will not be condemned. Forgive, and you will be forgiven." Luke 6:37

Fun Fact
Fred Merkle became the Giants' full-time first baseman in 1910 and was a regular for the Giants, Dodgers, and Cubs for another ten years. He played in five World Series, all for the losing team. Bitter over the events of the "bonehead" game, Merkle avoided baseball after his playing career finally ended in 1926. When he finally appeared at a Giants old-timers' game in 1950, the fans gave him a standing ovation.

Wrestling

On this day in 2000, Rulon Gardner (USA) beat Alexander Karelin of Russia to win the Olympic gold medal in the super heavyweight class, Greco-Roman wrestling.

This was a huge upset. Alexander Karelin had won gold at the Seoul, Barcelona, and Atlanta Olympics. Before this match, he had never lost in international competition and had been unbeaten in all competitions in thirteen years. He hadn't even surrendered a single point in a decade. In contrast, Rulon Gardner, Karelin's opponent, had never earned an NCAA championship or a world medal. Yet Rulon Gardner won!

The next year, Gardner won again, adding a world championship to his resume and making him the only American to ever win both a World and Olympic title in Greco-Roman wrestling. When Gardner wrestled these favored opponents, he knew that despite their string of victories, they could be beaten. They were, after all, just flesh-and-blood men like him. He prepared, wrestled well, and won.

We face a powerful wrestling opponent, too.

Our battle isn't about winning medals, however, but about advancing the kingdom of God. Here's what the apostle Paul had to say: "We wrestle not against flesh and blood but against principalities, against powers, against the rulers of the darkness of this world, against spiritual wickedness in high places" (Ephesians 6:12, KJV). That sounds serious, and it is. These wicked opponents are from Satan and are very powerful. So, Paul says, we must be prepared, ready for anything they throw at us.

This battle, spiritual warfare, is real. The devil will do everything possible to encourage us to disobey God, to give in to temptation and do what we know is wrong, to turn away from our faith. And he doesn't play by the rules—he can approach from any angle, at any time. Suppose a junior high school wrestler decided to take on Karelin—no contest; it would be over in a few seconds. Satan is way more powerful than an undefeated Russian wrestler, so we dare not underestimate him or try to win in our own strength. Instead, Paul adds, we should "Pray in the Spirit at all times and on every occasion. Stay alert and be persistent in your prayers for all believers everywhere" (Ephesians 6:18, NLT). In God's strength, we can be victorious.

Are you ready? Take it to the mat.

....

ALSO ON THIS DAY . . .

1938—Don Budge became the first tennis player to accomplish the Grand Slam.

1977—Ken Hinton of the Canadian Football League Columbia Lions returned a punt 130 yards.

2004—Laila Ali won the IWBF light heavyweight title, knocking out Gwendolyn O'Neal in three rounds at Atlanta, Georgia.

2008—Seven-time Tour de France winner Lance Armstrong, who had come out of retirement earlier that month, announced that he would ride for the Astana Team, managed by Johan Bruyneed, his team manager for all seven of his Tour titles.

Finally, be strong in the Lord and in his mighty power. Put on the full armor of God so that you can take your stand against the devil's schemes. Ephesians 6:10–11

BIRTHDAYS:

1946—"Mean" Joe Greene, Hall-of-Fame NFL tackle (Pittsburgh Steelers) and four-time Super Bowl champion

1970—Jeanette Kollasch, Evanston, IL, WPVA volleyball player

1974—Matt McKeon, Florissant, MO, soccer midfielder, winner of the Olympic gold medal, 1996

Fun Fact After the 2000 Olympics, Rulon had numerous injuries from accidents, including an amputated toe and a dislocated wrist. But he still won the US Olympic trials for his weight class. At the 2004 Olympics, he won the bronze medal. After that match, he left his shoes on the mat as the traditional symbol of retirement from competitive wrestling.

Accomplished **Receiver**

On this day in 2005, Marvin Harrison and Peyton Manning of the Indianapolis Colts broke the record for most passing yardage between two teammates with 9,568 yards.

In this game, the Colts beat the Browns 13-6 in a defensive battle, but an offensive record was set. The previous one was held by Jim Kelly and Andre Reed, who had combined for 9,538 yards with the Buffalo Bills.

Obviously setting a record like this takes two excellent athletes, with skills and determination, and hundreds of hours of practice. Half of the credit goes to the quarterback who has to throw the football at just the right time to the right spot at the right speed. But to make the combination work, the receiver has to be in the right place at the right time; then, when the ball is thrown, this athlete has to actually catch it. And all of this must be done while huge, muscular, fast, and determined opponents are trying to stop both the quarterback and receiver. The keys to catching the ball are body position and concentration, watching it all the way into the hands and not being distracted by anything, especially not the defender who will try to intercept the ball, bat it away, or rip it out of the receiver's hands—no easy task. One thing is for sure—to catch the ball, the receiver must be looking in the right direction and have eyes and hands wide open. Imagine a basketball, baseball, or football athlete trying to catch a ball with their back to the passer or with fists tightly clenched or eyes closed—not gonna happen.

Actually that last statement is true about receiving anything—a letter, handshake, gift, football . . . or a gift from God. We have to be open and ready to receive it. Some people wonder why they haven't received anything from God, not a football, but a message or a blessing. Yet they aren't turned toward him and, in many ways, have their eyes and hands closed. For all they know, God has been tossing blessings their way for years; they just haven't been ready and open. Being ready to receive God's gifts means staying focused on him (reading his Word, looking for his work, praying for guidance) and being open (willing to do whatever he says, thanking him, confessing our sins and asking for help).

Are you open? (Tip: Try praying with your hands open.) God to you—a great passer-receiver combination!

BIRTHDAYS:

1976—Chauncey Billups, NBA guard (Celtics, Raptors, Nuggets, Magic, Timberwolves, Pistons)

1985—Calvin Johnson, Tyrone, GA, NFL wide receiver (Detroit Lions)

1990—Mao Asada, Japanese figure skater, the winner of the Olympic silver medal, 2010

They sought God eagerly, and he was found by them. So the Lord gave them rest on every side. **2 Chronicles 15:15b**

Fun Fact Against the Detroit Lions on December 14, 2008, Marvin Harrison caught his 1,095th career reception, putting him in third place, all time. Then on December 28, he moved into second on the all-time NFL reception record list with 1,102 receptions during a 23-0 Colts victory over the Titans. Following that season, Harrison asked for and was granted his release by the Indianapolis Colts. He spent the 2009 season out of football.

26 Trusting **the Team**

On this day in 2006, Greg Maddux threw just seventy-six pitches in six innings of work as the Los Angeles Dodgers beat the Colorado Rockies 11-4.

This might not seem like a big deal, but Maddux had a reputation for being economical with his pitches. Normally a major-league manager and pitching coach like to keep a hurler's pitch count to just over 100 to protect his arm, and they want him to pitch at least six innings. Maddux would routinely reach the seventh or eighth inning with pitch counts below eighty, one time using just seventy-eight in all nine innings—very unusual in the modern era of baseball.

In 1944, the record was set for the fewest pitches in a nine-inning game. On August 10, Red Barrett, a right-handed pitcher for the Boston Braves, pitched a 2-0 shutout of the Cincinnati Reds on just fifty-eight pitches. Amazing. In a game that took just one hour and fifteen minutes, he faced the minimum twenty-seven batters, surrendered two hits, walked no one, and struck out no one. The absolute least amount of pitches that could be thrown in a nine-inning game would be twenty-seven—one per batter (pretty much impossible). To throw only fifty-eight comes out to just over two pitches for each batter.

Pitchers like Greg Maddux and Red Barrett were successful because of their pinpoint accuracy, their control, and because they trusted their teammates behind them. They didn't give up walks and didn't try for strikeouts (each one requires at least three pitches). Instead, they let the batters hit the ball, giving the fielders the opportunities to make the put-outs.

Working with teammates and trusting them is important in all sports but in many other areas as well. School assignments and church groups often use teams. In the team we're most familiar with, the family, every person needs to do his or her job for the team to function well. The opposite approach is one person trying to do everything alone, ignoring the rest of the team or not valuing what they can contribute. The most important team is what the Bible calls "the Body of Christ"—the Church, the fellowship of believers.

No matter what your age or experience, as a follower of Christ, you are an important member of his team, with a vital contribution to make. Trust your team.

ALSO ON THIS DAY . . .

1978—New York District Court Judge Constance Baker Motley ruled that women sportswriters could not be banned from locker rooms.

2003—Lyn-Z Adams Hawkins won the Triple Crown overall Street Title at the Xbox World Championships of Skateboarding with consistent finishes at all three Vans Triple Crown events.

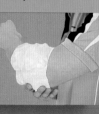

2004—Morten Anderson of the Minnesota Vikings played in the game against the Chicago Bears, his 341st appearance in an NFL game, breaking George Blanda's record.

2006—Barry Bonds hit his 734th career home run to set a new National League record.

BIRTHDAYS:

1974—Gary Hall Jr., Cincinnati, OH, swimmer (50-meter, 100-meter, 400-meter freestyle relay) and winner of ten Olympic medals (five gold, three silver, two bronze)

1979—Jaycie Phelps, Indianapolis, IN, gymnast, winner of the Olympic gold medal, 1996

1981—Serena Williams, Palm Beach Gardens, FL, world-class tennis professional, winner of 12 Grand Slam tennis tournaments

Instead, speaking the truth in love, we will in all things grow up into him who is the Head, that is, Christ. From him the whole body, joined and held together by every supporting ligament, grows and builds itself up in love, as each part does its work. **Ephesians 4:15–16**

[un]fact The most pitches thrown in a major-league baseball game was 172. On April 27, 1993, Pirates' knuckleball pitcher Tim Wakefield did this over ten plus innings in a 6-2 victory against the Braves.

True **Colors**

On this day in 1881, the Chicago Cubs beat Troy 10-8 before a record small "crowd" of twelve.

Baseball sure has come a long way since those days—in many ways, but especially attendance. The game has become big business, involving billions of dollars annually, and more fans equal more money. The salaries for just one team total millions of dollars—so ticket prices continue to climb in order to meet the increasing payroll. In 1993, the Colorado Rockies drew 4,483,350 fans, an average of 55,350 for every home game. That's a lot better than twelve. Attendance matters in all sports: the greater the crowd, the greater the revenue. In perhaps the largest sporting event anywhere, more than 400,000 attend the Indianapolis 500 race every Memorial Day weekend.

Vocal support is another advantage of having a large home crowd. A stadium packed with ardent fans cheering their lungs out in support of their athletic heroes is sure to help the home team. And most of them wear the team colors, forming a sea of blue or red or green or orange . . . Sometimes they'll wave hankies or towels or bang "thunder sticks." Many will wear distinctive headgear (cheeseheads anyone?) or paint themselves in the team colors to show their support—even in sub-zero temperatures, a few brave (foolhardy) guys will spell out the team name on their bare chests. No one can doubt where their hearts are—they are true fans!

Many team supporters also display their athletic loyalties during the week. Today and tomorrow, count the number of jerseys, jackets, shirts, and caps with team logos. You'll see a bunch. Team merchandise is another lucrative aspect of the sports business. We love our sports and their stars.

What about the Christian team? Not on an athletic field but in everyday life. What are the team colors? How do we know who's on the team anyway?

It's easy; believers are those who love others. At least that's what Jesus said should set us apart. Having a Christian bumper sticker, wearing a T-shirt with a Christian message, and playing Christian radio are all fine, but the true mark of Christ-followers should be how we love each other, our neighbors, and even our opponents ("enemies").

Display your true colors.

....

ALSO ON THIS DAY . . .

1987—The NFL players went on strike.

1998—Mark McGwire became the first man to hit seventy homers in one season in Major League Baseball.

2004—Diana Taurasi of the Phoenix Mercury was named the WNBA's rookie of the year.

2009—In volleyball the Dominican Republic beat Puerto Rico to win the RCECA Women's Championship in Bayamón, Puerto Rico for the first time and qualify for the World Grand Champions Cup.

BIRTHDAYS:

1939— Kathy Whitworth, Monahans, TX, professional golfer, seven-time LPGA Player of the Year

1965—Steve Kerr, Beruit, Lebanon, NBA guard (Suns, Cavaliers, Magic, Bulls, Spurs, Trailblazers), winner of five NBA Championships, and president and general manager of the Phoenix Suns

1975—Tajama Abraham, Kecoughton, VA, WNBA center (Sacramento Monarchs)

1984—John Lannan, Long Beach, NY, major-league pitcher (Washington Nationals)

[Jesus said], "So now I am giving you a new commandment: Love each other. Just as I have loved you, you should love each other. Your love for one another will prove to the world that you are my disciples." **John 13:34–35, NLT**

FUN FACT The bestselling football merchandise is dominated by quarterbacks. Over 3 million Tony Romo jerseys moved through the stores in a recent year. That number of Eli Manning jerseys were sold, too. Other quarterbacks in the top ten include Ben Roethlisberger (2.8 million), Mark Sanchez (1.8 million), and Peyton Manning (1.5 million).

Fun**Quiz** • September 28 & 29

1. In what Olympic sporting event in 2000 did Nancy Johnson compete? (September 16)

2. What country did 1960 Olympic marathon champ Abebe Bikila call home? (September 10)

3. In what track race did Derek Redmond compete? (September 3)

4. What is the most pitches thrown by one pitcher in a single Major League Baseball game? (September 26)

5. What year did the American League and National League umpires form a new Association of Major League Umpires? (September 30)

6. At what tennis event did John McEnroe get fined for his tirades? (September 5)

7. What college did Todd Beamer attend? (September 11)

8. What type of kayaking did Clay Wright pioneer? (September 17)

9. How old was Jim Morris when he made his major-league debut for the Tampa Bay Devil Rays? (September 18)

10. How many fans attended the Chicago Cubs–versus–Troy baseball game in 1881? (September 27)

11. On what team did Peyton Manning and Marvin Harrison play? (September 25)

12. Who was the first American League player to hit a grand-slam home run in his first career at bat? (September 2)

13. In 2004, what caused the Tampa Bay Rays to be late to their game against the New York Yankees? (September 6)

14. How many injuries has Donovan McNabb had? (September 20)

15. Who is the only woman to ever win the gold medal three times for the 200-meter sprint at the Athletics World Championships? (September 12)

16. Who did Rulon Gardner (USA) defeat for gold in Greco-Roman wrestling at the 2000 Olympic Games? (September 24)

17. What was the first major broadcast network in the United States? (September 9)

18. How many players in Major League Baseball history have won thirty games in a season? (September 19)

19. In how many World Series did Fred Merkle play? (September 23)

20. Who did the Appalachian State University football team upset in 2007? (September 4)

21. Who was the first American to win a medal at the World Gymnastics Championships? (September 13)

You Make **the Call**

ON THIS DAY IN 1968, THE AMERICAN LEAGUE AND THE NATIONAL LEAGUE UMPIRES FORMED A NEW ASSOCIATION OF MAJOR LEAGUE UMPIRES.

Officials—every sanctioned athletic contest has them: referees, linesmen, scorers, judges, starters, timers, and umpires. These men and women have the responsibility of guiding the event within the rules and making tough but assertive calls. They are in charge, and players and fans, even when they disagree, should respect their judgment. They can be wrong, of course (they're human, too), but they are paid to judge impartially, according to the rules. Without these men and women, a game would dissolve into chaos.

Not everyone has the temperament to be an athletic official, to withstand the pressures of making quick judgments and getting grief from athletes, coaches, and fans. And sometimes the job can be dangerous when a close call goes against the home team.

We all like to judge, whether we admit it or not. Sitting in the stands, far from the field of play, we are sure that the pitch shouldn't have been called a strike or that the puck actually went over the line before the goalie pulled it back. Our judging isn't limited to sporting events. We often make snap decisions about who is guilty ("She broke my bike!"), a person's motives for doing something ("You did that just to annoy me!"), or why someone was late or seemed to ignore us or didn't call. Making judgments can harm or even destroy relationships. And, more often than not, eventually we usually are proven to be wrong.

Jesus said, "Do not judge, or you too will be judged. For in the same way you judge others, you will be judged, and with the measure you use, it will be measured to you" (Matthew 7:1–2). Often we criticize others for the very behavior that we are guilty of doing. We can easily overlook our own mistakes, failures, and sins while pointing them out in someone else. We expect them (parents, siblings, friends, neighbors, and others) to be almost perfect, while we want them to accept us as we are, faults and all. In this passage, Jesus is saying that we need to be careful or we'll be judged with the same criteria. We should leave the judging up to God.

Instead of judging, be forgiving and loving, assuming the best of others.

You make the call.

....

ALSO ON THIS DAY . . .

1927—Babe Ruth hit his record-setting sixtieth home run (off Tom Zachary).

1988—Louise Ritter (USA) highjumped 6'8" to win the Olympic gold medal.

1994—The National Hockey League players went on strike.

2007—Germany won the FIFA Women's World Cup (soccer), beating Brazil; the United States beat Norway to take third.

BIRTHDAYS:

1959—Kim Bauer, New Orleans, LA, LPGA golfer

1972—Jamal Anderson, Newark, NJ, NFL running back (Atlanta Falcons)

1981—Dominique Moceanu, Hollywood, CA, gymnast, winner of Olympic gold medal in 1996

Brothers, do not slander one another. Anyone who speaks against his brother or judges him speaks against the law and judges it. When you judge the law, you are not keeping it, but sitting in judgment on it. There is only one Lawgiver and Judge, the one who is able to save and destroy. But you—who are you to judge your neighbor? James 4:11–12

Fun Fact In 2005, a soccer referee with twenty years of experience decided to quit after a player spit in his face. This Welsh referee said that the level of abuse directed at officials on Wales' football pitches (soccer fields) had become intolerable. In that season alone, referees had been assaulted fourteen times.

Making His Mark **in History**

On this day in 1965, Masanori Murakami made his last appearance in Major League Baseball.

Exactly thirteen months earlier, in Shea Stadium in New York City, baseball fans witnessed history in the making when Masanori Murakami stepped in to pitch for the San Francisco Giants in the eighth inning. Murakami was the first Japanese man to play Major League Baseball.

And there he was, with the National League Pennant at stake. This was Masanori's first day in New York, his first day in the majors. Although he didn't know English, he didn't have to speak the language to understand that his team was losing to the Mets.

So, how did the twenty-one-year-old southpaw wind up with the Giants? It all started back in Japan when Murakami was just in high school. His pitching arm earned him a spot on the Nankai Hawks, a team in Japan's Nippon Professional Baseball League. An exchange program, however, later earned Murakami a trip to the States and a minor-league team in Fresno California. His 11-7 pitching record with that team gained him notice and a trip to New York.

Although the Giants wound up losing that game, Murakami pitched a near perfect inning, giving up only a single. Although Murakami wound up going back to Japan after just over a year, he had made his mark.

Like Murakami, Daniel was a fish out of water who also made his mark in history. He had been brought to Babylon not as part of an exchange program but as a captive of an invading army. But God had plans for Daniel that involved his being chosen as one of the advisors of the king of Babylon (Nebuchadnezzar). Daniel's skill as an interpreter of dreams—a skill powered by God—gained him the respect and praise of Nebuchadnezzar (Daniel chapters 2 and 4). Over the years, Daniel became Nebuchadnezzar's wisest advisor, one who didn't hesitate to share his faith in the God of Israel.

Maybe someday you'll make your mark in history. A good start to that is by following Daniel's example and trusting God. God helps his people to make wise decisions. Check out what Daniel says in the passage below. God promises to provide what you need.

ALSO ON THIS DAY . . .

1922—The former Chicago Staleys played their first NFL game as the Chicago Bears, winning 6-0.

1932—In the fifth inning of the World Series in Chicago, after two strikes Babe Ruth pointed to the center field bleachers and hit the next pitch there.

2000—The Sydney Summer Olympics closed, with the United States having won the most medals (ninety-seven) and the most gold medals (forty).

2004—Japanese player Ichiro Suzuki (Seattle Mariners outfielder) set the major-league record for base hits in a season, breaking George Sisler's eighty-four-year-old record of 257.

BIRTHDAYS:

1956—Leslie Burr-Howard, equestrian show jumper, winner of Olympic gold medal in 1984 and silver medal in 1996

1964—Marcia Pankratz, Wakefield, MA, field hockey forward (Olympics, 1988 and 1996)

1984—Matt Cain, Dothan, AL, major-league pitcher (San Francisco Giants)

Praise be to the name of God for ever and ever; wisdom and power are his. . . . He gives wisdom to the wise and knowledge to the discerning. **Daniel 2:20–21**

Fun Fact
In 1965, Murakami struck out over one batter per inning pitched, posted an earned run average under four, and earned eight saves. He had to return to his original Japanese club the next season, however, because of contractual obligations. Murakami continued his successful baseball career for another seventeen years.

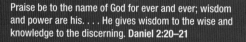

Down but **Not Out**

On this day in 2004, Felix Trinidad rose from a knockdown in round three and dropped Ricardo Mayorga three times in round eight to score an eighth-round knockout.

The outlook wasn't good, especially from the canvas. Felix Trinidad had been knocked down early in his ten-round battle. But in what some experts called the fight of the year, Trinidad got to his feet, continued boxing, and won.

Boxing can be a brutal sport. At its worst, it looks like two grown men (or women) trying to kill each other. And through the years, many fighters have been seriously injured, and some have lost their lives. At other times, a match can look like a choreographed dance, with boxers moving quickly around the ring, in and out, up and down. The sport is much safer in the Olympics, where, in addition to the gloves, the competitors wear headgear, and they only box for three rounds. Most fights are won on points, not on KOs or TKOs.

Regardless, this match serves as a good illustration about life. Although we aren't fighting like Trinidad and Mayorga were, we still can get knocked down. The

hit may be a setback at school, such as an F in a class. It could be in a relationship, being wrongly blamed for something by a friend. Perhaps the family has to move to another city. Or maybe the situation is even more serious—a terrible tragedy for someone you love. Everyone suffers blows like that. Sometimes they come out of nowhere, catching us by surprise and knocking us flat. But what happens next is what's important—how we react to those knockdowns. Will we lie there and be counted out? Or will we struggle to our feet, regain our strength, and rejoin the fight? Failures don't have to be permanent!

The apostle Paul experienced several knockdowns in life: abandonment, false accusations, imprisonments, beatings, shipwreck, and more. Yet he kept getting up and moving on. He knew that with God's strength he could do God's will. Paul told the

Romans, "No, in all these things we are more than conquerors through him who loved us" (8:37). We've read that passage before, and it's true. Through Christ we can get off the mat and defeat any foe, even death; for when we die we get to live with the Savior forever.

You may be down, but you're not out. Get up and join the battle.

ALSO ON THIS DAY . . .

1991—Steffi Graf became the youngest woman to win 500 professional tennis matches.

2003—Richie Velasquez won the trick competition at the Gravity Games in Cleveland, Ohio.

2006—Rebecca Ward (USA) won the women's saber at the 2006 World Fencing Championships in Turin.

2007—Carlos Peña of the Tampa Bay Rays and Dmitri Young of the Washington Nationals were given the MLB Comeback Player of the Year Award for the American League and National League, respectively.

BIRTHDAYS:

1932—Maury Wills, Washington, DC, all-star major-league shortstop and base-stealing leader (Dodgers, Pirates, Expos), National League MVP in 1962, three-time World Champion

1974—Anthony Johnson, Charleston, SC, NBA point guard/shooting guard (Kings, Hawks, Magic, Cavaliers, Nets, Pacers, Mavericks)

1985—Craig Davis, New Orleans, LA, NFL wide receiver (San Diego Chargers)

We are pressed on every side by troubles, but we are not crushed. We are perplexed, but not driven to despair. We are hunted down, but never abandoned by God. We get knocked down, but we are not destroyed. Through suffering, our bodies continue to share in the death of Jesus so that the life of Jesus may also be seen in our bodies. 2 Corinthians 4:8, NLT

Fun Fact Cassius Clay (Muhammad Ali) had an amateur record of 100 wins with five losses. That includes the 1960 Summer Olympics in Rome, where he won the light heavyweight gold medal. In his 1975 autobiography, Ali wrote that he threw his Olympic gold medal into the Ohio River after being refused service at a "whites-only" restaurant and fighting with a white gang. He was given a replacement medal during the 1996 Olympics in Atlanta, where he lit the torch to start the games.

Surf's **Up!**

On this day in 2008, Kelly Slater won his ninth title as world champion of surfing at the Billabong Pro Mundaka.

Kelly Slater lives in Florida and surfs worldwide. More than a decade ago, he had become the most successful champion in surfing history. So this ninth title added to his legacy and legend. He is both the youngest (at twenty) and the oldest (at thirty-six) to win the title. In the final heat of a competition in 2005, Slater became the first surfer ever to be awarded two perfect scores for a total of twenty out of twenty points under the ASP two-wave scoring system. This man knows his boards and waves, and he knows how to ride.

As with all sports, surfing has unique words and descriptions, such as *tube, cutback, floater, snaking, goofy foot, grom, tubular,* and *pearl.* Some surfing terms have become well known, such as, *catch the wave, hang ten,* and *wipe-out.*

Another familiar expression, "Surf's up!" is a call to all surfers to grab their boards and get to the beach because conditions are right (wind and waves) for surfing. Most people who enjoy the beach and ocean probably have a different take on that day's weather forecast. Seeing the clouds, many think, "Not a good day to catch some rays." Others, seeing the waves rising and crashing, think, "Not a good day to swim or water ski" (or go fishing). When the conditions seem negative and almost threatening to some people, to surfers they sound perfect. They see opportunity.

One day Jesus was talking with his disciples, just after his encounter with the Samaritan woman at the well. That incident must have confused the disciples because most Jews didn't like Samaritans very much. Anyway, Jesus said, "I tell you, open your eyes and look at the fields! They are ripe for harvest" (John 4:35). Jesus was telling them to look differently at people. Instead of seeing problems and threats, they needed to see opportunities. The disciples were surrounded by people who were hurting and lost, without hope, desperate for God's good news.

Like the disciples, we need a Jesus nudge, a reminder to look differently at our circumstances. Just as surfers who can't wait to hit the waves, we should be eager to tell others about Christ, seeing the opportunities that God gives us to ride his wave.

Surf's up!

ALSO ON THIS DAY . . .

1951—With the "shot heard round the world," Bobby Thomson's home run in the bottom of the ninth inning of their playoff game gave the Giants the National League pennant over the Dodgers.

1982—Scott Weiland ran the Detroit marathon backwards in less than five hours.

2008—Candace Parker of the WNBA's Los Angeles Sparks became the first player to be named the league's MVP and Rookie of the Year in the same season.

2009—Mariel Zagunis (USA) won the women's sabre in the fencing World Championships in Antalya, Turkey.

BIRTHDAYS:

1940—Mike Troy, American butterfly swimmer, winner of two Olympic gold medals, 1960

1954—Dennis Eckersley, Oakland, CA, Hall-of-Fame starting and relief pitcher (Indians, Red Sox, Cubs, Athletics, Cardinals)

1970—Tyji Armstrong, Inkster, MI, NFL tight end (Buccaneers, Cowboys, Rams)

When he saw the crowds, he had compassion on them, because they were harassed and helpless, like sheep without a shepherd. Then he said to his disciples, "The harvest is plentiful but the workers are few. Ask the Lord of the harvest, therefore, to send out workers into his harvest field." **Matthew 9:36–38**

FUN FACT In his spare time, Slater enjoys playing the guitar and strolling on the beach. His favorite surfing spots are Pipeline in Hawaii, Sandspit in California, Kirra in Australia, Miramar in Buenos Aires, Argentina, Taghazout in Morocco, Jeffrey's Bay in South Africa, Soup Bowls in Barbados, and Sebastian Inlet near his home in Florida.

Taking **His Stand**

On this day in 1963, A. C. Green was born in Portland, Oregon.

A.C. Green played sixteen seasons in the NBA as a power forward or center. Known for his defense and rebounding, he contributed to the success of several teams: Lakers, Suns, Mavericks, and Heat. He was an all-star and a three-time NBA champion, too. But here's an amazing fact: he played in more consecutive games than any other player in NBA and ABA history (1,192). So he was durable and dependable.

For this NBA star, however, more important than any awards, achievements, or records is his faith. He gave his life to Christ while in high school, and ever since he has tried to live the way a Christ-follower should. This isn't easy for a college and professional athlete, with temptations at every turn.

But A.C. was determined, with God's help, to be faithful to his convictions. He even went public, taking a stand for abstinence—waiting until marriage to have sex. And he doesn't mind saying that he began and ended his NBA career as a virgin. At times during his basketball career, his teammates would send women to tempt him to compromise his morals. But A.C. would just calmly quote Bible verses to them. These days he runs youth camps through his A. C. Green Youth Foundation promoting abstinence until marriage.

The Bible is very clear about this issue. God created sex, so it is good. But God also said that it should happen with a man and a woman only in marriage. Because A.C. was serious about his faith, he also was serious about reading and applying God's Word, living God's way.

Whether or not you ever play a professional sport, you will be tempted to do all sorts of things that you know you shouldn't, that go against Scripture. Right now, every day you face them, and they'll only increase as you get older. At times you may think, "Well if everyone is doing it . . ." Don't fall for that line of thinking. Everyone is not doing it. A. C. Green is a great example of this. And if A.C. could keep his morality, anyone can.

You can do it, too. Take your stand.

ALSO ON THIS DAY . . .

1996—Liz Johnson won the BPAA US Women's Bowling Open.

2005—John Hart resigned as the general manager of the Texas Rangers. John Daniels, at the age of twenty-eight years, is named his replacement, becoming the youngest general manager in any sport.

2008—In mixed martial arts, Seth Petruzelli defeated Kimbo Slice by TKO on strikes in fourteen seconds to win the EliteXC in Sunrise, Florida.

2009—Ben Spies (USA) won the Magny-Cours Superbike World Championship in Magny-Cours, France.

BIRTHDAYS:

1934—Sam Huff, Edna Gas, WV, Hall of Fame NFL linebacker (New York Giants, Washington Redskins)

1952—Anita Lucette Defrantz, Philadelphia, PA, rower, winner of an Olympic bronze medal in 1976 (eight-oared shell), member of United States and International Olympic Committees

1972—Joanna Stone, Australian javelin thrower, 1996 Olympics

But whatever was to my profit I now consider loss for the sake of Christ. What is more, I consider everything a loss compared to the surpassing greatness of knowing Christ Jesus my Lord, for whose sake I have lost all things. I consider them rubbish, that I may gain Christ. **Philippians 3:7–8**

FUN FACT During his NBA career, A.C. suffered from singultus (chronic hiccups). The hiccups only stopped when he was running or working out. He never slept more than two hours at a time because of the condition. He has since recovered. A.C. got married in 2002, to Veronique.

Baseball World Series

1. In the 2009 World Series, which Phillies pitcher threw a complete game masterpiece in the first game to take the win?
   a. Pedro Martinez
   b. Cliff Lee
   c. Mariano Riviera
   d. A. J. Burnett

2. What nickname was given by the fans and media to the 2000 World Series?
   a. Freeway Series
   b. Windy City Series
   c. Lone Star Series
   d. Subway Series

3. In the game-four thriller in 2009, who stole second base and then third and scored on an Alex Rodriguez double to win the game for the Yankees?
   a. Mark Teixeira
   b. Jorge Posada
   c. Nick Swisher
   d. Johnny Damon

4. In 2005, which team won their first World Series title since 1917?
   a. Chicago Cubs
   b. Philadelphia Phillies
   c. Cleveland Indians
   d. Chicago White Sox

5. Which team, playing in only their fourth season in Major League Baseball, shocked the New York Yankees in the 2001 World Series?
   a. Florida Marlins
   b. Arizona Diamondbacks
   c. Colorado Rockies
   d. Tampa Bay Devil Rays

6. The Boston Red Sox won the 2007 series with a 4-0 win over which team, making their World Series debut?
   a. Colorado Rockies
   b. Milwaukee Brewers
   c. Washington Nationals
   d. San Diego Padres

7. The Florida Marlins upset the New York Yankees in the 2003 World Series. Which Marlin pitched a complete game shutout in game six at Yankee Stadium to clinch the series?
   a. Brad Penny
   b. Josh Beckett
   c. Carl Pavano
   d. Mark Redman

8. Which MLB curse was finally laid to rest in the 2004 World Series?
   a. Curse of the Bambino
   b. Curse of Billy Penn
   c. Curse of the Billy Goat
   d. Curse of the Black Sox

9. The first walk-off home run to ever win a World Series title was in 1960, defeating the New York Yankees. Who hit this historic shot?
   a. Roger Maris
   b. Bill Mazeroski
   c. Mickey Mantle
   d. Yogi Berra

10. Which National League team won the 1901 World Series?
    a. No one (no World Series in 1901)
    b. New York Yankees
    c. Boston Red Sox
    d. Los Angeles Angels

ANSWERS: 1.b, 2.d, 3.d, 4.d, 5.b, 6.a, 7.b, 8.a, 9.b, 10.a

Covenant-**Keeper**

On this day in 1975, the Major League Players Association filed a suit on behalf of Dodgers pitcher Andy Messersmith.

John Alexander "Andy" Messersmith pitched twelve seasons in the major leagues (Dodgers, Braves, and Yankees) and had some success, a four-time all-star and two-time Gold Glove winner. But he is most famous for the historic ruling in 1975 that led to the end of the MLB reserve clause and began the era of free agency.

In 1975, Andy was negotiating his new contract with the Dodgers and asked for a no-trade clause. The Dodgers refused. Evidently the negotiations took a nasty, personal turn, but he went ahead and pitched that year without a contract, leading the league in complete games and shutouts, with an ERA of 2.29. Marvin Miller of the players union filed a grievance on behalf of Messersmith and another player.

They won and were free to sign with any team, which Andy did. In an interview, Andy said, "It was a matter of being tired of going in to negotiate a contract and hearing the owners say, 'Okay, here's what you're getting. Tough luck.'" Now contract negotiations and free agency are a huge part of all professional sports.

In a typical contract, two parties each agree to perform a certain way for specific considerations (usually payment of money). In publishing, an author agrees to write a book to a specified standard by a certain time, and the publisher agrees to pay the writer and publish the book by a certain time. In sports, an athlete agrees to play for an organization for a specific length of time and money. If either party fails to meet the contract terms, the contract no longer applies, and that party may be penalized. Our world runs on these legal documents, and lawyers make a living off them.

Fortunately, God doesn't treat his people that way. Instead of a contract, he makes covenants. A covenant is similar to a contract, but get this: the covenant isn't cancelled by our poor performance. God is perfect, so his covenants are perfect, and he would never violate them. Here's the best part—God keeps his promises. Even if we totally mess up, which we do, he still does what he has promised.

Let that truth soak in and make your day. God has promised that because you trusted in Christ as Savior, he will never leave you and will get you home, no matter what. Wow!

....

ALSO ON THIS DAY . . .

1928—Paavo Nurmi (Finland) ran a world-record ten miles (50:15.0).

1985—Lynette Woodward was chosen as the first woman on the Harlem Globetrotters.

1992—The Tampa Bay Lightning became first National Hockey League expansion team to win its opening game.

2007—Former Ram Kurt Warner threw for 190 yards and a touchdown and ran for another after starting Cardinals quarterback Matt Leinart left with a broken collarbone as Arizona beat St. Louis 34-31.

> Then he took the cup, gave thanks and offered it to them, saying, "Drink from it, all of you. This is my blood of the covenant, which is poured out for many for the forgiveness of sins." **Matthew 26:27–28**

Fun Fact After winning his case, Messersmith signed a three-year deal with the Atlanta Braves. Braves owner Ted Turner suggested the nickname "Channel" for Andy and jersey number seventeen, in order to promote his television station that broadcast the Braves games. Major League Baseball said no.

BIRTHDAYS:

1957—Jayne Torvill, English ice skater of Torvill and Dean, winner of the Olympic gold medal in 1984 and the bronze medal in 1994

1975—Billy Walsh, Summit, NJ, soccer midfielder, winner of Olympic gold medal, 1996

1985—Evan Longoria, Downey, CA, major-league third baseman (Tampa Bay Rays)

1986—Lee Nguyen, Richardson,

OCTOBER

8 No **Fool**

ON THIS DAY IN 1927, JIM ELLIOTT WAS BORN IN PORTLAND, OREGON.

Growing up, Jim had several hobbies and loved sledding on the mountainside—one of the extreme sports of his time. And in high school, he played football and participated in many other activities, including the school newspaper, dramatic productions, and the speech club. He would take long hikes, go canoeing, and go camping with his friends.

After high school, Jim enrolled at Wheaton College in Illinois, a long way from home. There he competed on the wrestling team. In 1948, Jim decided to attend a missions conference over Christmas break. There he felt called to minister in South America. After graduating from college, he began working to make that dream a reality.

Eventually he and four others who were working with the Quichua Indians in Ecuador decided to try to reach a violent Indian tribe known then as the Aucas (now Waurani). Jim and his companions, Ed McCully, Roger Youderian, Pete Fleming, and their pilot, Nate Saint, made contact from their airplane with these Indians using a loudspeaker and a basket to pass down gifts. Then the men landed on a beach near the Auca village. All seemed to be going well; they were building trust. But suddenly, on January 8, 1956, the world was shocked to hear that all five had been murdered by the people they had been trying to reach. The world couldn't understand the dedication and drive of these young men and the "waste" of lives.

Certainly those were tragic deaths, but their lives weren't wasted. They were doing God's work, and their deaths inspired hundreds to become missionaries, too.

Many years earlier Jim had settled the matter, determining to go wherever God would lead him to share the gospel, regardless of hardships and risks. In his journal he had written, "He is no fool who gives what he cannot keep to gain that which he cannot lose." Jim had also written, "Consume my life, my God, for it is [yours]. I seek not a long life, but a full one, like you, Lord Jesus." Clearly this athlete, this man of God, was living not for earthly victories but for his Lord and Savior Jesus Christ.

We should do the same.

....

ALSO ON THIS DAY . . .

1956—Don Larsen of the New York Yankees pitched the only perfect World Series game, against the Brooklyn Dodgers, winning 2-0.

1995—Miami Dolphin quarterback Dan Marino broke Fran Tarkenton's NFL career completions record.

2005—Northwestern College, an NCAA Division III school in St. Paul, Minnesota, became the first school in modern history to play two games in the same day. They started with a noon home game against Trinity Bible College, winning 59–0; then they traveled a few miles for a night game against Macalester College and won 47–14.

2009—The International Olympic Committee voted to add golf and rugby to the Olympic program for the 2016 Games in Rio de Janeiro.

BIRTHDAYS:

1965—Matt Biondi, Palo Alto, CA, 100-meter swimmer and winner of three Olympic gold medals, 1984, 1988, and 1992

1973—Donnie Abraham, Orangeburgh, SC, NFL cornerback (Tampa Bay Buccaneers, New York Jets)

1983—Travis Pastrana, Annapolis, MD, extreme motorsports driver

I have been crucified with Christ and I no longer live, but Christ lives in me. The life I live in the body, I live by faith in the Son of God, who loved me and gave himself for me. I do not set aside the grace of God, for if righteousness could be gained through the law, Christ died for nothing! Galatians 2:20–21

Fun Fact The documentary film *Beyond the Gates of Splendor* (2002) tells the story. In 2003, *Love Above All*, a musical based on the story of Jim and Elisabeth Elliot, was staged at the Victoria Concert Hall in Singapore by Mount Carmel Bible-Presbyterian Church, and again, in 2007, at the NUS University Cultural Centre. In 2006, *End of the Spear*, a theatrical movie, was released. It tells the story of the pilot, Nate Saint, and the return trip of Saint's son attempting to reach the natives of Ecuador.

Getting **Even**

On this day in 1991, the San Jose Sharks beat the Calgary Flames 4-3 for their first National Hockey League win.

Now that's how to start a franchise. Not many teams begin that way. In fact, on this day in 1974, the Washington Capitals lost their first-ever game 6-3 to the New York Rangers. That began a thirty-seven-game road losing streak for the Capitals. These days, both the Sharks and Caps are enjoying success in the league.

Hockey is a tough, demanding sport, involving great conditioning and skill. And because the action occurs on a lightning-fast surface in a small space, the game can get quite physical. Checks are part of the game, but also, unfortunately, are fights. These fights begin when someone takes offense at something a player on the other team said or did. Soon the gloves are dropped, jerseys grabbed, and punches thrown . . . and both players head to the penalty box.

When two players are penalized, one from each team, play continues at equal strength, four aside. But when just one player is sent off, the other team enjoys a one-player advantage and goes to the power play. Obviously a team would like to have many more power plays than penalty-killing opportunities. Often infractions happen by accident; a stick gets too high or a skate trips a player—with so much action, those are bound to occur. But winning teams learn how to avoid foolish penalties. Those happen when a player gets caught up in the heat of the moment and decides to retaliate. Great discipline is needed to refrain from returning the punch or cheap shot or to ignore the trash-talk insult. But oh how we love to get even!

That attitude pops up in many areas. Someone cuts off a driver in traffic, so that driver speeds up and returns the favor. A kid at school makes fun of us or makes us look foolish, and we think of what we can say to cut him down to size. Someone hurts a friend, and we think of what we can do to get back at her. Not only are those foolish actions, but they go against the way God wants us to respond. Jesus told his disciples (us too), "If someone slaps you on the right cheek, offer the other cheek also" (Matthew 5:39, NLT).

Don't take a foolish penalty. Leave the retaliation up to God.

....

ALSO ON THIS DAY . . .

1960—Cowboy quarterback Eddie LeBaron threw the shortest touchdown pass (two inches).

1974—Frank Robinson became the first black baseball manager (Cleveland Indians).

1997—Dean Smith, North Carolina-Chapel Hill, the winningest college basketball coach, retired.

2006—Haris Charalambous, a twenty-one-year-old backup center for Toledo, originally from England, died after collapsing during practice.

BIRTHDAYS:

1959—Mike Singletary, Houston, TX, Hall-of-Fame NFL middle linebacker (Chicago Bears) and head coach (San Francisco 49ers)

1970—Annika Sorenstam, Stockholm, Sweden, one of the all-time great golfers, winner of seventy-two LPGA tournaments

1982—Travis Rice, Jackson Hole, WY, professional snowboarder, winner of X Games gold medals, 2003 (slopestyle) and 2009 (big air)

ear friends, never take revenge. Leave that to the righteous anger of God. For the criptures say, "I will take revenge; I will pay them back," says the Lord. Instead, "If your nemies are hungry, feed them. If they are thirsty, give them something to drink. In doing his, you will heap burning coals of shame on their heads." **Romans 12:19–20, NLT**

[UN FACT] In their game on March 5, 2004, the Ottawa Senators and Philadelphia Flyers had a record total of 419 minutes in penalties between them. Obviously many of the penalties were being served at the same time, since a hockey game has three twenty-minute periods—total, sixty minutes!

10 Spin

On this day in 2006, Vitaly Efimov and Diogo José Dos Santos Pinho from Portugal won the men's doubles table tennis at the 2006 Lusophony Games in Macau.

Table tennis may not seem like a sport, especially when played in the basement with a friend, but world-class table tennis is a fast-paced game that involves quickness, coordination, and skill. Watch an Olympic competition some time, and you'll be amazed. Most of the best players in the world come from Asia. In this case the team from Portugal won. One of the best US players was Wang Chen, a woman who immigrated to the States from China.

Experienced table tennis players know how to put spin on the ball. That involves hitting the ball in a slicing motion with the paddle, spinning it so that it changes direction after hitting the table. Sometimes it's backspin, causing the ball to bounce more vertically. Or the spin can cause a ball to go to one side or another or change the speed of the ball after a bounce. A skilled player can use several types of spin, limiting an opponent's options to great advantage. Putting spin on a ball is also used in pool, tennis, bowling, golf, soccer—just about every sport that uses a round ball. Causing the misdirection can be very effective in a game.

Putting "spin" on a story is another way to use this technique. When a politician says something embarrassing, a publicist quickly explains that the person really didn't mean what was said or that the statement was taken out of context. We react the same way when we're caught doing something we shouldn't. We say something like, "I was just . . ." and try to make what we did sound okay. That's "spin." It makes the ball, or the incident in these examples, go in another direction. But putting spin on our words and actions is nothing more than lying, bouncing the truth in another direction.

Jesus expects his people to be truthful, to live and speak honestly. Simply defined, lying is the attempt to deceive. So when we spin a situation, we're really trying to divert attention away from the truth—to deceive. And that's wrong. People should be able to trust us and to know that we will own up to our mistakes, failures, and sins.

Be committed to the truth; don't try to spin your way out.

ALSO ON THIS DAY . . .

1920—Second baseman Bill Wambsganns of the Cleveland Indians made the first unassisted World Series triple play, against the Brooklyn Dodgers.

1976—Greece's ninety-eight-year-old Dimitrion Yordanidis became the oldest man to compete in a marathon, finishing in 7:33.

1992—Paula Newby-Fraser became the first woman to go sub-nine hours in a record-setting performance in the Ironman Triathlon.

2004—The New England Patriots set a record for the number of consecutive NFL games ever won, at nineteen, after beating the Miami Dolphins 24–10.

BIRTHDAYS:

1969—Brett Favre, Gulfport, MS, all-pro NFL quarterback (Packers, Jets, Vikings), eleven-time pro bowl, five-time NFC MVP

1974—Ralph Dale Earnhardt Jr., Kannapolis, NC, NASCAR driver

1984—Troy Tulowitzki, Santa Clara, CA, major-league shortstop (Colorado Rockies)

But most of all, my brothers and sisters, never take an oath, by heaven or earth or anything else. Just say a simple yes or no, so that you will not sin and be condemned. **James 5:12, NLT**

Fun Fact
The most popular racket sport in the world, table tennis has over 300 million active players. The game is controlled by the International Table Tennis Federation (ITTF), founded in 1926. Since 1988, table tennis has been an Olympic sport. From 1988 until 2004, the events were men's singles, women's singles, men's doubles, and women's doubles. Since 2008 the doubles have been replaced by team events.

Full **Protection**

On this day in 2009, Peyton Manning became only the third quarterback, after Steve Young and Kurt Warner, to throw for 300 or more yards in each of the season's first five games.

After an all-American college career at the University of Tennessee, Peyton Manning continued his success in the pros with the Indianapolis Colts. Since drafting Peyton in 1998, the Colts have had a series of successful seasons, culminating with their Super Bowl victory 2007, where Peyton was named MVP. In addition to being a great team leader and calling all the plays from a no-huddle alignment, Peyton's passing has been spectacular. He is the all-time Colts franchise leader in career passing yards, pass completions, and passing touchdowns. He also holds the NFL records for consecutive seasons with over 4,000 yards passing and the most total seasons with 4,000 or more yards passing. No wonder Manning is already considered one of the best quarterbacks of all time.

Peyton Manning hasn't achieved this by himself, of course—he has a team surrounding him—receivers, backs, and linemen. While the quarterback, running backs, and receivers receive all the attention (and glory) on the offensive side of the ball, the unsung heroes are the center, guards, and tackles. These men block, putting their bodies between the defense and their running backs and quarterback. In the case of the quarterback, they provide protection. Not even the most talented quarterback in the world can complete a pass lying face-down on the turf. And very few are successful when they have to throw before they want to or on the run. Quarterbacks like Peyton Manning understand this; they know that much of their success depends on their line.

Protection and security are needed in a world that seems to be pressed against us. At times we can feel like a quarterback attempting to pass but surrounded by hostile, attacking forces. The protection supplied by an offensive line sounds a lot like what we read in the Bible as a "wall" or "hedge." Walls protected cities from attacking armies; thus, King David and others would ask God to protect them, personally, the same way.

Just like a quarterback can't succeed on his own, we need God's protection—from danger, temptation, and Satan himself. At the same time, we need to stay within that wall and not venture out on our own.

Ask God to guide and protect you. He will.

....

ALSO ON THIS DAY . . .

1911—Ty Cobb (AL) and Frank Schulte (NL) became Major League Baseball's first MVPs, and each man received a car as an award.

1992—Deion Sanders played for the Atlanta Falcons (NFL) and the Atlanta Braves (MLB).

2008—In the highest combined scoring game (eighty points) in the Red River Rivalry, the Texas Longhorns got fifteen unanswered points in the final eight minutes to knock off the top-ranked Sooners, 45-35, and leap to the top of the AP survey.

2009—The United States won the President's Cup for the third straight time, with the final score, US Team 19½–14½ International Team.

BIRTHDAYS:

1961—Steve Young, Salt Lake City, UT, Hall-of-Fame NFL quarterback (Tampa Bay Buccaneers, San Francisco 49ers), three-time Super Bowl champion and winner of numerous awards, including Super Bowl MVP (XXIX)

1969—Ty Murray, Phoenix, AZ, rodeo cowboy, nine-time world champion

1989—Michelle Wie, Honolulu, HI, professional golfer, the youngest to qualify for an LPGA tour event

You are my hiding place; you will protect me from trouble and surround me with songs of deliverance. **Psalm 32:7**

Deliver me from my enemies, O God; protect me from those who rise up against me. **Psalm 59:1**

FUN FACT Outside of football, Peyton Manning has appeared in many television commercials and was featured on the covers of the NFL Fever games. He has also hosted *Saturday Night Live* and guest-voiced on *The Simpsons*, along with his brothers, Eli and Cooper.

Sports Potpourri

1. After turning amateur in 1954 and winning the Canadian Open in 1955, Arnold Palmer won his first Masters tournament in which year?
   a. 2005
   b. 1943
   c. 1992
   d. 1958

2. The first female driver to race in an Indianapolis 500 was Janet Guthrie—in which year?
   a. 1945
   b. 1913
   c. 2006
   d. 1977

3. The Buffalo Bills not only lost four Super Bowls in the same decade but did it in four consecutive years. In which decade did this unfortunate NFL situation occur?
   a. 1990s
   b. 1940s
   c. 1960s
   d. 1910s

4. In what year did NHL all-star Wayne Gretzky retire?
   a. 2001
   b. 2000
   c. 1999
   d. 1998

5. What WNBA team won four championships in a row from 1997-2000?
   a. Detroit Shock
   b. Houston Comets
   c. Los Angeles Sparks
   d. New York Liberty

6. Who won the most World Cups (soccer) in the 20th century?
   a. Argentina
   b. Italy
   c. Brazil
   d. West Germany

7. Who won the first Kentucky Derby?
   a. Aristides
   b. Man o' War
   c. Sir Barton
   d. Donerail

8. Which of the following Hall-of-Fame major-league pitchers never pitched in a World Series?
   a. Don Drysdale
   b. Jim Palmer
   c. Catfish Hunter
   d. Ferguson Jenkins

9. What NBA team closed out the 20th century winning the most NBA championships?
   a. Chicago Bulls
   b. Philadelphia 76ers
   c. Los Angeles Lakers
   d. Boston Celtics

10. Which of the following twenty-five-game winners and Hall-of-Fame inductees never won a Cy Young Award?
    a. Sandy Koufax
    b. Tom Seaver
    c. Whitey Ford
    d. Walter Johnson

ANSWERS: 1.d, 2.d, 3.a, 4.c, 5.b, 6.c, 7.a, 8.d, 9.d, 10.d

Hi, **Mom!**

On this day in 2007, Vinny Testaverde was signed by the Carolina Panthers, allowing him to become the oldest starting quarterback to win a game in NFL history.

Vinny Testaverde was born on November 13 in 1963; that means in this game he would have been almost forty-four years old—ancient for a professional football player. But he played and set the record. He also extended his record of consecutive seasons with at least one TD pass to twenty-one (every year of his career). Oh yes, and the Panthers beat the Cardinals 25-10.

Usually, when a football player makes a big play, such as scoring a touchdown, returning a punt for a score, recovering a fumble, or sacking the quarterback, the television camera will zoom in on the player to catch his reactions and interactions with his

teammates. Often the player will look directly into the camera and say, "Hi mom!" That immediately tells us two things: first, the player thinks his mom is watching; second, he loves his mother.

Family ties are important to everyone, even tough, 250-pound, muscular, all-pro football players. Many of them come from very modest economic backgrounds, some from single-parent households, meaning that their parents scrimped and sacrificed to raise them right. For some, sports became the way out of poverty and the road to maturity and success. And they remember Mom.

The Bible tells children to obey their parents. This applies to all children while they are young and unable to support themselves and live on their own. Adults aren't required to obey. But God also tells us to honor father and mother. That command always applies, no matter how old we are. We honor our parents by

treating them with respect, thanking them for all they have done for us, and telling others about our love and appreciation for them, perhaps even on TV.

Think about the family God has given you. Sure, each person can be aggravating at times, but they love you and want nothing but the best for you—especially your parents. How can you honor them today?

....

ALSO ON THIS DAY . . .

1968—Gruener and Watson (US) set scuba depth record (436.35 feet) in the Bahamas.

1990—San Francisco 49er Joe Montana passed for six touchdowns in the win against the Atlanta Falcons (45-35).

2008—Steven López (USA) won the men's eighty kg at the Taekwondo World Championships in Copenhagen, Denmark.

2009—Jessie Vetter, goalie for the US women's ice hockey team, was awarded Sportswoman of the Year at the Women's Sports Foundation's thirtieth Annual Salute to Women in Sports Awards Dinner.

BIRTHDAYS:

1950—Sheila Young, Birmingham, MI, speed skater and track cyclist, winner of three Olympic speed skating medals, one gold, one silver, and one bronze (1976)

1964—Joe Girardi, East Peoria, IL, major-league catcher (Cubs, Rockies, Yankees, Cardinals) and manager (Florida Marlins, New York Yankees)

1974—Kim Williams, WNBA guard (Starzz)

hildren, obey your parents in the Lord, for this is right. "Honor your father and other"—which is the first commandment with a promise—"that it may go ell with you and that you may enjoy long life on the earth." **Ephesians 6:1–3**

un Fact Vinny's dad, Al, had not seen his son play in person since 1988, after heart attack. Instead, he would watch videotapes of each weekend's game on the lowing Tuesday. Vinny's mother, Josie, would attend Jets games at Giants Stadium. en he would drive her home to Elmont, N.Y. "I'd call [Dad] from the car and tell him out the game," Vinny said. "Then when we got near his house, we'd call again and meet at a restaurant for a big Sunday dinner." Al Testaverde died in 1999 of heart lure. He was just sixty-six years old. "I'm glad I was able to come home for the last or seven months of his life. I know that made him happy."

15 Working Out **for Good**

On this day in 1985, Shelley Taylor-Smith of Australia made the fastest swim ever around Manhattan Island, doing it in six hours, twelve minutes, twenty-nine seconds.

Shelley Taylor-Smith was born in Perth, Western Australia, and early in life was diagnosed with scoliosis, a curvature of the spine. Much of her childhood she had to wear a special back brace because of the condition. Despite the scoliosis, Shelley became an excellent swimmer and won many competitions growing up. She was awarded a swimming scholarship to the University of Arkansas, but the increased, heavy training routine at that level caused some lower body paralysis. As Shelley was recovering, her coach could see that she was doing well in the longer distances, so he encouraged her to take up marathon swimming. This sport would allow her to avoid the potentially back-damaging flip turns. Shelley took her coach's advice and eventually broke the world four-mile record (1983). Eventually she won the Australian Marathon Swimming Championship three times and seven consecutive FINA Marathon World Cups. Shelley broke the record for the Manhattan Island Marathon Swim in 1985 and won that race five times, breaking the world record again in 1995. She swam the 48km (29.83 miles) distance in 5 hours, 45 minutes, and 25 seconds.

Shelly Taylor-Smith is a good example of how something bad can be turned into good. Because of a condition that limited her in certain activities, she turned to swimming and became a world champion.

When confronted with a setback like that, we may have very negative thoughts about life, looking at a bleak future. But that's because we can only see a small part of the picture. We don't know all of our hidden talents and potentials. But God does. And he can take us the way he made us and use us to do very significant things for him. He can also turn bad into good. Some of the best doctors have suffered physically. Some of the most successful comedians had difficult childhoods. Some of the most effective counselors have come through emotional and relational issues. Almost all of the great Christian leaders had early life struggles.

Instead of thinking about our bad breaks in life and what we can't do, let's trust God to work his good in us and ask him to show us what we can do for him.

....

ALSO ON THIS DAY . . .

1912—Tris Speaker of the Boston Red Sox made the only World Series unassisted double play from the outfield.

1977—Don Ritchie ran 100 miles in world-record time (11:30:51).

1995—The Carolina Panthers won their first game ever, beating the New York Jets 26-15.

2005—The USC Trojans won their twenty-eighth straight game in wild fashion. With Notre Dame up by three, quarterback Matt Leinart fumbled out of bounds on the one-yard-line, the clock expired, and fans crowded the field. But the officials said the game had seven seconds left. USC signaled as though they would throw the ball away to stop the clock and try a field goal, but Leinart snuck into the end zone to win the game, 34-31.

BIRTHDAYS:

1945—Jim Palmer, New York, NY, Hall-of-Fame major-league pitcher (Baltimore Orioles), six-time all-star, three-time World Series champion, three-time Cy Young Award winner, and sportscaster

1962—Susan DeMattei, San Francisco, CA, cyclist, winner of the Olympic bronze medal, 1996

1987—Jesse Levine, Nepean, Ontario, Canada, American professional tennis player

And we know that in all things God works for the good of those who love him, who have been called according to his purpose. **Romans 8:28**

Fun Fact In 1998, Shelley Taylor-Smith was diagnosed with chro fatigue syndrome because of her constant exposure to polluted water and Gia lamblia infection and was told she had six months to live. But she then won he fifth consecutive Manhattan Island marathon and then retired from swimming now lives in Sydney, where she works as a motivational speaker. Her autobiog *Dangerous When Wet: The Shelley Taylor-Smith Story*, was published in 1996.

Wrong Assumptions

On this day in 1974, Oakland A's pitcher Ken Holtzman, who hadn't batted all season, belted a third-inning home run in game four of the World Series and got the win over the Dodgers, 5-2.

Ken Holtzman was an outstanding major-league pitcher with a fourteen-year career in the big leagues. During that time, he played for the Chicago Cubs, Oakland As, Baltimore Orioles, and New York Yankees. He pitched two no-hit games (both for the Cubs), was selected to the all-star team twice, and was a three-time world champion. He was a major factor in Oakland's championship seasons (1972-1975). Holtzman had some experience as a hitter because of his years in the National League with the Cubs. But the American League employed the designated hitter (adopted in 1973), so most pitchers didn't bat for themselves. Hitting major-league pitching is difficult, especially if you haven't tried it in a while. But Ken Holtzman came to the plate and hit a home run against one of the league's best pitchers, Andy Messersmith, in a pressure-packed situation, the World Series. No one expected him to get a hit, much less a home run. But he did.

Making assumptions about people is easy—it happens all the time. We may see a physical characteristic (height, weight, looks) and think the person is good or bad at a certain sport. Or we may hear someone speak with a strong accent—either from a region of America or another country—and assume the person isn't very bright. Or we may just figure that a person can't perform in a situation because he or she doesn't have lots of experience (similar to Ken Holtzman's situation). That's a mistake, and it's not the way God wants us to look at people.

Not every person can do everything well—to make that assumption would be going too far in the other direction. But we should allow people the opportunity to prove themselves and not prejudge them. Just because a guy has muscles on his muscles doesn't mean he can't think. Just because a girl is blond doesn't mean she's empty-headed. Just because someone gets good grades doesn't mean he or she isn't athletic. The only assumption that is totally fair to make is that every person is a sinner who needs Christ.

The idea is to treat people the way we would like to be treated. That's a great rule to follow.

....

e completely humble and gentle; be patient, bearing with one another in love.
phesians 4:2

FUN FACT After baseball, Ken Holtzman had a successful career as a stock broker and in insurance. For a few years, he coached the St. Louis baseball team for the Maccabi games and managed the Petach Tikva Pioneers in the inaugural 2007 season of the Israel Baseball League. He is a member of the Chicagoland Sports Hall of Fame.

17 The Weight **of the World**

On this day in 1932, Paul Anderson, light super heavyweight lifter, was born in Toccoa, Georgia.

The Strongest Man in the World" was how Paul Anderson would be billed. And he was! Though only five feet ten inches tall, he weighed between 350-375 pounds and was powerful. His public feats of strength began in the 1950s, at the height of the Cold War. After winning the USA National Amateur Athletic Union Weightlifting Championship, Paul traveled to the Soviet Union for an international competition.

People in the States saw a newsreel of the event. The person narrating the film of the event said this as he walked up to lift: "Then, up to the bar stepped a great ball of a man, Paul Anderson. The Soviets snickered as Anderson gripped the bar, which was set at 402.5 pounds, an unheard-of lift. But their snickers quickly changed to awe and all-out cheers as up went the bar, and Anderson lifted the heaviest weight overhead of any human in history."

That was just the beginning. Later in October at the 1955 World Championships, Anderson broke two more world records (the press and total weight cleared). A year later, in Melbourne, Australia, he won the Olympic gold medal in the super-heavyweight class while suffering with a 104-degree fever. After the Olympics, Paul turned professional and toured the country doing strength demonstrations. At one time he was listed in the *Guinness Book of World Records* for a back-lift of 6,270 pounds.

A dedicated Christian, Paul's mission was to share the good news about Jesus with young people. He toured the country, speaking in high schools, youth rallies, and other events. He and his wife, Glenda, also founded a home for troubled youth in 1961. It was supported from Paul's speaking engagements and strength exhibitions.

No matter who is the strongest person in the world these days, God's strength is way beyond. Humans can lift barbells, free weights, and huge loads with their arms, backs, and legs, but God can move mountains. Even more amazing, he can remove the weight of sin and change lives. Paul Anderson would be the first to say: Don't count on human strength to solve problems, resist temptation, and do what is right. Depend on your heavenly Father who will give you everything you need.

Feel like you're carrying the weight of the world? Give your burden to God.

....

ALSO ON THIS DAY . . .

1885—Major League Baseball set all players' salaries at $1,000–$2,000 for the 1885 season.

1959—Queen Elizabeth of England was fined $140 for withdrawing her race horse.

2004—Valentino Rossi (Italy) won the World Moto GP title for the third successive year.

2009—Cuba defeated the United States (3-1) to win the NORCECA Men's Championship (volleyball) in Bayamón, Puerto Rico, and qualify for the World Grand Champions Cup.

BIRTHDAYS:

1946—Bob Seagren, Pomona, CA, pole vaulter, winner of the Olympic gold medal in 1968

1966—Danny Ferry, NBA forward (Cleveland Cavaliers and San Antonio Spurs) and general manager (Cleveland Cavaliers)

1987—Jaroslaw Fojut, Polish footballer (soccer player) in Poland and England

Give your burdens to the Lord, and he will take care of you. He will not permit the godly to slip and fall. Psalm 55:22, NLT

Fun Fact Paul Anderson could not compete in the 1960 Olympics because he had been paid for some of his weightlifting and strength exhibitions. In the 1960 Olympics the Russian heavyweight Yury Vlasov beat Paul's records set at the 1956 Olympics. A short time later, not to be outdone by the Russian and to verify his positi as World's Strongest Man, Paul lifted the same weight as the Russ three times in quick succession, demonstrating unbelievable streng

Falling **Short**

On this day in 1968, Bob Beamon (USA) set the long-jump record (29 ft. 2 1/2 in.) at the Olympics in Mexico City, Mexico.

Bob Beamon was reared by his grandmother because his father had been abusing his mother and had threatened to kill little Bob if her mother had brought him home. In high school, he was discovered by a famous track coach. Later Bob became part of the all-American track and field team, and he won a college track scholarship. Bob qualified for the Olympics four months before being suspended from school for refusing to compete against a university that he believed had racist policies. This left him without a coach, and fellow Olympian Ralph Boston began to coach him unofficially.

At the Olympics, Bob's new world record shattered the old one by 21 ¾ inches. The distance was announced, but Bob wasn't affected because it was given in meters. When Ralph Boston told him that he had broken the world record, Bob fell to his knees and placed his hands over his face in shock. The record stood for twenty-three years until Mike

Powell broke it in 1991.

How would you do in the long jump against Bob Beamon or Mike Powell in their primes? So comparing yourself to them, you could feel like a failure, right? But if you compared your long-jumping ability to your six-year-old neighbor, would you feel like a champion.

We make comparisons with others all the time. We may think, for example, "I'm not so bad, especially compared to that guy!" And if we compare our actions to someone worse, we justify ourselves. But that's just as foolish.

Here's the point: many people think they're good enough to get into heaven because they've never committed "terrible" sins such as armed robbery, drug dealing, or murder. But how would they do compared to perfection? After all, heaven's perfect. Comparing ourselves to others in relationship to God's standard is like trying to long-jump across the Grand Canyon. We might jump pretty far, and Bob and Mike would get out farther than anyone, but we'd all

fall way short. Here's the deal: we can't get there on our own. Instead of comparing ourselves to others and trying to be good enough, we need to quit all the trying and start depending . . . on Christ. He's the only One who can take us there. We just need to put our lives in his hands.

That long-jump record will last forever!

··

ALSO ON THIS DAY . . .

1992—Randall Cunningham, quarterback for the Philadelphia Eagles, set the NFL quarterback-scramble (run) record of 3,683 yards in a career.

1997—Liz Heaston became the first female to play and score in a men's NAIA college football game, played between Willamette University and Linfield College.

2009—Kevin Reiterer (Austria), Sam Harvey (New Zealand), and Alessander Lenzi (Brazil) were the pro champions crowned during the finale of the 28th Annual Quakysense International Jet Sports Boating Association (IJSBA) World Finals (jet skiing).

2009—Sixteen-year-old Julie Watson (Australia) began her solo sailing trip round the world, which she completed on May 15, 2010, becoming the youngest person to accomplish this.

BIRTHDAYS:

1939—Mike Ditka, Carnegie, PA, Hall-of-Fame NFL tight end (Chicago Bears, Philadelphia Eagles, Dallas Cowboys), NFL head coach (Chicago Bears, New Orleans Saints), five-time pro bowl selection, three-time Super Bowl winner, and broadcaster

1956—Martina Navratilova, Prague, Czechoslovakia, American tennis great, winner of eighteen Grand Slam tournaments

1984—Lindsey Vonn, St. Paul, MN, world-class skier, winner of the Olympic gold medal in the downhill (2010)

For everyone has sinned; we all fall short of God's glorious standard. **Romans 3:23, NLT**

For the wages of sin is death, but the free gift of God is eternal life through Christ Jesus our Lord. **Romans 6:23, NLT**

[**FUN FACT**] After Bob Beamon's record jump, the defending Olympic champion, Lynn Davies of Great Britain, told him, "You have destroyed this event." Bob's world record stood for twenty-three years and was named by *Sports Illustrated* as one of the five greatest sports moments of the 20th century. More than forty years later, it still is the second longest of all time.

Baseball Stadiums

Match the MLB team to its stadium.

1. Chicago Cubs
2. Milwaukee Brewers
3. New York Yankees
4. Boston Red Sox
5. Houston Astros
6. Seattle Mariners
7. Los Angeles Dodgers
8. San Francisco Giants
9. Atlanta Braves
10. Cleveland Indians
11. Philadelphia Phillies
12. Chicago White Sox
13. Minnesota Twins
14. Detroit Tigers
15. New York Mets
16. Arizona Diamondbacks
17. Colorado Rockies
18. Kansas City Royals
19. Tampa Bay Rays
20. Toronto Blue Jays

a. Target Field
b. Dodger Stadium
c. Coors Field
d. Turner Field
e. Citizens Bank Park
f. Tropicana Field
g. Miller Park
h. Chase Field
i. Comerica Park
j. Yankee Stadium
k. Kauffman Stadium
l. Fenway Park
m. Progressive Field
n. Wrigley Field
o. Rogers Centre
p. Safeco Field
q. Citi Field
r. Minute Maid Park
s. U.S. Cellular Field
t. AT&T Park

ANSWERS: 1.n, 2.g, 3.j, 4.l, 5.r, 6.p, 7.b, 8.t, 9.d, 10.m, 11.e, 12.s, 13.a, 14.i, 15.q, 16.h, 17.c, 18.k, 19.f, 20.o

Glory

On this day in 1980, the Philadelphia Phillies won their first World Championship in their ninety-eight-year history, beating the Kansas City Royals.

What's the greatest prize or award that someone can win? How about the World Series? When a team such as the Phillies wins their first ever, you can imagine the celebrations (Philadelphia won again in 2008, beating the Tampa Bay Rays). Winning a World Series is a big deal in sports—a world championship. The same goes for winning the Super Bowl, Stanley Cup, World Cup, WNBA Championship, and world championships in every sport. And that's just in professional sports. We can't overlook the Olympics, all the NCAA tournaments, and the Heisman Trophy winner.

Champions are named beyond sports, too. Our society seems intent on presenting almost a continuous stream of award ceremonies: Oscar, Emmy, Tony, Golden Globe, People's Choice. . . . And we can't forget the Nobel Prize or Pulitzer Prize.

All these awards recognize excellence in specific fields of endeavor, and winners can be justifiably proud—and should celebrate their victories and bask in the glory.

Let's face it, everyone wants some glory—to be recognized and honored, to be praised and admired, to be famous, a star (at least for a while). But these earthly glories are nothing compared to what God has prepared for us. Listen to this: "Now there is in store for me the crown of righteousness, which the Lord, the righteous Judge, will award to me on that day—and not only to me, but also to all who have longed for his appearing" (2 Timothy 4:8). Paul wrote this, contrasting God's future glory to athletic glory: "Everyone who competes in the games goes into strict training. They do it to get a crown that will not last; but we do it to get a crown that will last forever" (1 Corinthians 9:25).

So when you're feeling down because your team came in second (or last), because you didn't win MVP, or because no one noticed your outstanding work, remember the glory that is yours to come. But also remember that our main goal should be to glorify God, not with a metal-and-wood trophy or an awards ceremony, but with how we live: "to the only God our Savior be glory, majesty, power and authority, through Jesus Christ our Lord, before all ages, now and forevermore! Amen" (Jude 1:25).

ALSO ON THIS DAY . . .

1973—Fred Dryer of the Los Angeles Rams became the first player in NFL history to score two safeties in the same game.

1979—Ozzie Newsome of the Philadelphia Eagles began his NFL streak of 150 consecutive games in which he had at least one pass reception.

1984—Niki Lauda (Austria) became the motor racing world champ for the third time.

2004—A three-judge panel of the Court of Arbitration for Sport upheld the awarding of the gold medal in the gymnastics men's all-around to American Paul Hamm, rejecting the appeal of South Korea.

And when the Great Shepherd appears, you will receive a crown of never-ending glory and honor. 1 Peter 5:4, NLT

FUN FACT

The Philadelphia Phillies Major League Baseball team is the oldest continuous, one-name, one-city franchise in all of professional American sports, dating to 1883. In addition to their two World Series Championships, they have won seven National League pennants, the first in 1915. The team also holds the record for having lost the most games of any team in the history of American professional sports—mainly because they've been around so long!

BIRTHDAYS:

1965—Chris Duplanty, Palo Alto, CA, water polo goalkeeper, 1996 Olympics

1983—Zack Greinke, Orlando, FL, major-league pitcher (Kansas City Royals)

1984—Kenny Cooper, Baltimore, MD, soccer forward (U.S. National team)

1990—Ricky Rubio, Spanish basketball player, drafted by the Minnesota Timberwolves in 2009

Seeing the **Signals**

On this day in 2005, Joe Paterno earned his 350th victory as Penn State coach in a rout of the Fighting Illini, 63-10.

Joe Paterno has had an illustrious coaching career, especially at Penn State, where he has been the head football coach for more than sixty years (that's right—sixty). He holds the records for the most seasons for any football coach at any university, the most victories for a Football Bowl Subdivision (Division 1) coach, and the most bowl-game wins. Through all those years, every player in the program knew who was in charge, calling the shots.

Following instructions and signals is important in all sports but especially in football. In big-time college programs and in the pros, teams station coaches way above the action at the top of the stadium in every game, constantly watching the action (on TV monitors and through binoculars), analyzing the opposition's moves, commenting on individual players, and calling plays. The head coach and others on the sidelines receive the information and then call the play for their team on the field (either offense or defense) through a series of hand signals (or headset to the quarterback). Then the defensive captain or the quarterback relays the play to the players, sometimes making last-second changes, audibles, before the snap of the ball. After the dust settles, the whole process repeats.

In a successful team, all the players listen and watch carefully for the signals and then carry out their assignments. Each one is expected to trust the wisdom and perspective of the coaches and then to submit, to obey their commands. The quickest route to a loss is for individual players to think they know better than the coaches and to do whatever they want. Talk about foolish!

We can think of the game of life the same way. God is way above the action, taking it all in. He knows us best—our abilities, strengths, spiritual gifts, and weaknesses. He also knows everything that is going on, events that are way out of our knowledge or understanding. He also calls the plays. He sends those plays—his will for how we should live—through the Bible and through the Holy Spirit working in us. And our job is to listen carefully and then to submit and obey him. Anything else would be foolish, and we would lose.

God wants to make the calls in your life. Listen to his signals, submit, and obey.

....

ALSO ON THIS DAY . . .

1968—Kip Keino (Kenya) won an Olympic gold medal for the 1,500-meter race.

1979—Billy Martin, manager of the New York Yankees, was involved in a barroom altercation with Joseph Cooper, a Minnesota marshmallow sales-man, and required fifteen stitches.

1997—New York Ranger Wayne Gretsky's wife, Janet, was knocked unconscious and cut when a Plexiglas panel fell on her while she was watching the hockey game.

2008—Emil Andersson (Sweden) won the World Running Target Championships in Plzen, Czech Republic, 6-1, scoring seven consecutive tens in the first ever ten-meter running target championship to be decided in a knockout format.

BIRTHDAYS:

1963—Brian Boitano, Mountainview, CA, figure skater, winner of the Olympic gold medal in 1988

1974—Dani Tyler, born in Denver, CO, softball infielder, winner of the Olympic gold medal in 1996

1982—Heath Miller, Richlands, VA, NFL tight end (Pittsburgh Steelers), two-time Super Bowl champion

1986—Kara Lang, Canadian soccer player (UCLA and Canada National Team) and already Canada's second-leading all-time international women's goal-scorer

Yet I am always with you; you hold me by my right hand. You guide me with your counsel, and afterward you will take me into glory. **Psalm 73:23–24**

[UN][ACT] In this game, the Nittany Lions' fifty-six points in the first half set an all-time school record. On December 16, 2008, a news report stated that Coach Paterno, "JoePa," had agreed in principle to a contract extension that would extend his tenure at Penn State by at least three years.

Win or **Die Trying**

On this day in 2005, the Chicago White Sox came back twice to beat the Houston Astros 7-6 in the second game of the World Series.

A motto for the Chicago White Sox in 2005 was "Win or die trying!" They certainly lived up to their motto in this game by coming from behind twice. After a grand-slam home run by Paul Konerko had put them ahead for the first time, the Astros got two runs in the top of the ninth to tie the score. But then Scott Podsednik hit a one-out

walk-off home run in the bottom half to give the Sox the win. This victory put the White Sox up two games to none. They went on to sweep the Astros and win the championship.

That slogan "Win or die trying," would make a pretty good motto for life. First, however, we should decide what we mean by "win." Some people think victory, success in life, means accumulating wealth, getting lots of money; so they literally spend their lives working, saving, and investing—getting rich. For others a victory means finding the perfect romantic partner— the wife or husband of their dreams. That, then, becomes almost an obsession as they date and fall in and out of love. Many want to be famous, to have their name in the headlines or in lights, so they exhaust every possible avenue toward stardom. Others seek power and influence—they begin climbing the political ladder.

All of those goals are okay— but not worthy of our lives. In fact, the Bible would call that idolatry (putting something in God's place). Instead, our victory should be to do what God wants, resisting the temptation to live any other way. We will face fierce opposition when we

live this way, but we can prevail. "For everyone born of God overcomes the world. This is the victory that has overcome the world, even our faith. Who is it that overcomes the world? Only he who believes that Jesus is the Son of God" (1 John 5:4–5). John and the other disciples lived this, giving their all in order to be God's person in the world and to tell others about the Savior.

God wants us to be victorious, to win his victory. That's worth every resource, every ounce of strength. Let's win or die trying!

ALSO ON THIS DAY . . .

1920—A Chicago grand jury indicted Abe Attell, Hal Chase, and Bill Burns as go-betweens in the "Black Sox" World Series scandal.

1949—Emile Zatopek, Czech running great, ran a world record in the 10,000-meter race (29:21.2).

1960—Cassius Clay won his first fight as a professional boxer.

But whatever was to my profit I now consider loss for the sake of Christ. What is more, I consider everything a loss compared to the surpassing greatness of knowing Christ Jesus my Lord, for whose sake I have lost all things. **Philippians 3:7–8**

Fun Fact Game three turned out to be the longest game in World Series history, time wise, and tied for the longest in terms of number of innings. Eventually, the White Sox, after using nine pitchers to the Astros' eight, won in the fourteenth inning. The teams had played for five hours and forty-one minutes. The final score was Chicago 7, Houston 5.

BIRTHDAYS:

1940—Edison Arantes do Nascimento (Pelé), soccer legend

1970—Scott Drew, Kansas City, KS, head men's basketball coach (Baylor University)

1972—Tiffeny Milbrett, Portland, OR, soccer forward (US Women's National Team)

1973—Ichiro Suzuki, Kasugai, Japan, all-star major-league outfielder (Seattle Mariners)

261

24 Internal **War**

On this day in 1974, Billy Martin was named the American League Manager of the Year (Texas Rangers).

Billy Martin played second base but is known more as a brilliant field manager who could turn losing teams into winners. He had success with the Minnesota Twins (1969), Detroit Tigers (1971–1973), Texas Rangers (1973–1975), and Oakland Athletics (1980–1982), but he spent the most time with the New York Yankees, where he managed at five different times (hired, fired, rehired, fired, etc.). Martin was known for his heated arguments with umpires and his aggressive style of play, called "Billy Ball."

We might wonder why Martin changed teams so often if he was such a good baseball manager. The turnover rate for this occupation is high, but Martin's record is unique, the way he hopped around. The main reason was his aggressive personality—he had trouble getting along with veteran players and owners. He actually got into several fights as a player and as a manager. In the middle of a game as manager, the Yankees against the Red Sox, he removed Reggie Jackson from the game for not hustling on a fielding play. Martin was so angry that he had to be held back by his coaches to keep him from getting into a fight in the dugout. Much of this behavior off the field was fueled by drinking—Martin was an alcoholic. He was always fighting his demons.

Great manager—bad manager. Good behavior—bad behavior. We wonder how someone can swing so quickly between extremes. But every human being is capable of the same. We all have tremendous potential for good; after all, we're created by God in his image. But we also have potential for bad; we're sinners—that's our nature. Even the apostle Paul had this struggle, and he wrote honestly about it in Romans 7:14–25, admitting that often he didn't do what he should and that often he did what he shouldn't.

Believers still have the war of the two natures: sinful vs. spiritual

The good news is that we have the Holy Spirit in us giving us the power to conquer sin. God empowers us to make the right choices, to say no to sin and yes to him.

So don't be discouraged at sin in your life. Instead, confess it to God and ask him for help in doing what is right the next time.

ALSO ON THIS DAY . . .

1984—Steffi Graf played her first professional tennis match.

1989—After a week's delay because of the earthquake, World Series game three was played.

2004—Jimmie Johnson's sixth win of the 2004 NASCAR season, at the Martinsville Speedway, was overshadowed by the crash of a private plane belonging to his racing team, Hendrick Motorsports; all ten people on board the plane were killed, including four relatives of team owner Rick Hendrick.

2009—Meryl Davis and Charlie White (USA) won the ISU Grand Prix: Rostelcom Cup in Moscow, Russia (ice dance).

BIRTHDAYS:

1953—James and Jonathan di Donato, twins who swam the butterfly 406 miles

1970—Todd Riech, Polson, MT, javelin thrower, 1996 Olympics

1983—Brian Vickers, Thomasville, NC, NASCAR driver (Red Bull Racing Team)

I love God's law with all my heart. But there is another power within me that is at war with my mind. This power makes me a slave to the sin that is still within me. Oh, what a miserable person I am! Who will free me from this life that is dominated by sin and death? Thank God! The answer is in Jesus Christ our Lord. Romans 7:22–25, NLT

[UN]ACT In 1986, the Yankees retired Martin's uniform, number one, and dedicated a plaque in his honor. The plaque contains the words, "There has never been a greater competitor than Billy." Martin told the crowd, "I may not have been the greatest Yankee to put on the uniform, but I am the proudest." Sadly, Martin died in a one-car, alcohol-related accident in 1989.

WWJD

On this day in 1999, Payne Stewart died in an airplane accident at the age of forty-two.

On June 20, 1999, professional golfer Payne Stewart had just won his second US Open by one stroke over Phil Mickelson, after sinking a fifteen-foot putt on the last hole, the longest putt to decide that championship. A few months later, he was part of the winning Ryder Cup team. Payne was at the pinnacle of his sport. The winner of three majors, he was third on the all-time money list and in the top ten of the world golf rankings. But tragically his life was cut short when the private plane in which he was traveling with five others crashed in South Dakota. He was survived by his wife, Tracey, and their two children, Chelsea and Aaron. Payne had been a favorite of both fans and photographers, renowned for his tam caps and knickerbocker golf pants. Everyone knew him for his golfing

talent, and people were beginning to learn about his faith. After accepting the trophy for his US Open victory, he said, "First of all, I have to give thanks to the Lord. . . . I'm proud of the fact that my faith in God is so much stronger, and I'm so much more at peace with myself than I've ever been in my life." He had become a follower of Christ and had a WWJD bracelet on his wrist. He was wearing that bracelet at the US Open and the Ryder Cup and on the day he died. "What Would Jesus Do?" had become the guiding question for Payne, as he related to his family and friends, as he competed on the golf course, as he lived.

Payne wasn't ashamed to let the world know about his faith in Christ although he knew it might cost him and put him under pressure to live up to his profession. But he knew that it was what Jesus would do.

All Christ-followers should be asking that question. When faced with a conflict: "What would Jesus do? How would he respond?" When dealing with

temptation: "WWJD?" How would he react? When interacting with parents, siblings, friends, teachers, classmates, co-workers, and neighbors: "WWJD?" How would he relate? When seeing someone hurting, how would he meet that person's need? Jesus is our Lord and our perfect example.

In every situation, consider what Jesus would do. Then be Jesus, then and there.

....

ALSO ON THIS DAY . . .

1964—Jim Marshall of the Minnesota Vikings recovered a fumble but ran sixty-six yards with it the wrong way, into his own end zone, resulting in a safety for the 49ers.

2005—Atlanta Braves pitcher John Smoltz won the Roberto Clemente Award for community service.

2008—Somebeachsomewhere took the final leg of the Pacing Triple Crown (harness racing) when he won the Messenger Stakes in 1:52.1 over Shadow Play.

2009—Ben Spies won the Superbike World Championship (his rookie season).

BIRTHDAYS:

1938—Bob Webster, Berkeley, CA, diver, winner of the Olympic gold medal in 1960 and 1964

1940—Bobby Knight, Massillon, OH, college basketball coach (Army, Indiana, Texas Tech), winner of the NCAA National Championship (1976, 1981, 1987) and Olympic gold medal (1984)

1948—Dan Gable, Waterloo, IA, one of the all-time great college and Olympic wrestlers, winner of the Olympic gold medal in 1972 (lightweight)

1980—Ilana Goldfogel, Denver, CO,

> To this you were called, because Christ suffered for you, leaving you an example, that you should follow in his steps. **1 Peter 2:21**

[un][act] Tracey Stewart's reflects, "Payne and I started reading devotionals together, but before long I noticed that he was much farther along than I was. He'd read the Scripture from the devotional every night before he went to bed. He also began reading the Bible. . . . The Scriptures themselves were the most powerful influence on Payne's life."

Sports Terms, part 2

1. **Salcow**
2. Pike
3. **Takedown**
4. Clean & jerk
5. **Check**
6. Triple double
7. **Wipe-out**
8. Foil
9. **Ringer**
10. Tack
11. **Sacrifice**
12. Test match
13. **Side out**
14. Corner
15. **Half-pipe**
16. Eagle
17. **Love**
18. Spare
19. **Gate**
20. Pit road
21. **Wake**
22. Individual pursuit
23. **Medley**
24. Hitting the wall
25. **Scrum**
26. Landing
27. **Off-road**
28. Free-riding
29. **Boast**

a. **Surfing**
b. Water Skiing
c. **Golf**
d. Figure Skating
e. **Rugby**
f. Soccer
g. **Squash**
h. Diving
i. **Baseball**
j. Swimming
k. **Snowboarding**
l. Weight Lifting
m. **Track Cycling**
n. Fencing
o. **Cricket**
p. Wrestling
q. **NASCAR Racing**
r. Skateboarding
s. **Long-Distance Running**
t. Basketball
u. **Gymnastics**
v. Volleyball
w. **Motocross**
x. Tennis
y. **Sailing**
z. Ice Hockey
aa. **Slalom Snow Skiing**
bb. Bowling
cc. **Horseshoes**

Match the sport to the term.

ANSWERS: 1.d, 2.h, 3.p, 4.l, 5.z, 6.t, 7.a, 8.n, 9.cc, 10.y, 11.i, 12.o, 13.v, 14.f, 15.r, 16.c, 17.x, 18.bb, 19.aa, 20.q, 21.b, 22.m, 23.j, 24.s, 25.e, 26.u, 27.w, 28.k, 29.g

Playbook

On this day in 2007, the New England Patriots beat the Washington Redskins, 52-7.

The New England Patriots have been at or near the top of the NFL since 2000, winning the Super Bowl in 2001, 2003, and 2004. After winning this game against the Redskins, they were 8-0 and preparing for a showdown with the Indianapolis Colts the next weekend (they won, 24-20). The Patriots made the Super Bowl again in 2007 but were upset by the New York Giants. Obviously winning teams have great players—and New England has many, but each of the great teams also has a great head coach. Here, he's Bill Belichick, since 2000.

In addition to winning championships, Belichick was named the AP NFL Coach of the Year twice, for 2003 and 2007. In 2007, the Patriots became the first team ever to finish the regular season with a 16-0 record. Every coach has a personal coaching philosophy and approach that includes choosing and relating to players, hiring and supervising the right assistant coaches, and designing and implementing a playbook.

In successful teams, the players trust their coach and follow his instructions. That begins by knowing the playbook. The typical NFL playbook can be as massive as 800 pages, filled with offensive and defensive alignments, position responsibilities, and, of course, plays. It's the first thing rookies get when their preseason workouts begin in the spring and the last thing taken from them when they're cut by the team.

Football, while simple in the basics, is a complicated game, with twenty-two well-conditioned athletes quickly carrying out their assignments at every snap of the ball. So the playbook can be intimidating and confusing for the ordinary person. But players who want to stay have to study their books and learn fast.

Your playbook is the Bible—not for winning at sports but for winning at life. So reading, studying, and applying it just makes sense. And this playbook is perfect, the words from your perfect Coach. (He's undefeated, by the way, from eternity to eternity.)

Where's your playbook? Do you know the plays?

ALSO ON THIS DAY . . .

1962—New York Giant quarterback Y. A. Tittle passed for seven touchdowns as the Giants beat the Washington Redskins 49-34.

1997—The NBA announced the hiring of Dee Kantner and Violet Palmer as the first women to officiate a major-league all-male sports league.

2005—In an attempt to cut down the number of home runs being hit in their park, the Philadelphia Phillies announced that the fence in left field would be moved back.

2007—Rob Smith set the World Indoor Rowing Record for 500 meters (1:15.9) at the Welsh Indoor Rowing Championships.

All Scripture is inspired by God and is useful to teach us what is true and to make us realize what is wrong in our lives. It corrects us when we are wrong and teaches us to do what is right. 2 Timothy 3:16, NLT

Fun Fact NFL center Matt Birk is a Harvard graduate who knew the old Viking playbook inside and out. But a new head coach brought a new coaching philosophy, so Birk spent his spare time studying his new playbook. Soon he could tell any of his line mates where to be. "It is a very cerebral game," he said. "We spend hours and hours in meetings every single day. This is my tenth year in the league, and I still take my playbook home." Matt now plays for the Ravens and has had to learn a new playbook.

BIRTHDAYS:

1949—Bruce Jenner, Mount Kisco, NY, decathalete, winner of the Olympic gold medal in 1976

1971—Tracy Hanson, Coeur D'Alene, ID, LPGA golfer

1982—Jeremy Bonderman, Kennewick, WA, major-league pitcher (Detroit Tigers)

OCTOBER 29 Reason **to Live**

On this day in 1941, Harvey Hendrick, major-league outfielder, died.

Little is known about Harvey Hendrick—just a few statistics. He was born in Mason, Tennessee, in 1897, and attended Vanderbilt University. In 1923, he began his major-league baseball career with the New York Yankees and won the World Series. He played for six more teams (Indians, Robins, Reds, Cardinals, Cubs, Phillies), with his longest stay with any one team at five years with the Brooklyn Robins. During Harvey's eleven-year career in the big leagues, he hit .308, with an on-base percentage of .364 and a slugging percentage of .443—decent numbers. But at forty-four years of age, in Covington, Tennessee, Harvey

Hendrick committed suicide.

That information, and a few more baseball stats, is about all we know. Most baseball players would give anything to just play one game in the majors—Harvey played in 922 over eleven years. Most Major League Baseball players would love to hit .300—Harvey's lifetime average was .308. Most professional athletes dream about winning a championship—Harvey's first team won the World Series. We can safely say that in athletic terms, Harvey Hendrick was a success. But something caused him such pain, such despair, that he thought he would be better off dead—and he took his own life. We could speculate— perhaps he was dealing with a terminal illness; maybe he had a terrible financial reversal; he could have lost a loved one. Whatever the reason, suicide was the result.

Today many people struggle with loneliness and depression, sometime so severe that they take that last resort.

Looking down at their lives and their problems, they see no way out. That's often the way it works; we focus on our problems and lose hope. Instead, we should look up to God who loves us. Our heavenly Father values life, every life, and he want us to experience life to the full, with joy. He loves us so much, in fact, that he sent Jesus to die for us. So we can be forgiven and freed from guilt. And when we give our lives to him, the Holy Spirit lives in us, increasing our hope and filling us with joy.

Even if everyone leaves us and life seems to be falling apart, God is with us, around us, and in us. He gives us a reason to live.

Celebrate life!

ALSO ON THIS DAY . . .
1967—Danny Abramowicz began an NFL streak of 105 consecutive games with a pass reception.

1987—Thomas "Hitman" Hearns won an unprecedented fourth (different weight) boxing title.

1995—The United States beat Japan, 19-17, at the Nichirei International LPGA Golf Tournament.

2006—Phil Taylor (England) won his seventh darts World Grand Prix title, beating Terry Jenkins 7-4 in the final.

BIRTHDAYS:
1954—Herman Ronald Frazier, Philadelphia, PA, 400-meter and 4x400-meter relay runner, winner of an Olympic gold medal in 1976

1970—Chris Thorpe, Waukegan, IL, doubles luger, 1994 Olympics

1981—Amanda Beard, born in Newport Beach, CA, 100-meter and 200-meter breaststroke, winner of two Olympic silver medals in 1996

The thief comes only to steal and kill and destroy; I have come that they may have life, and have it to the full. **John 10:10**

FUN FACT Harvey Hendricks was 6'2" and weighed 190 pounds. During his baseball career, he played first base, third base, and the outfield. In 1927, his rookie year, he hit .310 with 4 home runs and 50 RBI. His best year was 1929, when he hit for a .354 average and knocked in 82 runs.

One Way **Out**

On this day in 2005, in the Marine Corps Marathon, over 325 runners were disqualified for cutting the course.

A marathon is a 26.2 mile race on a specially designed course, in this case on the streets of Arlington, Virginia, and Washington, DC. The Marine Corps Marathon is usually run on the last Sunday in October, a few weeks before the Marine Corps' birthday on November 10. The race is called The People's Marathon because it is the largest race that doesn't offer prize money or appearance fees to elite runners. In the 2005 race, more than 300 runners took a shortcut and were disqualified.

Similar marathon cheating has happened before. In one famous incident, Rosie Ruiz Vivas seemed

to have won the Boston Marathon in 1980, crossing the finish line before all the other women and in record time. Officials learned, however, that she hadn't run the course. Instead she had

just jumped in from the crowd late in the race. She was stripped of her title. Looking deeper, reporters learned that Rosie had also cheated in the New York Marathon (hopping the subway in that one), so she was disqualified there, too.

Everyone understands that in a race, especially one that winds through a city, all the runners must run the same course; only one correct path goes from start to finish. Getting there any other way means disqualification.

In talking about the "marathon" of getting to heaven, Jesus told his disciples, "I am the way and the truth and the life. No one comes to the Father except through me" (John 14:6). He was saying, in other words, that God had laid out only one way, only one course, one road or path— through his Son, Jesus. No other way is right or even possible.

Some people don't like that, thinking it sounds so narrow, unfair. But instead of a race, imagine standing at a canyon's edge. You want to get to the

other side, but you see no way, no bridge. Then someone says, "Just three miles north of here, you'll find a bridge. Go there and you can get across. It's the only way." You probably wouldn't be upset that only one way across had been constructed. Instead, you'd gladly get to that bridge.

Thank God that he has provided a way—the only way. We'd be worse than disqualified, we'd be lost forever without it, without our Savior.

....

ALSO ON THIS DAY . . .

1945—Jackie Robinson signed a major-league contract with the Brooklyn Dodgers.

1984—Detroit Tigers reliever Willie Hernandez won the AL Cy Young Award.

1993—The Toronto Maple Leafs lost their first game of the season after going 10-0-0.

2004—The city of Boston held a victory parade for the Red Sox after they won their first World Series since 1918, breaking the "curse of the Bambino."

BIRTHDAYS:

1918—Ted Williams, San Diego, CA, Hall-of-Fame major-league left fielder (Boston Red Sox) and perhaps the greatest hitter of all time, the last one to hit over .400 for a season, the AL MVP in 1946 and 1949, and the triple crown winner in 1942 and 1947

1960—Diego Maradona, Lanús, Argentina, world-class soccer midfielder, Argentina national team

1970—James Pedro, Danvers, MA, lightweight judoka, winner of the Olympic bronze medal in 1992 and 1996

1989—Nastia Liukin, Moscow, Russia, American gymnast (artistic

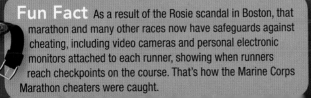

For Jesus is the one referred to in the Scriptures, where it says, 'The stone that you builders rejected has now become the cornerstone.' There is salvation in no one else! God has given no other name under heaven by which we must be saved." Acts 4:11–12, NLT

Fun Fact As a result of the Rosie scandal in Boston, that marathon and many other races now have safeguards against cheating, including video cameras and personal electronic monitors attached to each runner, showing when runners reach checkpoints on the course. That's how the Marine Corps Marathon cheaters were caught.

Blood in **the Surf**

On this day in 2003, while surfing, Bethany Hamilton encountered a shark.

On Halloween, thirteen-year-old Bethany Hamilton went for a morning surf. This was normal because she lived in Hawaii, both her parents were surfers, and she had already been surfing competitively. In fact, when only eight, she had won first place in a contest for both longboard and shortboard. Bethany had dreams of a surfing career, so she had begun competing more seriously, continued winning, picked up a sponsor, and eventually joined the National Scholastic Surfing Association circuit.

That morning, surfing with a friend and her friend's father and brother, Bethany was lying sideways on her board, her left arm dangling in the water. Suddenly a fourteen-foot tiger shark attacked, ripping that arm off just below the shoulder (two more inches would have meant death). Bethany knew she had to get to shore. Bleeding from the long gash, she used her right arm to paddle to shore where her friend's father used his surfing shirt to make a tourniquet. Bethany prayed, asking God to help her get to the beach, and she remembers hearing his calm voice say that she was in his hands. During the ride to the hospital, a paramedic whispered in her ear, "God will never leave you or forsake you."

Despite this terrible accident, just three weeks later she returned to her board and went surfing. After teaching herself how to surf with one arm, she began competing again. In 2005, Bethany took first place in the NSSA National Championships. In 2008, she began competing full-time on the Association of Surfing Professionals World Qualifying Series.

More impressive, she uses her story to share her faith in Christ. Her book, *Soul Surfer*, made the bestseller lists. In a CNN interview, Bethany said, "I mainly wrote the book just to tell my faith with God and to let everyone know that he loves them, and just how much he took care of me that day. I wouldn't be here because I lost 70 percent of my blood that morning, and it was kind of rare for me to even make it. I was just praying the whole way in."

Bethany Hamilton shines as one who loves her Lord and knows that he is working everything together for good in her life, and she lives to tell others. Like Bethany, may we live with faith, hope, and love.

ALSO ON THIS DAY . . .

1921—Federation Sportive Feminine International, the first women's track-and-field association, was formed.

1987—A pair in Coventry, England, tied the world record for the longest singles tennis match played—eighty hours, twenty-one minutes.

1987—Chris Antley became the first jockey to win nine races in one day (at Belmont).

1999—Yachtsman Jesse Martin returned to Melbourne after eleven months of circumnavigating the world, solo, non-stop, and unassisted.

BIRTHDAYS:

1951—Nick Saban, Fairmont, WV, NCAA college football head coach (Toledo, Michigan State, LSU, Alabama) winner of the national championship in 2003 (LSU) and 2009 (Alabama)

1960—Janice Harrer, Torrance, CA, WPVA volleyball player and member of the 1996 Olympics team

1973—Ross Verba, Des Moines, IA, NFL tackle (Packers, Browns, Lions), winner of Super Bowl XXXI

"The Lord himself goes before you and will be with you; he will never leave you nor forsake you. Do not be afraid; do not be discouraged."
Deuteronomy 31:8

Fun Fact
Bethany has appeared on many TV shows, including *20/20*, *Good Morning America*, *Inside Edition*, *The Oprah Winfrey Show*, and *The Tonight Show*. In addition to her book, the documentary film *Heart of a Soul Surfer* tells her story. Bethany even appeared on a 2010 episode of *Extreme Makeover: Home Edition*. In 2011, the film, *Soul Surfer*, will be released.

Calling the Pitches

On this day in 1951, Brooklyn Dodger's catcher Roy Campanella won the first of his three National League Most Valuable Player awards.

Roy Campanella was elected to the baseball Hall of Fame in 1969, and he certainly deserved the honor. His first game in the major-leagues was April 20, 1948, and he played in every all-star game from 1949 through 1956.

He won the National League MVP award three times: in 1951, 1953, and 1955. In each of those seasons, he batted over .300, hit over thirty home runs, and had over 100 RBI. Over his career, he threw out fifty-seven percent of the base runners who tried to steal a base on him, the highest by any catcher in major-league history.

The catcher plays a crucial part in every baseball game. Along with the pitcher, this player touches the ball on every play when in the field. Together, they're called the "battery." The catcher also calls the game. In other words, he relays signals, down low and next to his mitt, telling the pitcher what pitch to throw and where. Catchers have to know their pitchers and the strengths and weaknesses of every batter. When the catcher is calling a good game, and the pitcher has good command of his pitches, the batters don't have much of a chance. It's all about making the right pitch, one that the batter will have a difficult time hitting hard.

So who, then, makes the decisions—whose will is carried out? Fans may think the pitcher controls the game, but usually the catcher calls the pitches. Obviously the pitcher has a huge role to play, but he will only be successful if he and the catcher are working together, with the pitcher submitting his will to the will of the catcher. So both wills are involved.

That's the way the Christian life works. God doesn't make us into robots or force us to do what he wants. Instead, he calls the pitches and expects us to submit our wills to his and do what he says, what he expects.

This happens day by day, moment by moment. That's why we read the Bible—to see his signs. It's also why we ask, "What would Jesus do?" in tough situations. And when we submit and follow through, we win.

You and God working together—what a battery!

ALSO ON THIS DAY . . .

1959—Jacques Plante became the first National Hockey League goalie to wear a mask.

1964—George Blanda of Houston threw an NFL-record thirty-seven passes in sixty-eight attempts.

1987—Fukumi Tani won the Nichirei Ladies Cup US-Japan Team Golf Championship.

2004—The Phoenix Suns decided to keep Yuta Tabuse as the last player on their regular season roster, making him the first Japanese-born player ever to participate in an NBA season.

BIRTHDAYS:

1961—Anne Donovan, Ridgewood, NJ, basketball player, winner of the Olympic gold medal in 1984, and WNBA head coach (Fever, Sting, Storm, Liberty)

1968—Kent Graham, Winfield, IL, NFL quarterback (Giants, Lions, Cardinals, Steelers, Redskins, Texans, Jaguars)

1983—Josh Wicks, Landstuhl, Germany, American soccer goalkeeper (Los Angeles Galaxy, D.C. United)

For it is God who works in you to will and to act according to his good purpose. **Philippians 2:13**

Fun Fact
On January 28, 1958, Campanella was driving home when he hit a patch of ice and skidded into a telephone pole. The accident left him paralyzed from the shoulders down. Eventually he was able to feed himself, shake hands, and gesture while speaking, but he needed a wheelchair for the rest of his life. Simon & Schuster announced plans to publish a new biography of Roy Campanella scheduled for a 2010 or 2011 release.

Featured Events in **October**

1. For what team did Andy Messersmith play in 1975? (October 7)
2. Who is the oldest starting quarterback to win a game in NFL history? (October 14)
3. For what is American League baseball manager Billy Martin known? (October 24)
4. In what year did the Philadelphia Phillies win their first World Series title? (October 21)
5. From what condition did marathon swimmer Shelley Taylor-Smith suffer? (October 15)
6. Who did the Oakland A's play in the 1974 World Series? (October 16)
7. In what year did Masanori Murakami make his last appearance in Major League Baseball? (October 1)
8. How many years has Kelly Slater had the title of world champion of surfing? (October 3)
9. Peyton Manning is the quarterback of what NFL team? (October 11)
10. Who upset the New England Patriots in the 2007 Super Bowl? (October 28)
11. What legendary football coach has won over 350 games with Penn State? (October 22)
12. Who did Felix Trinidad defeat on an eighth-round knockout in 2004? (October 2)
13. What team did the San Jose Sharks beat for their first NHL win? (October 9)
14. How many runners were disqualified in the 2005 Marine Corps Marathon? (October 30)
15. Who was considered "The Strongest Man in the World"? (October 17)
16. What baseball position did Harvey Hendrick play? (October 29)
17. Worldwide, how many active players does table tennis have? (October 10)
18. How old was golfer Payne Stewart when he died? (October 25)
19. What position did A. C. Green play in the NBA? (October 4)
20. Who beat the Houston Astros to win the 2005 World Series? (October 23)
21. Where did Jim Elliot attend college? (October 8)
22. What record did Bob Beamon set at the 1968 Olympics in Mexico City, Mexico? (October 18)
23. How old was Bethany Hamilton when a shark bit off her arm? (October 31)

Magic or **Miracle?**

On this day in 1989, the Orlando Magic played their first NBA game, losing to the New Jersey Nets, 111-106.

Disney World is known as the "Magic Kingdom," and Orlando grew like magic after that world-famous theme park opened. So we know where the team got its name. That word, *magic*, is used to describe just about everything special that happens. We might say, "She appeared, as if by magic," or we might hear someone on TV talk about the "magic" of an opening night or in a romantic relationship. Magic Johnson got his nickname because of his spectacular passes. And the popular Harry Potter books and movies are filled with imaginative magic.

Watching a magician's tricks, we can be amazed by the illusions and slight-of-hand. When we're very young, we might think these performers have special powers. We soon learn, however, that they just know how to fool us, that every magic trick has a secret to make it work: hidden strings or compartments, distractions, mirrors, and other techniques. And we know movies are make-believe. So although we know the Magic Kingdom is wonderful fun and the Magic basketball team can do amazing moves with a ball and a hoop, we don't think anything supernatural is happening.

Then what do we do about the miracles described in the Bible? The Red Sea parted, the sun stood still, Jericho's walls fell, Gideon's army won, Elijah called down fire from heaven, Naaman's leprosy disappeared, a donkey talked, a man survived three days inside a huge fish, and Jesus healed, brought people back to life, and was raised from the dead himself! Many people will say that those were just tricks or that the people writing about them were wrong. Folks like that may have been tricked before (perhaps by a magician) or just don't believe that miracles are possible.

But with God, anything is possible. And that's the difference between magic and miracles. True miracles come from God. Does God still intervene in history and suspend the laws of nature from time to time? Sure. And he doesn't mind us asking for them. But he expects us to do what he has already told us in his Word and to depend on him for strength day by day.

If you want to see a miracle, just think of the lives he has changed, including yours!

ALSO ON THIS DAY . . .

1972—The Los Angeles Kings scored three goals within forty-five seconds against the New York Islanders.

2001—The Arizona Diamondbacks won the World Series, beating the New York Yankees four games to three.

2007—Adrian Peterson of the Minnesota Vikings set an NFL record with 296 rushing yards and became the first player ever with two 200-yard rushing games in his rookie season.

2008—Matthew Emmons (USA) won the fifty-meter rifle three positions in the 2008 ISSF World Cup Final (rifle and pistol) in Bangkok, Thailand.

BIRTHDAYS:

1929—Jimmy Piersall, Waterbury, CT, all-star major-league outfielder (Red Sox, Indians Senators, Mets, Angels)

1933—Millie "Tex" McDaniel, Atlanta, GA, high jumper, winner of the Olympic gold medal in 1956

1982—Devin Hester, Riviera Beach, FL, NFL returner and wide receiver (Chicago Bears), two-time all-pro

Jesus replied, "What is impossible with [people] is possible with God." Luke 18:27

Fun Fact The Orlando Magic began in 1989 as an expansion franchise and has had several big stars in its short history, including Shaquille O'Neal, Grant Hill, Vince Carter, and Tracy McGrady. The team has made the playoffs twelve times so far and has been the most successful of the four teams brought into the NBA in 1988 and 1989. It must be magic!

5 Tough **Love**

Owens was suspended after he had given an interview with ESPN in which he had criticized the Eagles for not publicly recognizing his 100th career receiving touchdown two weeks before. He also had said that if Brett Favre were their quarterback instead of Donovan McNabb, the Eagles would be undefeated. In other words, Terrell Owens was bad-mouthing his team, especially the owners, the coaches, and his leader (the quarterback), and thinking only of himself. He was acting like a spoiled child. And like the parent of a child who acts that way, the head coach, Andy Reid, exercised "tough love" and disciplined him. Terrell Owens is a tremendous talent, and the team would miss his spectacular pass receptions. But the coach did what was ultimately best for him and for the team.

Discipline often involves punishment, as in this case. The basic meaning of this word, however, is more like instruct, correct, or self-control. That's why loving parents discipline their children, trying to teach them to do what is right, to exercise self-control. Sometimes, their discipline involves punishment. Parents don't do this because they want to hurt their kids. Just the opposite: they love their children so much that they want them to learn the right way. At times the discipline involves pain—that's why it's called tough love. These actions are tough on the parents and on the kids.

We call God "Father" and he is—our loving, heavenly Father—and we are his children. We were born and adopted into his family when we trusted Christ as Savior. So we shouldn't be surprised when he disciplines us. Our Father's discipline may involve punishment, but usually he just gives us opportunities, challenges to strengthen our faith and trust in him. These circumstances may be tough, but God allows them because he loves us. Good questions to ask whenever we encounter difficulties are, "What does God want me to learn from this?" and "What do you want me to do now, Lord?"

How do you respond to God's tough love?

Because the Lord disciplines those he loves, and he punishes everyone he accepts as a son. **Hebrews 12:6**

[un]ACT After the ESPN interview incident, Owens was suspended four games. Then, after Owens served his suspension, the Eagles deactivated him from their roster for the remainder of the season. After the Eagles, Owens played for the Cowboys and the Bills.

When No One is **Watching**

On this day in 2006, Paul Azinger was named captain of the American Ryder Cup Team, replacing Tom Lehman, the captain for the 2006 team.

A golfing competition between the United States and Europe, the Ryder Cup matches are held every other year. Being named captain is a great honor and also a great responsibility. Although a certain number of players make the team because of their tournament wins, the captain chooses a few others. The captain also decides who plays with whom in which specific matches. Interestingly, both Paul Azinger and Tom Lehman are strong Christians.

Paul Azinger won eleven PGA tournaments from 1987 to 1993, ending with the 1993 PGA Championship. Soon after he was diagnosed with non-Hodgkin's lymphoma, so he had six months of chemotherapy and five weeks of radiation treatments. In 1995, he received the GWAA Ben Hogan Award, given to the person who has

continued to be active in golf despite serious illness or physical handicap. He returned to the tour and won the Sony Open in 2000. Paul has been public about his faith, and he gave the eulogy at the memorial service for his friend Payne Stewart, who died in a plane crash in 1999.

Tom Lehman has also enjoyed success as a professional golfer, winning the British Open in 1996. But his faith is much more important than golf. He explains, "The Bible says, 'All men are like grass and their glory is like the flowers of the field. The grass withers and the flowers fall.' So what is it that lasts? The only thing that has given my life true meaning—my relationship with Jesus Christ."

At a critical point in a tournament early in his career, Tom hit his drive down the fairway. A little later he gave himself a penalty, explaining to the official that in getting ready for his next shot, he had accidently touched his ball.

When discussing this, someone asked why he had penalized himself; after all, no one had seen him—no one knew. Tom simply replied, "I did." A person's character is defined by how that person acts when no one is looking. Usually people try to get away with stuff if they can. But Tom Lehman understood that even if his was a small infraction, he had to do what was right and report it. Tom is a man of strong Christian character.

How do you act when no one is watching? Let your character shine.

ALSO ON THIS DAY . . .

1961—The US government issued a stamp honoring the 100th birthday of James Naismith, inventor of basketball.

1972—The first intercollegiate Ultimate (Frisbee) competition was held between Rutgers University and Princeton University, the 103rd anniversary of the first intercollegiate game of American football featuring the same schools competing in the same location.

1976—Former Twins relief ace Bill Campbell became the first free agent to sign with a new team, joining the Red Sox for $1 million over four years.

2009—Shani Davis (USA) won the 1,000-meter in the Speed Skating World Cup in Berlin, Germany (1:08.53).

BIRTHDAYS:

1976—Laurie Baker, Concord, MA, ice hockey forward, winner of Olympic gold medal (1998) and silver medal (2002)

1976—Pat Tillman, San Jose, CA, NFL linebacker (Phoenix Cardinals) and soldier

1989—Josmer Volmy "Jozy" Altidore, Livingston, NJ, soccer striker, member of the US National Team

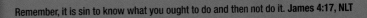

Remember, it is sin to know what you ought to do and then not do it. James 4:17, NLT

FUN FACT Tom Lehman wrote, "I think that everything you go through helps you develop character. And the Bible talks about how God allows you to go through good times and bad times so you'll be trained by what you go through. Then you'll learn how to persevere, how to develop character, how to be more open and, hopefully, how to be more like God. I really feel like every good thing and every bad thing you actually go through is experienced in order to make you more like Christ—if you'll allow it to train you in that way."

7 A Wheel **and a Way**

On this day in 2009, Jeremy Horgan-Kobelski and Alison Dunlap (both from Colorado) won the twenty-eight-mile Iceman Cometh mountain bike race in Kalkaska, Michigan.

The largest single-day mountain-bike race in America, this specific race had the largest group of competitors ever—4,400. Starting in downtown Kalkaska, the course wound through brush and mud and up and down hills, ending in Traverse City. Horgan-Kobelski, who competed in the 2004 Olympics and is the current US national champion, won the men's professional race in one hour, thirty-four minutes, two seconds. Dunlap, a two-time Olympian and thirteen-time national champ, claimed the women's race by one second in 1:46:40.

Mountain bikes take lots of abuse, pounding over rocks and ruts, through mud and dust, and over bumps and, well, mountains. Every part of the bike must be strong, especially the wheels.

Nothing ends a race quicker than a broken wheel.

Wheels have to be made just right. A good wheel must be round (ovals, triangles, squares, and pentagons won't work). It also should be balanced. Good tires are important, too. And the supports from the hub to the rim need to be strong. Other important steps go into the manufacture of quality wheels, depending on their use.

Look at a bicycle wheel, a regular one for tooling around town, a mountain bike, or even a little kid's version. You'll see the tire and the rim, then the spokes that offer the strong support. Follow a spoke toward the center, and you'll come to the hub. This is the most important part—everything revolves around it and depends on it. With a weak one, the wheel falls apart.

A bicycle wheel can be a good picture of our lives. We have a hub, an organizing core, around which everything is centered. That hub is whatever is most important to us. If someone loves football more than anything, that person will almost eat and sleep football (probably even wear logo pajamas). A person or family can be the hub. Some adults center their lives on a career or making money. But all of those hubs are weak—they can't support our lives and will break under the strain. Jesus Christ wants to be at the center, and he wants every aspect of our lives to revolve around him. He's worthy, he's strong, and he will take us safely to our destination. Keep him as your hub and you'll be able to ride . . . anywhere.

....

ALSO ON THIS DAY . . .

1973—New Jersey became the first state to allow girls into little league.

1989—Baltimore's Greg Olson became the first relief pitcher to win the AL Rookie of the Year.

1991—Magic Johnson announced that he had the HIV virus and retired from the Los Angeles Lakers.

2009—Charles Hamelin (Canada) won the 500-meter short-track speed skating World Cup in Montreal, Canada, beating Apollo Anton Ohno (USA) and Jeff Simon (USA).

I want to know Christ and experience the mighty power that raised him from the dead.
Philippians 3:10, NLT

Fun Fact The largest wheels with passengers don't need or use tires. They're Ferris wheels. Right now, the world's tallest Ferris wheel is the Singapore Flyer—541 feet tall. It opened to the public on March 1, 2008. This wheel won't take you anywhere, but you'll have a great view. The world's biggest bicycle was built by Didi Senft from Germany. It is 25 feet, 7 inches long, and 12 feet, 2 inches high. Good luck riding that one! (Hint: don't take it off-road.)

BIRTHDAYS:

1938—James Kaat, Zeeland, MI, major-league pitcher (Twins, White Sox, Phillies, Yankees, Cardinals), three-time all-star, World Series Champion (1982), and sportscaster

1957—Kathy McMillan, Raeford, NC, long jumper, winner of Olympic silver medal in 1976

1976—Mark Philippoussis, Australian professional tennis player

Prows and **Pitons**

On this day in 1958, Warren Harding, Wayne Merry, and George Whitmore made the first official climb of El Capitan (Yosemite).

El Capitan, in Yosemite National Park, California, has two towering rock faces, the southwest and the southeast. Between them sits the "Nose," a massive prow. Once considered impossible to climb, El Capitan is now the standard for big-wall climbing. The first to successfully make the ascent was Warren Harding and team. Beginning with Mark Powell and Bill Feuerer, the three

began climbing the 2,900-foot prow. But Powell broke his leg and dropped out. Then Feuerer became disillusioned and quit. Harding decided to keep trying, and eventually Wayne Merry and George Whitmore joined him, with Merry sharing lead climbing chores with Harding. In the fall, two pushes got them to the 2,000-foot level. Finally, in the late fall in what probably would be their last try, they worked their way slowly

upward, taking seven days to push to within the last 300 feet. After sitting out a storm for three days at this level, they hammered their way up the final portion. Harding struggled fifteen hours through the night, hand-placing twenty-eight expansion bolts up an overhanging headwall before topping out at 6 a.m.

The complete climb had taken forty-five days, with more than 3,400 feet of climbing, including huge pendulum swings across the face, the incredible labor of hauling bags, and harrowing rappel descents. But they had succeeded!

Climbing mountains, especially ones like El Capitan, can be tedious and extremely difficult. But like any great accomplishment and sporting victory, nothing can match the feeling when you succeed. In the middle of the mountain, when faced with a formidable section of rock, most climbers wish for an easier way, knowing the effort that will be needed to make it past this point and higher. But they persevere and push on.

A wise person has said, "If

the mountain were smooth, we couldn't climb it." Think about it: a flat slope might seem to be nice, but we'd quickly slip back. We need the ridges, crevasses, and ledges to push and pull our way along. Smooth sounds good, but it isn't.

As we climb in life, we may have similar thoughts: if only the way were smoother; if only we didn't have these obstacles to overcome . . . . But each difficulty helps us along, helps us climb, taking us to our God-directed destination.

What bumps are in your path? How can you use those as footholds for your climb?

....

ALSO ON THIS DAY . . .

1970—Tom Dempsey of the New Orleans Saints kicked an NFL-record sixty-three-yard field goal.

2008—John Brzenik won the arm-wrestling, right ninety-six-kg championships at the Nemiroff World Cup in Warsaw, Poland.

2008—The United States beat Uruguay 43-9 in the Rugby Union, End-of-Year tests in Sandy, Utah.

2009—Travis Pastrana landed the famous Rodeo 720 (freestyle motocross) and filmed it in his newest movie, *Nitro Circus— Country Fried.* After landing the trick, he named it the TP7, because he was 20 degrees short of 720.

BIRTHDAYS:

1929—Bobby Bowden, Birmingham, AL, Hall-of-Fame college football coach (Florida State University, 1976–2009), winner of two national championships, 1993 and 1999, and twelve ACC championships

1942—Angel Cordero Jr., Santurce, Puerto Rico, all-time great jockey, winner of over 6,000 races, including all of the American Classic Races

1968—Michelle Kline, Circle Pines, MN, speed skater, 1994 Olympics

He lifted me out of the slimy pit, out of the mud and mire; he set my feet on a rock and gave me a firm place to stand. **Psalm 40:2**

Fun Fact
Harding and his team finished one of the classics of modern rock climbing. The Nose Route is often called the most famous rock climbing route in North America, and these days, in good fall weather, can have anywhere between three and ten different parties strung out along its thirty rope lengths to the top. On the fiftieth anniversary of the first successful ascent, the US House of Representatives passed a resolution honoring the original party's achievement.

Match the team name to the description.

1. 747s
2. Hostile attackers
3. Various iron workers
4. Caused by being upset over the massage
5. Suntanned bodies
6. Toy baby with arms
7. Crooked carriers of electricity
8. Credit card users
9. Indian leaders
10. Used to be a girl
11. Six shooters
12. Rodeo horses
13. Coming in first with someone with bronze skin
14. Poe's foes
15. I.O.U.s
16. Residents of a huge state

a. Patriots
b. Chargers
c. Jaguars
d. Bills
e. Colts
f. Steelers
g. Bengals
h. Texans
i. Titans
j. Jets
k. Ravens
l. Browns
m. Dolphins
n. Chiefs
o. Raiders
p. Broncos

AFC Football

ANSWERS: 1.j, 2.o, 3.f, 4.a, 5.l, 6.m, 7.c, 8.b, 9.n, 10.g, 11.e, 12.p, 13.i, 14.k, 15.d, 16.h

The Best is **Yet to Come**

On this day in 1981, Fernando Valenzuela became the first rookie ever to win a Cy Young Award.

When the Los Angeles Dodgers acquired Fernando Valenzuela, they thought he would do well in the major leagues, but no one predicted his amazing first year. In 1981, this rookie left-hander started 8-0 with five shutouts and an ERA of 0.50. Although a strike wiped out 38 percent of the major-league schedule, he still finished with a 13-7 record, a 2.48 ERA, and a league-leading 180 strikeouts. He also pitched a complete game three of the World Series against the Yankees, helping the Dodgers to their first World Championship since 1965. The result: Valenzuela won both the Rookie of the Year and the Cy Young Award for that season.

Fernando was born on November 1, 1960, in Mexico. Although he began his American baseball career with the Dodger and pitched eleven seasons for them, he also played for five other teams (Angels, Orioles, Phillies, Padres, Cardinals), pitching his last game in the majors in 1997.

After that first amazing year, Valenzuela became a workhorse starter and one of the league's best pitchers. In perhaps his best season (1986), he finished 21-11 with a 3.14 ERA and led the league in wins, complete games, and innings pitched. In that year's all-star game, he tied a record by striking out five consecutive American League batters. In 1987, he began to slump, and in 1988, he won just five games and missed much of the season.

Every great athlete experiences a similar career path—strong beginning, great performances for a number of years, and then decline because of injury or age (or both). Most hit their prime in their early 30s, so they have many more years after their playing days. Some adjust well, but some can't handle the loss of abilities and spotlight.

Diminishing physical skills are a fact of life. All human beings decline physically and eventually die. Nothing lasts forever.

Wrong. God is forever and has created us, our souls, to live on after death. And for those who believe in Christ, the best is yet to come! While we strive for excellence and success on earth, we know that perfection in heaven awaits. Thank you Lord!

ALSO ON THIS DAY . . .

1989—Tish Johnson won the Sam's Town Bowling Invitational.

1996—John Smoltz of the Atlanta Braves won the National League Cy Young Award.

2006—Evan Lysacek won the ISU Grand Prix of Figure Skating in Nanjing, China.

2007—Jimmie Johnson won the Checker Auto Parts 500 at Avondale, Arizona, his fourth straight race, becoming the first driver to do so in the Cup since current teammate Jeff Gordon in 1998, and virtually clinching the NASCAR title.

BIRTHDAYS:

1934—Paula Myers-Pope, Lackawanna, NY, platform diver, winner of three Olympic silver medals (1952, 1960) and one bronze (1956)

1969—LaRee Pearl Sugg, Petersburg, VA, LPGA golfer

1980—Willie Parker, Clinton, NC, NFL running back (Pittsburgh Steelers, Washington Redskins), two-time Super Bowl champion

Praise be to the God and Father of our Lord Jesus Christ! In his great mercy he has given us new birth into a living hope through the resurrection of Jesus Christ from the dead, and into an inheritance that can never perish, spoil or fade—kept in heaven for you. **1 Peter 1:3–4**

[UN][ACT] At the beginning of his career, with all his success, Fernando set off a craze, especially in the Los Angeles Latino community, called "Fernandomania." He was also nicknamed "El Toro."

12 True **Colors**

On this day in 1927, the Notre Dame Fighting Irish changed their blue jerseys to green.

We can guess the reason for the change—perhaps because green is more Irish than blue. The change probably didn't help or hinder their athletes in their performance. These days, when teams make uniform changes, they do it for money.

Whether we put on a uniform, sweat suit, dress clothes, or shorts, we try to wear the right outfit for each occasion. Usually we want to look our best, especially if we expect to be seen. Clothes make a statement about a person and his or her personality, and some go to great lengths to get that message out. Think of those musical groups with the outrageous outfits—what are they trying to say? How about movie stars on the red carpet—what image are they trying to project? And then we have professional wrestlers—very serious about their public images.

Let's face it—we spend lots of time on our appearance, not just the style and color of our clothes. We know that, as the Bible reminds us, "People judge by outward appearance" (1 Samuel 16:7, NLT). We do, and we know that others do too. We see a person wearing leather and chains and dismounting a Harley, and we make assumptions. A middle-aged man in an expensive suit and carrying a briefcase walks by, and we think we know something about him. The same could be said for someone wearing a cowboy hat, someone dressed in Goth, a woman in a burqa, a man with muscles bulging through his T-shirt, or a fan decked out in team merchandise. We judge by outward appearances. But here's the kicker (and the rest of the verse), "the LORD looks at the heart." God had given Samuel the job of finding the next king of Israel and was telling him what to look for.

This truth has two immediate lessons. First, we shouldn't be quick to judge others by their looks, their projected image. Second, although we may be able to fool people by our appearance, we can't fool God. He knows what we're really like. We also should remember that only God can change people, us included. Regardless of how we dress, the real person is on the inside, the heart. That's what God sees and what he wants to change. And his changes are for real and forever.

ALSO ON THIS DAY . . .

1892—Pudge Heffelfinger received $500 and became the first professional football player.

1964—Paula Murphy, the first woman to drive the Indianapolis Motor Speedway, set a female land speed record, 226.37 mph.

1995—Dan Marino (Dolphins) broke Fran Tarkenton's (Vikings) NFL all-time passing yardage mark of 47,003.

2006—Asafa Powell, who equaled the 100 meters world record twice in 2006 and won all six Golden League meetings, was named IAAF Athlete of the Year in the men's category. Sanya Richards won the women's award for her achievements in this year, breaking Valerie Brisco-Hooks' 1984 US national record and winning all the Golden League meetings at her distance, the 400 meters.

> But the Lord said to Samuel, "Don't judge by his appearance or height, for I have rejected him. The Lord doesn't see things the way you see them. People judge by outward appearance, but the Lord looks at the heart." 1 Samuel 16:7, NLT

FUN FACT Many teams choose the color of their uniforms based on the city or country they represent or their mascot (leprechaun?). But a study has discovered that the color red can actually affect a referee's split-second decisions and even promote a scoring bias, especially in combat sports such as taekwondo.

BIRTHDAYS:

1945—Al Michaels, Brooklyn, NY, sportscaster for *ABC Monday Night Baseball/Football*

1961—Nadia Comaneci, Romanian gymnast, winner of three Olympic gold medals (1976), the first gymnast ever to be awarded a perfect score of ten, and winner of two gold medals at the 1980 Summer Olympics

1971—Heidi Burge, Fairfax, CA, WNBA forward (Los Angeles Sparks, Washington Mystics)

Like Father, **Like Son**

On this day in 1997, Ken Griffey Jr. won the American League Most Valuable Player in a unanimous vote.

Ken Griffey played nineteen years in the major leagues, mostly with the Cincinnati Reds. As a member of the Big Red Machine, he was a three-time all-star (1976, 1977, 1980), a two-time World Series champion (1975, 1976), and the 1980 MLB All-Star Game MVP. But that's the father. Most people know about his son, Ken Griffey Jr.

Now there's a baseball player. Junior, a sure Hall of Famer, is one of the most productive home run hitters and best defensive outfielders in the long history of baseball. He stands fifth in number of career home runs and has the most of any active major-league player. He has led his league many times in hitting categories and has won ten Gold Glove awards, mostly for his play in center field (1990–1999). Selected by the Seattle Mariners as the first overall pick in the 1987 amateur draft, he got to the majors in 1989 and made an immediate impact on his team and the league. And his career continues: after stops with the Cincinnati Reds and Chicago White Sox, he returned to the Mariners as their designated hitter.

In addition to stats in the usual categories, the Griffeys share another important distinction, becoming the first son and father to play on the same team at the same time (1990–1991). They also are the only father-and-son pair to hit back-to-back home runs.

Most parents appreciate their children following in their footsteps, at least as they copy Mom or Dad's positive characteristics. And let's face it, we will be like our parents in many ways—values, priorities, character, sense of humor, and more—even if we don't choose their vocation. What a thrill for Ken Griffey Sr. to be on the same team as his son and playing at that level.

We have a Father who is proud of us and who loves to see us follow in his footsteps. Our accomplishments will never overshadow his, of course, for he is perfect. But we should look up to him and copy him in every aspect of life. And if we want to know exactly what our heavenly Father looks like, we can look at our big brother, Jesus—the perfect representation. And get this: we're all on the same team!

....

ALSO ON THIS DAY . . .

1982—Korean boxer Duk Koo Kim was fatally injured when knocked out by Ray Mancini.

2005—Chad Hedrick set a new world record for the 5,000 meters at the ISU World Cup in Calgary, Alberta, Canada, with the time 6:09.68, beating the previous record by nearly five seconds.

2008—Lindsey Vonn won the Women's World Cup slalom in Levi, Finland.

2009—Harry Statham, head basketball coach at the NAIA school McKendree College, became the first men's coach at a four-year school to reach 1,000 career wins.

For God knew his people in advance, and he chose them to become like his Son, so that his Son would be the firstborn among many brothers and sisters. **Romans 8:29, NLT**

Fun Fact
Ken Griffey Jr.'s defense in center field was considered the standard of elite fielding. With great range, he would make spectacular diving plays, dazzling over-the-shoulder basket catches, leaping and reaching balls over the fence to rob opposing hitters of home runs. He was featured on a Wheaties box and had his own Nike signature sneaker.

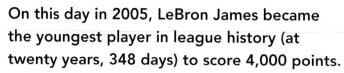

On this day in 2005, LeBron James became the youngest player in league history (at twenty years, 348 days) to score 4,000 points.

LeBron James has been setting high standards in basketball for more than a decade. Born in 1984, LeBron was reared by a very young single mother—life was a struggle. He loved basketball and played as a child. LeBron grew quickly and by the eighth grade stood six feet tall. He learned to play all five positions and developed a sense for the game. In high school LeBron dominated and was named Mr. Basketball of Ohio three years. Called King James, sportswriters were saying he'd be a great pro when he was just a sophomore. Right after graduation, LeBron was chosen by the Cleveland Cavaliers as the overall first pick in the 2003 NBA Draft. Unlike other high school phenoms who turn out to be NBA busts, LeBron has lived up to the hype, winning many awards and setting records.

As a high school sophomore, LeBron was called Chosen One by *Sports Illustrated* and the nickname stuck. Chosen One may mean that LeBron would be the next great NBA player, or perhaps it means that he was chosen to lead the Cavaliers to the championship. But anyone labeled *chosen one* carries a heavy burden of expectations. So far LeBron has played with excellence, but is that enough . . . for the one?

Thousands of years ago, the Jewish people were looking for their chosen one. They didn't expect this person to win athletic championships but something much bigger, to lead the whole nation to freedom, military might, peace, and prosperity. Talk about expectations! This one would be their Messiah. Then Jesus arrived. And he said he was the One they had been awaiting—sent from God. Many didn't think Jesus looked or acted the part and rejected him. But some believed and followed, even though they wondered at times, "Are you the one who was to come, or should we expect someone else?" (Matthew 11:3).

Jesus proved that he was the Messiah, the Christ, through his life, teachings, actions, death, and resurrection. His mission was not to defeat earthly armies, however, but to defeat Satan, to suffer and die for sin, taking our place on the Cross, and to defeat death. He is our Chosen One, our Savior—and now he chooses us.

The true Chosen One has chosen you. Follow him.

ALSO ON THIS DAY . . .

1981—Paul "Bear" Bryant tied Amos Alonzo Stagg with 314 football wins.

1993—Uta Pippig won the twenty-third New York City Women's Marathon in 2:26:24.

1993—Don Shula became the winningest coach in NFL history.

2004—Alecko Eskandarian scored two goals as DC United defeated the Kansas City Wizards 3–2 to take the 2004 Major League Soccer championship, the franchise's fourth title.

You did not choose me, but I chose you and appointed you to go and bear fruit—fruit that will last. Then the Father will give you whatever you ask in my name. **John 15:16**

[U N ‖ ꓱ C T] LeBron has become a definite triple-double threat, averaging 27.8 points, 7.0 assists, and 7.0 rebounds per game so far in his career in the regular season. As of the 2009–2010 season, he has recorded thirty-four triple-doubles in his career. On offense, LeBron uses his size, strength, and quickness to get past defenders and for absorbing contact while finishing at the basket, with a variety of spectacular dunks and lay-ups.

BIRTHDAYS:

1955—Jack Sikma, Kankakee, IL, NBA center/power forward (Seattle Supersonics, Milwaukee Bucks), seven-time all-star

1964—Silken Suzette Laumann, Mississauga, Ontario, Canadian champion rower

1982—Kyle Orton, Altoona, IA, NFL quarterback (Chicago Bears, Denver

Playing for **the Glory**

On this day in 2005, Albert Pujols of the St. Louis Cardinals was named the winner of the National League Most Valuable Player Award.

To say that first baseman Albert Pujols has been tearing up the National League the past nine years would be an understatement. According to a poll of all thirty major-league managers, he is the most feared hitter in baseball. Since his first game with the Cardinals in 2001, Albert has been selected an all-star eight times and has been named the National League's MVP three times. He hits for power and batting average; in fact, at the end of the 2009 season, he led all active players in slugging percentage (.628), batting average (.334), and on-base percentage (.427). He also is one of the leading home run hitters in MLB history.

At 6'3" and 231 lbs., Albert Pujols is an intimidating figure on the baseball field, but he is anything but scary in person. He and his wife, Deidre, are strong and active Christians who let people know about their faith and what it means to them. In 2005, they started the Pujols Family Foundation, whose purpose is "the love, care and development of people with Down's syndrome and their families," as well as helping the poor in the Dominican Republic (Albert's country of birth). The website for the foundation states, "In the Pujols family, God is first. Everything else is a distant second." Albert and Diedre often travel back to the DR to bring supplies as well as teams of doctors and dentists and to represent the work of Compassion International.

When asked about all his charity work, Albert replied, "Helping other people—that is what you play for. I think that is my responsibility. As a baseball player, God has blessed me with more than what I even deserve and I want to make sure I get the opportunity to keep blessing others." In another interview, Albert explained his purpose for playing baseball, "I don't play for numbers. I play first of all to glorify God."

Does Albert Pujols play hard? Yes. Does he care about winning? Definitely; just like any major leaguer he wants to win the World Series (he did once). But all his playing, winning, losing, and living he does for God's glory, not his own.

What a great example.

. . . .

ALSO ON THIS DAY . . .

1964—Mickey Wright shot a sixty-two, the lowest golf score for a woman professional golfer.

1992—Praveen Amre scored more than 100 runs himself in his Test Cricket debut (103 for India vs. South Africa).

2006—Despite being fired by the Florida Marlins, Joe Girardi was named winner of the National League Manager of the Year.

2009—The United States men won the team pursuit in the World Cup (speed skating).

BIRTHDAYS:

1963—Michele McAnany, Los Angeles, CA, baseball infielder, Colorado Silver Bullets (women's baseball team)

1974—Susan Jean (Susie) Maroney, Cronulla, New South Wales, Australian marathon swimmer

1981—Lorena Ochoa, Guadalajara, Mexico, LPGA golfer with twenty-seven LPGA tour victories, including two majors, considered to be the best Mexican golfer of all time

Religion that God our Father accepts as pure and faultless is this: to look after orphans and widows in their distress and to keep oneself from being polluted by the world. **James 1:27**

FUN FACT

"The home runs and whatever it is—obviously it is great. That is the platform God has given me, but what matters is what you have done for the Lord and for people who really look at you as a role model. That is what I try to be. I try to pass on the blessing that God has given to me." —Albert Pujols, St. Louis Cardinals

Match the name of the person born in November with the sport he or she played.

1. Pat Tillman

a. Football—quarterback

2. **Bobby Bowden**

b. **Gymnastics**

3. Dan Marino

c. Track and Field—100-meter sprinter and hurdler

4. **Lorena Ochoa**

d. **Football—Washington Redskins head coach and NASCAR owner**

5. Allyson Felix

e. Tennis

6. **Gail Devers**

f. **Baseball—outfielder/designated hitter**

7. Kerri Strug

g. Football—defensive back

8. **Stan Musial**

h. **Motocross**

9. Ken Griffey Jr.

i. Track and Field—200-meter sprinter

10. **Billy Jean King**

j. **Baseball—center fielder**

11. Joe DiMaggio

k. Football—FSU coach

12. **Joe Gibbs**

l. **Golf**

13. Ricky Carmichael

m. Baseball—first baseman

Significant **Birthdays**

Heart of a **Champion**

On this day in 1966, Jean Driscoll was born in Milwaukee, Wisconsin.

Jean was born with spina bifida (an open spine), which affected her ability to walk and brought other problems. Jean's feet turned to the side, so she had to wear ugly brown stainless-steel braces on her feet and drag her legs behind. She fell down easily and had to endure stares and teasing. Growing up was mostly a sad time. Despite these childhood challenges, Jean was always determined to be active, to push the limits of what she could do.

At fifteen, Jean began using a wheelchair; then, through the suggestion from a friend, she got involved in wheelchair basketball—she loved it. After high school, she went to the University of Illinois, where she excelled in basketball and racing. Eventually Jean started participating in marathons, and she excelled, to say the least. She won the Boston Marathon every year from 1990 through 1996

and then again in 2000, giving her more Boston wins than anyone in any division. Through the years at the Paralympic Games, her medal count is five gold (1988, 1992, 1996, and 2000), three silver, and four bronze.

During college, Jean accepted Christ as her Savior, but her faith remained immature. But after winning her first Boston Marathon and beating the previous record by seven minutes, she felt unhappy, as though she had a hole inside her, and she wondered what was wrong. A good friend helped explain that her relationship with God was a loving relationship, that God wasn't judging her and waiting to punish her for sins. Realizing that truth, her heart softened, and she began to grow in her faith. She also realized that God had a purpose for her life, the way she was.

In a TV interview, Jean explained, "God has healed me, not physically, not the way I thought I wanted to be healed,

but he has healed my heart and healed my mind and given me a perspective that enables me now to encourage people." And she does. Since retiring from racing in 2000, she spends her time encouraging and motivating people around the world—and telling them about Christ. Through a partnership that began in 2001 with Joni and Friends, Inc., Jean began working with people who have disabilities in Ghana, West Africa.

God changed Jean's heart and transformed disability into an ability. What an amazing woman serving our amazing God.

....

ALSO ON THIS DAY . . .

1984—The Winnipeg Blue Bombers defeated the Hamilton Tiger-Cats, 47–17, to win the seventy-second CFL Grey Cup.

1987—Andre Dawson of the Chicago Cubs became the first player from a last-place major-league team ever to win the MVP.

2005—Steve Hengeveld won first overall, open pro, at the Baja 1,000 off-road race.

2006—Anna Meares of Australia set a new world record at the 500-meter individual time trial at the 2007 UCI Track Cycling World Cup Classics meeting in Sydney (33.944 seconds).

BIRTHDAYS:

1954—Gail Marquis, New York, NY, basketball player, winner of the Olympic medal in 1976

1957—J. C. Watts, Eufaula, OK, football quarterback (University of Oklahoma and the Canadians Football League) and US Congressman

1985—Allyson Felix, Los Angeles, CA, sprinting star, winner of an Olympic gold medal (2008, 4x100 relay) and two silver medals (2004, 2008 – 200 meters)

Three times I pleaded with the Lord to take it away from me. But he said to me, "My grace is sufficient for you, for my power is made perfect in weakness." Therefore I will boast all the more gladly about my weaknesses, so that Christ's power may rest on me. 2 Corinthians 12:8–9

Fun Fact
The University of Rhode Island and the Massachusetts School of Law awarded Jean Driscoll honorary doctorate degrees in 1997 and 2002, respectively. She is also in the Fellowship of Christian Athletes' Hall of Champions and the Wheelchair Sports, USA, Hall of Fame. In addition to her speaking, Jean is the associate director of development in the College of Applied Health Sciences at the University of Illinois.

19 Qualified?

On this day in 1989, the United States men's soccer team beat Trinidad, 1-0, qualifying for the 1990 FIFA World Cup.

For the US men to qualify for the World Cup was a big deal. Actually, this was their first qualification since 1950. Here's how it works. Leading up to the World Cup, FIFA (International Federation of Football Association) holds qualifying tournaments in six zones (Africa, Asia, North and Central America and Caribbean, South America, Oceania, Europe). Beforehand, FIFA decides how many spots will be awarded in each zone. Eventually thirty-two teams make the final tournament.

Other sports have qualification systems. In golf, for example, aspiring professionals go to Qualifying School, where a certain number of winners of those special tournaments are given a tour card and allowed to participate in PGA events the following year. To qualify for the Olympics, athletes have to win their way onto their nation's squad. And all major sports have playoffs where just the top teams get to play for the championship. We're well aware of this

process elsewhere. To get into many schools, especially colleges and universities, students must do well on certain tests. Men and women have to pass physical exams to see if they qualify for service in the military and elsewhere. Some opportunities have an age requirement; a person might be too young or too old. Sometimes citizenship or where a person was born is a factor (a US President must be born in the United States, for example), or finances might be (in getting a loan). And every amusement park has height requirements ("You must be this tall to ride").

Most of those qualifying situations make sense. But learning that we don't qualify still stinks. It's like being turned away at a party or not being chosen for a team on the playground. Or being told we're not good enough or smart enough or cool enough. We want to belong.

That's one reason the good news about Jesus is so good.

Any person, regardless of age, height, gender, race, background, finances, physical abilities, appearance, nationality, political affiliation, or social status can receive salvation through Christ. No special characteristics needed, no qualifying exam. Just turn from sin and turn to Christ and we're in! That's grace, and that's God. Amazing!

....

ALSO ON THIS DAY . . .

1932—Joe Kershalla scored seventy-one points in a college football game.

1983—Edmonton Oilers beat the New Jersey Devils, 13-4, after which Wayne Gretzky of the Oilers called the Devils "a Mickey Mouse organization."

2004—With less than a minute to go in a game between the Pacers and the Pistons, an on-court altercation between the teams over a foul became a massive brawl as Pacers players assaulted heckling Pistons fans. The game was called off, with the Pacers winning by default, 97-82.

2006—Peter Norfolk (England) defeated David Wagner (USA) in the Wheelchair Tennis Masters quads gold medal match, in Amsterdam.

BIRTHDAYS:

1966—Gail Devers, Seattle, WA, 60-meter and 100-meter hurdler, winner of two Olympic gold medals, 1992, 1996

1977—Kerri Strug, Tucson, AZ, gymnast, winner of the Olympic gold medal, 1996, and bronze medal, 1992

1971—Jeremy McGrath, San Francisco, CA, supercross racer who has won a record of seventy-two 250 cc Main Event wins and captured seven 250 cc Championships between 1993 to 2000

1988—Patrick Kane, Buffalo, NY, NHL forward (Chicago Blackhawks)

[Jesus said], "For God so loved the world that he gave his one and only Son, that whoever believes in him shall not perish but have eternal life." **John 3:16**

Fun Fact For the World Cup, the host country is automatically qualified. Unlike some other sports, results of the last World Cup and continental championships don't matter. Until 2002, the defending champions were also automatically qualified; but since 2006, they also need to enter qualifying.

Sacked!

On this day in 1966, Dallas sacked Pittsburgh quarterbacks an NFL-record twelve times.

We've already discussed what happens when the offensive line in football does its job (see October 11). On passing plays, they protect the quarterback, allowing him to stand in the pocket, scan the field, see the receivers, and deliver the ball. Their job is to keep the defensive players out. But the job of those defensive players is to get to the quarterback and tackle him in the backfield. That's called a sack. If a player tackles the quarterback at the same time as someone else, he gets credit for half of a sack. The current NFL single-season record for sacks belongs to Michael Strahan, who had 22.5 in 2001. NFL teams average about sixty offensive plays per game. If half of those are passing plays, you can see that getting twelve quarterback sacks in one game is a ton.

What do you think Pittsburgh's second-string quarterback thought when he saw the Dallas tackles and ends pouring through the line? How about when the coach told him to strap on his helmet and get in the game? He was in for an adventure, for sure—trying to run the offense, but running for his life instead.

We can feel that way at times. Somehow, some way, opposing forces keep breaking through, charging right at us and knocking us flat. We know that will happen occasionally, but so many times, so soon? We get up; then down we go again. A terrible argument with a friend. A punishment from Mom or Dad. A lost prized possession. A lingering sickness. Just when we think we're in the clear, another one hits, and we're tasting turf. And sometimes the hits come because of our faith in Christ. So we may even wonder how God could allow us to go through so much.

Just remember this: the true measure of a person's character and commitment is how that person responds to hard times. We know that God allows us to struggle and suffer for his reasons. We probably won't ever know those reasons while we're here on earth, so we just have to trust him. And like those intrepid quarterbacks, we have to get up, wipe off the mud and blood, and call the next play. We may get sacked a few times, but we're in the game to stay.

....

ALSO ON THIS DAY . . .

1969—Pele scored his 1,000th soccer goal.

1977—Walter Payton (Bears) rushed for NFL-record 275 yards in one game.

1997—A. C. Green set a new NBA record of 907 consecutive games played.

2005—Shani Davis (USA) set the men's 1,000-meter record (1:07.03), and Cindy Klassen (Canada) set the women's 1,500-meter record (1:51.79) at the ISU World Cup meet in the Utah (speed skating).

BIRTHDAYS:

1976—Dominique Dawes, Silver Spring, MD, gymnast, winner of the Olympic gold medal in 1996 and three bronze medals in 1992, 1996, and 2000

1953—Susan Notorangelo, ultracyclist

1981—Carlos Boozer, Aschaffenburg, West Germany, NBA power forward (Cleveland Cavaliers, Utah Jazz), winner of the Olympic gold medal in 2008

But we have this treasure in jars of clay to show that this all-surpassing power is from God and not from us. We are hard pressed on every side, but not crushed; perplexed, but not in despair; persecuted, but not abandoned; struck down, but not destroyed. We always carry around in our body the death of Jesus, so that the life of Jesus may also be revealed in our body. **2 Corinthians 4:7–10**

FUN FACT Deacon Jones, NFL Hall-of-Fame defensive end, coined the phrase, "quarterback sack," comparing it to an ancient city being devastated when it was sacked by an invading army.

Running with **Purpose**

On this day in 1925, Red Grange played his final University of Illinois football game and signed with the Chicago Bears.

Harold Edward "Red Grange," "The Galloping Ghost," was an elusive runner. Grange's athletic career began at Wheaton High School in Illinois, where he earned sixteen varsity letters in four sports—football, basketball, track, and baseball. During his four years of football, he scored seventy-five touchdowns and 532 points.

After high school, Grange enrolled at the U. of I., planning only to compete in basketball and track, but he changed to football when he got to campus. In his first game, against Nebraska, he scored three touchdowns. In seven games that year, he ran for 723 yards and twelve touchdowns. His biggest college game was probably against Michigan in 1924. Grange returned the opening kickoff 95 yards for a touchdown and scored

three more on runs of 67, 56, and 44 yards in the first quarter. Michigan had allowed just four touchdowns in the two previous seasons combined. Grange sat out the second quarter but returned in the second half to score again. He amassed 402 yards—212 rushing, 64 passing, and 126 on kickoff returns. His senior year was better yet. After college, Grange continued his excellent play with the Chicago Bears. He was a charter member of both the College and Pro Football Hall of Fame, and in 2008, ESPN named Red Grange the greatest college football player of all time.

Red Grange was strong and elusive, but he ran with purpose. He knew that his job was to put the ball in the end zone, so he got there as quickly as possible, regardless of who stood in his way. When the apostle Paul compared the Christian life to sports, it sounds like he had someone like Red Grange in mind: "Do you not know that in a race all the runners run, but only one gets

the prize? Run in such a way as to get the prize…Therefore I do not run like a man running aimlessly" (1 Corinthians 9:24, 26).

Running aimlessly means expending a lot of energy but going nowhere. Imagine a back running in circles or straight to the sidelines. Running with purpose means keeping the goal in sight, in mind, and then going straight for it, over and around the opposition.

God's purpose for us is to glorify him, to make a difference in the world for him. Don't run aimlessly; run with purpose.

ALSO ON THIS DAY . . .

1905—The first game in the Australian Tennis Open was played.

1971—The New York Rangers score an NHL-record eight goals in one period.

2006—Australian Ian Thorpe, a five-time Olympic gold medalist, announced his retirement from the sport at the age of twenty-four.

2009—John Napier/Charles Berkeley (USA) won the two-man bob sled at the World Cup in Lake Placid, New York (1:53.62).

BIRTHDAYS:

1920—Stan Musial, Donora, PA, Hall-of-Fame major-league outfielder/first baseman (St Louis Cardinals), twenty-four-time all-star, seven-time NL batting champion, three-time World Series champion, three-time NL MVP

1969—George Kenneth "Ken" Griffey Jr., Donora, PA, major-league outfielder (Mariners, Reds, White Sox), thirteen-time all-star, ten-time Gold Glove winner, seven-time Silver Slugger winner

1971—Michael Strahan, all-pro NFL defensive end (NY Giants), seven-time pro-bowl selection, Super Bowl winner, broadcaster

Above all, you must live as citizens of heaven, conducting yourselves in a manner worthy of the Good News about Christ. Then, whether I come and see you again or only hear about you, I will know that you are standing together with one Spirit and one purpose, fighting together for the faith, which is the Good News. **Philippians 1:27, NLT**

Fun Fact "I asked George Halas who is the greatest running back you ever saw? And he said, 'That would be Red Grange.' And I asked him if Grange was playing today, how many yards do you think he'd gain? And he said, 'About 750, maybe 800 yards.' And I said, 'Well, 800 yards is just okay.' He sat up in his chair and he said, 'Son, you must remember one thing: Red Grange is seventy-five years old.'" Chris Berman on ESPN's *SportsCentury*.

Catch the **Wind**

On this day in 2008, Doug Douglass' *Goombay Smash* (USA) won the Rolex Farr 40 North American Championship.

Sailboats can be as small as a sunfish, at 13 feet 10 inches long and weighing 120 pounds, or as large as a three-masted schooner such as the mega-yacht *Athena*, at 295 feet long and weighing 1,126 tons. The Farr 40 is a 40-foot one-design sailboat. In 1997, the world's first Farr 40 One Design was launched. By 2008, the class numbered over 137 boats. Today this class of sailboats has an extensive international racing schedule. The ultimate competition is the Rolex Farr 40 Worlds.

Sailboats of all classes and sizes have a number of things in common, but the most obvious is sails. A sail is any type of surface that is used to harness the power of the wind, much like a wing, but vertical. For centuries, sails were made of cloth: flax (linen), hemp, or cotton in various forms including canvas. Most modern sails are made from synthetic fibers ranging from low-cost nylon or polyester to expensive aramids or carbon fibers. Sails must be lightweight, and they rise vertically from the hull of the boat, attached to masts, yards, and rigging. The purpose of a sail is to harness wind-power. As the wind blows, it hits the sail and moves the vessel forward.

Good sailors know how to catch the wind whether they're traveling with the wind, against the wind, or cross wind. As long as the wind is blowing they can move.

The Bible uses *wind* as a picture of the Holy Spirit. In fact, the Greek word for *spirit* (*pneuma*) means "breath" or "wind." When the disciples were filled with the Holy Spirit, the Bible says, "Suddenly a sound like the blowing of a violent wind came from heaven and filled the whole house where they were sitting" (Acts 2:2). That's powerful. And that's exactly what Jesus told his disciples would happen after the Spirit came—they would receive power (Acts 1:8).

When we trust in Christ as Savior, the Holy Spirit begins living in us, changing us from the inside out and giving us power to obey God and to tell others about him. We just need to be available—to put up those sails and catch the wind.

Ask God to empower you through his Spirit. Sail on with him.

ALSO ON THIS DAY . . .

1950—Just 7,021 saw the lowest NBA score as the Ft. Wayne Pistons beat the Minneapolis Lakers, 19-18.

1984—In one of the all-time great college football games, Doug Flutie and Boston College beat Miami University and Bernie Kosar on one last, desperate play.

2009—Peter Marshall (USA) set a world record in the fifty-meter backstroke at the FINA Swimming World Cup—Series five in Singapore (22.61).

2009—Steven Holcomb/Justin Olsen/Steve Mesler/Curtis Tomasevicz (USA) won the four-man bobsled at the World Cup in Lake Placid, New York (1:49.60).

BIRTHDAYS:

1943—Billie Jean King, Long Beach, CA, tennis player, winner of 12 Grand Slam singles titles, 16 Grand Slam women's doubles titles, and 11 Grand Slam mixed doubles titles

1955—Sue Novara-Reber, Flint, MI, cyclist, world sprint champ, 1975

1986—Oscar Leonard Carl Pistorius, South African Paralympic runner

[Jesus told Nicodemus], "The wind blows wherever it pleases. You hear its sound, but you cannot tell where it comes from or where it is going. So it is with everyone born of the Spirit." **John 3:8**

Fun Fact On May 16, 2010, sixteen-year-old Jessica Watson cruised into Sydney Harbor in her pink, thirty-four-foot sailboat, *Ella's Pink Lady*, to become the youngest person to sail around the globe solo, nonstop, and unassisted. Jessica had spent 210 days guiding her boat through raging storms and forty-foot waves and seven knockdowns during the 23,000-nautical-mile journey.

College Football Rivalries

Match the rivalry with the nickname.

1. Egg Bowl
2. Old Oaken Bucket
3. Little Brown Jug
4. Little Brass Bell
5. Red River Shootout
6. Iron Bowl
7. Sunshine Showdown
8. Border Showdown
9. Civil War
10. Commonwealth Cup
11. Bayou Bucket
12. Victory Bell
13. Bedlam Series
14. Holy War

a. Oregon vs. Oregon State
b. Wheaton vs. North Central
c. Oklahoma vs. Texas
d. Virginia vs. Virginia Tech
e. Kansas vs. Kansas State
f. Mississippi State vs. Mississippi
g. Brigham Young vs. Utah
h. Rice vs. Houston
i. Minnesota vs. Michigan
j. Oklahoma vs. Oklahoma State
k. North Carolina vs. Duke
l. Alabama vs. Auburn
m. Indiana vs. Purdue
n. Florida vs. Florida State

ANSWERS: 1.f, 2.m, 3.i, 4.b, 5.c, 6.l, 7.n, 8.e, 9.a, 10.d, 11.h, 12.k, 13.j, 14.g

It's Not **All About You**

On this day in 1993, Leon Lett of the Dallas Cowboys muffed a fumble recovery to help the Dolphins win the game.

Defensive tackle Leon Lett could dominate at the point of attack and often had to be double-teamed. With all of his success, however, Lett is most remembered for two blunders.

This Thanksgiving day in snowy Dallas, the Cowboys were leading the Dolphins 14-13 with fifteen seconds left in the game. The Dolphins attempted a field goal. The kick was blocked, and Lett's Cowboy teammates began celebrating. But in trying to pick up the ball, he touched it, slipped on the ice, and allowed Miami to recover the "muff" on the Dallas one-yard line. If he had just stayed away from the ball,

time would have expired, and the Cowboys would have won. Instead, the Dolphins retained possession and kicked the game-winning field goal.

Leon Lett's more infamous play occurred in Super Bowl XXVII. Late in the fourth quarter, he recovered a fumble and proceeded to run it toward the end-zone. When he reached the ten-yard line, he slowed down and held out the ball in one hand. He didn't realize that Don Beebe of the Bills was chasing him. Beebe knocked the ball out of Lett's hand just before he crossed the goal line, costing him the touchdown. The Cowboys still won the game, but everyone remembers Leon's blunder.

In both cases, Lett acted instinctively, but he wasn't thinking of his team, only of himself—looking for the glory. But before being too hard on Leon, we have to admit that we have the same tendency. Every day we make choices in our own self interest, looking for what

makes us look good or feel good. This could be letting someone else do the dirty work while we get the credit or, at least, get to relax. It might involve trying for individual glory at the expense of the team. Or it just might be waiting and hoping for someone else to step up and take care of a problem instead of getting in and trying to solve it ourselves. Each time we blunder, we hurt the cause of Christ—and often those are the actions that people remember.

Ask God to show you how to be a humble, sacrificial team player on his team.

....

ALSO ON THIS DAY . . .

1980—Sugar Ray Leonard defeated Roberto Duran to regain the WBC welterweight championship.

1985—White Sox shortstop Ozzie Guillen was named the American League Rookie of the Year.

2007—The Chicago Bears beat the Denver Broncos 37-34 in overtime with the Bears' Devin Hester returning a punt and a kickoff for touchdowns in the second quarter, the first player since the AFL-NFL merger to do both in a quarter.

2009—Viktoriya Safvenko (Russia) won women's sixty-three-kg snatch in the weightlifting World Championships in Goyang, South Korea (112 kg).

BIRTHDAYS:

1914—"Joltin'" Joe DiMaggio, Martinez, CA, Hall-of-Fame outfielder (New York Yankees), one of the greatest baseball players ever

1940—Joe Gibbs, Enka, NC, NFL head coach and NASCAR owner, winner of three Super Bowl championships and two NASCAR championships

1965—Cris Carter, Troy, OH, all-pro NFL wide receiver (Eagles, Vikings, Dolphins)

1976—Clint Mathis, Conyers, GA, professional midfielder/forward (Galaxy, MetroStars, Real Salt Lake, Rapids, Red Bulls)

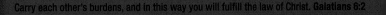
Carry each other's burdens, and in this way you will fulfill the law of Christ. Galatians 6:2

[UN][ACT] Leon Lett from NCAA Division II Emporia State University in Kansas, played eleven years in the NFL (1991–2001), ten with the Dallas Cowboys. When he retired after the 2001 season, he had 22.5 career quarterback sacks and seven fumble recoveries in 121 games, and he was on the Cowboys' Super Bowl championship teams in 1992, 1993, and 1995.

With Time Running **Out . . .**

On this day in 2007, Jeff Reed kicked a field goal with seventeen seconds left in the game to give the Pittsburgh Steelers a victory over the Miami Dolphins, 3-0.

The field was a mess. With heavy rain before and during the game, soon the players were slogging through mud, trying without much success to move the ball. Eventually the four quarters of futility came down to a final twenty-four-yard field goal with time running out—the only points of the game. Many athletic contests are timed events. That is, winners are the teams or individuals who score the most points during a specific time period. In others—such as baseball, cricket, bowling, table tennis, skateboarding, diving, high jump, figure skating, and so forth—success is measured solely by point totals, with no clock involved. But in sports such as ice

hockey, water polo, basketball, soccer, and football, often a last-second shot wins the contest. Players, coaches, and fans are well aware of the amount of time left in a quarter/period/half and, especially, in the game. Tensions rise when the score is razor thin and the seconds tick off. Some athletes fold under pressure; others thrive on it. But all the players in the game are subject to the clock.

Every life has a time limit—some have more time than others, but everyone's time eventually expires. Game over. When we're young, we don't like to think about it. Even twenty-five years seems like a long time to live, so seventy years can seem like an eternity and way too far off in the future to consider right now. That kind of thinking isn't limited to children, kids, and teens; people of all ages can act as though they have all the time in the world, as though they will live forever. We know that way of thinking doesn't turn out well in sports, where we have to be aware of the time limits and prepare for the end or

we'll lose.

The clock is ticking. Time is running out. So the questions are these: What's our game strategy? What plays will we call to win the game? To win in this life means to use whatever time we have to glorify God, doing what he wants, including loving others and spreading his word. Whether conditions are great or a mess, we should make every second count for our Lord.

Tick tock.

....

ALSO ON THIS DAY . . .

1956—Vyacheslav Ivanov (USSR) won the Olympic single sculls gold medal, but in his excitement he jumped for joy and lost his medal as it sank into the river.

1979—The International Olympic Committee voted to readmit China after twenty-one years.

2005—In sumo wrestling, Asashoryu Akinori (Mongolia) won his eighty-third bout of the year to clinch the championship in the November basho (tournament), sweeping all six basho in 2005 and winning his seventh one in a row (all were new records).

2006—Nicol David (Malaysia) defeated Natalie Grinham (Australia) to with the Women's World Open Squash Championship, successfully defending her title.

Do not boast about tomorrow, for you do not know what a day may bring forth.
Proverbs 27:1

Fun Fact In the 2010 Big Ten basketball tournament, Michigan was leading Ohio State 68-66 with 2.2 seconds left on the game clock. Evan Turner took the inbounds pass, dribbled up court and drained a thirty-seven-footer at the buzzer to give Ohio State the 69-68 win. "You can't really practice for those moments; you just have to come out and come ready," said the Big Ten player of the year. Turner's final attempt was so close to the buzzer that the play was reviewed. Officials signaled the shot was good, and Ohio State fans went crazy.

BIRTHDAYS:

1943—Jan Stenerud, Fetsund, Norway, NFL place kicker (Chiefs, Packers, Vikings), seven-time all-pro and winner of Super Bowl IV

1966—Sue Wicks, Center Moriches, NY, WNBA forward (NY Liberty)

1983—Matthew Scott Garza, Selma, CA, major-league pitcher (Tampa Bay Rays)

Predictions and Assumptions

On this day in 2009, Duke University beat the University of Connecticut 68-59 in the National Invitational Tournament Season Tip-off.

Before every college athletic season, sports experts predict the top teams in the country and rate them. Then, at early tournaments like this, they begin to see if they were right or wrong (or close). As the season unfolds, the ratings change, depending on the outcomes of games, the quality of teams played, and the margin of victory. In a basketball regular season of more than thirty games, the polls and ratings change often from week to week, especially at the top. At the end of the regular season, the top sixty-four or so teams get invited to the big tournament, and March Madness begins. As the season began, both Duke and UConn were highly rated. In 2009–2010, UConn had a decent regular

season but lost fairly early in the tournament. Duke, on the other hand, won their conference and then the National Championship.

Predictions, assumptions, and ratings are fine for sports, but we should beware of them in other areas of life, especially relationships. We may, for example, come to conclusions about a person because of the way he or she looks, that person's friends, or something that happened. We may assume that someone is athletic because of that person's race. We may think someone is intelligent because of clothes, glasses, and personality. We may think someone is prideful because he or she doesn't say much to us. Or we could assume that a person is tough or a troublemaker because of some of that person's friends.

We don't like to be treated that way; for example, when a teacher seems to predict how we'll do in class when we walk in the room. Or when someone assumes that we did something

for a reason that wasn't even close to the truth. Or when a coach doesn't give us a chance to get on the field. We want to be treated fairly, to be accepted and respected, to have the opportunity to prove ourselves.

Jesus taught what we now call the Golden Rule, treating other people the way we want to be treated. And we want to be like Jesus. His poll is the only one that matters.

Leave the predicting to the sports reporters.

....

ALSO ON THIS DAY . . .

1947—Joe DiMaggio won his third American League MVP award, beating Ted Williams by one vote.

1960—Gordie Howe became the first NHL player to score 1,000 points.

1966—The Washington Redskins defeated the New York Giants 72-41, the highest-scoring NFL game.

2007—At the International Club Friendly at Telstra Stadium, Sydney, New South Wales, Australia, Sydney FC (A-League, beat the Los Angeles Galaxy (MLS) 5-3, despite David Beckham scoring on a bending free kick in the first half.

BIRTHDAYS:

1966—Chryssandra Hines, Bristol, CT, team handball wing, 1996 Olympics

1979—Ricky Carmichael, Clearwater, FL, called the "greatest motocross racer of all time"

1984—Domata Peko, Pago Pago, American Samoa, NFL defensive tackle (Cincinnati Bengals)

So in everything, do to others what you would have them do to you, for this sums up the Law and the Prophets. Matthew 7:12

[UN] [ACT In one preseason poll for the 2009–2010 basketball season, the top ten were as follows: 1-Kansas, 2-Michigan State, 3-Purdue, 4-Kentucky, 5-West Virginia, 6-Connecticut, 7-North Carolina, 8-Butler, 9-Duke, 10-Villanova. North Carolina didn't make the tournament at all, and the championship game was between Duke and Butler.

28 How Much **is Enough?**

On this day in 1989, Rickey Henderson signed a contract for a record $3,000,000 per year with the Oakland Athletics.

When this headline appeared, many people were amazed that an athlete could get that much money for playing just 162 regular season games. That works out to just under $19,000 per game—pretty good for a few hours of hitting, catching, running, and sliding. Since then, contracts have skyrocketed. In 2008, for example, Alex Rodriquez of the Yankees signed a ten-year contract totaling $275 million ($27.5 million a year).

His teammate, Derek Jeter, is in the last year of his ten-year contract for $18.9 million per year. Of the ten highest contracts, eight belong to baseball players (two to race car drivers). Way down at number thirty-eight sits Albert Haynesworth of the Redskins, getting paid a measly $14,285,714 per year (for sixteen regular-season football games). Those numbers don't include endorsement money.

Many defend the salaries: If athletes can get that kind of money in the free enterprise system, then good for them. And we know that many professional athletes set up foundations and use their newfound wealth for good, feeding the poor, helping young people, giving to their schools and communities, and more. Albert Pujols, Tim Tebow, A. C. Green, and others are great examples of this. But what frustrates us are those athletes who squander their money, much like most lottery winners. What drives us crazy are the multimillionaire athletes who want to renegotiate their contracts to get even more. "How much is enough?" we wonder. And we think, "Just give me a million, and I'll be satisfied!"

But would we? The truth is that we tend to always want more—more fun, more food, more toys, and, especially, more money. Many years ago, a very wealthy man was asked how much money would make him happy. He answered, "Just a little bit more." That approach to life always leaves us unsatisfied, unfulfilled, and unhappy. Money isn't bad—and God wants us to use it for good—but it cannot satisfy our deepest longings. We can only find meaning and true happiness in Christ; he alone truly satisfies. And when we trust him and live for him we will discover what Paul told young Timothy: "godliness with contentment is great gain" (1 Timothy 6:6).

Work hard and do your best, of course. But thank God for all you have. Then use it well and be content.

....

ALSO ON THIS DAY . . .

1895—America's first auto race started; six cars traveled fifty-five miles with the winner averaging seven miles per hour.

1981—Bear Bryant won his 315th game to pass Alonzo Stagg and become college football's winningest coach.

1982—The United States beat France to win the seventy-first Davis Cup, 4-1.

2004—The entire Boston Red Sox team was named *Sports Illustrated*'s Sportsmen of the Year for their 2004 World Series victory over the St. Louis Cardinals, the first time that an entire professional sports team had received that honor.

I am not saying this because I am in need, for I have learned to be content whatever the circumstances. I know what it is to be in need, and I know what it is to have plenty. I have learned the secret of being content in any and every situation, whether well fed or hungry, whether living in plenty or in want. **Philippians 4:11–12**

Fun Fact According to *Sports Illustrated*, here's what some athletes made in 2006. The totals include endorsement money, usually much more than the salary or winnings: Michael Schumacher—$80 million, Tiger Woods—$97 million, David Beckham—$50 million, Phil Mickelson—$46 million, Shaquille O'Neal—$34 million, Kobe Bryant—$34 million, Carson Palmer—$32 million, LeBron James—$29 million, Dale Earnhardt Jr.—$26 million, Maria Sharapova—$20 million.

BIRTHDAYS:

1942—Paul Warfield, Warren, OH, NFL wide receiver (Cleveland Browns, Miami Dolphins)

1958—Dave Righetti, San Jose, CA, major-league starter and relief pitcher (Yankees, Giants, Athletics, Blue Jays, White Sox), two-time all-star, threw a no-hitter (1983)

1984—Andrew Bogut, Melbourne, Australia, NBA center (Milwaukee Bucks)

Extreme **Rivalries**

On this day in 2008, Georgia Tech beat Georgia in the "Clean, Old-Fashioned Hate" game, 45-42.

Traditional sport rivalries are common. Every high school has another school in the conference or community that they play annually with great fanfare. Those rivalries can divide a community (north vs. south or one side of the river vs. the other, etc.). Colleges and universities have these rivalries, too. Some have very colorful names such as "Border Showdown" (Kansas vs. Kansas State), "Civil War" (Oregon vs. Oregon State), "Bayou Bucket" (Rice vs. Houston), "Holy War" (Brigham Young vs. Utah), "Egg Bowl" (Mississippi vs. Mississippi State), and "Red River Shootout" (Oklahoma vs. Texas).

This annual football game between Georgia and Georgia Tech has probably the most interesting title: "Clean, Old-Fashioned Hate." Going into this game, the Georgia Bulldogs had

hopes for a postseason BCS bowl. But the Yellow Jackets came back from being sixteen points down in the first half and with a 26-0 run in the third quarter pulled out the win. Emotions run high and play a big factor in a game like this, but should it be called the "hate" game?

Certainly whoever came up with that title meant it in a humorous way, especially with the words "clean" and "old-fashioned" in it, but the title carries a lot of truth. Unfortunately anger and hate come into play in many of these games, among players and especially among fans, with fights breaking out on the field and in the stands. Too often we'll hear of ugly incidents when players or fans lost it. Reports of vandalism and worse arise every year. And some athletes try to harm their opponents with cheap shots or worse.

Sports should be about having fun and using skills and abilities. Yes, winning is important, but not at the expense of integrity and character. Good sportsmanship

means playing hard and fair, shaking hands afterward, and respecting our opponents on and off the field. Christians, especially, should be known for playing, winning, and losing the right way. In football, some Christian college athletes help up their opponents after knocking them down. And they huddle to pray for an injured player on the other team. Jesus tells us to love our enemies. Certainly that applies to athletic opponents. Athletes who have to work up anger and hate to play hard should switch sports.

Play your best and with emotion, but not with anger and hate.

ALSO ON THIS DAY . . .

1934—The Chicago Bears beat the Detroit Lions 19-16 in the first NFL game broadcast nationally.

1987—Joe Montana of the San Francisco 49ers completed twenty-two consecutive passes for an NFL record.

2006—For the second time in less than a week, the top team in the Associated Press NCAA Men's Division I basketball poll lost, as this week's number one team, Ohio State, was beaten by number six, North Carolina, 98-89, in the "Dean Dome."

2008—Simon Amman (Switzerland) won the ski jumping World Cup in Kuusamo, Finland.

BIRTHDAYS:

1927—Vin Scully, Bronx, NY, long-time radio broadcaster for the Brooklyn and Los Angeles Dodgers

1969—Kasey Keller, Olympia, WA, professional soccer goalie (Seattle Sounders and US National Team)

1982—Ashley Force, Yorba Linda, CA, funny car drag racer for John Force Racing

1985—Shannon Brown, Maywood, IL, NBA guard (Cavaliers, Bulls, Bobcats, Lakers)

[Jesus is speaking] "You have heard that it was said, 'Love your neighbor and hate your enemy.' But I tell you: Love your enemies and pray for those who persecute you." **Matthew 5:43–44**

Fun Fact
Separated by seventy miles, the University of Georgia and Georgia Tech have been heated rivals since 1893. Georgia's Chapel Bell and Bulldog statue and Tech's Ramblin' Wreck (Ford Model A) have been stolen numerous times by students from the other school. Many fans refuse to even have any clothing, food, or other materials of their rival's school colors; for example, Georgia fans not eating mustard or Georgia Tech fans not using red pens.

1. What team did Terrell Owens play for when he scored his 100th career receiving touchdown? (November 5)

2. What NFL Hall-of-Fame defensive end coined the phrase "quarterback sack?" (November 20)

3. How many years did Ken Griffey Jr. play in the major leagues? (November 13)

4. How many National League MVP awards did catcher Roy Campanella win? (November 1)

5. What is the Rolex Farr 40 North American Championship? (November 22)

6. What two college teams compete in the annual "Clean, Old-Fashioned Hate" game? (November 29)

7. What position did Jeff Reed play for the Pittsburgh Steelers? (November 26)

8. What is the largest single-day mountain-bike race in America? (November 7)

9. Who was the youngest player in NBA history to score 4,000 points? (November 14)

10. In what year did the Orlando Magic play their first NBA game? (November 4)

11. In what year did Bear Bryant win his 315th game as a college football coach? (November 28)

12. Who did the United States men's soccer team beat to qualify for the 1990 World Cup? (November 19)

13. To what color did Notre Dame change its football jerseys in 1927? (November 12)

14. Who made the first official successful climb of El Capitan in 1958? (November 8)

15. With what team did Red Grange play in college? (November 21)

16. Who was the first NHL player to score 1,000 points? (November 27)

17. How many PGA tournaments did Paul Azinger win from 1987 to 1993? (November 6)

18. In what country was Albert Pujols born? (November 15)

19. How many years did Leon Lett play in the NFL? (November 25)

20. In what sports did Jean Driscoll compete? (November 18)

21. Who was the first rookie ever to win the Cy Young award? (November 11)

Featured Events in **November**

Reference **Point**

On this day in 2007, boats left San Sebastián de La Gomera to begin the Atlantic Rowing Race, finishing in the English Harbor, Antigua.

This annual event is a challenging ocean rowing race from the Canary Islands to the West Indies, a distance of almost 3,000 miles. Ocean rowing is as much a psychological as a physical

challenge. Rowers often have to endure long periods at sea, with no land in sight and with help often many days if not weeks away. Then there's the weather. Instead of the normal trade winds that help rowers, often they have to contend with strong cross- or headwinds, often associated with a nearby tropical storm.

One of the challenges in rowing is staying on course, especially on an open body of water like the ocean or a lake. That's because rowers sit with their backs to the front of the boat as they pull on the oars. So they're moving backwards and can't see where they're going. Ocean rowers have sophisticated navigation equipment to help keep them on course, but for our journey, we'll need another guidance system.

So how does a single rower trying to get to a spot on the other side of the lake keep a straight line while rowing backwards? Actually, the answer is simple: we need to choose a reference point on the opposite bank, a fixed object directly in line with the direction we want to go. Then we keep our eyes on that point as we row. It works. The reference point makes the difference. But we need to choose the right object, one that is stationary, such as a tree or a house. And it needs to be in the right place. Then we need to

keep our eyes on it, not looking side to side or behind but trusting that point and keeping on line.

As we "row" through life, we can have worthy goals. We can even have great equipment and training (very important). But we'll only stay on track by keeping focused on our Reference Point—our Lord and Savior Jesus Christ. We do this by reading God's Word, talking to our Father in prayer—about everything—and following Jesus as our example. If we do that, even in bad weather and high waves, with God's help we'll get to the other shore.

....

ALSO ON THIS DAY . . .

1963—The Major League Baseball Rules Committee banned oversized catcher's mitts, effective in 1965.

1989—Andre Ware (quarterback) of the University of Houston won the fifty-fifth Heisman Trophy Award.

1990—The United States won the seventy-ninth Davis Cup, beating Australia 3-2.

2006—Lincoln University beat Ohio State at Marion, 201-78, to win the consolation game at the Division III Salem University Invitational. The 123-point margin of victory is the largest in NCAA history.

Fix your thoughts on Jesus, the apostle and high priest whom we confess. Hebrews 3:1

Fun Fact Although ocean rowing competitions have grown in recent years, as of a few years ago, fewer people had rowed an ocean than had climbed Mt. Everest or been into space. This 2007 race was won by Pura Vida (a four), finishing on January 19, 2008, and taking 48 days, 2 hours, and 52 minutes to complete the journey.

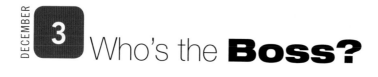

3 Who's the **Boss?**

ON THIS DAY IN 1997, GOLDEN STATE WARRIOR GUARD LATRELL SPREWELL'S FOUR-YEAR, $32-MILLION CONTRACT WAS TERMINATED FOR ATTACKING HIS COACH, P. J. CARLESIMO.

During practice on December 1, 1997, Coach Carlesimo yelled to Sprewell to "put a little mustard" on his passes. Sprewell responded that he was not in the mood for criticism and told the coach to stay away. When the coach approached, Sprewell threatened to kill him and dragged him to the ground by his throat, choking him for ten to fifteen seconds before being pulled off by his teammates. About twenty minutes later, Sprewell returned and took a swing at his coach before being dragged away again.

Latrell Sprewell was actually a decent ballplayer, a four-time NBA all-star who played fourteen years in the league. But this incident has defined his career. Because of his attack on his coach, Sprewell was suspended the remainder of the season (sixty-eight games) and then traded to New York. We don't know what led up to the confrontation—maybe Sprewell was just in a bad mood. But there's no excuse for that kind of behavior, especially not to that extreme.

The Bible is clear about how we should respond to those in authority over us, beginning with our parents. Scripture also talks about the government, bosses, teachers, and spiritual leaders. In all cases, while under their authority we are to submit to them, pray for them, and respect them. The exception would be if they told us to sin, to disobey God—he's our ultimate authority.

At some time or another, we all have someone over us who rubs us the wrong way. It may be a teacher who doesn't like our work, a yelling, negative coach; a business or political leader with strange ideas; or even a Sunday school teacher or pastor. We won't always be under their authority, but while we are, we should work at having a good attitude and be respectful—as though we were working for God.

Actually, we are. And by being good children, workers, students, employees, citizens, and church members, we glorify him.

Submit, endure, and see what lessons God is teaching you with this "boss."

....

ALSO ON THIS DAY . . .

1999—Tori Murden became the first American and the first woman to row alone across the Atlantic, from the Canary Islands to the Caribbean, taking eighty-two days and covering 3,000 miles.

2005—USC beat UCLA 66-19 to earn a trip to the Rose Bowl, where they would play Texas (for the national championship), thanks to Heisman Trophy candidate Reggie Bush's 260 yards rushing and two touchdowns.

2006—Poland defeated Brazil 12-25, 22-25, 17-25 to win the gold medal at the volleyball FIVB Men's World Championships.

2009—Hofstra University voted to eliminate football after this season because of large monetary losses. The school became the second in the Colonial Athletic Association to drop the sport in two weeks.

BIRTHDAYS:

1960—Mike Ramsey, Minneapolis, MN, NHL defenseman (Sabres, Penguins, Red Wings) and winner of the Olympic gold medal, 1980

1965—Katarina Witt, born in Staaken, East Germany, figure skater, winner of two Olympic gold medals, 1984 and 1988

1970—Lindsey Hunter, Utica, MS, NBA guard (Pistons, Bucks, Lakers, Raptors, Bulls), two-time NBA Champion (2002, 2004)

Slaves, obey your earthly masters with deep respect and fear. Serve them sincerely as you would serve Christ. Try to please them all the time, not just when they are watching you. As slaves of Christ, do the will of God with all your heart. Work with enthusiasm, as though you were working for the Lord rather than for people. Remember that the Lord will reward each one of us for the good we do, whether we are slaves or free. Ephesians 6:5–8, NLT

Fun Fact Over his career, Sprewell started 868 of 913 games he played in, averaging 18.8 points, 4.2 assists, and 4.1 rebounds per game. He was named to the All-NBA First Team and the All-NBA Defensive Second Team at the end of his second season. Sprewell's career ended unexpectedly when he refused a $21-million three-year contract offer from the Timberwolves and no other teams in the league were able to make a deal with him. These days he's out of basketball and seems to be in financial trouble.

Overconfident

On this day in 1996, the Orlando Magic tied the NBA record of fewest points scored since the inception of the twenty-four-second clock, losing to Cleveland Cavaliers 84-57.

Almost anything can happen in a basketball game to determine the outcome. Players can get hurt, a good shooter can be off while a poor shooter can't miss, and the ball can take some lucky, or unlucky, bounces. But how could a team of highly paid, skilled, and in-shape professional athletes get only about half of what they usually score? For Orlando to only score fifty-seven points and to lose to Cleveland is remarkable. The previous season, the Magic had finished with a 60-22 record, first in the Atlantic Division. The Cavaliers' record was

45-37, third in the Central Division. So what was the problem this night? Perhaps the Magic players were overconfident. They had a better team and had just beaten the Cavaliers a few days before (November 30). So they came out expecting to win easily . . . and were surprised.

We should never underestimate an opponent, assuming that all we have to do is show up to win. The Magic should have known that, of course. After all, the Cleveland team was also comprised of former all-American athletes who got paid for playing basketball.

Although life can be compared to a game in many ways (which we've done several times in this book), our contest is much more serious, with much more at stake and with a much more powerful opponent than a team of professional athletes. Our adversary, Satan, "prowls around like a roaring lion looking for someone to devour" (1 Peter 5:8). Imagine seeing a lion slowly walking around your

house and thinking: "No big deal. I'll go out and yell at it to scare it away. Better yet, I'll take this water gun—that ought to work!" Talk about being overconfident . . . and foolish . . . and the lion would have lunch.

God is way more powerful than the devil—no contest. But we should take Satan seriously and never try to defeat him in our own strength. And understand this—he knows where we are weak and will attack us there, tempting us to sin and trying to separate us from other believers.

Be prepared—it's a battle.

ALSO ON THIS DAY . . .

1956—Paul Hornung (Notre Dame quarterback) won the twenty-second Heisman Trophy Award.

1988—Amy Benz/John Huston won the LPGA JC Penney Golf Classic (teams consisted of one PGA Tour player and one LPGA Tour player).

2005—In the final of the 2005 College Cup (soccer), the Portland Pilots, behind two goals by Canadian Christine Sinclair, shut out UCLA 4-0, made even more incredible by the fact that the Bruins had shut out all their previous five NCAA tournament opponents before this game.

2009—Meryl Davis and Charlie White (USA) won the Senior Ice Dance at the Grand Prix Final in Tokyo, Japan (169.44).

BIRTHDAYS:

1979—Jay DeMerit, Green Bay, WI, soccer center back (US National Team)

1985—Andrew Brackman, Cincinnati, OH, baseball pitcher (New York Yankees organization)

1986—Martell Webster, Edmonds, WA, NBA small forward (Portland Trailblazers)

> If you do what is right, will you not be accepted? But if you do not do what is right, sin is crouching at your door; it desires to have you, but you must master it. **Genesis 4:7**

Fun Fact Two of the biggest NBA upsets: 1969—the Boston Celtics, who barely made the playoffs, upset the Western Division Champion Los Angeles Lakers in seven games; 1975—the Warriors, who had a regular season of 48-34, shocked the Washington Bullets, who were 60-22, by winning the NBA title in a four-game sweep.

Mountains and **Valleys**

On this day in 2008, Lindsey Vonn (USA) won the downhill event at the Women's World Cup in Lake Louise, Alberta, Canada (1 minute, 26.10 seconds).

What goes up must come down (because of gravity). Also, whoever wants to come down must go up. That's certainly true in skiing. Of all the sports, skiing probably depends on gravity the most, as skiers slip and slide down a variety of slopes. But to be able to slide down a mountain, skiers must first get to the top. Lindsey Vonn has experienced her share of ups and downs in this sport, and not just in her victories and defeats. She has been injured several times, a result of hurtling down at such high speeds. Each time, after healing, she returns to the slopes—to great success.

In 2008, Lindsey won the overall World Cup title, becoming only the second American woman to do so, following Tamara McKinney in 1983. The next year, she repeated as overall World Cup champion, as well as repeating as champion in the downhill and also winning the season championship in Super G by winning the season's final race. At the 2010 Olympics, she was predicted to win several medals, but injuries kept her from dominating. She did, however, win the gold in the downhill and bronze in the Super G.

Life is filled with ups and downs—we experience highs and lows, joys and sorrows, excitement and disappointment, victories and defeats. We can feel as though we're on a roller-coaster ride of emotions. Between mountains, the high points, lie valleys, the low points. And just as in nature, often the valleys follow the mountains. In other words, we may have a mountaintop experience—feeling happy, excited, and on top of the world. But soon after, we may crash emotionally and hit bottom. That's a frustrating, and exhausting, way to live.

A better way would be to not get too carried away by the highs and be better prepared to face the lows. And in both places, to be content, thanking God for what he is doing in our lives and for his presence and asking for his direction for our next steps.

Let God even out your path and make it straight.

ALSO ON THIS DAY . . .

1973—Ron Santo of the Chicago Cubs became the first MLB player to veto his trade.

1981—Marcus Allen (USC running back) won the forty-seventh Heisman Trophy Award.

1996—Portland's Jermaine O'Neal, eighteen, became the youngest NBA player.

2009—Daniel Ross (Australia) won the ASP World Qualifying Series (WQS) at Sunset Beach, Oahu, Hawaii, further cementing his reputation as one of the most dangerous surfers on the 2010 ASP Dream Tour.

BIRTHDAYS:

1947—Jim Plunkett, San Jose, CA, NFL quarterback (Patriots, 49ers, Raiders), two-time Super Bowl champion (XV, XVIII), Super Bowl MVP (XV)

1964—Pablo Morales, Chicago, IL, butterfly swimmer, winner of three Olympic gold medals (1984, 1992) and two silver medals (1982)

1973—Corissa Yasen, Omaha, NE, WNBA forward and guard (Sacramento Monarchs)

1985—Josh Smith, College Park, GA, NBA forward (Atlanta Hawks)

> I am not saying this because I am in need, for I have learned to be content whatever the circumstances. I know what it is to be in need, and I know what it is to have plenty. I have learned the secret of being content in any and every situation, whether well fed or hungry, whether living in plenty or in want. **Philippians 4:11–12**

FUN FACT In December 2009, Lindsey bruised her arm badly in a large crash during the opening run of the World Cup giant slalom. Because the arm wasn't fractured, she continued. Despite skiing with her arm in a brace, she won three straight races (two downhills and a Super G) in Austria from January 8–10, 2010. The wins raised her to second among American skiers on the all-time career list for World Cup wins with twenty-eight, passing Phil Mahre and trailing only Bode Miller.

Faith in **Action**

On this day in 2008, Mathieu Crepel (France) won the Men's Big Air at the Snowboarding World Cup in Grenoble, France.

In big air competitions, snowboarders perform tricks after launching high off a special jump built for the event. The competitors aim for height and distance and perform tricks in the air. Then they hope to land cleanly. The winners do all three well. Needless to say, this is not easy, and in their countless hours of practice, snowboarders endure many slips, nasty spills, and crash landings. Obviously monsieur Crepel has put in his hours and has mastered the sport.

Just about anyone can buy a typical snowboarder's outfit and a board and show up to a ramp. But being successful in this sport involves more than looking the part. Or let's take it a step further. Suppose someone decides to become an authority on snowboarding. This person reads articles in books and on the Internet and even learns the lingo, understanding and using words like *jib*, *rail jam*, and *shred*

the gnar. This snowboarding expert could ace any written test on the sport. But would that make this person a snowboarder? Not even close. The proof is in the performance—not the professing or even the knowing, but in the doing.

That pretty much sums up what James is telling us about the Christian life. He says, "Faith by itself, if it is not accompanied by action, is dead. But someone will say, 'You have faith; I have deeds.' Show me your faith without deeds, and I will show you my faith by what I do" (James 2:17–18).

At every snowboarding event, competitors demonstrate what they know by what they do. Knowing about big-air aerodynamics and the construction of the board is fine, but it doesn't mean much when the prize is on the line. It's the same with the Christian life. Yes we should read and study and learn, but we need to put our faith into practice. People will learn about God—his love and plan—and that following Christ makes a difference by looking at us. If our walk doesn't match our talk, then it's big "hot" air.

Learn it, but live it!

ALSO ON THIS DAY . . .

1992—San Francisco 49er Jerry Rice caught a NFL record 101st touchdown.

2004—Vijay Singh won the PGA Tour Player of the Year award, fending a five-year streak by Tiger Woods.

2005—The first international X games began in Dubai.

2009—Steven Holcomb, Justin Olsen, Steve Mesler, and Curtis Tomasevicz (USA) won the four-man bobsled World Cup in Cesana, Italy.

BIRTHDAYS:

1960—Jasmina Perazic Gipe, WNBA guard/forward (NY Liberty)

1982—Alberto Contador, Spanish cyclist and 2007 Tour de France winner

1982—Robbie Gould, Jersey Shore, PA, NFL placekicker (Chicago Bears)

Do not merely listen to the word, and so deceive yourselves. Do what it says. **James 1:22**

[un] [ACT] Snowboarding was inspired by skateboarding, surfing, and skiing. It was developed in the USA in the 1960s and the 1970s and became a Winter Olympic sport in 1998. Many believe that the first snowboard was invented and manufactured in Utah in the early 1970s, but some trace it to Muskegon, Michigan, in 1965. Whatever—it's gnarly.

Well-known Sporting Events

Match the nickname to the yearly event.

1. Frozen Four

2. March Madness

3. Granddaddy of Them All

4. Fall Classic

5. Run for the Roses

6. Crosstown Cup

7. Honda SuperClasico

8. Midsummer Classic

9. Subway Series

10. Super Series

a. New York Yankees vs. New York Mets

b. World Series

c. Chicago Cubs vs. Chicago White Sox

d. MLS Los Angeles Galaxy vs. Chivas USA

e. Rose Bowl Game

f. MLB all-star Games

g. NCAA Division I Men's Basketball Championship

h. Exhibition games between Soviet and NHL, '76-'91

i. Kentucky Derby

j. NCAA Men's Ice Hockey Championship

ANSWERS: 1.j, 2.g, 3.e, 4.b, 5.i, 6.c, 7.d, 8.f, 9.a, 10.h

Fearless

On this day in 2006, B. J. Schumacher won the Bull Riding event at the Wrangler National Finals Rodeo in Las Vegas.

Bull riding has been called "the most dangerous eight seconds in sports." That figures, since it involves a rider getting on the back of a huge, violent animal (that doesn't want someone on its back) and trying to stay on for at least eight seconds while the animal attempts furiously to buck off the rider.

In another event at this rodeo, K. C. Jones was able to wrestle a steer to the ground in 3.5 seconds to win the Steer Wrestling competition. In this contest, also called bulldogging, a horse-mounted rider chases a steer, then drops from the horse and wrestles the steer to the ground by twisting its horns. This is another event with a high risk of injury to the cowboy.

Many sports are risky—mountain climbing, skateboarding, skiing, and racecar driving, to name a few. Others, such as table tennis, golf, fly-fishing, and curling, not so much. But for the risky sports, athletes have to overcome their fears. Knowing they could be seriously injured or worse, they go ahead and compete.

Some people are so tentative and afraid that they try to avoid anything that even hints of risk. But let's face it—all of life is risky. Even in the mildest of activities, something could go terribly wrong. Not that we should take foolish chances, but we need to step out in faith, to take risks in recreation, relationships, career, and just living in general. The only way to be almost totally safe would be to stay inside, in a padded house, all the time.

God wants us to live without fear. This means being sensible about what we do and where we go but trusting him every step of the way. He has promised to be with us, to protect us, and to get us home safely. Check out Deuteronomy 31:6: "So be strong and courageous! Do not be afraid and do not panic before them. For the Lord your God will personally go ahead of you. He will neither fail you nor abandon you" (NLT).

These promises don't guarantee a life without pain, struggles, and losses. But we know that no matter what happens our loving Father is in control and that his way is best, for us and for our world.

Live without fear.

. . . .

ALSO ON THIS DAY . . .

1925—Professional football was a hit in New York City as 73,000 fans watched Red Grange and the Chicago Bears beat the New York Giants.

1961—Wilt Chamberlain of the Philadelphia Warriors scored sixty-seven points against New York.

1978—In the first game of the Women's Pro Basketball League (WBL), the Chicago Hustle played the Milwaukee Does.

1995—Eddie George (Ohio State running back) won the sixty-first Heisman Trophy Award.

BIRTHDAYS:

1942—Dick Butkus, Chicago, IL, NFL Hall-of-Fame linebacker (Bears), eight-time Pro Bowl selection, sportscaster

1968—Kurt Angle, Pittsburgh, PA, 220-pound, freestyle wrestler, winner of the Olympic gold medal, 1996

1978—Mandy James, Jacksonville, FL, rhythmic gymnast (1996 Olympics)

[Jesus said] "Don't be afraid of those who want to kill your body; they cannot touch your soul. Fear only God, who can destroy both soul and body in hell. What is the price of two sparrows—one copper coin? But not a single sparrow can fall to the ground without your Father knowing it. And the very hairs on your head are all numbered. So don't be afraid; you are more valuable to God than a whole flock of sparrows. **Matthew 10:28-31, NLT**

Fun Fact Here are a few rodeo records. The highest score in bull riding: 100 points—perfect score scored by Wade Leslie (Central Point, OR, in 1991). The fastest time in steer wrestling: 2.2 seconds posted by Oral Zumwalt in 1930 (no "barrier"—breakaway rope pulled across the roping chutes—at this time); 2.4 seconds posted by Jim Bynum and Todd Whatley (Marietta, OK, in 1955), Gene Melton (Pecatonia, IL, in 1976), and Carl Deaton (Tulsa, OK, in 1976).

10 Wins and Losses

On this day in 2006, the Minnesota Vikings beat the Detroit Lions 30-20.

This event may not seem like a big deal; after all, what's one game out of many on one Sunday out of sixteen in the regular season? But for the Detroit Lions players, it was a typical day of frustration. The team had begun the decade in decent shape, going 9-7 in the 2000–2001 season. But since then, the losses have mounted (including this one). Their record from that season through 2009 stands at 33 wins and 95 losses, including 2008, where they became the only team in NFL history to go winless, at 0-16. This decade has definitely turned into one of football futility for the Lions and their fans. How do you think the players felt as they prepared for the next game on the schedule, especially in 2008, strapping on the pads, listening to the coaches' plans and pep talks, trying to get motivated, psyched up? Anyone who has endured loss after loss begins to feel like a loser. And even if they didn't admit it, subconsciously at least, those Lions probably expected to lose.

That happens. It's the reason some coaches try hard to win the preseason games, even though those games don't count. They want the players to get used to winning and expecting to win.

Everyone wants to be on a winning team, to have a winning streak: the salesperson with sales, the student with grades, the politician with votes, the author with book sales, and everybody with friendships. We know we can't win every game—life has downs as well as ups. But when the losses begin to add up, one after another with no end in sight, we can lose hope and feel discouraged—like losers.

That's when we should remember God's encouraging words—that he loves us, created us with a purpose and plan for our lives, is working together all of our experiences for our good and his glory, is with us every step and in every situation, and will get us safely home. And get this, when we read the end of his book, Revelation, we learn that in the end, God is totally victorious—we win!

Feeling like a loser? Get your head up. You're on a winning streak that lasts into eternity.

ALSO ON THIS DAY . . .

1896—Wesleyan beat Yale 4-3 in the first intercollegiate basketball game.

1961—Houston Oiler Billy Cannon gained a record 373 yards against the New York Titans (AFL).

1983—Martina Navratilova beat K. Jordan in the fifty-eighth Australian Women's Tennis Open.

2008—C. C. Sabathia signed a seven-year, $160-million deal with the New York Yankees, making Sabathia the highest-paid pitcher in baseball history, with the deal averaging out to nearly $23 million a year.

Then, together with them, we who are still alive and remain on the earth will be caught up in the clouds to meet the Lord in the air. Then we will be with the Lord forever. 1 Thessalonians 4:17, NLT

[UN]ACT In 2008, the Detroit Lions began their seventy-ninth season in fine fashion, going 4-0 in the preseason. But then it fell apart as they lost all sixteen regular-season games. They were mathematically eliminated from playoff contention after week eleven, and their general manager lost his job.

BIRTHDAYS:

1963—Michael Lofton, Montgomery, AL, fencer—sabre, 1996 Olympics

1973—Bernard Holsey, Rome, GA, NFL defensive tackle (Giants, Colts, Patriots, Redskins)

1985—T. J. Hensick, Howell, MI, NHL center (Colorado Avalanche), US National Team

Trading **Places**

On this day in 1975, the New York Yankees traded George "Doc" Medich to the Pittsburgh Pirates for Willie Randolph, Dock Ellis, and Ken Brett.

This was one of the best trades the Yankees have ever made. "Doc" Medich was a good major-league pitcher, but Dock Ellis and Ken Brett were good players, too, and Willie Randolph turned out to be a six-time all-star and the Yankees' team captain. One for three . . . and an all-star! When the Pirates agreed to the trade, they probably thought they had made a wise move. They didn't see the potential in Randolph, but he became a key member of a great team, at the plate and in the field. Sometimes trades work out that way. In sports, when two clubs trade players, both teams expect that it will be good for them. No one tries to make a bad deal. And when one happens, when we get taken, we become skeptical the next time an offer is made. The Pirates probably didn't rush into more trades with the Yankees any time soon.

How would you react if someone proposed an amazing deal that seemed too good to be true? Let's say, for example, that a guy offered you $1,000 for your old bicycle—that would be a great trade, right? You might think, "Wow—I'll take it!" but you probably also would have doubts, wondering what could be so valuable about your bike. And if you had been swindled or cheated before, you probably wouldn't make the deal, no matter how great it sounded.

So along comes Jesus, and he says, "I'll make you a trade. You give me your sin and weakness and death, and I'll give you forgiveness and strength and eternal life."

When most people hear that, they think, "What's the catch? That's sounds much too simple and way too good to be true."

And Jesus answers, "All three. It's simple, too good, and true. The best part—it's free. Just give me your life, and I'll give you mine! I love you, you know."

That's the transaction. It's the gospel message. Thank God for this amazing deal through his amazing grace.

....

ALSO ON THIS DAY . . .

1866—The first yacht race across the Atlantic Ocean took place.

1983—Mats Wilander beat Ivan Lendl in the seventy-second Australian Men's Tennis Open.

2008—Alexe Gilles (USA) won the Junior Ladies Short Program and the Figure Skating Junior Grand Prix Final in Goyang, South Korea.

2009—Following a tumultuous two weeks in which he faced allegations of numerous extramarital affairs, Tiger Woods admitted to infidelity and announced he would be taking an indefinite leave from professional golf in an attempt to save his marriage.

BIRTHDAYS:

1967—Jackie Gallagher-Smith, Marion, IN, LPGA golfer

1972—Francisco Rodriguez, Brooklyn, NY, major-league pitcher (Minnesota Twins)

1988—Tim Southee, Whangarei, New Zealand, cricket right-arm fast-medium bowler and hard-hitting lower-order batsman.

> For all have sinned and fall short of the glory of God, and are justified freely by his grace through the redemption that came by Christ Jesus. **Romans 3:23–24**

Fun Fact
Eventually Willie Randolph played for six major-league teams: Pirates (1975), Yankees (1976–1988), Dodgers (1989–1990), Athletics (1990), Brewers (1991), and Mets (1992). He has also been a major-league coach (Yankees and Brewers) and field manager (Mets). In these roles he has won six world championships.

12 Giving **Back**

On this day in 2009, Ndamukong Suh (Nebraska) came in fourth in the voting for the Heisman Trophy.

Fourth? Yes, behind winner Mark Ingram (Alabama), Toby Gerhart (Stanford), and Colt McCoy (Texas) and just ahead of Tim Tebow (Florida). Having a defensive lineman seriously considered for this award is highly remarkable. Usually, offensive players, such as a quarterback or running back (as with Mark Ingram) win. Suh had already won the 2009 Bronko Nagurski Trophy as the top defensive player in the nation. He also won the AP College Football Player of the Year, the Chuck Bednarik Award, and the Outland Trophy. Clearly this man can play football. The professional scouts agreed, and he was drafted as second overall in the 2010 NFL Draft by the Detroit Lions.

More remarkable than football ability, however, is Suh's character and generosity. Even before being drafted by the NFL and signing a lucrative contract, he announced that he would be donating $2.6 million to his alma mater, the University of Nebraska. Two million dollars of his gift would go to the athletic department for its strength and conditioning program, and the rest would be used as an endowed scholarship for the College of Engineering. This gift will be the largest single charitable contribution by any former player, and he made the pledge before receiving a penny as a professional player. After the draft, he said he looked forward to working with kids in the inner city.

Now that's a man with his priorities in order—giving back before he has been given anything. What a great example and contrast to so many athletes who get the big bucks and squander it on selfish indulgence. Soon the temptations will come, so let's pray that Suh can keep his values in line.

Suh's attitude of giving back to those who helped him along the way and of reaching out to those in need reminds us of Jesus' teachings. He told the rich young man to give up his wealth and follow him (Luke 18:22), and he said that what we did to the "least of these" we did to him (Matthew 26:40). Money, fame, power, and possessions aren't important and should never be first in our lives. Only Jesus should live in that space.

What can you do to give back, even now, way before you sign that big contract?

ALSO ON THIS DAY . . .

1899—George F. Bryant of Boston patented the wooden golf tee.

2004—The Indiana Hoosiers defeated the UCSB Gauchos 3-2 on penalties (they tied 1-1) to win the NCAA Division I men's soccer championship.

2009—In the Freestyle Skiing World Cup at Suomu, Finland: Jesper Bjoernlund of Sweden beat Bryon Wilson (USA) and Nathan Roberts (USA) to win the men's moguls; Hannah Kearney (USA) won the women's moguls.

BIRTHDAYS:

1952—Cathy Rigby McCoy, Los Alamitos, CA, gymnast, 1968 Olympics

1965—Laurie Grover-Tavares, Newark, NJ, biathlete, 1994 Olympics

1967—John Randle, Hearne, TX, Hall-of-Fame NFL defensive tackle (Minnesota Vikings, Seattle Seahawks), seven-time Pro Bowl selection, six-time all-pro

1981—Ronnie Brown, Rome, GA, NFL running back (Miami Dolphins)

Remember this: Whoever sows sparingly will also reap sparingly, and whoever sows generously will also reap generously. Each man should give what he has decided in his heart to give, not reluctantly or under compulsion, for God loves a cheerful giver. **2 Corinthians 9:6–7**

Fun Fact
Suh's mother, Bernadette, (an elementary school teacher) was born in Jamaica and is a graduate of Southern Oregon University. His father (a machinist) is from Cameroon. His parents met in Portland, Oregon, and were married there. In the Ngemba ethnic group of Cameroon, Ndamukong means "house of spears." Suh is the second oldest of four children, with three sisters.

Preparing **the Way**

On this day in 2008, Scotland beat Norway to win the men's European Curling Championship in Örnsköldsvik, Sweden, and Switzerland defeated Sweden for the women's title.

In curling, two teams, with four players each, take turns sliding heavy, polished granite stones down a sheet of ice toward a circular target, called the "house" (similar to shuffleboard). Each team has eight stones, and the goal is to get the highest score. Points are scored for the stones resting closest to the center of the target at the conclusion of each round (called "end"). A full game may have eight or ten ends. The player sliding the stone (the "curler") can spin the stone and cause it to curve, but two "sweepers" also help, using brooms to sweep the ice in front of the stone to influence it to go faster or alter its direction.

These sweepers play a crucial role as they prepare the way for the stone to take. Their purpose is to reduce friction underneath the stone and to decrease the amount of curl. Because stones curl more as they slow down, sweeping early tends to increase distance as well as straighten the path. Sweepers need to measure the pressure and speed of their brushes and know when to sweep. When the ice in front of the stone is swept, a stone will usually travel both farther and straighter. The stone moves toward the house with sweepers preparing the way.

The phrase "prepare the way" may sound familiar. It's how the Bible describes John the Baptist's role: "This is he who was spoken of through the prophet Isaiah: 'A voice of one calling in the desert, "Prepare the way for the Lord, make straight paths for him"'" (Matthew 3:3). Sounds a little like curling.

John preached boldly to anyone who would listen, and his message was simple: turn from your sins; get ready for the coming Messiah. And when Jesus arrived, he declared, "Look, the Lamb of God, who takes away the sin of the world!" (John 1:29). John pointed people to Jesus.

God expects us to do the same, to prepare the way for the Savior. We can do that by how we live and by what we say. When people ask about our actions and words, we can direct them to Jesus.

Got your broom ready? Prepare the way for the Lord; make a straight path for him.

....

ALSO ON THIS DAY . . .

1956—The Brooklyn Dodgers traded Jackie Robinson to the New York Giants for pitcher Dick Littlefield and $35,000; Robinson retired.

1983—In the highest-scoring NBA game, the Detroit Pistons beat the Denver Nuggets 186-184 (3 overtimes).

2008—Madison Chock and Greg Zuerlein (USA) took first, with Madison Hubbell and Keiffer Hubbell (USA) taking second in the junior ice dance; Becky Bereswill (USA) won first in the junior ladies, with Alexe Gilles taking third; Jeremy Abbott (USA) won the senior men's competition at the figure skating Grand Prix and Junior Grand Prix in Goyang, South Korea.

2009—In nine-ball, Team USA won the Mosconi Cup in Las Vegas for the first time in four years and the eleventh time overall.

Preach the Word; be prepared in season and out of season; correct, rebuke and encourage—with great patience and careful instruction. 2 Timothy 4:2

Fun Fact Some curling tournaments offer cash prizes, but full-time professional curlers are few. In 1998, curling returned to the Winter Olympics with men's and women's tournaments after not having been on the official program since 1924. Because strategy, skill, and experience are more valuable in curling than speed, stamina, and strength, most competitive curlers are older than their counterparts in other sports. Curling is particularly popular in Canada. In 2008, the United States Curling Association celebrated its fiftieth anniversary and had more than 13,000 curlers and 135 clubs.

Nicknames in Sports History

Match the nickname to the historical event, team, or player.

1. The Immaculate Reception
2. Sweetness
3. Purple People Eaters
4. Phi Slamma Jamma
5. The Greatest Show on Turf
6. Steel Curtain
7. The Thrilla in Manila
8. The Miracle on Ice
9. The Drive
10. The Great One

a. University of Houston Men's basketball team, '82–84
b. Al Michaels' call in Olympic Hockey
c. Ali vs. Frazier boxing match
d. Denver beats Cleveland
e. Pittsburgh Steelers pass play in 1972
f. St. Louis Rams offense 1999–2001
g. Walter Payton
h. Wayne Gretzky
i. Pittsburgh Steelers defense
j. Minnesota Vikings defensive line 1970s

ANSWERS: 1.e, 2.g, 3.j, 4.a, 5.f, 6.i, 7.c, 8.b, 9.d, 10.h

Challenging Opportunities

On this day in 1996, mountain climber Todd Huston was mentioned in an article in *Forbes* magazine.

This may seem like a strange event to highlight, but *Forbes* (a business magazine) doesn't often mention athletes, especially a mountain climber. But Todd Huston is an unexpected person to engage in this sport because he has only one leg. Actually, the article was about the latest advances in artificial limbs and also mentioned Oscar Pistorius, whom we highlighted on May 16. But let's talk about Todd Huston.

Fourteen-year-old Todd was waterskiing and was in the water a few feet behind the boat, trying to get free of the ski rope and ready to be pulled up. Suddenly the boat was accidently put into reverse and began moving toward him. Todd tried to swim away, but he was tangled in the rope, and his legs got sucked into the propellers. As he was pulled from the bloody water, he could see that both legs were badly mangled. He almost died a couple of times, but the doctors saved his life and his legs. Eventually, however, his right leg had to be amputated just below the knee. So Todd decided to make the most of his life as a one-legged man. A few years later, he joined a team that wanted to climb the highest points in all fifty states. That would be challenging for anyone, especially someone with just one good leg. But he did it, shattering the record for all climbers. The previous record had been 101 days; Todd accomplished this in 66, from June 1 to August 7, 1994. Climbing the heights of Nebraska or Kansas wouldn't be dangerous, but what about Alaska, where Mt. McKinley stands a formidable 20,320 feet. Todd did it.

A strong Christian, Todd now spends his life telling people about his experiences and about Christ. He says that anyone who has done anything great has taken falls on the way to reaching his or her goals. The fall is not important, just that we get back up every time. He wants his audiences to remember that every challenge has an opportunity. Todd never knew he'd climb mountains—but he did. Todd never knew he'd inspire and motivate thousands by telling his story—but he does. See what God can do!

How have you "fallen" recently? What challenges do you face? What opportunities do you see? God wants to use every experience to make you more like Christ and to glorify him.

ALSO ON THIS DAY . . .

1929—The Chicago Blackhawks beat the Pittsburgh Pirates in their first game at the Chicago stadium, 3-1.

1972—The Miami Dolphins became the first undefeated NFL team (14-0-0).

2005—Appalachian State defeated Northern Iowa 21-16 to win the NCAA Division I-AA national football championship, the first football title for the Mountaineers and the school's first team NCAA title in any sport.

2006—Theo Bos (Holland) set a new world record at the 200-meter sprint distance in track cycling in Moscow during a 2007 UCI Track Cycling World Cup Classics meeting.

BIRTHDAYS:

1962—William "The Refrigerator" Perry, Aiken, SC, NFL defensive lineman (Chicago Bears, Philadelphia Eagles), winner of Super Bowl XX

1971—Cathy Symon, Washington, DC, rower, 1996 Olympics

1979—Trevor Immelman, Cape Town, South Africa, PGA golfer, Rookie of the Year in 2006, Masters winner in 2008

I have kept my feet from every evil path so that I might obey your word. **Psalm 119:101**

[un]ACT In addition to *Forbes*, Todd has been featured in thousands of publications throughout the world, including *Sports Illustrated*, the *Wall Street Journal*, *Chicken Soup for the Soul—A Second Helping*, and this one. He has been a special guest on *CBS Year in Sports* and *Robert Schuller's Hour of Power* and has been interviewed on ABC, NBC, CBS, CNN, TNN, *Inside Edition*, and *Extra*, plus numerous radio programs.

Color-blind

On this day in 1965, the Texas Western men's basketball team beat Fresno State University 75-73.

The 1965–66 basketball season was a game-changer in basketball history. Don Haskins was the coach of the Texas Western Miners, and they started this season in fine fashion. This victory ran their record to 5-0. They had a good team and were just learning how good they could be. Eventually their winning streak got to twenty-three when they beat New Mexico State on March 2, 1966. More than the wins, what made this season remarkable is that Coach Haskins started five black players, unheard of in the South. The Miners lost their next game, the last one of the regular season, but then they resumed their winning ways in the NCAA tournament. Eventually they made it to the championship game on March 19 in College Park, Maryland, where they would face mighty Kentucky and its Hall-of-Fame coach, Adolph Rupp. The game would pit Haskins' all-black team against Rupp's all-white squad. At this time in our nation's history, people assumed white players were more intelligent than blacks, so the Wildcats would be able to outsmart and outthink the Miners. Coach Rupp even came into the game saying that five blacks would never beat his team. But Texas Western won the championship, defeating Kentucky 72-65. This game helped integrate college basketball teams in the South. The courage of Don Haskins and his team made a difference.

If you are a "minority," you know the sting of prejudice and discrimination. Even these days, people decide what you are like because of your race. If you aren't a minority person, imagine how you would feel if people assumed that Italians or Norwegians or Greeks or redheads or blue-eyed people were inferior (if one of those characteristics applies to you). You'd hate it, and you would know how unfair it would be. In addition to a person's color or race, we often make assumptions about people based on how they look or dress or speak. But every person has much more to him or her than what is seen on the surface. We should never judge someone based on appearance.

All people, male, female, old, and young of every color, race, and nationality are special creations of God, who loves and values them. And he expects us to do the same.

Don't give prejudice an opening—it's sin. Give every person a chance.

> Then Peter began to speak: "I now realize how true it is that God does not show favoritism." Acts 10:34

Fun Fact On January 13, 2006, Disney released *Glory Road*, a film telling the story of the Texas Western (now the University of Texas at El Paso) 1966 championship season. Coach Haskins was disappointed at the cutting of the movie scenes of his one-on-one games with his African American boyhood friend, Herman Carr. The scenes would have shown Carr's influence on Haskins' game of basketball. Haskins appeared in the movie as an extra by playing a gas station attendant. The year before the movie's release, the city of El Paso renamed the street between its two basketball arenas "Glory Road."

A Bumpy **Ride**

On this day in 2008, Hannah Kearney (USA) won the moguls women's competition at the freestyle skiing World Cup in Meribel, France.

Hannah Kearney loves freestyle skiing, and it shows. Although only in her early twenties (born in 1986), she has enjoyed great success. In addition to this World Cup championship, she had previously won the World Championship in moguls in 2005 and has since won the gold medal in moguls at the 2010 Olympics in Vancouver.

In the mogul competition, skiers must navigate a course with a bunch of large bumps (moguls). As if that weren't difficult enough, on the way down they have to complete at least two trick jumps. They have to do all of this fast and without falling.

Obviously, some skiers (like Hannah) love to ski moguls. They attack the slope, twisting, turning, bouncing, and flying through the course. They see a hill that could strike fear inside many skiers as an exciting challenge. And they work hard at perfecting this mogul-skiing skill.

Life is filled with bumps, and while some are tiny, others would qualify as world-class moguls—losses, conflicts, illnesses, disappointments, reversals, tough times. Given a choice, most people would rather have a smooth, bump-free journey—no moguls, please. We certainly don't seek out problems. But like it or not, we will encounter them, much like a skier poised at the top of a hill, with the only way down through moguls galore. When that happens, what do we do? Well, we have a choice to make and it's not about whether we'll go down the hill.

In life, we don't get to choose our family, the weather, and lots of other things (many more when we're young). But we can always choose our attitude. We can stand at the top of the slope and pout and complain about our lot in life. Or we can pull a Hannah and attack the hill with gusto. It's all in the attitude.

What moguls stand before you, between you and your goal in school, in relationships, at home, or about your future? Choose to see these as exciting opportunities to learn some lessons and even catch some air. Then, with God's help, attack the hill and go for the gold!

....

ALSO ON THIS DAY . . .

1932—The Chicago Bears beat the Portsmouth Spartans 9-0 in the first NFL playoff game.

1990—Baseball's National League announced Buffalo, Denver, Miami, Orlando, Tampa-St. Petersburg, and Washington DC as the six finalists for 1993 expansion (Miami and Denver won)—the teams became the Florida Marlins and the Colorado Rockies.

1994—Greg Norman, Fred Couples, and Paul Azinger won the PGA Wendy's 3-Tour Golf Challenge.

2004—The Stanford Cardinal defeated the Minnesota Lady Gophers three games to one (30-23, 30-27, 30-21) to win the NCAA Division I Women's National Volleyball Championship.

Consider it pure joy, my brothers, whenever you face trials of many kinds, because you know that the testing of your faith develops perseverance. Perseverance must finish its work so that you may be mature and complete, not lacking anything. **James 1:2–4**

FUN FACT Hannah Kearney grew up and still lives in Norwich, Vermont. She graduated from Hanover High School, where she played the trumpet on the school's jazz band into her sophomore year. In Hannah's free time, she likes knitting, riding horses, reading, playing soccer, and watching her brother play hockey.

On this day in 1961, Reggie White was born in Chattanooga, Tennessee.

Reggie White made an impact on the football field. In his fifteen NFL seasons, he was a two-time defensive player of the year, a thirteen-time Pro Bowl selection, and a twelve-time all-pro. He also is a leader in career quarterback sacks, with 198.5. He had great years with the Philadelphia Eagles and Green Bay Packers, and along with his football talent, he brought great leadership to both teams. In one year for the Packers, even though he had knee and hamstring problems, he still put pressure on quarterbacks and had several sacks. Reggie could be ferocious on the field, playing hard and within the rules.

Reggie retired after the 1998 season with the Packers, but then he came out of retirement to play one last year with the Carolina Panthers in 2000, where he started all sixteen games and had six sacks and one forced fumble.

Reggie White also made an impact off the field. A strong Christian, he used every opportunity to tell people about Christ. Reggie said, "Talking about my relationship with Jesus Christ is as natural as breathing for me. I say relationship because it's a day-by-day, night-by-night, ongoing communication between Jesus and me." Reggie's faith-sharing earned him the nickname "Minister of Defense." After his playing days, Reggie shared his testimony all over the country and pastored an inner-city church in Tennessee.

On the morning of December 26, 2004, Reggie was rushed from his home to a hospital, where he was pronounced dead. He had suffered a fatal heart problem. He is buried in Mooresville, North Carolina.

If you've ever played a contact sport like football (basketball, hockey, lacrosse, rugby, soccer, and so forth), you know how quickly emotions like anger and hate flare up. We can feel like hurting our opponent or doing almost anything to win, including dirty plays and cheap shots. Reggie White shows that athletes don't have to resort to that kind of play. Tough, all-out, aggressive, and intense, he played fair and won or lost with class. In other words, he lived out what he preached and became one of the most respected athletes of his generation—both the Eagles and the Packers have retired his number, ninety-two.

You don't have to choose between being a winning athlete or a good Christian. You can be both. Play and live for God's glory.

ALSO ON THIS DAY . . .

1904—The Dawson City hockey team began a nine-day walk to get a boat to Seattle to catch a train to Ottawa to play in the Stanley Cup on January 13, 1905.

1983—The original FIFA World Cup trophy, the Jules Rimet Trophy, was stolen from the headquarters of the Brazilian Football Confederation in Rio de Janeiro.

2004—Norway defeated Denmark, 27-25, to win the European Women's Handball Championship.

2008—In snowmobiling, Tucker Hibbert won the Milwaukee Mile National Snocross Race in West Allis, Wisconsin, in a Monster Energy/Arctic Cat.

As a prisoner for the Lord, then, I urge you to live a life worthy of the calling you have received. **Ephesians 4:1**

Fun Fact On February 4, 2006, Reggie White was elected to the NFL Hall of Fame on the first ballot and was enshrined at the ceremony on August 5, 2006, in Canton, Ohio. Reggie's widow, Sara, gave the acceptance speech. She was introduced by their son, Jeremy, who also released the first copies of his autobiography, *In His Shadow: Growing Up With Reggie White.*

BIRTHDAYS:

1971—Jennifer Dore, Kearny, NJ, rower, 1996 Olympics

1972—Warren Sapp, Orlando, FL, all-pro NFL defensive tackle (Tampa Bay Buccaneers, Oakland Raiders), seven-time Pro Bowl selection, Super Bowl champion (XXXVII)

1985—Jessie Vetter, Cottage Grove, WI, hockey goalkeeper (US National Women's Hockey Team), winner of the Olympic silver medal in 2010

Legacy

On this day in 1981, the San Francisco 49ers beat the New Orleans Saints 21-17 in their last game of the regular season.

In the 49ers' next game, in the playoffs, they beat the New York Giants . . . then the Dallas Cowboys . . . and, finally, the Cincinnati Bengals to win Super Bowl XVI. Two years earlier, the team had won just two games. What a remarkable turnaround. The difference? Head coach Bill Walsh.

The San Francisco 49ers had been playing poorly for a few years. In 1978, their record was 2-14. In Walsh's first season, they had the same record. But the next season, 1980, he turned over the starting quarterback job to Joe Montana (drafted from Notre Dame in the third round the year before), and the 49ers improved to 6-10. Then they won the championship! Bill Walsh's final record with the 49ers was 102-63-1. He won ten of fourteen postseason games, six division titles, three NFC Championship titles, and three Super Bowls. In 1981 and 1983, Walsh was the NFL Coach of the Year, and in 1993, he was elected to the Hall of Fame.

No doubt Bill Walsh was a great football coach. He was also a great coach producer. That is, many coaches who served as Walsh's assistants learned from him and went on to have successful NFL head-coaching careers. Here are a few of the notables in the Walsh "coaching tree": Mike Holmgren, Steve Mariucci, Andy Reid, Jon Gruden, Jim Fassel, Sam Wyche, George Seifert, Dennis Green, Mike Shanahan, Jeff Fisher, Brian Billick, and Tony Dungy. Bill Walsh died in 2007 from leukemia, but he left a coaching legacy.

Great leaders do that— they pass on their values and knowledge to the next generation. The Bible has several examples of this, including Paul with Timothy and Barnabas and Peter with Mark. If these faithful followers of Jesus hadn't passed on their faith to others who would pass it on, we may never have heard about Christ and his salvation.

You are part of this legacy of faith. One or more adults shared the gospel with you and are modeling and teaching you what being a Christian means—parents, grandparents, Sunday school teacher, youth leader, older sibling . . . . And you will find someone for whom you can be a good example, leader, and teacher.

Thank God for your legacy of faith. And pass it on.

....

ALSO ON THIS DAY . . .

1921—The American League voted to return to a best-of-seven World Series, but the National League voted for a best-of-nine, so Commissioner Judge Kenesaw Mountain Landis cast the deciding vote for best-of-seven.

2008—Seth Wescott (USA) won the snowboardcross men's competition at the Snowboarding World Cup in Arosa, Switzerland.

2008—Bill Demong won the Nordic combined ten-km Gudnerson title at the World Cup in Ramsau am Dachstein, Austria.

2009—Lindsey Jacobellis and Faye Gulini (USA) won the women's team snowboard cross at the World Cup in Telluride, United States.

I have been reminded of your sincere faith, which first lived in your grandmother Lois and in your mother Eunice and, I am persuaded, now lives in you also. For this reason I remind you to fan into flame the gift of God, which is in you through the laying on of my hands. 2 Timothy 1:5–6

Fun Fact Bill Walsh's pro-coaching career began in 1966 as an assistant coach with the Oakland Raiders. He was on the Cincinnati Bengals staff from 1968 to 1975; then he went to the San Diego Chargers. Known as an offensive genius, he is credited with shaping Ken Anderson of the Bengals, Dan Fouts of the Chargers, and Joe Montana of the 49ers into great quarterbacks. He also created the "west coast offense," which has been used by most NFL teams.

Fun**Quiz** • December 21 & 22

Match the athlete to the sport.

1. Monica Seles
2. **Katarina Witt**
3. Dick Butkus
4. **John Randle**
5. Sandy Koufax
6. **Ty Cobb**
7. Reggie White
8. **Bill Rogers**
9. Carlton Fisk
10. **Ozzie Smith**
11. Susan Butcher
12. **Tiger Woods**
13. LeBron James

a. Football—linebacker

b. **Football—defensive end**

c. Baseball—shortstop

d. **Golf**

e. Baseball—catcher

f. **Tennis**

g. Dog sled racing

h. **Baseball—pitcher**

i. Football—defensive tackle

j. **Basketball**

k. Baseball—outfielder

l. **Marathon running**

m. Figure skating

ANSWERS: 1.f, 2.m, 3.a, 4.i, 5.h, 6.k, 7.b, 8.l, 9.e, 10.c, 11.g, 12.d, 13.j

Making **the Play**

On this day in 1972, the Pittsburgh Steelers turned around a 7-6 defeat with a last-second touchdown reception against the Oakland Raiders to win 13-7.

This play has been called "the greatest play in [NFL] football history" (NFL films) because of how it happened and the result. This was the AFC divisional playoff game at Three Rivers Stadium in Pittsburgh. The Steelers had the ball on their own forty-yard line, but they were losing, it was fourth down, and only twenty-two seconds were left in the game. As quarterback Terry Bradshaw dropped back, he was pressured by the defensive linemen but was able to fire the football downfield to his halfback, Frenchy Fuqua. Defensive back Jack Tatum arrived with the ball and knocked Fuqua to the ground, sending the ball sailing backward several yards and headed for a game-ending incompletion. But just before the ball hit the ground, Steelers fullback Franco Harris grabbed it and headed for the end zone. He avoided one linebacker; the tight end blocked another. Then he stiff-armed the last defender and

scored, giving the Steelers the fantastic finish and improbable win. Because everything happened so quickly and just right, the play is known as the "Immaculate Reception."

Many factors contributed to the completion, but the most important was Franco Harris continuing to hustle after completing his original assignment. After making his initial block—the normal job of a fullback—he ran downfield in case Bradshaw needed another eligible receiver. Thus he was in the right place at the right time and made the play.

Many daily tasks can seem boring and unimportant. Blocking certainly isn't as glamorous as throwing or catching a pass. But God expects us to faithfully do our jobs and, then, to be alert and aware of other opportunities he gives us to make a difference for him.

You might be teaching a Sunday school class of little kids, and no one seems to be paying attention. But then a child asks why Jesus died on the

cross. You would be there, at the right place and right time, and make the play. Other typical daily or weekly activities could include doing chores, studying, babysitting, or cleaning your room. Sometimes you can wonder if it's worth all the trouble, especially when you're having a bad day. But keep at it; keep doing what you know God wants you to do. Hey, you never know—maybe you'll get an "immaculate reception"!

....

ALSO ON THIS DAY . . .

1946—The University of Tennessee refused to play Duquesne University because of the possibility that Duquesne might use a black player in their basketball game.

1978—The New York Islanders scored seven goals in one period against the New York Rangers; Brian Trottier scored eight points in the game, including five goals and set the NHL record of six points in a single period.

2006—Bob Knight tied Dean Smith's NCAA's Division I record for most wins with his 879th win as Texas Tech defeated Bucknell, 72-60.

2007—The Packers botched four punts on a wintry day and lost any chance of winning the top seed in the NFL playoffs, losing to the Chicago Bears 35-7.

BIRTHDAYS:

1947—Bill Rodgers, Hartford, CT, marathon runner, former American record holder and winner of both the Boston Marathon and New York City Marathon four times

1963—Carol Peterka, Little Falls, MN, team handball backcourt, 1992 and 1996 Olympics

1983—Hanley Ramírez, Samana, Dominican Republic, major-league shortstop (Florida Marlins), two-time all-star, 2006 NL Rookie of the Year

> The one who plants and the one who waters work together with the same purpose. And both will be rewarded for their own hard work. For we are both God's workers. And you are God's field. You are God's building. **1 Corinthians 3:8–9, NLT**

[un ACT] This victory seemed to turn around the Steelers fortunes, although they lost the AFC championship the next week to the Miami Dolphins (who went on to be undefeated champions). The Steelers became the dominant NFL team of the decade, winning four Super Bowls.

24 Playing **Special**

On this day in 2006, the Denver Broncos beat the Cincinnati Bengals 24-23 and moved one step closer to a wild-card spot when the Bengals botched an extra-point attempt with thirty-seven seconds remaining.

Football coaches talk about the three phases of the game: offense, defense, and special teams. They'll often add that teams need to be solid in all three. But that last one seems like the least important of the three. Most football players don't want to spend the game colliding with other big guys running full speed on kickoffs, punts and blocking for kickers—or trying to block kicks—on extra-point and field-goal attempts. People aren't drafted for those positions, and they seem to be the leftovers, where non-starters and rookies play. Some special team plays are especially dangerous—kickoffs and punt returns. But the extra points are just plain boring, and in the pros, automatic.

Not exactly—as this game demonstrated. The Bengals messed up one simple, final extra point and lost the game. Little things matter, and special teams can make a huge difference.

Actually, making a field goal or extra point takes skill and coordination. The center must snap the ball just right; the holder must catch the ball and put it down just right; and the kicker must kick the ball just right. The other eight players must stand their ground to keep the defenders from running through or around them to block the kick. That takes skill, too—knowing who to block and how to hit them so they can't get their hands high.

Because blocking, hiking, and holding are not valued football tasks, good special team players can be hard to find. But they can make the difference in the game.

Every venture has its "special teams." It might be the set-up or take-down crew for an event or program, the keeper of the props for a play, the IT person for a business, or the accompanist for a soloist. In families special-team jobs can involve taking out garbage, cutting grass and pulling weeds, or cleaning the house. And just think of all those special teams at church, fixing meals, setting up rooms, picking up attendance pads and bulletins, visiting the sick, working in the nursery . . . .

These tasks and teams are called special for a reason. Their players may not get the headlines, and people may only notice when they mess up, but they matter.

What's your special team? Your heavenly Coach is watching, and he thinks you're special. So play like it.

. . . .

ALSO ON THIS DAY . . .

1889—Daniel Stover and William Hance patented a bicycle with a back pedal brake.

1950—The Cleveland Browns won the NFL Championship, beating the Los Angeles Rams 30-28.

1982—Chaminade University, with a student body of only 850, beat number one ranked Virginia 77-72 in a Honolulu holiday basketball classic.

2004—Johnny Oates, popular major-league baseball player (Orioles, Braves, Phillies, Dodgers, Yankees) and manager (Orioles, Rangers)—and strong Christian—died of a brain tumor.

There are different kinds of spiritual gifts, but the same Spirit is the source of them all. There are different kinds of service, but we serve the same Lord. God works in different ways, but it is the same God who does the work in all of us. 2 **Corinthians 12:4–6, NLT**

BIRTHDAYS:

1965—Nancy Reno, Elmhurst, IL, WPVA volleyball player, 1996 Olympics

1973—Eddie Pope, Greensboro, NC, soccer defender (DC United, MetroStars, Real Salt Lake), winner of the Olympic gold medal, 1996

1985—David Ragan, Unadilla, GA, NASCAR driver

FUN FACT According to SI.com, these are the NFL All-Pro Special Teams players for 2009: kicker—Sebastian Janikowski, Oakland; punter— Shane Lechler, Oakland; kick returner—Josh Cribbs, Cleveland; punt returner—DeSean Jackson, Philadelphia; all-around player—Blake Costanzo, Cleveland, with fourteen tackles, two forced fumbles, and three fumbles recovered.

Good **News**

On this day in 2001, the Washington Redskins told Justin Skaggs that he would be suiting up for their last regular-season game.

That might not seem like such a big deal, but to Justin Skaggs it probably was the best Christmas gift he could receive. Most NFL players come from huge universities with big-time football programs, such as USC, Oklahoma, Ohio State, Florida, Texas, Penn State, Nebraska, Notre Dame, and Alabama. The schools at the next level down produce a few NFL players. But hardly ever does an athlete from a small school like Evangel University make it, and that's where Justin played his college ball. Evangel has less than 2,000 students. Compare that enrollment to the University of Michigan with 26,000 undergraduates and a total of more than 41,000 students. Think of the amount of money invested in football there!

At 6'4" and 205 pounds, Justin was a sprinter and a wide receiver. He was confident in his abilities and didn't let his small-college experience stop him from pursuing his dream. Justin began his professional career by playing arena football and then sent a personal highlight tape to NFL teams. A few teams showed interest, but the Redskins eventually signed him, on his twenty-second birthday—quite a birthday present. After a strong preseason, he made the team and was assigned to the practice squad. Then on Christmas day came the gift.

Good news on Christmas—sounds familiar doesn't it? Remember what the angels told the shepherds—"Do not be afraid. I bring you good news of great joy that will be for all the people. Today in the town of David a Savior has been born to you; he is Christ the Lord. This will be a sign to you: You will find a baby wrapped in cloths and lying in a manger" (Luke 2:10–12).

"Good news of great joy"—certainly that's what Justin felt when he got the word from the Redskins coaches. But as a follower of Jesus Christ, he knew that the best news of all had been delivered about 2,000 years ago in Bethlehem when God came to earth and was born as a baby—our Savior, Christ the Lord.

What good news are you waiting to hear? No matter how great it is, nothing compares to the truth about God's Son. Today, when we celebrate his birth, thank God for sending Jesus and for having eternal life through him.

....

ALSO ON THIS DAY . . .

1894—The first midwestern football team to play on the west coast, the University of Chicago, defeated Stanford 24-4 at Palo Alto, California.

1908—Jack Johnson knocked out Tommy Burns to become the first black heavyweight champion.

1973—Tommy Chambers (Scotland) finished his fifty-one-year cycle tour (799,405 miles).

2004—In their first matchup since the Los Angeles Lakers traded Shaquille O'Neal to the Miami Heat (at least in part because of animosity with Kobe Bryant), O'Neal and the Heat defeated Bryant and the Lakers, 104-102 in overtime in Los Angeles.

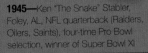

BIRTHDAYS:

1945—Ken "The Snake" Stabler, Foley, AL, NFL quarterback (Raiders, Oilers, Saints), four-time Pro Bowl selection, winner of Super Bowl XI

1962—Mary Ellen Clark, Abington, PA, diver, winner of two Olympic bronze medals, 1992 and 1996

1988—Eric Gordon, Indianapolis, IN, NBA guard (Los Angeles Clippers)

And this is what God has testified: He has given us eternal life, and this life is in his Son. Whoever has the Son has life; whoever does not have God's Son does not have life. **1 John 5:11–12, NLT**

Fun Fact
In his brief NFL career, Justin Skaggs played for the Redskins, 49ers, and Buccaneers. He also played for the Orlando Predators and Utah Blaze of the Arena Football League and the Amsterdam Admirals of NFL Europe. Sadly, on June 15, 2007, Justin died of inoperable brain cancer—he was only twenty-eight. But now he has received the greatest gift of all—eternal life with Jesus.

"I don't know the word **quit!**"

On this day in 1954, Susan Howlet Butcher was born in Cambridge, Massachusetts.

At just 5'6" and 135 lbs., Susan Butcher was one tough woman. Susan loved dogs and the outdoors. After high school, she studied at Colorado State University and became a veterinary technician. She especially loved huskies and became interested in dogsled racing, so she moved to the Wrangell Mountains area of Alaska—a long way from Massachusetts. She decided to compete in the Iditarod Trail Sled Dog Race and began training for this test of skill and endurance. In this race, mushers and their dogs spend about two weeks traveling more than 1,100 miles through arctic blizzard conditions across the spectacular but brutal Alaskan wilderness. Competitors have to endure blinding snow, 100-mph skin-ripping winds, and

temperatures reaching seventy degrees below zero.

Susan entered her first Iditarod in 1978 and finished in the top five from 1980 through 1984. In 1985 she was leading until a pregnant moose wandered into her path and killed two of her dogs and severely injured six others, forcing her to withdraw. The following year, Susan won. She won again in 1987 and 1988. In 1989, she finished second, but returned to win again in 1990. She had achieved four first-place finishes in only five years, an Iditarod record. In all, Susan would finish in the top five in twelve Iditarods. No musher has ever so dominated the sport.

These quotes from Susan reveal her spirit and what made her such a fierce competitor:

"I have been known to walk in front of my team for fifty-five miles, with snow shoes, to lead them through snowstorms, in non-racing situations, where I could have just as easily radioed a plane to come and get me."

"I do not know the word *quit*. Either I never did, or I have abolished it."

We may not face blizzards and angry moose, but other conditions can tempt us to quit, to abandon the important task that God wants us to do. And at times we can feel as though we are mushing through a barren wilderness, alone, totally cut off. But God is with us—we can never be lost to him—and he whispers, "Keep going. I am with you. You can do this in my strength."

"Be strong in the Lord and in his mighty power" (Ephesians 6:10). You can do it. You can make it. Endure!

ALSO ON THIS DAY . . .

1925—A NHL-record 141 shots were taken as the New York Americans (73) beat the Pittsburgh Pirates (68), 3-1.

1946—USA beat Australia to win the thirty-fifth Davis Cup, in Melbourne (5-0).

1991—Chuck Knoll retired as a head coach after twenty-three years in the NFL.

2004—Reggie White, who was regarded as the dominant defensive lineman in the NFL in the 1990s as a player for the Philadelphia Eagles and Green Bay Packers, died of a heart attack at age forty-three.

BIRTHDAYS:

1947—Carlton Fisk, Bellows Falls, VT, Hall-of-Fame major-league catcher (Red Sox, White Sox), 11-time all-star

1954—Ozzie Smith, Mobile, AL, Hall-of-Fame major-league shortstop (San Diego Padres, St. Louis Cardinals), fifteen-time all-star, thirteen-time Gold Glove winner, World Series champion in 1982

1973—Ryan Berube, Tequesta, FL, swimmer, 800-meter freestyle relay, Olympic gold medal winner, 1996

> For I am convinced that neither death nor life, neither angels nor demons, neither the present nor the future, nor any powers, neither height nor depth, nor anything else in all creation, will be able to separate us from the love of God that is in Christ Jesus our Lord. Romans 8:38–39

Fun Fact
Susan won the US Victor Award for Female Athlete of the Year two years in a row. In 1985, Susan married fellow dog racer David Monson, and they successfully competed in major sled-dog races around the world. Susan Butcher died on August 5, 2006, from leukemia. On March 1, 2008, Susan Butcher was honored by the state of Alaska when, just prior to the start of the 2008 Iditarod, Governor Sarah Palin signed a bill establishing the first Saturday of every March as Susan Butcher Day.

Job **Security**

On this day in 1919, Boston Red Sox owner Harry Frazee announced that the team would be willing to trade any player except Harry Hooper. Hooper was sent to the Chicago White Sox after the 1920 season.

You've probably never heard of Harry Hooper, but he was a four-time World Series champion (1912, 1915, 1916, and 1918), he had a .300+ batting average for four seasons, and he scored over 100 runs in three seasons. Hooper was a solid leadoff hitter and excellent right fielder. Hooper in right, Tris Speaker in center, and Duffy Lewis in left formed one of the finest outfields in baseball history. Until Rickey Henderson duplicated this feat eighty years later, Hooper was the only player to hit a home run to lead off both games of a doubleheader. He also was the first player to hit two home runs in a single World Series game (1915). So if anyone's job was secure, it would have been Harry Hooper's especially after his club owner said so.

Yet less than a year later he was gone, traded to the White Sox.

Everyone wants security, to know that where they stand is solid. People get good jobs and work for financial security, enough income, savings, insurance, and retirement funds to take care of any life situation. So they struggle when they get laid off or suffer financial loss and don't know how to pay their bills. People also want to be secure in relationships, knowing they can count on friends and loved ones. So they feel devastated when someone they care about leaves. People want to be secure and safe in their homes as well. So after a burglary they feel afraid and question whether they can ever be safe again. And everyone wants to be assured of their health. So a bad medical report makes them wonder about the future.

Here's the truth: nothing in this world is totally secure. You're better off learning this now rather than later. People (all sinners, by the way) will let us down because no one's perfect—that includes employers, friends, and family members. Possessions will become old, outdated, and broken. And nothing can completely protect us from harm and illness.

But here's another truth: God is perfect, stays the same, and will never leave us. We can and should find our security in him. And we need to remember that even if the world seems to be falling apart around us, nothing surprises or frustrates him.

Rest secure—God is in control.

···

ALSO ON THIS DAY . . .

1980—Calvin Murphy of the Houston Rockets began the longest NBA free-throw streak of hitting seventy-eight in a row.

1987—Steve Largent set the all-time NFL record for career catches when he caught his 752nd pass.

2004—In English fox hunting, approximately 250 hunts were taking place in England and Wales for what could be the last-ever traditional Boxing Day meet, because hunting with hounds was set to become illegal in England and Wales in February.

2009—The New York Jets beat the Indianapolis Colts 29-15, ending the Colts' record regular-season winning streak after twenty-three games; most of the Colts starters sat out much of the game in preparation for the playoffs, angering most Colts fans.

And he who is the Glory of Israel will not lie, nor will he change his mind, for he is not human that he should change his mind!" **1 Samuel 15:29, NLT**

Jesus Christ is the same yesterday and today and forever. **Hebrews 13:8**

FUN FACT Henry Frazee, the owner of the Boston Red Sox who traded Hooper away, was known for several controversial moves. But the most well-known and biggest one Frazee ever made was selling Babe Ruth to the Yankees for $125,000 plus a $300,000 mortgage on Fenway Park. This sale supposedly began the "curse of the Bambino" (Babe).

FunQuiz • December 28 & 29

1. What is curling? (December 13)

2. What is considered the greatest play in [NFL] football history? (December 23)

3. In what sport does Lindsey Vonn compete? (December 5)

4. What was the Detroit Lions' 2008 regular-season record? (December 10)

5. What 2006 Disney movie was released about Texas Western (now the University of Texas at El Paso)? (December 17)

6. For what feat did Travis Pastrana set a new world record in 2009? (December 31)

7. For what teams did NFL legend Reggie White play? (December 19)

8. Where did the 2007 Atlantic Rowing Race finish? (December 2)

9. Who was the San Francisco 49ers football coach in 1981 when they won Super Bowl XVI? (December 20)

10. What was NFL player Jim Marshall's nickname? (December 30)

11. For whom did the New York Yankees trade George "Doc" Medich in 1975? (December 11)

12. To what team did the Orlando Magic lose 84-57 in 1996? (December 4)

13. In what type of skiing event does Hannah Kearney (USA) participate? (December 18)

14. For what college did Washington Redskins player Justin Skaggs play football? (December 25)

15. What year did Susan Butcher first win the Iditarod? (December 26)

16. Why was Golden State Warrior guard Latrell Sprewell's four-year contract terminated in 1997? (December 3)

17. What is the Big Air Competition in snowboarding? (December 6)

18. What's so special about Todd Huston? (December 16)

19. What football position does Ndamukong Suh play? (December 12)

20. What caused Major League Baseball player and manager Johnny Oates to die in 2004? (December 24)

21. To what team did the Boston Red Sox trade Harry Harper after the 1920 season? (December 27)

22. What is the highest score in bull riding? (December 9)

Featured Events in December

Turn **Around!**

On this day in 1937, Jim Marshall was born in Danville, Kentucky.

After a stellar high school career, Jim Marshall played football at Ohio State University. Before his senior year he left for the Canadian Football League. In 1960, he was drafted by the Cleveland Browns, where he played one season. Marshall then spent the rest of his career (1961–1979) with the Minnesota Vikings. He played in 282 consecutive games (of those games, he started in 270 in a row). No wonder he was called "Iron Man." During Marshall's great career, he recovered thirty fumbles, had 127 career quarterback sacks, and was a member of the Vikings' famous "Purple People Eaters" defensive line. With all of that, however, he may be most remembered for what many consider one of the most embarrassing moments in sports history.

On October 25, 1964, against the San Francisco 49ers, Marshall recovered a fumble and ran sixty-six yards to the end zone—the wrong end zone! Thinking he had scored a touchdown, he tossed the ball into the stands in celebration, resulting, instead, in a safety for the 49ers. The Vikings eventually won the game, but Marshall had a tough time living down his wrong-way run.

Years ago, another football player, Roy Riegels, made a famous run in the wrong direction. On New Year's Day, 1929, the center picked up a fumble. Just thirty yards from the end zone, he somehow got turned around and ran 65 yards the wrong way. His teammates screamed for him to stop, and finally one of them caught him at the three-yard line. From then on Roy was known as "Wrong-way Riegels."

Imagine watching a teammate headed in the wrong direction and trying to persuade him to turn around. Very frustrating, to say the least—but those were just games.

Today, millions of people are moving quickly the wrong way. They think they are headed for success and glory, but only disaster awaits. Instead of heaven, they'll make it to hell. We see what they're doing, the direction they're going, and we want to stop them. What can we do? We can pray, asking God to open their eyes to the truth. And we can share the good news about Jesus—the only way, truth, and life.

Look around—who needs to be told the truth, to be turned around? Pray that they will turn the right way, to eternal life.

ALSO ON THIS DAY . . .

1954—The twenty-four-second shot clock was first used in a professional basketball game (Rochester vs. Boston).

1981—Wayne Gretzky set an NHL record of scoring fifty goals by his thirty-ninth game of the season.

2005—Tony Dungy stated that he would return to coach the Indianapolis Colts on Sunday (January 1, 2006) against the Arizona Cardinals, a week after his son's death.

2006—In ski jumping, sixteen-year-old Gregor Schlierenzauer (Austria) won the first of four competitions in the 2006–2007 Four Hills Tournament.

BIRTHDAYS:

1935—Sandy Koufax, Brooklyn, NY, Hall-of-Fame major-league pitcher (Brooklyn/Los Angeles Dodgers), Cy Young Award winner in 1963, 1965, and 1966, seven-time all-star, four-time World Series champion, pitched four no-hitters, including a perfect game in 1967

1975—Tiger Woods, Cypress, CA, world's best professional golfer, winner of seventy-one PGA tournaments, including fourteen Majors

1977—Laila Ali, Miami Beach, FL, undefeated super middleweight boxer (twenty-four fights)

1984—LeBron James, Akron, OH, all-star NBA small forward (Cleveland Cavaliers), Rookie of the Year (2004), six-time all-star, scoring champion

We are therefore Christ's ambassadors, as though God were making his appeal through us. We implore you on Christ's behalf: Be reconciled to God. 2 Corinthians 5:20

Fun Fact After his celebratory toss into the stands, Marshall was a bit confused when the 49ers' center, Bruce Bosley, came over and said, "Thanks, Jim." Suddenly Marshall realized what he had done and bent over and held his head in his hands. Marshall later received a letter from Roy Riegels with the message, "Welcome to the club." In 1994, NFL films listed Marshall's wrong-way run as their greatest "folly."

31 Faith **Landing**

On this day in 2009, New Year's Eve, Travis Pastrana set a new world record—274 feet —for jumping a rally car.

Travis Pastrana has won X Games gold medals in many events, including supercross, motocross, freestyle motocross, and rally racing. He rose to fame back in 1999 when, at the age of fifteen, he won a gold medal in the first-ever MotoX Freestyle event at the X Games, scoring the highest-ever run of 99.00 points. Travis is also known for being the first to perform a double backflip on a motorbike. Recently, on August 29, 2009, Pastrana claimed the overall victory at the Ojibwa Forests Rally, his fifth of the season, sealing his fourth consecutive Rally America driver's title, the most in series history.

In this New Year's Eve event, Pastrana's goal was to beat the previous jump record, and he shattered it by a whopping 103 feet. At Long Beach, California's Pine Street Pier, several thousand people watched Travis peal out on the 1,000-foot run-in, fly over 200 feet of water, and land on a barge anchored in the harbor. Happy New Year!

Some spectators probably thought Pastrana was crazy to try such a stunt. But he didn't just decide to jump in a car and ride it fast on a ramp and over water. (Don't try this at home.) He had years of experience and practice and the best safety precautions. All this being said, Pastrana still exercised a lot of faith on New Year's Eve. He had faith in his skill and experience, in the car, and in the ramp. But it wasn't a blind leap of faith into the dark sky over the harbor. He also knew where he was going to land.

Often when people look at Christians, they can think we're foolish to believe the gospel and the Bible, to give our lives to Christ and live for him. And when we talk about living by faith, it sounds like a blind jump into the dark. But it's not. Yes, everything is "by faith," but we know that God doesn't lie, we have his Word, we know the truth about Jesus, and we've seen many others make this jump, this step of faith. We know where we'll land.

In trusting in Christ as Savior, we land in his arms. And, eventually, we land in his home. Happy New Year!

....

ALSO ON THIS DAY . . .

1958—Willie Shoemaker became the first jockey to win the national riding championship four times.

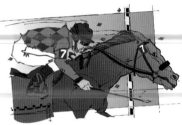

1989—Heavy fog rolled in as the Chicago Bears defeated the Philadelphia Eagles 20-12 in a playoff game dubbed "The Fog Bowl."

1997—Marv Levy retired as head coach of the Buffalo Bills.

2008—Vanderbilt University beat Boston College 16-14 in the Music City Bowl, fifty-three years to the day after the Commodores' last football bowl victory.

BIRTHDAYS:

1939—Willye White, Money, MS, long jumper and sprinter, winner of two Olympic silver medals in 1956 and 1964, participated in five Olympic Games

1971—Heath Shuler, Bryson City, NC, NFL quarterback (Washington Redskins, New Orleans Saints), congressman and strong Christian

1987—Javaris Crittenton, Atlanta, GA, NBA point guard (Lakers, Grizzlies, Wizards)

> I have fought the good fight, I have finished the race, I have kept the faith. Now there is in store for me the crown of righteousness, which the Lord, the righteous Judge, will award to me on that day—and not only to me, but also to all who have longed for his appearing. 2 Timothy 4:7-8

FUN FACT Pastrana is one of the most talented, popular people ever to ride a motorcycle, but he is riding his bike less in order to concentrate more time on rally car racing. Travis, an awesome trick innovator, is easily the most successful rider in the history of the event. "My strengths and weaknesses are the same: I've got the willingness and stupidity to try anything. If I think it's even remotely possible, I'll do it."—Travis Pastrana

Scripture Index for the Devotionals

Verse	Date Used	Theme	Sport
Genesis 4:7	December 4	Temptation	Basketball
Genesis 50:20	July 2	Timing	Baseball
Exodus 20:3	April 18	Comebacks	Cycling
Exodus 20:15–16	March 5	Cheating	Baseball
Deuteronomy 3:18	October 31	God's Presence	Surfing
Deuteronomy 31:6	July 23	Strength	Gymnastics
Joshua 4:23–24	April 3	Confidence	Basketball
Joshua 24:15	June 19	Choices	Basketball
1 Samuel 2:30	January 16	Priorities	Track
1 Samuel 6:7	November 12	Judgments	General
1 Samuel 15:29	December 27	Security	Baseball
1 Kings 18:21	July 29	Decisions	Football
2 Chronicles 15:15	September 25	Receiving	Football
Psalms 19:1	July 31	Creation	Fishing
Psalms 32:7; 59:1	October 11	Protection	Football
Psalms 33:4	July 17	Dependability	Baseball
Psalms 40:2	November 8	Perseverance	Climbing
Psalms 46:4	September 17	Life	Kayaking
Psalms 51:10	January 17	Loyalty	Football
Psalms 73:23–24	October 22	Guidance	Coaching
Psalm 55:22	October 17	Burdens	Weightlifting
Psalms 118:6	April 2	Overcoming	Baseball
Psalms 119:9	February 16	Fleeting Fame	Skiing
Psalms 119:11	July 16	Receptivity	Golf
Psalms 119:101	December 16	Perseverance	Climbing
Psalms 121:1–2	August 5	Persistence	Climbing
Psalms 133:1	July 9	Unity	Tennis
Psalms 139:1–3	March 11	God Sees	Football
Psalms 139:14	August 6	Creativity	Skateboarding
Psalms 139:16b	May 13	God's Sovereignty	Tennis
Proverbs 3:5–6	May 3	E.P.S.	Geocaching
Proverbs 4:10–12	July 3	Competition	Track
Proverbs 4:25–27	June 4	Concentration	Golf
Proverbs 10:9	June 13	Integrity	Baseball
Proverbs 22:1	January 11	Reputation	Baseball
Proverbs 22:29	July 15	Hard Work	Track
Proverbs 27:1	November 26	Time	Football
Ecclesiastes 9:2	February 29	Passion	Baseball
Ecclesiastes 9:10	May 16	Potential	Track
Ecclesiastes 12:1	February 28	Conditioning	Running
Song of Songs 2:4	February 23	Naming Rights	General
Isaiah 40:29	August 28	Strength	Baseball
Isaiah 52:7	September 10	Sharing Good News	Track

Verse	Date Used	Theme	Sport
Jeremiah 12:5	April 19	Hustle	Baseball
Jeremiah 17:14	September 20	Injuries	Football
Lamentations 3:22–23	February 21	Overtimes	Basketball
Ezekiel 11:19–20	April 4	Transformation	Baseball
Ezekiel 22:30	March 2	Standing Strong	Hockey
Ezekiel 33:10–11	September 12	Removing Weight	Track
Daniel 2:20–21	October 1	Impact	Baseball
Joel 2:28	September 18	Dreams	Baseball
Micah 6:8	July 10	Legacy	Motorsport
Zechariah 4:6	February 8	Limitations	Basketball
Matthew 5:9	January 25	Peacemaking	Olympics
Matthew 5:16	August 16	Gospel in Action	Soccer
Matthew 5:43–44	November 29	Love	Football
Matthew 6:19–21	March 22	Fame	General
Matthew 6:24	March 6	Keeping Score	Golf
Matthew 6:33	January 2	Commitment	Soccer
Matthew 6:33	April 8	Priorities	General
Matthew 6:33	July 5	Fame	Tennis
Matthew 7:12	November 27	Perspective	Basketball
Matthew 8:26–27	August 29	Confidence	General
Matthew 9:36–38	October 3	Participation	Surfing
Matthew 10:28–31	December 9	Fear	Bull Riding
Matthew 10:39	May 31	Sacrifice	Football
Matthew 14:27	April 10	Courage	Baseball
Matthew 17:5	June 27	Attentiveness	Baseball
Matthew 22:37–40	January 24	Rules	General
Matthew 23:11–13	February 7	Greatness	Boxing
Matthew 25:35–36, 40	August 14	Compassion	Track
Matthew 26:27–28	October 7	Covenants	Baseball
Mark 2:27	February 20	Sabbath-keeping	General
Mark 10:27	January 12	Impossibilities	Football
Luke 1:37	May 6	Possibilities	Track
Luke 2:52	May 30	Balanced Life	Skateboarding
Luke 6:37	September 23	Forgiveness	Baseball
Luke 14:11	April 15	Humility	General
Luke 16:11	February 6	Faithfulness	Baseball
Luke 17:33	June 6	Risk-taking	Football
Luke 18:27	November 4	Miracles	Basketball
John 3:8	November 22	Holy Spirit	Sailing
John 3:16	September 16	Sin	Track
John 3:16	November 19	Qualified	Soccer
John 8:12	August 8	Light	Baseball
John 10:10	October 29	Life	Baseball
John 13:14–17	February 27	Serving	Basketball
John 13:14	April 5	Teamwork	Basketball

Verse	Date Used	Theme	Sport
John 13:14–15	July 1	Sacrifice	Baseball
John 13:34–35	September 27	Love	Baseball
John 14:6	May 22	Narrow Way	Golf
John 15:15	March 18	Nicknames	General
John 15:16	November 14	Chosen	Basketball
John 17:15–17	September 6	Home and Away	Baseball
Acts 4:11–12	October 30	Only way	Marathoning
Acts 5:29	February 9	Priorities	Basketball
Acts 9:10	September 2	Availability	Baseball
Acts 10:34	December 17	Courage	Basketball
Romans 3:23; 6:23	October 18	Comparisons	Track
Romans 3:23–24	December 11	Trades	Baseball
Romans 5:6	August 23	Timing	Baseball
Romans 5:8	May 9	Errors	Baseball
Romans 5:8	August 21	Redemption	Golf
Romans 5:10–11	March 29	Included	Hockey
Romans 6:23	August 13	Consequences	Track
Romans 7:22–25	October 24	Temper	Coaching
Romans 8:28	February 19	Failures	Bowling
Romans 8:28	October 15	Weaknesses	Swimming
Romans 8:29	November 13	God's Pleasure	Baseball
Romans 8:31–32	July 24	Losses	Baseball
Romans 8:35, 37	March 21	Crashes	Skiing
Romans 8:37	August 2	God's Help	Basketball
Romans 8:38–39	December 26	Consistency	Dog Sledding
Romans 12:2	March 27	Cheating	General
Romans 12:4–5	August 12	Attitude	Baseball
Romans 12:17	April 26	Class	Hockey
Romans 12:17–18	February 26	Fighting	Hockey
Romans 12:19–20	October 8	Penalties	Hockey
1 Corinthians 1:26–29	March 20	Excellence	Basketball
1 Corinthians 1:27	July 22	Opportunities	Football
1 Corinthians 3:5–7	August 30	Coordination	Rowing
1 Corinthians 3:5–9	April 22	Teamwork	Driving
1 Corinthians 3:8–9	December 23	Service	Football
1 Corinthians 9:24	February 14	Purpose	Car Racing
1 Corinthians 9:24	May 23	Perseverance	Cycling
1 Corinthians 9:25	August 1	Potential	Track
1 Corinthians 10:12	May 1	Errors	Baseball
1 Corinthians 10:12	August 19	Pride	Snowboarding
1 Corinthians 12:4–6	June 14	Contentment	BMX
1 Corinthians 12:4–6	December 24	Roles	Football
1 Corinthians 12:12	April 16	Teamwork	Baseball
1 Corinthians 12:18–20	March 15	Variety	Fly-fishing
2 Corinthians 2:15	July 25	Impact	Football

Verse	Date Used	Theme	Sport
2 Corinthians 4:7	March 1	Excellence	World Class
2 Corinthians 4:7	May 8	Endurance	Basketball
2 Corinthians 4:7–10	November 20	Perseverance	Football
2 Corinthians 4:8–9	October 2	Down; not out	Boxing
2 Corinthians 4:8–10	June 18	Comebacks	Baseball
2 Corinthians 5:15	January 18	Stand-in	Baseball
2 Corinthians 5:17	February 22	Miracles	Hockey
2 Corinthians 5:17	March 25	Names	General
2 Corinthians 5:20	June 26	Representation	Soccer
2 Corinthians 5:20	September 9	Examples	Broadcasting
2 Corinthians 5:20	December 30	Reconciliation	Football
2 Corinthians 6:2	June 25	Salvation	Baseball
2 Corinthians 6:17	May 20	Righteousness	Baseball
2 Corinthians 9:6–7	December 12	Generosity	Football
2 Corinthians 12:8–9	November 18	Weakness	Paralympics
2 Corinthians 12:8–10	October 17	Strength	Weightlifting
2 Corinthians 12:9	August 7	Power	Baseball
Galatians 2:20–21	October 8	Life	General
Galatians 3:26–28	March 19	Equality	General
Galatians 3:28	January 4	Inclusion	Baseball
Galatians 6:2	May 28	Compassion	Football
Galatians 6:2	September 2	Cooperation	Track
Galatians 6:2	November 25	Teamwork	Football
Galatians 6:3	June 11	Priorities	Motorsports
Galatians 6:4	May 2	Dependability	Baseball
Galatians 6:7	January 22	Consequences	Boxing
Galatians 6:10	April 24	Rivalries	Baseball
Ephesians 2:8–9	August 27	Heaven	Football
Ephesians 2:8–10	January 10	Fame/Faith	Baseball
Ephesians 3:17–19	January 9	Confidence	Football
Ephesians 3:20–21	January 3	Hope	Football
Ephesians 4:1	December 19	Consistency	Football
Ephesians 4:2	October 16	Humility	Baseball
Ephesians 4:15–16	March 13	Cooperation	Baseball
Ephesians 4:15–16	September 26	Teamwork	Baseball
Ephesians 4:22–23	April 9	New Creation	Baseball
Ephesians 4:25	May 17	Truthfulness	Fishing
Ephesians 4:26–27	April 30	Anger	Baseball
Ephesians 5:8	April 25	Spotlight	Football
Ephesians 5:15–16	July 26	Death	Coaching
Ephesians 6:1–3	October 14	Love	Football
Ephesians 6:5–8	December 3	Submission	Basketball
Ephesians 6:10–11	September 24	The Enemy	Wrestling
Ephesians 6:13	January 26	Defense	Football
Philippians 1:6	June 3	Chosen	Baseball

Verse	Date Used	Theme	Sport
Philippians 1:21	July 4	Life	Baseball
Philippians 1:21	September 11	Death	General
Philippians 1:27	November 21	Purpose	Football
Philippians 2:4	January 29	Sportsmanship	Basketball
Philippians 2:12–13	January 19	Endurance	Cycling
Philippians 2:13	November 1	Control	Baseball
Philippians 2:15	July 8	Examples	Baseball
Philippians 3:7–8	October 4	Priorities	Basketball
Philippians 3:7–8	October 23	Goals	Baseball
Philippians 3:10	November 7	Center of life	Cycling
Philippians 3:12	March 12	Excellence	Basketball
Philippians 3:12	May 27	Fun	Soccer
Philippians 3:13	March 26	Perseverance	Basketball
Philippians 3:13	April 15	Attention	Walking
Philippians 3:13–14	January 1	Resolutions	Football
Philippians 3:13–14	June 21	Performance	Football
Philippians 4:11–12	November 28	Greed	Baseball
Philippians 4:11–12	December 5	Resilience	Skiing
Philippians 4:13	March 7	Determination	Baseball
Colossians 1:28–29	March 8	Persistence	General
Colossians 1:28–29	April 17	Witness	Baseball
Colossians 2:6–7	February 5	True Living	Wrestling
Colossians 2:6–7	May 15	Consistency	Baseball
Colossians 2:6–7	July 11	Follow-through	Golf
Colossians 3:11	August 9	Racism	Track
Colossians 3:13	June 12	Forgiveness	Baseball
Colossians 3:17	February 1	Playing	Basketball
Colossians 3:23–24	March 28	Clutch Players	Basketball
1 Thessalonians 4:17	December 10	Winning	Football
1 Thessalonians 5:16–18	June 24	Prayer	Baseball
1 Timothy 4:7–8	May 14	Burn out	Tennis
1 Timothy 4:12	June 10	Potential	Baseball
1 Timothy 5:8	March 14	Family	Hockey
1 Timothy 6:9–10	January 5	Greed	Baseball
2 Timothy 1:5–6	December 20	Legacy	Coaching
2 Timothy 1:7	May 10	Self-control	Baseball
2 Timothy 1:7	August 26	Control	Baseball
2 Timothy 2:2	August 22	Hand-offs	Track
2 Timothy 2:4–5	April 23	Focus	Football
2 Timothy 2:15	February 12	Equipment	Baseball
2 Timothy 2:15	June 5	Attentiveness	Baseball
2 Timothy 3:16	October 28	God's Word	Coaching
2 Timothy 4:2	December 13	Preparation	Curling
2 Timothy 4:7–8	August 15	Achievement	Baseball
2 Timothy 4:7–8	December 31	Faith	Motocross

Verse	Date Used	Theme	Sport
Titus 2:12	January 23	Consistency	Archery
Titus 2:13	January 15	Sudden	Basketball
Hebrews 3:1	December 2	Guidance	Rowing
Hebrews 5:13–14	September 13	Diet	Gymnastics
Hebrews 11:6	June 28	Boldness	Baseball
Hebrews 12:1	January 30	Perseverance	Basketball
Hebrews 12:1	June 7	Priorities	Horseracing
Hebrews 12:1–2	August 20	Courage	Track
Hebrews 12:2	May 24	Focus	Baseball
Hebrews 12:2	July 30	Coaching	Baseball
Hebrews 12:2–3	January 8	Ultimate Hero	Baseball
Hebrews 12:6	November 5	Tough Love	Football
Hebrews 12:11	May 29	Discipline	Golf
Hebrews 13:7–8	February 13	Styles and Fads	Skating
James 1:2–3	June 17	Endurance	Speed Skating
James 1:2–4	July 19	Preparation	Marathoning
James 1:2–4	December 18	Overcoming	Skiing
James 1:17	May 7	Security	Baseball
James 1:22	December 6	Pretending	Snowboarding
James 1:25	June 20	Righteousness	Baseball
James 1:27	November 15	Priorities	Baseball
James 3:7–10	September 5	Trash Talk	Tennis
James 4:7	November 6	Integrity	Golf
James 4:11–12	September 30	Judgments	Umpires
James 4:14–15	February 2	Life	Basketball
James 4:14–15	April 12	Commitment	Running
James 5:12	October 10	Truth-telling	Table Tennis
1 Peter 1:3–4	November 11	Heaven	Baseball
1 Peter 5:8	July 12	Warnings	Baseball
1 Peter 3:15	January 31	Hope	Baseball
1 Peter 3:15	April 11	Witness	Golf
1 Peter 5:4	October 21	Rewards	Baseball
2 Peter 1:5–8	September 19	Milestones	Baseball
2 Peter 2:21	October 25	WWJD	Golf
1 John 4:7	May 21	Love	Tennis
1 John 5:4	July 18	Victory	Baseball
1 John 5:4	September 4	Underdogs	Football
1 John 5:4–5	February 15	Winning	Basketball
1 John 5:11–12	December 25	Good News	Football
3 John 1:11	April 29	Imitating	Driving

Photo Credits by monthly dates:

January

Photos.com —1, 2, 3, 4, 5, 8, 9, 10, 11, 12, 15, 18, 19, 22, 23, 24, 26, 29, 30, 31
iStockphoto — 1, 2, 3, 4, 9, 11, 12, 16, 17, 18, 22, 23, 26, 30
Bigstock — 3, 5, 8, 9, 11, 12, 15, 18, 22, 23, 24, 25, 26
Jupiter Images — 12, 30, 31
Corbis Images — 16, 31

February

Photos.com —1, 2, 3, 5, 6, 7, 8, 9, 12, 13, 14, 21, 23, 26, 27, 28, 29
iStockphoto — 1, 5, 7, 9, 13, 14, 15, 16, 21, 26, 29
Bigstock — 1, 2, 6, 7, 8, 12, 13, 15, 16, 19, 20, 21, 22, 23, 26, 27, 28
Corbis Images — 22

March

Photos.com —1, 4, 5, 6, 7, 8, 11, 12, 13, 15, 18, 19, 20, 21, 22, 25, 26, 27, 28, 29
iStockphoto — 1, 4, 5, 6, 13, 14, 18, 20, 21, 22, 26, 27
Bigstock — 1, 4, 11,12, 13, 15, 18, 19, 20, 21, 25, 26, 27, 28, 29
Jupiter Images — 6, 8, 11, 14, 15
Corbis Images — 7, 28

April

Photos.com —1, 2, 3, 4, 5, 8, 9, 10, 11, 12, 17, 19, 22, 23, 26
iStockphoto — 1, 2, 3, 4, 9, 11, 12, 15, 16, 17, 18, 19, 22, 23, 24, 25, 26, 29, 30
Bigstock — 4, 5, 8, 9, 10 12, 15, 17, 18, 19, 23, 24, 25, 29, 30
Larry Taylor — 8
Corbis Images — 10

May

Photos.com —1, 2, 7, 8, 15, 17, 20, 21, 22, 24, 28, 29
iStockphoto — 1, 2, 6, 14, 16, 20, 28, 29
Bigstock — 1, 2, 3, 6, 7, 8, 9, 10, 13, 14, 15, 17, 20, 21, 22, 23, 24, 27, 28, 29, 30, 31
Corbis Images — 31

June

Photos.com —1, 3, 4, 5, 6, 7, 10, 11, 12, 13, 14, 18, 20, 21, 24, 25, 27, 28
iStockphoto — 1, 7, 12, 13, 17, 18, 25, 28
Bigstock — 3, 4, 5, 6, 7, 11, 12, 13, 14, 17, 19, 20, 21, 24, 25, 26, 27, 28,
Larry Taylor — 27
Corbis Images — 18

July

Photos.com —1, 2, 3, 4, 8, 9, 11, 12, 15, 16, 17, 18, 19, 22, 26, 30
iStockphoto — 9, 18, 22, 29, 31
Bigstock — 1, 2, 3, 4, 5, 8, 9, 10, 12, 15, 16, 17, 18, 22, 23, 24, 25, 26, 29, 30, 31
Corbis Images — 16, 25

August

Photos.com —2, 5, 6, 7, 8, 9, 12, 15, 19, 20, 21, 22, 23, 26, 27, 28, 29, 30
iStockphoto — 5, 6, 7, 8, 9, 20, 21, 23, 28
Bigstock — 1, 2, 7, 8, 9, 12, 14, 15, 16, 19, 21, 22, 27, 28, 29, 30

September

Photos.com —2, 3, 4, 5, 6, 9, 10, 11, 12, 13, 16, 17, 18, 19, 20, 23, 24, 25, 26, 27, 30
iStockphoto — 2, 3, 11, 18, 19, 23, 24, 25, 26
Bigstock — 2, 4, 5, 10, 12, 13, 16, 17, 18, 20, 24, 27, 30
Corbis Images — 12

October

Photos.com —1, 2, 3, 4, 7, 8, 9, 10, 11, 14, 15, 16, 17, 18, 21, 22, 23, 24, 25, 28, 29, 30, 31
iStockphoto — 1, 2, 3, 8, 9, 10, 11, 14, 15, 16, 24, 25, 28, 29
Bigstock — 8, 10, 14, 17, 18, 21, 23, 24, 25, 28, 29, 30, 31
Corbis Images — 4, 25

November

Photos.com —1, 4, 5, 6, 7, 8, 11, 12, 14, 15, 18, 19, 20, 25, 26, 28, 29
iStockphoto — 1, 4, 5, 7, 8, 11, 12, 13, 14, 18, 19, 20, 21, 22, 25, 26, 27, 28, 29
Bigstock — 8, 20, 25
Corbis Images — 15
Fotolia — 6

December

Photos.com — 2, 3, 4, 5, 6, 9, 10, 11, 12, 13, 16, 17, 18, 19, 20, 26, 30, 31
iStockphoto — 2, 3, 4, 5, 9, 10, 12, 13, 16, 18, 19, 24, 25, 27
Bigstock — 2, 3, 20, 23, 24, 25, 26, 27, 30, 31

Dave Veerman

Dave played high school basketball and football and college football; he has finished six marathons; he has coached football, baseball, soccer, and basketball; and he's a die-hard Cubs fan. A graduate of Wheaton College (B.A.) and Trinity Evangelical Divinity School (M.Div), Dave has written more than 60 books, including *Trivia Twist Devotions, Letting Them Go, Dads that Make a Difference,* and *If I Knew Then What I Know Now.* He also served as a Senior Editor of the *Life Application Study Bible* and *Student's Life Application Study Bible.* The father of two athletic daughters and a founding partner of The Livingstone Corporation, Dave and wife, Gail, live in Naperville, IL.

Dana Niesluchowski

Dana played a variety of sports in junior high and high school and received her B.S. degree in Kinesiology from Wheaton College and her M.A. in Exercise Physiology from the University of North Carolina, Chapel Hill. She loves all sports and is an avid runner, and she especially enjoys cheering for the Chicago Cubs, Bears, Blackhawks, and Fire. While with Livingstone, Dana contributed to many resources, including the *Legacy Bible, Lose It for Life,* and *iStand—the Power of Courageous Choices.* Dana recently left Livingstone to be a stay-at-home mom for her new son, Edmund. She and husband, Walter, live in Oswego, IL.

The Livingstone Corporation

Formed in 1988, The Livingstone Corporation partners with Christian publishers to produce Bibles, books, Bible studies, curricula, and other resources.

AVALON studio